AF616836

INTRODUCTION TO MICROPROCESSORS USING THE MC6809 OR THE MC68000

McGraw-Hill Series in Electrical and Computer Engineering

Senior Consulting Editor
Stephen W. Director, *Carnegie Mellon University*

Circuits and Systems
Communications and Signal Processing
Computer Engineering
Control Theory
Electromagnetics
Electronics and VLSI Circuits
Introductory
Power and Energy
Radar and Antennas

Computer Engineering

Bartee: *Computer Architecture and Logic Design*
Bell and Newell: *Computer Structures: Readings and Examples*
Garland: *Introduction to Microprocessor System Design*
Gault and Pimmel: *Introduction to Microcomputer-Based Digital Systems*
Givone: *Introduction to Switching Circuit Theory*
Givone and Roesser: *Microprocessors/Microcomputers: Introduction*
Hamacher, Vranesic, and Zaky: *Computer Organization*
Hayes: *Computer Organization and Architecture*
Horvath: *Introduction to Microprocessors Using the MC6809 or the MC68000*
Kohavi: *Switching and Finite Automata Theory*
Lawrence-Mauch: *Real-Time Microcomputer System Design: An Introduction*
Levine: *Vision in Man and Machine*
Peatman: *Design of Digital Systems*
Peatman: *Design with Microcontrollers*
Peatman: *Digital Hardware Design*
Ritterman: *Computer Circuit Concepts*
Rosen: *Discrete Mathematics and Its Applications*
Sandige: *Modern Digital Design*
Sze: *VLSI Techology*
Taub: *Digital Circuits and Microprocessors*
Wear, Pinkert, Wear, and Lane: *Computers: An Introduction to Hardware and Software Design*
Wiatrowski and House: *Logic Circuits and Microcomputer Systems*

INTRODUCTION TO MICROPROCESSORS USING THE MC6809 OR THE MC68000

Ralph Horvath

College of Engineering
Michigan Technological University

McGraw-Hill, Inc.

New York St. Louis San Francisco Auckland Bogotá
Caracas Lisbon London Madrid Mexico Milan Montreal
New Delhi Paris San Juan Singapore Sydney Tokyo Toronto

This book was set in Times Roman by Publication Services, Inc.
The editors were Anne T. Brown and John M. Morriss.
The cover was designed by Carol Couch.
Project supervision was done by Publication Services, Inc.
R. R. Donnelley & Sons Company was printer and binder.

Cover photograph: © Srulik Haramaty/Phototake NYC.

INTRODUCTION TO MICROPROCESSORS USING THE MC6809 OR THE MC68000

1 2 3 4 5 6 7 8 9 0 DOC DOC 9 0 9 8 7 6 5 4 3 2

ISBN 0-07-030507-2

Library of Congress Cataloging-in-Publication Data

Horvath, Ralph.
Introduction to microprocessors using the MC6809 or the MC68000/
Ralph Horvath.
p. cm. — (McGraw-Hill series in electrical and computer engineering. Computer engineering)
Includes index.
ISBN 0-07-030507-2
1. Motorola 6809 (Microprocessor) 2. Motorola 68000 (Microprocessor) I. Title. II. Series.
QA76.5.H72 1992
004.165—dc20 91-42488

ABOUT THE AUTHOR

Ralph Horvath is an Associate Professor of Electrical Engineering at Michigan Technological University, Houghton. His teaching interests range from continuing education courses in microprocessors taught to engineers in industry through graduate courses offered on the NTU satellite network, and he has also taught at universities in Europe and Australia. He has received several teaching excellence awards at the local, state, and international levels.

While Dr. Horvath was a Member of the Technical Staff at Bell Telephone Laboratories from 1960 to 1962, he helped to develop some of the earliest electronic telephone switching systems. He later did real-time computerized research on the electrical activity of the brain at the Worcester Foundation for Experimental Biology. He also designed one of the first digital cardiac pacemakers. This and several other medically related devices for which he holds patents have become commercially successful products which are used throughout the world.

His current professional interests include investigations of fires of electrical origin, microprocessor applications, biomedical applications of computers, and continuing technical education. His nonprofessional interests include fishing, house design and construction, racketball, and acting in theatre productions.

CONTENTS

PREFACE

INTENDED AUDIENCE

An *Introduction to Microprocessors Using the MC6809 or the MC68000* is intended for the typical sophomore engineering student who has had little formal electronic training and whose computer experience is probably limited to elementary programming in a higher level language such as FORTRAN or Pascal. In addition, it should be useful to engineers in the field as well as to managers who need an introduction to the area of microprocessors. It will provide any engineer with an adequate background so that he or she can intelligently use, program, modify, and maintain microprocessor systems or supervise people who do.

DEPTH OF COVERAGE

The approach emphasizes the point of view of the microprocessor system user. It introduces only those facts which will be of value to the engineer who must program, use, or maintain microprocessor systems or design hardware to couple with a microprocessor chip. It does not delve into the internal electronic aspects of the integrated circuits involved.

Many introductory books on microprocessors go into much more detail in logic design than is necessary for such a presentation, or they presume a strong background in logic design and relegate that subject to an appendix. These books are written primarily for electrical engineering (or computer engineering) students who are emphasizing the computer area and have a strong interest in understanding the internal workings of microprocessor chips. Not all electrical engineers and very few non-electrical engineers need this sort of preparation.

The coverage of logic circuits in this book is just sufficient to provide a satisfactory basis for an understanding of microprocessors. It is not intended to replace the traditional electrical engineering logic and switching course. In fact, it may serve to stimulate the reader to study this field in more depth.

The book introduces the reader to combinational circuits from a functional point of view with the emphasis on understanding the sorts of things they can accomplish. No design concepts are introduced other than to describe the minimization problem.

The discussion of sequential circuits is a descriptive one with enough detail to show the reader how simple registers can be constructed from flip-flops and gates. These topics have been included because I feel that at least a minimal coverage of both combinational and sequential logic circuits is a necessary prerequisite for a basic understanding of microprocessors.

TARGET PROCESSOR(S)

As is stated in the title, the book introduces two Motorola microprocessors as examples or targets, the MC6809 and the MC68000. The MC6809 is a very important processor from the pedagogical point of view. It is a simple enough machine to serve very well as an introductory vehicle to the world of microprocessors, yet it is complex enough to find extensive use in control applications in the real world. The MC68000 is the senior member of one of the major families of processors used in current personal computer systems and it too is used extensively in real time control applications.

For the first exposure to the material in the book, the reader should select one of the two processors and concentrate on it to the exclusion of the other. It would be a difficult and discouraging task to attempt to learn the details of both processors simultaneously. To support this approach, all processor specific sections, tables, figures, and problems are clearly labeled as such. When studying the details of one processor, those segments dealing with the other may be readily identified and omitted.

The choice of which processor to study initially will probably be determined by the availability of a laboratory system which may be used to prepare and run programs. It is very important that the student have such a system for the first (or only) processor to be studied.

After the initial exposure and after gaining an understanding of the details of the selected processor, the other may be studied for the purpose of contrast and comparison. However, such a comparison is not as important as the depth of coverage of the primary processor and the availability of a suitable laboratory platform.

ORGANIZATION OF MATERIAL

Following a brief presentation of the general aspects of computer systems, the book introduces the reader to the two primary digital areas of logic circuits and number systems. The basic aspects of microprocessors are then presented. As each new topic is introduced it is first discussed in a general way. The terms are defined, general examples are shown, and the fundamental concepts are established. Then, the specifics of the topic as related to the MC6809 are discussed followed by a similar presentation for the MC68000. The specifics are presented in such a way that either could stand alone; i.e., the coverage of each processor is independent of the other.

Following a brief historical overview, Chapter 1 introduces some very basic and important concepts and terminology. This chapter must be covered carefully and in detail, as it forms the basis for much of the material of the book.

Chapters 2 and 3 provide the introduction to logic circuits and number systems. These chapters include the minimum required exposure to these basic subjects which are so important to understanding the subsequent material. Unless the subjects have been covered in a prior course, these chapters must also be covered in detail.

Chapter 4 describes the architectural and functional structures of microprocessors in general, including such concepts as the programming model, accumulator and general register processors, condition codes, the fetch/execute cycle, basic memory types, and bus cycles. It ends with a presentation of the programming models and simple example programs for each of the target processors.

Chapter 5 discusses instruction sets and addressing modes in general and includes a detailed description of the modes available with the target processors. The emphasis is on describing the sorts of things which the individual machine language instructions may accomplish in order to support the discussion of the details of the addressing modes. Understanding the addressing modes in detail is of particular importance. The lack of such an understanding is often the major stumbling block to the student's grasp of the subsequent material on assembly language programming.

Chapter 6 introduces assembly language programming and presents a more detailed discussion of the instruction sets of the target processors, with the emphasis on their mnemonic forms and addressing mode limitations.

Chapters 5 and 6 are by far the longest chapters in the book. The material in them should be thoroughly understood by the student before going on to the subsequent material. Some instructors may prefer to cover the latter part of Chapter 6 before introducing assembly language programming. However, I recommend the order followed in the book.

Chapter 7 presents several examples of program segments which illustrate such things as double precision and BCD arithmetic, loop structures, relocatability, bit level manipulations, and BCD/binary number conversions.

Chapter 8 introduces stacks and their uses and includes extensive subroutine techniques, including parameter passing and dynamic memory allocation.

Structured modular programming is introduced in Chapter 9. This programming discipline is intentionally introduced late in the book. I feel that the student must have a thorough understanding of the capabilities of the processor before the material in this chapter can be of benefit. However, some instructors may prefer to present this material earlier, perhaps immediately after Chapter 6. It has been written in such a way as to support this approach.

Chapters 10 and 11 describe the general aspects of I/O and interrupt structures and present the details of these structures as implemented in the target processors. In addition, Chapter 10 introduces the three primary Motorola interface chips: the PIA, the PTM, and the ACIA. Chapter 12 presents some additional material on memory types and structures including address decoding and interfacing. The material in these three chapters is less detailed than earlier material. Some of it may be deferred to a follow-on interfacing course. Alternatively, the material may be supplemented with detailed manufacturer's specifications on specific chips and expanded to include some interfacing techniques.

Chapter 13 includes the pin-by-pin hardware descriptions of the target processors, including instruction timing and bus cycle timing. Chapter 14 introduces some of the more common development tools. Some or all of this material need not be covered formally and may be left for a reading assignment. The material in Chapter

13 should be covered in detail if the choice is made to expand the material to include interfacing.

LABORATORY WORK

When first learning about microprocessors it is important that the student be able to perform supporting experiments as new material is presented. Such experiments may be done on real hardware such as logic kits and microprocessor educational kits. On the other hand, they may be simulated quite well on a general purpose computer. Either approach seems to work satisfactorily, although many instructors and students do prefer to see the actual components.

Two simulator programs are available for use with this book, ASSYM000 for the MC68000 and ASSYM09 for the MC6809. Each program can assemble a source program into machine code and then simulate the execution of the program on its processor. They run in the DOS operating system on any IBM compatible personal computer. These programs accompany the instructor's problem-solution manual which may be obtained from McGraw-Hill when the book is adopted for classroom use.

The assembler/simulator programs were written at Michigan Technological University and rights to the programs are retained by the university. They may be loaded on only one computer with copies allowed only for back-up purposes. Additional copies may be obtained by contacting Michigan Technological University at (906) 487-2487.

ACKNOWLEDGMENTS

McGraw-Hill and I would like to thank the following reviewers for their many helpful comments and suggestions: Ashok Krishnamurthy, Ohio State University; Stephen Prigozy, United States Merchant Marine Academy; Barna Szabados, McMaster University; and William Trotter, Jr., University of Maryland.

Ralph Horvath

INTRODUCTION TO MICROPROCESSORS USING THE MC6809 OR THE MC68000

CHAPTER 1

INTRODUCTION TO COMPUTERS

Welcome to the exciting and dynamic world of computers! The computing power which in the 1950s filled several entire rooms is now available on an electronic component small enough to fit on the tip of your finger. This tiny device, known as a *microprocessor,* is ushering in a new era of technological progress through its widespread application in every realm of human endeavor. In addition to their uses in computers, microprocessors are now used to control household appliances, automobile engines, laboratory equipment, factory machinery, robots, consumer electronic devices, chemical processing plants, steel mills, and medical diagnostic and treatment equipment; the list goes on and on. They have made it possible to capture a bit of the essence of human intelligence and apply it to the control of inanimate devices. Speaking facetiously, it is now possible to purchase a spark of human genius for $1.98! In this chapter we will look at some of the broader aspects of computers and microprocessors, including some historical developments, the evolution of the technology, and its division into hardware and software concerns.

1.1 HISTORICAL BACKGROUND

Most historians of technology agree that if any one person could be said to be the inventor or "father" of the computer it would be the English mathematician Charles Babbage. In the early part of the nineteenth century, Babbage first designed and attempted to build what he called an "Analytical Engine". This machine was intended to automatically compute values for mathematical tables. In those days before the invention of the calculator, mathematicians and engineers used tables to look up values of such things as logarithms, trigonometric functions, hyperbolic functions, factorials, and the like. The construction of these tables was a laborious and time-consuming task, and many people had attempted to devise machines to carry out the necessary calculations. Babbage's invention, however, was the first to attempt to automate the calculating process completely. It included the concept of a stored program and allowed the user to modify the program so as to alter the calculating behavior of the machine.

Unfortunately, with the limited technology of the nineteenth century, Babbage could not produce the mechanical components with sufficient accuracy to enable the machine to run properly. A machine built to his specifications in the early 1950s did perform as expected. By that time, however, the electronic computer had been developed and Babbage's invention was merely a historical curiosity.

During the early part of this century, much of the groundwork which led to the invention of the modern digital computer was accomplished by various telephone companies around the world, particularly by American Telephone and Telegraph's Bell Telephone Laboratories. Research in the design and development of the telephone switching network led to the invention of various components and design techniques that subsequently were implemented directly in the first successful computer. This computer was developed in the late 1930s to calculate ballistic information for use by the Allies during the Second World War. The computer used electromechanical devices known as *relays* to perform the various functions. Relays are electrically actuated mechanical switches that were used extensively in early telephone switching networks. (They are no longer used to perform logical functions of this type; now they are used simply to manipulate large electrical currents with small controlling currents.)

By the end of the Second World War several versions of the relay computer had been built, and their major shortcomings of speed and reliability were evident. In the early 1950s, however, a new generation of computers was conceived and built, using *vacuum tubes* rather than relays as its primary components. Vacuum tubes had been in use for many years in radio receivers and transmitters as well as in other electronic systems such as radar and sonar. In their new applications in computers they were used as electrically operated switches similar to relays in their behavior. In a relay, however, the switching action is enabled by the actual movement of a mechanical arm. In a vacuum tube switch, the switching action takes place through the movement of a stream of electrons flowing through a vacuum inside the device. As a consequence, the new computers were very much faster than their relay predecessors, performing hundreds of thousands of operations per second (as compared to tens of operations per second). They were also much more reliable because of their lack of mechanical motion. However, they eventually became so large that even with the best components available the mean time between failures was measured in hours!

Coincident with the development of the vacuum tube computer was the invention and subsequent development of the *transistor*. This device, which was destined to replace the vacuum tube in almost all of its applications, became the primary component in the next generation of computers, the transistorized solid-state computer.

When used as an electrically operated switch, the transistor has a significant advantage over the vacuum tube. In the transistor, the switching action takes place in streams of electric current flowing through the solid material of the device. This activity can take place at room temperature. In a vacuum tube, electrons must flow through a space between metal electrodes, and in order for an electrode to emit electrons into the space its temperature must be maintained at about 1000°C.

Because of its lower operating temperature and smaller size the transistor rapidly replaced the vacuum tube in the computers of the 1960s. The transistorized computer consisted of row upon row of printed circuit boards, each one containing as few as one or two or as many as 30 or 40 transistors together with associated components. A modest computer may have contained 5000 or so transistors, while a large one could contain as many as several hundred thousand transistors mounted on 20,000 or more printed circuit boards!

The next generation of computers had its roots in the space program of the 1960s, for which the United States expended enormous amounts of resources in order to put humans on the moon. Among the developments to come from this effort was the *integrated circuit,* which started as an attempt to assemble the equivalent of one printed circuit board's worth of components into a single component. The intent was to interconnect the components using the same process by which they were manufactured, with no manual intervention. This effort succeeded beyond imagination. The early integrated circuits contained the equivalent of one or two of the above-mentioned printed circuit boards, perhaps 10 transistors and about 100 other components. Modern integrated circuits can contain the equivalent of an entire computer, as many as several hundred thousand components.

The integrated circuit computer uses transistors that are similar to those of the earlier generation. The major difference is that the integrated circuit transistors are manufactured in integrated modules and interconnected with other components manufactured at the same time. Thus, a single component in this generation of computers may do the work of tens of thousands of components from the preceding generation. Yet this single integrated circuit component costs about the same and occupies about as much space as a dozen of the earlier components taken together. This is the basis of the computer revolution taking place today. The development cost of a modern computer may be comparable to that of one from an earlier generation, but the size and manufacturing cost are much lower. We are now manufacturing computers with the capabilities of the multi-million-dollar, multi-room-sized behemoths of the 1950s, but which cost only a few thousand dollars and fit on or under a (small) desk!

As a consequence of their reduced size and cost, modern integrated circuit computers are being used to do things that would never have been considered feasible in earlier generations. They are still used in the traditional applications of calculating mathematical results and performing various business support functions. But they are also used in the new area of computerized control, to monitor input signals from a system and to analyze these signals using traditional computation techniques. The results are then used by the computer to generate various signals which, in turn, control the system. The target system may be anything amenable to electrical monitoring and control.

1.2 THE DIGITAL COMPUTER

A computer is a machine, a very special machine, but a machine nonetheless. People often forget that fact and tend to attribute human-like powers to the computer. Perhaps that is because computer jargon includes such terms as *memory, read, write,* and *instructions,* and because we can "tell it what to do" in the program. Regardless of such terminology, the structure and operation of the computer can be readily understood in terms of a few basic concepts.

1.2.1 The PSBE Machine

The characteristics of a computer may be summarized as follows: a computer is a programmable, sequential, binary, electronic machine (a PSBE machine), which can do certain basic operations.

The fact that a computer is *programmable* means that it is capable of doing many different things and that what it does do in a specific instance is programmed or ordered by the user or designer of that specific application. Implicit in this definition is the understanding that the programming is easily accomplished with no change required in the physical components of the computer or in their interconnections.

The modern approach to the design of almost any physical process or system is to use a computer as a controller. One of the primary reasons is the computer's versatility—the relative ease with which its behavior may be modified. An industrial furnace control manufacturer thus needs to stock only one controller for dozens of different customers. Each different application requires a change in the program and not in the controller itself. An automobile manufacturer has a single engine-controller module; different engines, axle ratios, or transmissions are accommodated simply by changing the program in the controller.

The term *sequential* means that the computer does only one thing at a time. For instance, while it is incrementing a counter somewhere, it cannot be simultaneously writing a number into its memory for future reference. Instead, it must complete the current operation before it can start the next one. Fortunately, the time scale in which a modern computer operates is in the sub-microsecond realm. Thus, it may be able to perform millions of operations in one second. As a consequence, we may get the impression that it is doing many things simultaneously. However, this is not so; computers are sequential machines.

A *binary* machine is one in which every signal sent by one part of the machine to another is a binary or two-valued signal. Every communication between parts of the computer takes place by means of binary signals. Figure 1.1 illustrates the concept of a binary signal. Part *a* shows the acceptable levels (usually labeled 1 and 0). Correct system behavior is predicated upon the presence of input signals that fall within these ranges, and the response is undefined for any signal value outside of the two accepted ranges (i.e., in the forbidden range). All of the circuits inside of the computer respond to this type of signal. They also, in turn, generate this type of signal.

Figure 1.1*b* shows a typical binary signal that may be present within a computer. Note that any signal wire in the system will contain a signal that alternates between the two acceptable ranges. Note also that any value within one of the accept-

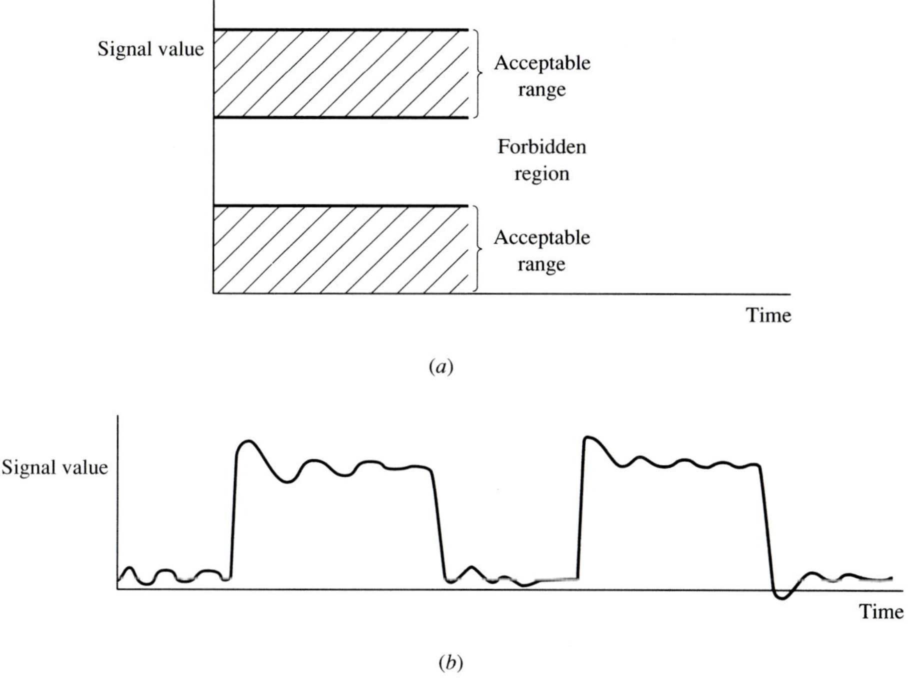

FIGURE 1.1
Binary signals: (*a*) signal ranges, (*b*) a typical binary signal.

able ranges is treated like any other value in that range. Thus, the typical "noise" or ringing in the signals shown in Figure 1.1*b* is of no consequence as long as the signal stays within the acceptable ranges. Because of this fact, binary signals are customarily shown as "clean" and noise free.

Electronic machines, of course, are machines that are constructed with electronic components: resistors, capacitors, inductors, transistors, integrated circuits, and so forth. The various parts of the machine communicate with each other by means of binary voltages and currents. The inputs and outputs to and from the machine are also binary voltages and currents. This book will not go into any of the electrical details of the operation of a computer; rather, it will be restricted to a discussion of its functional behavior.

1.2.2 The Functional Structure of a Computer

As shown in the block diagram of Figure 1.2, a computer consists of several functional units: the clock, the control unit, the arithmetic-logic unit (ALU), the memory, and the input/output (I/O) circuits. Binary signals flow between the units over a bus, which is a group of electrical conductors carrying signals that are functionally related to each other. The wide connecting paths shown here represent buses. An alternative depiction for a bus is to use a single line with a slash across it.

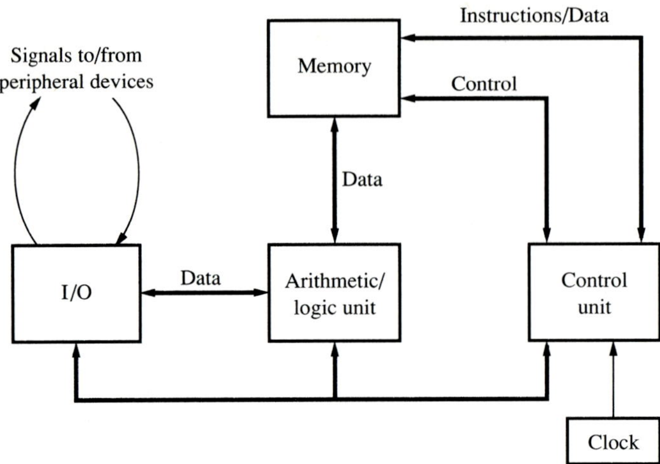

FIGURE 1.2
Block diagram of a computer.

The *clock* is an electronic circuit that generates a periodic binary signal as shown in Figure 1.3. The signal repeatedly alternates from one to zero at a precise rate, typically ranging between one and 100 MHz (megahertz, or million cycles per second). This corresponds to a period (T in Figure 1.3) between 10 nanoseconds (10 billionths of a second) and one microsecond. The rate is determined by a quartz crystal similar to the one that controls the rate in a digital watch. The clock signal serves to synchronize the operation of all parts of the computer. It ensures that the various steps that must be taken by the circuits throughout the computer will each take place at precisely the correct instant. As such, it is the part of the computer that establishes the rate at which the sequential operations will be performed. The types of components used in a specific computer determine the allowable clock rate, more expensive components generally allowing higher rates.

The *control unit* acts as the overseer and director of the rest of the computer. It establishes the basic step-by-step sequence of events known as the operation cycle of the computer. Taking its timing cues from the clock, the control unit sends signals

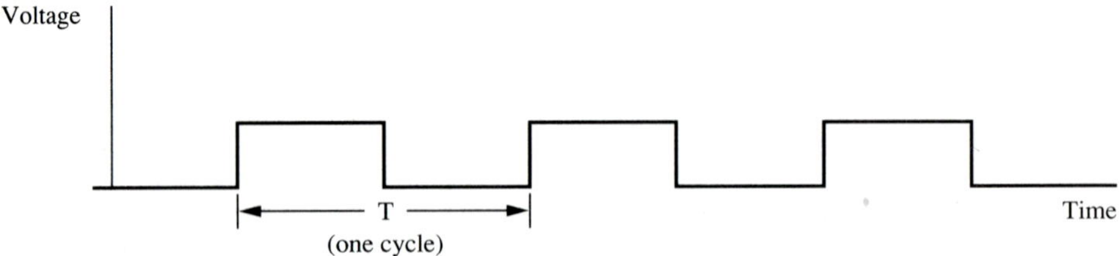

FIGURE 1.3
Computer clock signal.

out to the other units and electronically tells each one what to do and precisely when to do it.

The *arithmetic-logic unit,* or *ALU,* is the basic workhorse of the computer. As its name implies, it performs any arithmetic or logic operations that are called for in the program. It is capable of retaining information in electronic form long enough to accomplish its relevant tasks. Like all of the other parts of the computer, the ALU deals with electrical signals in binary form. Thus, any numerical or logic manipulation that it is to perform must be performed and understood in terms of operations upon binary signals. The arithmetic-logic unit operates under the direction of the control unit. Thus, the control unit interprets the steps called for in the program and directs the arithmetic-logic unit to perform these steps.

The *memory* is the unit that contains the program steps which the computer is to follow in performing the task at hand. It also serves to retain intermediate or temporary results obtained while the computer is operating. Again, it is an electronic unit that stores the requisite information in binary form. The information in the memory can be made available to the other parts of the computer in response to control signals sent to it by the control unit. This sort of transfer of information is called a *memory read* operation. In addition, a *memory write* operation is one in which information is encoded in the memory in such a form that it may later be retrieved.

The final unit, the *input/output* or I/O unit, links the internal structure of the computer with the external world. Various devices called *peripherals* are used to communicate with the outside world. Typical peripherals might include keyboards, printers, display lamps, switches, motors, solenoids, and so forth. The I/O circuits control the peripherals and provide the interface between them and the rest of the computer.

The electronic environment of the interior of the computer is a protected environment. The voltages and currents with which the circuits must deal are very precisely controlled and very precisely timed. Ordinarily there are no unexpected or spurious electrical signals. In contrast, the external world is much more variable. The peripheral devices generate signals at unpredictable times. The interconnections between these devices generate noise signals that combine with the desired ones. Very often, even the desired binary signals they generate are incompatible with the binary signals used inside the computer. The I/O circuits act to screen out the unwanted signals and to match the desired signals to those inside the computer.

1.2.3 Basic Operations

As stated earlier, a computer is a PSBE machine that can do certain operations. The operations may be summarized with another mnemonic, LATI, which stands for Load/store, Arithmetic/logic, Test/branch, and Input/output. The basic characteristics of these operations are described below. They will be discussed in much greater detail in later chapters on instruction sets and programming.

Load/store operations involve the ability of a computer to save information in its memory for later retrieval and use. The information to be saved, like all information inside the computer, is in the form of binary signals. The *load* operation is the operation of retrieving information from the memory of the computer. The *store* operation is the saving of information in the memory.

Arithmetic/logic operations are those operations that manipulate binary signals as if they represented numerical or logical values. For example, one group of binary signals may represent an integer value to which another integer value is to be added. Generating a group of binary signals that represents the sum of these two constitutes an arithmetic operation. Addition and subtraction are the minimum required arithmetic operations, although many computers can do other operations such as multiplication and division as well.

Logic values are inherently binary in nature and are commonly referred to as *true* or *false*. Logic operations combine two binary signals as if they were logic variables. For example, the *AND* operation combines them in such a way that the result is true if and only if both of the variables are true. This logic operation is illustrated in Figure 1.4. Computers typically include the *AND, OR, exclusive-OR*, and *NOT* operations. These will be discussed in detail in a later chapter.

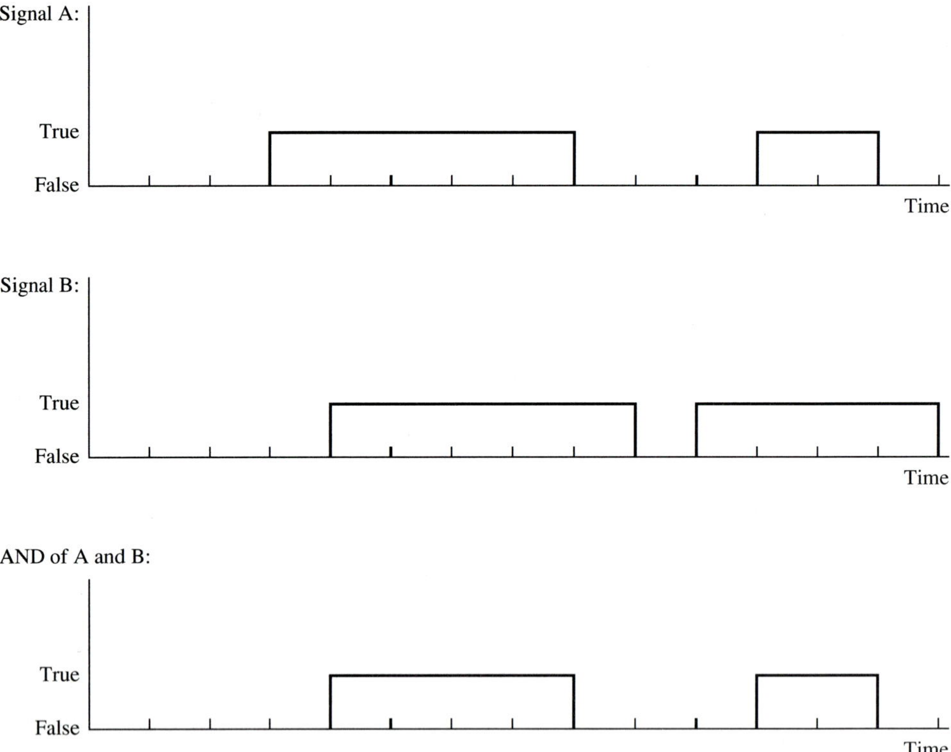

FIGURE 1.4
The logical AND operation on binary signals.

Test/branch operations allow for changes in the sequence of operations in the program. A test operation examines the result of a previous operation in order to determine whether some criterion has been met. Thus, the test may determine whether the result was zero, or positive, or whether it exceeded the capacity of the machine. Accompanying the test is a branch in the sequence of operations stated in the program. This test/branch process is implemented in all higher-level languages, often in the form of an IF, THEN, ELSE sequence.

Input/output operations are necessary in order for the computer to communicate with the outside world. These operations consist of sending binary signals to or receiving binary signals from the peripheral devices. The peripherals, in turn, are capable of using the signals in their binary form or of converting them to or from character or numerical patterns.

1.3 HARDWARE/SOFTWARE

The block diagram shown in Figure 1.2 represents the actual set of electronic components called a computer. It has a fixed form and consists of physical parts. In contrast, the program resides in the computer's memory in the form of binary electronic signals which may have no associated readily observable physical parts. To emphasize the difference between these two, the former is collectively called *hardware*, while the latter is called *software*.

1.3.1 Computer Hardware

The control unit and the arithmetic-logic unit blocks of Figure 1.2 taken together are called the *central processing unit,* or *CPU,* of the computer. A *microprocessor* is a single integrated circuit or *chip* that implements at least the circuitry of a complete CPU. Many microprocessors include the clock unit on the chip as well. Some even include some very limited I/O capabilities.

Typically, the memory and I/O circuits of a computer are manufactured separately and also in integrated circuit form. A computer might consist of a microprocessor together with several I/O chips and memory chips. Depending on the complexity of the processor and the size of the computer, the system may have from 2 to 20 or more I/O and memory integrated circuits. Perhaps 5 or 10 additional integrated circuits might be necessary to coordinate the others electronically. Thus, a typical computer constructed with a microprocessor may comprise some 10 to 40 integrated circuits in all.

Also available are integrated circuits that incorporate all of the functional units shown in Figure 1.2 into a single integrated circuit. Such circuits include not only the CPU but a certain limited amount of memory and I/O circuitry as well. They are known as *single-chip computers* or *micro-controllers*. They find common use in control systems such as the type used in appliances and some electronic equipment.

Regardless of the number of integrated circuits it possesses, a computer cannot function without the necessary power supply circuitry to energize its circuits.

In addition, a computer must have some peripheral devices to communicate with the outside world. When these parts are added, the result is a *computer system*. A microprocessor-based computer system that looks like a traditional computer and performs the traditional computer functions of number and alphabetic character manipulations is commonly called a *microcomputer* or a *personal computer*. A computer whose primary use is to control some physical system is often called a *microprocessor control system*. Whatever the name given it, such a system includes a microprocessor, memory circuits, I/O circuits, a power supply to energize the circuits, a chassis or case, and various peripherals.

Mainframe computers, which are larger and more complex, are often constructed from many hundreds of integrated circuits. Taken individually, these circuits are functionally much simpler than a microprocessor. However, the computers assembled from them are much more complex than microprocessors and are capable of operating at much higher speeds. Still, the internal structures and functions of these larger computers are very similar to those of microprocessors, so much so that a microprocessor serves as a good example with which to introduce the subject of computer engineering.

1.3.2 Computer Software

The software used in a computer must be in binary form within the computer's memory. It is very difficult for an unaided human even to understand programs represented in this *machine language*. To write programs directly in this form is not feasible. A more useful language known as *assembly language* has been devised for each type of central processor. In addition, there are common languages used with many different computers, the so-called *higher-level languages*. These include FORTRAN, Pascal, COBOL, BASIC, C, and others with which you may be familiar.

Although very little programming is actually done in assembly language nowadays, a large part of this book deals with assembly language programming. The primary reason for this is that using assembly language forces one to understand the basic structure and behavior of a computer. Writing a program in assembly language is impossible unless the programmer understands all of the intimate details of the structure and operation of the processor that will run the program.

1.4 THE MOTOROLA MC6809 AND MC68000 PROCESSORS

This book uses microprocessors and assembly language programming to introduce the subject of computer engineering. In particular, the microprocessors used are the *Motorola MC6809* and the *Motorola MC68000*. Each of these is treated independently so that the reader may readily concentrate on one to the exclusion of the other.

The MC6809 processor is very popular in applications involving the control of other equipment. It may be found, along with processors of similar complexity, in such applications as automobile engine controllers, robots, household appliances, consumer electronic devices, and so forth. It is a good example of a small, simple microprocessor that incorporates many modern features. It supports a relatively complex instruction set with many important addressing modes, and it has a powerful interrupt system. As such, it is an ideal target processor for an introduction to computers.

The MC68000 is used in more complex control applications and also is the first member of a family of microprocessors used in a popular series of personal microcomputers. Microprocessors such as this and others used in personal computers or workstations are larger and more complex than the MC6809. They operate at much higher speeds and incorporate many more features. However, if approached from the point of view of their internal structure and assembly-language programming, these more complex microprocessors can also be used successfully in introducing the subject of computer engineering.

SUMMARY

The development of computers from the earliest to the most modern has been brought about primarily by the evolution of the technologies involved. As one consequence of this evolution, the computer is now looked upon as a potential controller for almost any system that can be electrically monitored and manipulated.

A modern digital computer in its basic aspects may be defined as a programmable, sequential, binary, electronic machine that can do load/store, arithmetic/logic, test/branch, and input/output operations. It consists of a control unit, arithmetic-logic unit, memory, and I/O circuits that are synchronized by a binary clock. A microprocessor is a control unit and arithmetic-logic unit on a single integrated circuit chip. If the chip includes memory and I/O circuits also, it is referred to as a micro-controller.

Assembly language programming is a common way to introduce the subject of computer engineering since it requires that the programmer become familiar with the internal structure and functioning of at least the one processor that will run the program. Processors are similar enough that almost any processor will serve as an adequate vehicle for this purpose.

REVIEW PROBLEMS

1.1. List the primary devices used in computers in the past and compare their characteristics.

1.2. List some of the computer terms with which you are familiar that give the impression that the computer is something vaguely human and more than a machine.

1.3. Consider some computer program with which you are familiar. Write a description of what the program does.

1.4. Consider some device, instrument, or appliance that uses a microprocessor to control its operation. Write a description of what the microprocessor does in terms of the behavior of the device.

1.5. Estimate the time, as closely as you can, that you personally require to calculate the product of two five-digit decimal numbers using pencil and paper. Compare this with the time that a hand-held calculator requires.

1.6. Name the five primary parts of a computer and list their functions.

1.7. List the four primary types of operations that a computer can do and describe these operations in your own words.

1.8. Select some higher-level language in which you can program. Try to construct statements in that language corresponding to each of the four primary types of operations that a computer can do. Did you have difficulty with the load/store operations? Explain why these operations are not represented directly in higher-level languages.

1.9. What is an integrated circuit? What types of functions can be performed by integrated circuits? Do you know of any integrated circuits that are not used in computers or computer-based devices? What functions do they perform?

1.10. Select a small computer system with which you are familiar. What is the clock speed? What type of microprocessor does it use? How much memory does it have? What types of peripherals does it have? What languages does it use? List any other important facts that you know about it.

CHAPTER 2

LOGIC CIRCUITS

Logic circuits are the basic building blocks that make up the internal structure of a computer. They include a few simple, easily understood components known as gates and flip-flops. These basic components are commonly organized into more complex combinations such as adders, decoders, registers, and counters. These, in turn, can be combined to build an entire computer.

This chapter describes the basic gates and flip-flops in terms of their functional behavior. It then examines some of the more common combinations of these components. It is important to realize that a computer is a very complex interconnection of these relatively simple circuits. One of the keys to understanding and using computers intelligently lies in understanding the behavior of these basic structures.

2.1 THE BASIC GATES

The circuits that will be described here are known by many different names. They are referred to as binary circuits, digital circuits, switching circuits, logic circuits, gates, or Boolean circuits. The terms *binary* and *digital* refer to the nature of the input and output signals from the circuits. The circuits are used to control telephone switching networks, hence the term *switching circuits*. They are called *logic* circuits because they can be used to perform logic operations of the type referred to in Chapter 1. The term *gates* refers to the fact that these circuits act like gates, letting signals pass under some conditions and blocking them under others. The name *Boolean* refers to an algebraic system devised in the nineteenth century by an English mathematician named George Boole. In 1938 Claude Shannon, an engineer at Bell Telephone Laboratories, discovered that Boole's algebra could be applied to the design of telephone switching circuits. These circuits, in turn, evolved into the circuits described here. The algebraic system is now known as *Boolean algebra* and the circuits are known as *Boolean circuits*.

The inputs and outputs of logic circuits are binary signal voltages of the type described in Chapter 1. The following sections will introduce several ways in which these signals and their interactions may be described.

2.1.1 Binary Variables

A *binary variable* or a *logic variable* is a variable that can have either of two distinct values. Binary variables are commonly used to represent the inputs or outputs of logic circuits. The two values or states of a binary variable are most often referred to as 0 and 1, where 0 usually corresponds to the less positive of the two signals and 1, to the more positive, as in the example of the binary variable shown in Figure 2.1.

Other common labels for the states of a binary variable are *True* and *False* (when referring to logic statements), *High* and *Low* (signal voltage levels), *Actuated* and *Normal* (often used when referring to a switch), or *Asserted* and *Nonasserted* (when referring to signals that call for specific activities). This book will use the 1-0 notation as shown in Figure 2.1.

The rules of Boolean algebra describe the ways in which the variables can interact to produce other variables that represent combinations of the original ones. These same rules can be applied to describe the behavior of logic *circuits* where the original variables represent the inputs and the combinations represent the outputs. The simplest way to represent such a new variable is by tabulating all of the possible combinations of the original variables together with the corresponding values of the new variable. Such a tabulation is called a *truth table*. The following sections describe the basic combinations and the corresponding circuits and truth tables.

2.1.2 The AND Gate

The *AND* function is a combination of two or more input variables in which the output variable is a 1 if and only if each and every one of the input variables is a 1. The

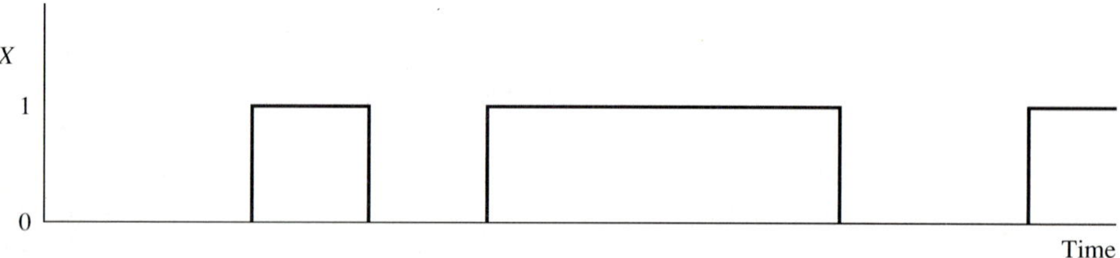

FIGURE 2.1
A binary variable *X*.

symbol for the corresponding circuit together with the truth table and the Boolean algebraic expression are shown in Figure 2.2. Notice that the output X is a 1 if A is a 1 AND B is a 1 AND C is a 1. Note also that the truth table shows a 0 output in each row corresponding to any other combination of the inputs. This is a consequence of the binary nature of the output variable: when the output is not a 1, it must be a 0; there is no other possibility.

The example in Figure 2.2 is a three-input AND gate. The AND function may include any number of inputs greater than or equal to 2. The extension to other numbers of inputs is obvious. The Boolean expression in Figure 2.2 is read as "X equals A AND B AND C". The symbol for the AND operation is the same one that is commonly used to indicate multiplication. As with normal algebraic multiplication, the symbol is often omitted and the variables simply written next to each other. In instances where the use of the multiplication symbol might lead to confusion, a different symbol may be used. A common alternative for the AND operator is the inverted V, called the "cap" symbol.

Note the shape of the AND gate circuit symbol in Figure 2.2. Each of the basic gates has its own uniquely shaped symbol to distinguish it from the others. A circuit diagram using this form of symbolic circuit representation is known as a *logic diagram*. Note that this shows none of the internal structure of the gate. (Of course, the electronic details of the gate are important to its proper operation; however, we will not discuss that aspect in this book.) Note also that the rows in the truth table are arranged in a standard order. This order ensures that no row will be omitted or duplicated and also makes the table easier to read. In the first row the variables are all 0s. Each successive row is obtained from the one immediately above it by changing the rightmost bit digit, if this does not duplicate any preceding row. If this action should result in a duplicate row, then the second digit from the right is also changed. Again, if this should result in a duplicate row, then the next digit is also changed, and so forth. Thus, the rows for four variables will be 0000, 0001, 0010 (change two digits), 0011, 0100 (change three digits), 0101, 0110 (change two), 0111, 1000 (all four changed here), and so forth.

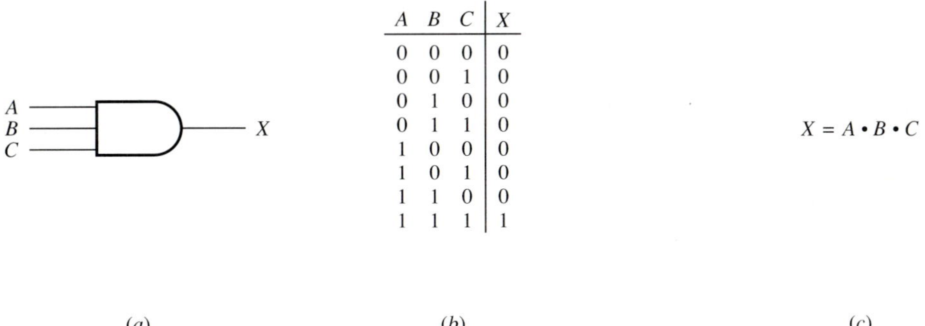

A	B	C	X
0	0	0	0
0	0	1	0
0	1	0	0
0	1	1	0
1	0	0	0
1	0	1	0
1	1	0	0
1	1	1	1

FIGURE 2.2
The AND function: (*a*) symbol; (*b*) Truth table; (*c*) Boolean expression.

If you understand the *binary* or *base-two number system*, you may recognize that the input rows on the truth table are merely the successive binary integers starting from 0. In the binary number system, each position has a weighting of an integer power of two starting with 2 to the power 0 on the right. With five bits the weights are (left to right) 16 (2^4), 8 (2^3), 4 (2^2), 2 (2^1), and 1 (2^0). Table 2.1 shows several examples of five-bit binary numbers.

Since the first row corresponds to the number 0, the sixth row in a four-variable truth table (0101) should then correspond to the number five expressed in binary. That is, 0 times 8 (2^3) plus 1 times 4 (2^2) plus 0 times 2 (2^1) plus 1 times 1 (2^0).

AND gates with various numbers of inputs are available pre-built in integrated circuit form. One popular family of integrated circuits (the 7400 series) includes a chip (component) containing 4 two-input AND gates, another chip with 3 three-input gates, and another with 2 four-input gates. To use these gates, one need only connect the necessary DC power (+5 volts and ground) to the chip and then connect to the input and output pins.

2.1.3 The OR Gate

Figure 2.3 shows the second basic circuit, the *OR* gate. The OR gate generates an output of 1 whenever any one (or more) of its inputs is a 1. In this example Y is a 1 if A is a 1 OR if B is a 1 OR if C is a one. Of course, if the output is not a 1 then it must be a 0. The corresponding Boolean expression is read as "Y equals A OR B OR C."

The most commonly used symbol for the OR operator is shown in Figure 2.3 as the plus sign. As with the AND symbol, this may be confusing in some situations, in which case the symbol V (read as "cup") is a commonly used alternative to the plus sign. OR gates may be designed with two or more inputs. They are available in integrated circuit form with numbers and sizes of gates per chip similar to those described above for AND gates.

TABLE 2.1
The binary number system

Weights					
2^4 (16)	2^3 (8)	2^2 (4)	2^1 (2)	2^0 (1)	
0	0	1	0	1	$0 + 0 + 1 \times 4 + 0 + 1 \times 1 = 5$ So 00101 = 5
0	1	1	1	1	$0 + 1 \times 8 + 1 \times 41 \times 21 \times 1 = 15$ So 011111 = 15
1	0	1	1	0	$1 \times 16 + 0 + 1 \times 4 + 1 \times 2 + 0 = 22$ So 10110 = 22
1	1	0	1	1	$1 \times 16 + 1 \times 8 + 0 + 1 \times 2 + 1 \times 1 = 27$ So 11011 = 27
1	1	1	0	1	$1 \times 16 + 1 \times 8 + 1 \times 4 + 0 + 1 \times 1 = 29$ So 11101 = 9

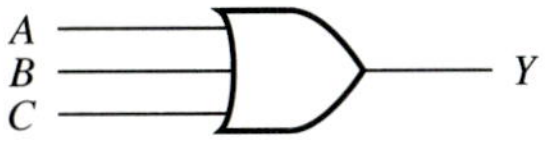

A	B	C	Y
0	0	0	0
0	0	1	1
0	1	0	1
0	1	1	1
1	0	0	1
1	0	1	1
1	1	0	1
1	1	1	1

$$Y = A + B + C$$

(*a*) (*b*) (*c*)

FIGURE 2.3
The OR function: (*a*) symbol; (*b*) Truth table; (*c*) Boolean expression.

2.1.4 The Inverter

The third basic circuit is the *inverter* or the *NOT* gate shown in Figure 2.4. Unlike the AND and OR gates, this circuit has only a single input. As its name implies, the output is NOT the input. The function is commonly referred to as the *complement* of the input. The inverter converts ones to zeros and vice versa.

The most common symbol for the complement operation is the one shown in Figure 2.4, the overstrike above the variable. The expression is read as "Y equals NOT A" or "Y equals A *bar*". With the advent of the personal computer and the proliferation of word processing, stand-alone symbols such as ′ or – are becoming more popular. The overstrike symbol will be used throughout this book.

The circuit symbol for the inverter is a small circle. When the inverter is shown alone, the symbol is drawn with a triangle as shown in Figure 2.4. Inverters are often combined with other basic gates to form more complex circuits. When that is the case, the inverter function will be shown directly as a part of another gate. See the NAND and NOR gates below for examples of this.

The AND, OR, and NOT gates constitute a complete set. Any logic function whatsoever can be realized as a combination of just these three types of gates. Theoretically, an entire computer could be built using just these three circuit types. However,

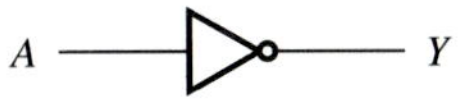

A	Y
0	1
1	0

$$Y = \overline{A}$$

(*a*) (*b*) (*c*)

FIGURE 2.4
The NOT function: (*a*) symbol; (*b*) Truth table; (*c*) Boolean expression.

A
B
C
Z

(*a*)

A	B	C	Z
0	0	0	1
0	0	1	1
0	1	0	1
0	1	1	1
1	0	0	1
1	0	1	1
1	1	0	1
1	1	1	0

(*b*)

$$Z = \overline{A \bullet B \bullet C}$$
$$= \overline{A} + \overline{B} + \overline{C}$$

(*c*)

FIGURE 2.5
The NAND function: (*a*) symbol; (*b*) Truth table; (*c*) Boolean expression.

other operations and corresponding gate types have been devised that represent combinations of these basic types. Some of these are commonly used in computers and other digital systems and will be described briefly below.

2.1.5 Some Other Gates

The *NAND* gate is the functional equivalent of an AND gate followed by an inverter, a NOT-AND gate. Figure 2.5 shows the symbol and the truth table for this gate as well as a Boolean expression describing its behavior. The circuit generates the NOT of the AND of its inputs. Notice from the truth table that the NAND function is also equivalent to the OR of the NOT of the inputs. That is, the truth table shows that the output is 1 whenever any one of the inputs is a 0.

Figure 2.6 shows the *NOR* gate, the equivalent of an OR gate followed by an inverter, the NOT of the OR of the inputs. Notice from the truth table that the output is a 1 whenever all of the inputs are 0. Thus, the output of the NOR gate could also be described as the AND of the NOT of its inputs.

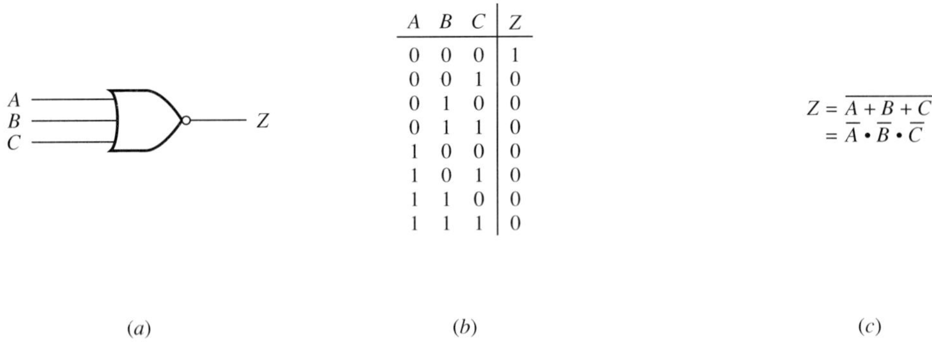

A	B	C	Z
0	0	0	1
0	0	1	0
0	1	0	0
0	1	1	0
1	0	0	0
1	0	1	0
1	1	0	0
1	1	1	0

$$Z = \overline{A + B + C}$$
$$= \overline{A} \bullet \overline{B} \bullet \overline{C}$$

FIGURE 2.6
The NOR function: (*a*) symbol; (*b*) Truth table; (*c*) Boolean expression.

A	B	Y
0	0	0
0	1	1
1	0	1
1	1	0

$$Y = A \oplus B$$
$$= \overline{A}B + A\overline{B}$$

(*a*) (*b*) (*c*)

FIGURE 2.7
The exclusive-OR function (XOR): (*a*) symbol; (*b*) Truth table; (*c*) Boolean expression.

Figure 2.7 shows the symbol and the truth table for the *exclusive-OR* or *XOR* gate. This circuit generates an output of 1 whenever either of its two inputs is a 1 but not when both are. That is, the output excludes the case when both inputs are 1, hence the name "exclusive"-OR. This exclusion definition makes sense only for two variables. However, the definition is often extended to three or more variables. When this is done, the function becomes the *odd inputs* (usually called the *odd parity*) function. The output is a 1 whenever an odd number of its inputs is a 1.

Notice from the truth table and the Boolean expression that the exclusive-OR function can be described as a combination of the basic operations. Thus, the output is 1 when A is NOT 1 AND B is 1, OR when A is 1 AND B is NOT 1. The common symbol for the exclusive-OR function is the OR symbol enclosed within a circle. When the cup symbol is used for the OR operation, a bar through the cup is used to indicate the exclusive-OR function.

2.2 BOOLEAN ALGEBRA

The principles of Boolean algebra are used to assist engineers in the design of the circuits used in digital computers. These circuits typically combine hundreds or even thousands of gates of the types described in Section 2.1. Boolean algebra provides a systematic approach to describing, implementing, and simplifying such circuits. Although this is not a logic design textbook, the following section will introduce some of the basic features of Boolean algebra.

2.2.1 Boolean Functions and Equations

Boolean algebra describes relationships between binary variables and constants. Variables are indicated by letters such as A, B, X, Y, and so forth, as in the standard algebra of numbers. The variables and their complements as they appear in Boolean expressions are collectively known as *literals*. Letters at the lower end of the alphabet are often reserved for independent variables or inputs to an interaction, while those at the upper end are used for dependent variables or outputs. Although this is not universal practice, it is the convention that will be followed here. Constants are the only two values which a binary variable may take, 0 and 1.

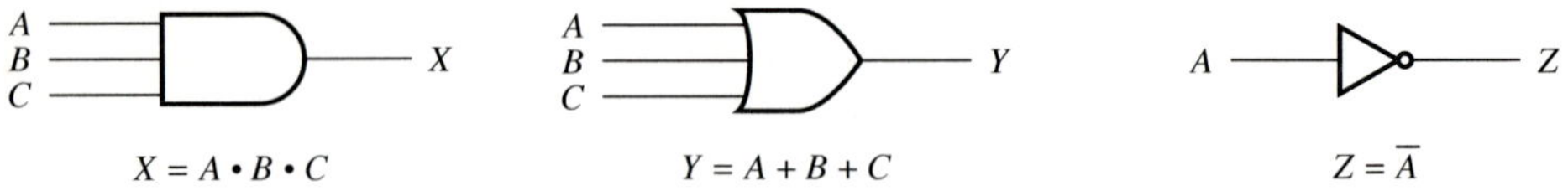

$X = A \cdot B \cdot C$

(a)

$Y = A + B + C$

(b)

$Z = \overline{A}$

(c)

FIGURE 2.8
The boolean algebra operations: (*a*) AND; (*b*) OR; (*c*) NOT.

The relationships between the variables and constants are combinations of the *Boolean operations* AND, OR, and NOT. The interactions are summarized by *Boolean functions* that describe them with the use of the symbols that were introduced in Section 2.1 and that are summarized in Figure 2.8 for convenience.

An example of a *Boolean equation* is the function Y, which describes the behavior of the exclusive-OR circuit:

$$Y = \overline{A}B + A\overline{B}$$

This equation states that the function Y is equal to 1 whenever NOT A is 1 AND B is 1, OR whenever A is 1 AND NOT B is 1. This, in turn, is equivalent to stating that Y is a 1 whenever A is a 0 AND B is a 1, OR whenever A is a 1 AND B is a 0.

As the example shows, a Boolean function states the conditions under which the function value will be 1. The function value will be 0 for any other condition since the function itself is a binary variable. As the example also illustrates, the variables within the body of the function are the independent or input variables and the function itself is a dependent or output variable.

2.2.2 Perfect Induction

A function of a finite number of variables has a finite number of combinations of input values. These combinations can be listed in a truth table together with the corresponding function values. This provides an important tool in Boolean algebra which is not available in standard algebra, *perfect induction*. With perfect induction, two Boolean functions can be shown to be equivalent by comparing their truth tables.

Consider the two functions X and Y as shown below:

$$X = AB\overline{C} + \overline{A}BC + ABC$$

$$Y = AB + BC$$

The truth tables for these functions may be constructed by placing 1s in the rows where the conditions on the right of the equal sign are satisfied. For X, these are rows where ABC are 110, 011, or 111. For Y, these are rows where AB are 11 or where BC are 11. All other rows should contain 0s. Both truth tables may be constructed with a common set of inputs as shown in Figure 2.9. The method of perfect induction

A	B	C	X	Y
0	0	0	0	0
0	0	1	0	0
0	1	0	0	0
0	1	1	1	1
1	0	0	0	0
1	0	1	0	0
1	1	0	1	1
1	1	1	1	1

$X = AB\overline{C} + \overline{A}BC + ABC$

$Y = AB + BC$

FIGURE 2.9
Truth tables for example functions.

proves that these two functions X and Y are, indeed, equivalent. Thus, we may write the Boolean equation:

$$AB\overline{C} + \overline{A}BC + ABC = AB + BC$$

2.2.3 The Rules of Boolean Algebra

In addition to the powerful tool of perfect induction, Boolean algebra includes a series of rules that can be used to modify the form of a Boolean expression. The fundamental rules of Boolean algebra together with their common names are listed in Table 2.2. Notice that every rule except the last has two forms, which are referred to as *duals* of each other. The dual of an expression is obtained by replacing each AND operator by an OR operator and vice versa, and by replacing each 1 by a 0 and vice versa. The principle of duality states that if a statement is valid then its dual is valid.

The first five rules are the *postulates* of Boolean algebra and as such form the framework of accepted definitions and properties of the Boolean operations and constants. Each of the remaining rules (numbers seven through eleven) are theorems that may be proved by perfect induction. Simply construct the truth tables for each side to show that they are equal.

TABLE 2.2
The fundamental rules of Boolean algebra

Name	First form	Dual form
1. Existence of 1,0	$0 + A = A$	$1A = A$
2. Complement	$A + \overline{A} = 1$	$A\overline{A} = 0$
3. Commutative	$A + B = B + A$	$AB = BA$
4. Associative	$(A + B) + C = A + (B + C)$	$(AB)C = A(BC)$
5. Distributive	$A + (BC) = (A + B)(A + C)$	$A(B + C) = AB + AC$
6. Null	$A + 1 = 1$	$0A = 0$
7. Idempotence	$A + A = A$	$AA = A$
8. Absorption I	$A + AB = A$	$A(A + B) = A$
9. Absorption II	$A + \overline{A}B = A + B$	$A(\overline{A} + B) = AB$
10. DeMorgan's law	$\overline{(A + B)} = \overline{A}\,\overline{B}$	$\overline{(AB)} = \overline{A} + \overline{B}$
11. Involution	$\overline{(\overline{A})} = A$	

A	B	AB	$A + AB$
0	0	0	0
0	1	0	0
1	0	0	1
1	1	1	1

(*a*)

A	B	AB	$\overline{AB}$	$\overline{A}$	$\overline{B}$	$\overline{A} + \overline{B}$
0	0	0	1	1	1	1
0	1	0	1	1	0	1
1	0	0	1	0	1	1
1	1	1	0	0	0	0

(*b*)

FIGURE 2.10
Truth table proofs for sample rules: (*a*) Absorption I rule; (*b*) dual of DeMorgan's law.

Figure 2.10 illustrates the perfect induction proof of the first absorption rule and the dual form of DeMorgan's law. Notice how a truth table for a more complex function may be constructed by first breaking it down into simpler components and then combining these components.

2.2.4 Circuit Representations

Any Boolean function can be represented by a logic diagram with gates used to implement the combinations between the input variables. The two functions X and Y shown in the truth tables of Figure 2.9 are represented by logic diagrams in Figure 2.11. Notice that the inputs to each of these diagrams are the variables A, B, and C, and that the outputs are the functions X and Y. In Figure 2.11*a* the 3 three-input AND gates create the three terms of X. These are then combined in the OR gate to generate the output X, which is the OR of the three terms. In Figure 2.11*b* the 2 two-input AND

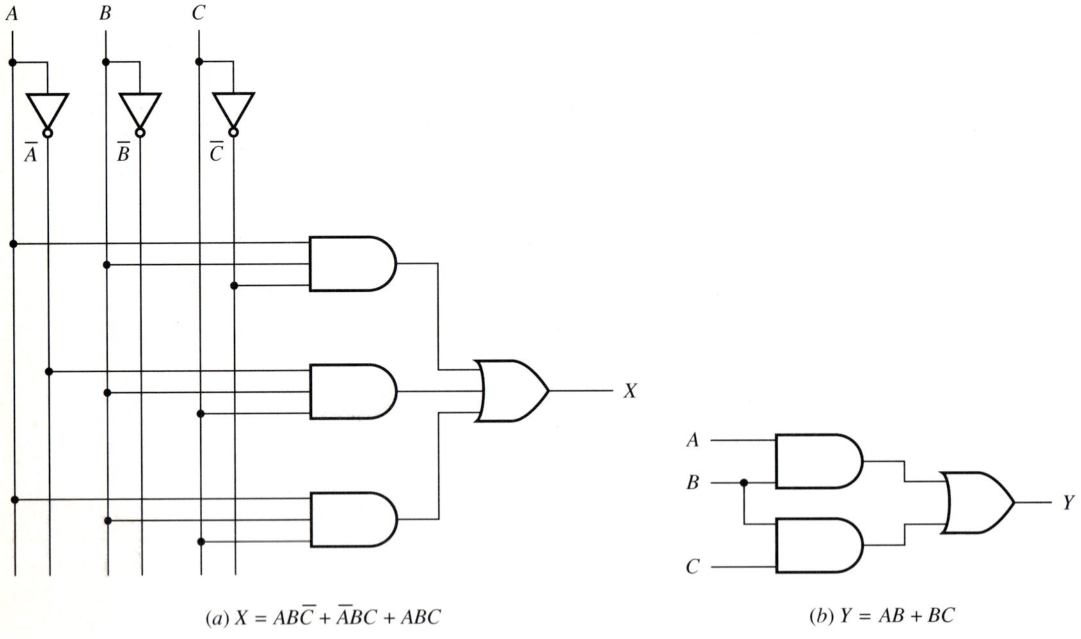

(*a*) $X = AB\overline{C} + \overline{A}BC + ABC$

(*b*) $Y = AB + BC$

FIGURE 2.11
Logic diagrams for the examples of Figure 2.9.

gates combine the inputs to create the two AND terms AB and BC, which are then combined in the OR gate to generate the output Y. The circuit for Y is simpler than the circuit for X and uses less expensive two-input gates rather than the three-input gates used in X.

Boolean algebra provides a means for generating a logic diagram for a circuit from a truth table description of the desired behavior of the circuit. It also assists in finding the most economical logic configuration to generate a required circuit behavior.

2.3 COMBINATIONAL LOGIC CIRCUITS

A *combinational logic circuit* is one in which the output is at all times a function of only the current inputs to the circuit. All of the examples discussed so far in this chapter have been combinational logic examples. Other types of logic circuits have outputs that are influenced by past inputs. Such circuits are said to exhibit the property of *memory*. Circuits with memory will be described in later sections.

2.3.1 Simplification of Circuits

The outputs from combinational logic circuits are Boolean combinations of the inputs and, as such, can be described by truth tables. The first step in going from a truth table description of the desired behavior to a simplified circuit is to write a Boolean function describing the truth table. This process is illustrated by the following example.

Consider the truth table shown in Figure 2.12 for a circuit to generate the function Z. The table implies that the circuit should generate a 1 whenever A and B and C are 000, 010, 011, 100, "or" 110. This says that the output is the OR of five terms. Each of the five terms is the AND of three literals (elements from the set of A, B, C, and their complements). Thus, a Boolean algebra description of the function Z would consist of the OR of five AND terms of three literals each. The result is called a *sum of products* or *SOP* form because of its similarity to a sum of products in ordinary algebra. The SOP form for Z is

$$Z = \overline{A}\,\overline{B}\,\overline{C} + \overline{A}B\overline{C} + \overline{A}BC + A\overline{B}\,\overline{C} + AB\overline{C}$$

The circuit diagram for Z can now be drawn to implement the function exactly as it is stated in the equation above. It would consist of 1 five-input OR gate and 5 three-input AND gates as shown in Figure 2.13.

A	B	C	Z
0	0	0	1
0	0	1	0
0	1	0	1
0	1	1	1
1	0	0	1
1	0	1	0
1	1	0	1
1	1	1	0

FIGURE 2.12
Truth tables for example function Z.

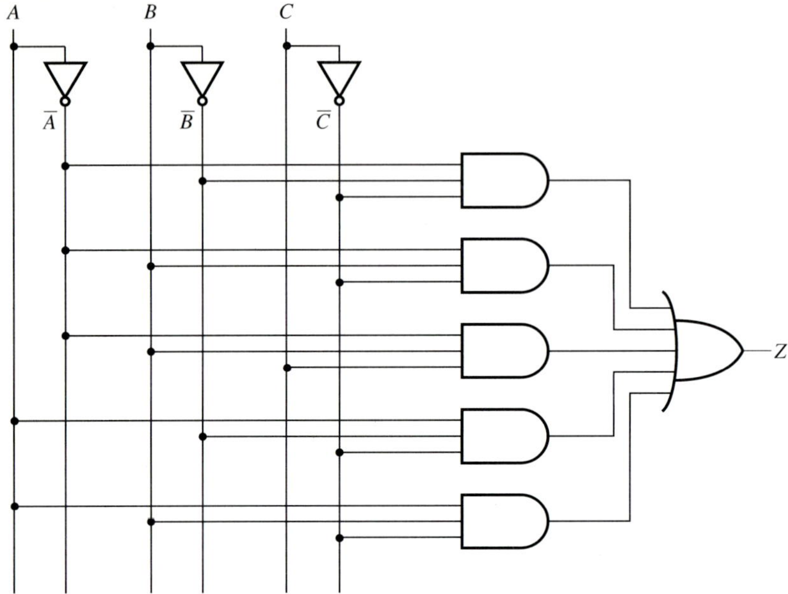

FIGURE 2.13
Circuit for Z from figure 2.12.

A less complex logically equivalent circuit for Z can be devised by first simplifying the expression for Z using the rules of Boolean algebra from Table 2.2 as outlined in the following steps:

$$Z = \overline{A}\,\overline{B}\,\overline{C} + \overline{A}\,B\overline{C} + (\overline{A}\,B\overline{C} + \overline{A}\,B\,\overline{C}) + \overline{A}BC + A\overline{B}\,\overline{C} + AB\overline{C} \qquad \text{Rule 7}$$

$$= \overline{A}\,\overline{C}\,(\overline{B} + B) + \overline{A}B(\overline{C} + C) + A\overline{C}(\overline{B} + B) \qquad \text{Rule 5, Dual, 3 times}$$

$$= \overline{A}\,\overline{C}1 + \overline{A}B1 + A\overline{C}1 \qquad \text{Rule 2, 3 times}$$

$$= \overline{A}\,\overline{C} + \overline{A}B + A\overline{C} \qquad \text{Rule 1, Dual, 3 times}$$

$$= \overline{C}(\overline{A} + A) + \overline{A}B \qquad \text{Rule 5, Dual}$$

$$= \overline{C}1 + \overline{A}B \qquad \text{Rule 2}$$

$$= \overline{C} + \overline{A}B \qquad \text{Rule 1, Dual}$$

Picture a circuit for Z based upon this simplified expression. It generates Z as the output of an OR gate having two inputs. One of the inputs is the literal $\overline{C}$ and the other is the AND of A and B. The circuit, shown in Figure 2.14, is obviously a more economical circuit than the original one shown in Figure 2.13.

The simplification of the function for Z in the above example can be expressed as a single rule that incorporates rules 1, 2, and 5 from Table 2.2. This important new rule may be written as follows:

$$\text{Rule 12:} \qquad AB + A\overline{B} = A$$

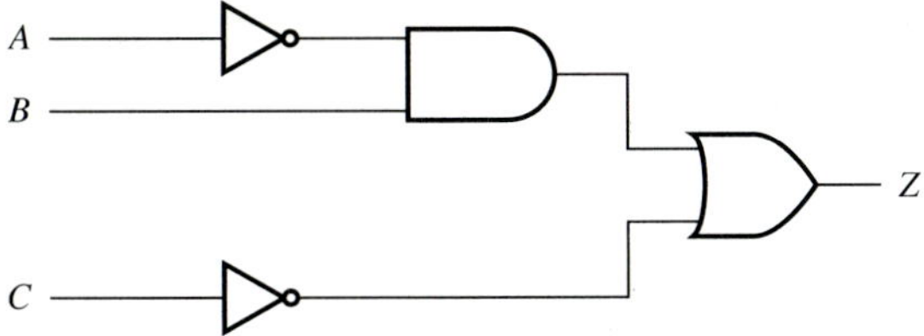

FIGURE 2.14
Simplified circuit for Z from Figure 2.12.

Rule 12 describes the case where an expression contains two terms that are identical in every way except that in one term a particular variable appears as an uncomplemented literal and in the other it is complemented. The two terms can be merged into one reduced term from which that variable is absent. This merging process is probably the most useful reduction step in designing minimized sum-of-product forms for combinational logic functions.

The task of designing combinational logic circuits consists of describing the required outputs and finding economical circuit configurations that will generate them. The steps to be followed in that process are similar to those followed in the above example. In addition, there may be constraints concerning the electrical and transient behavior of the circuits. Such constraints are a function of the technology used in implementing the gates. As stated earlier, this is not a logic design textbook and so no more will be said about the design of combinational logic circuits.

Combinational logic circuits may be implemented by interconnecting integrated circuit gates of the type mentioned earlier. These integrated circuits, each containing only a few gates, are known as *small-scale integrated (SSI) circuits*. When the system requires large amounts of circuitry the implementation is often directly into an integrated circuit that is custom-designed for the task at hand. Such integrated circuits are known as *ASICs*, or *Application Specific Integrated Circuits*.

An alternative to either of the above implementations is the use of arrays of gates known as *gate arrays* or *programmable logic arrays*. These are special integrated circuits, each consisting of several hundred gates that can be programmed to implement many different Boolean functions simultaneously. The specific functions that the array is to implement are defined by the user and programmed into the chip before it is used in a system.

Many combinational logic circuits are used extensively as building blocks in digital systems. The following sections describe the functions of the two most commonly used of these. Many such combinational logic circuits have been implemented in integrated circuits containing the equivalent of 10 to 100 individual gates. Integrated circuits of that size are known as *medium-scale integrated (MSI) circuits*.

2.3.2 Decoders

The *decoder* circuit (or *one-out-of-*2^n circuit) is a circuit that has n inputs and 2^n outputs. The n inputs can be considered to represent a binary number similar to the row patterns in a truth table. Thus, 2^n unique binary numbers can be represented by the inputs to the decoder. Each one of the outputs corresponds to one of these unique numbers. The decoder circuit selects the output corresponding to the applied input

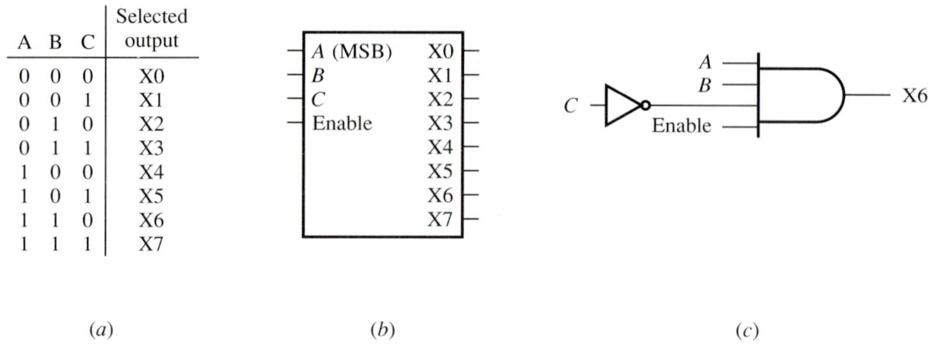

A	B	C	Selected output
0	0	0	X0
0	0	1	X1
0	1	0	X2
0	1	1	X3
1	0	0	X4
1	0	1	X5
1	1	0	X6
1	1	1	X7

FIGURE 2.15
A one-out-of-eight decoder: (*a*) Output coding; (*b*) Logic symbol; (*c*) Circuit for X6.

pattern and makes it equal to 1. It makes all of the other outputs equal to 0. Thus, it decodes the input pattern, or selects one output out of 2^n.

Figure 2.15 shows the logic symbol for a one-out-of-eight decoder and a table describing its behavior. Note that each output corresponds to a binary decoding of the inputs, with input C having a weight of one, B having a weight of two, and A having a weight of four. The label *MSB* on input A stands for *most significant bit*. This identifies the input *bit (binary digit)* which has the highest weight in the code for the selected output.

Decoders often include an additional input, the *enable* input shown in Figure 2.15. Unless the enable input is 1, all outputs are at logic level 0. This permits the user to select the condition of "no output" when such may be necessary.

Figure 2.15*c* shows the circuit required to generate the output X6. Each of the other eight outputs is generated in a similar fashion with a single four-input AND gate implementing the code corresponding to that particular output number.

Individual MSI circuits are available that implement one-out-of-four, one-out-of-eight, and one-out-of-sixteen decoders. One-out-of-ten decoders are also available which implement only the first 10 codes of the one-out-of-sixteen decoder.

2.3.3 The Full Adder

Another interesting and useful combinational logic circuit is the *full adder*. The full adder is used in computer arithmetic circuits to add numbers represented by binary patterns. The truth table is shown in Figure 2.16. The three inputs A, B and C_i represent three binary digits to be added together, where C_i stands for carry in. The two outputs C_o and S represent the sum of the inputs, where C_o stands for carry out and S stands for sum.

In the full adder the binary symbols 0 and 1 stand not only for two different electrical signals but also for numerical values that these electrical signals are supposed to represent. Thus, when the inputs contain no 1s, the outputs represent 0 ($C_oS = 00$ in binary). When the inputs contain a single 1, the outputs represent 1 ($C_oS = 01$ in binary). When the inputs contain two 1s, the outputs represent two ($C_oS = 10$ in

A	B	C_i	C_o	S
0	0	0	0	0
0	0	1	0	1
0	1	0	0	1
0	1	1	1	0
1	0	0	0	1
1	0	1	1	0
1	1	0	1	0
1	1	1	1	1

(*a*)

A B C_i
FADD
C_o S

(*b*)

FIGURE 2.16
The full adder: (*a*) Truth table; (*b*) Logic symbol.

binary). When the inputs contain three 1s, the outputs represent three ($C_oS = 11$ in binary). From the resulting truth table, using the techniques demonstrated earlier, the circuits to generate C_o and S can be designed. The full adder circuit block diagram is a square labeled FADD with the appropriate inputs and outputs, usually along the top and bottom edges as shown in Figure 2.16.

2.4 BASIC FLIP-FLOPS

Logic circuits in which the output depends upon past inputs as well as present inputs are known as *sequential circuits*, since the output depends upon the sequence leading up to the present conditions. Because of this dependency upon the past history of the inputs, such circuits are also said to exhibit memory. The simplest circuit to exhibit this memory for past conditions, the *flip-flop*, is available in several forms, each of which has a similar but somewhat different characteristic behavior.

2.4.1 The R-S Flip-Flop

The basic memory circuit is known as the *R-S* flip-flop from the names of its two inputs. It may be readily constructed from two cross-connected NOR gates as shown in Figure 2.17. The truth table for the NOR gate is shown next to the circuit for convenience. In order to understand the behavior of the circuit, assume that input R is 1 and input S is 0. Since R is 1, output Q is 0. This 0 together with the 0 at S will force output $\overline{Q}$ to be 1. This state, $Q = 0$ and $\overline{Q} = 1$, is referred to as the *reset*

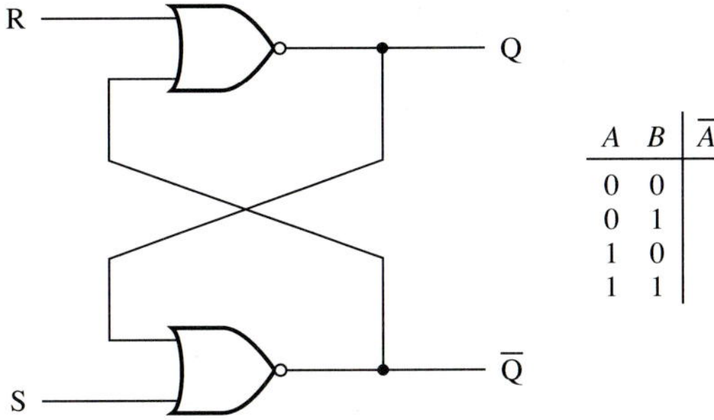

A	B	$\overline{A+B}$
0	0	1
0	1	0
1	0	0
1	1	0

FIGURE 2.17
The flip-flop circuit.

or *cleared* state for the flip-flop. Now make both R and S equal to 0. Notice that the outputs hold the reset state: $Q = 0$ together with $S = 0$ holds $\overline{Q}$ at 1, while $\overline{Q} = 1$ together with $R = 0$ holds Q at 0. Thus, once the flip-flop is in the reset state, it will remain there even when the inputs are both 0.

Now change the inputs to $R = 0$ and $S = 1$. This combination will force Q to 1 and $\overline{Q}$ to 0. This is evident from the symmetry of the circuit and can be verified by referring to the truth table for the NOR function. This state, $Q = 1$ and $\overline{Q} = 0$, is called the *set* state for the flip-flop. Again make both R and S equal to 0. This time the new "set" state is retained. Thus, the outputs will differ when both R and S are 0, depending upon the past history of the inputs.

Input R is called the *reset input,* and making R equal to 1 is said to *reset* or *clear* the flip-flop. Input S is called the *set* input, and making S equal to 1 is said to *set* the flip-flop. If both inputs are made 0, the flip-flop is neither set nor reset and retains its previous state, whatever that was.

If inputs R and S were both to be made equal to 1, the outputs would both become 0. For this case, the complementary labeling of Q and $\overline{Q}$ for the outputs is invalid. Also, if the inputs are afterward both made 0, there is a race between the outputs. That is, *whichever* output first reaches 1 will force the other to be 0. The result is not predictable. Thus, the condition of R and S both equal to 1 leads to an unpredictability in the behavior of the circuit. For these reasons, the input condition of R and S both equal to 1 is not permitted with the R-S flip-flop.

Since a flip-flop circuit is not a combinational circuit, its behavior cannot be described by a truth table. Instead, it is described by a *transition table.* A transition table lists the output from the flip-flop in terms of what it will become after the inputs are changed to the values shown in that row.

Figure 2.18 shows the transition table for the R-S flip-flop. Note that the output is shown in a time relationship to the inputs. In the first row, for example, the transition table states that $Q+$, the value of Q after the inputs are changed to 00, is equal to $Q-$, the value that Q had before that change.

It is common practice not to list the complementary output on the transition table. Only the value for Q is listed and not that for $\overline{Q}$, its complement, even though the complement must always be available internally as a consequence of the circuit construction. The signal $\overline{Q}$ is almost always brought out as an output even though it may not be listed in the transition table.

Figure 2.18 also shows the circuit symbol for an R-S flip-flop. This symbol is a square with inputs R and S entering from the left and outputs Q and $\overline{Q}$ leaving to

R	S	$Q+$
0	0	$Q-$
0	1	1
1	0	0
1	1	–

(*a*)

R Q
S $\overline{Q}$

(*b*)

FIGURE 2.18
The R-S flip-flop: (*a*) Transition table; (*b*) Logic symbol.

the right. The outputs from flip-flops often serve as inputs to other flip-flops and to combinational logic circuits. Thus, the outputs may instead be labeled A and $\overline{A}$, or B and $\overline{B}$, and so forth. When both the complemented and the uncomplemented forms of the literals are available in a system this is known as *double-rail logic*. Double-rail logic is the norm in computer circuits, since almost all of the variables are generated or retained in flip-flops.

Other types of flip-flops can be constructed from cross-connected inverting gates together with additional gates and other electronic components. The construction of such circuits will not be described in detail here. Instead, only the terminal behavior of some of the the more common types of flip-flops will be described.

2.4.2 The Clocked R-S Flip-Flop

A major modification of the R-S flip-flop results from the addition of a *clock* input. This input may be labeled C, Ck, or Cl. The clocked R-S flip-flop behaves in exactly the same way as the unclocked R-S flip-flop, except that changes in the output can occur only during either of the short periods when the clock input is changing. If the output change can occur only during the change from 0 to 1 (a rising or positive change), then the flip-flop is called a *positive-edge-triggered* or *leading-edge-triggered* clocked R-S flip-flop. If the change occurs on the other edge, it is said to be *trailing-edge-triggered* or *negative-edge-triggered*. Sometimes the clocked characteristic is shown in the transition table with the use of arrows as in Figure 2.19, which shows both the circuit symbol and the transition table for a negative-edge-triggered R-S flip-flop.

Sequential circuits in which changes may occur only at specified points in time are said to be *synchronous*, since any transitions in their outputs are synchronized with the clock. The clocked R-S flip-flop of Figure 2.19 is an example of a synchronous flip-flop. The R-S flip-flop described earlier and shown in Figure 2.18 is called an *asynchronous* R-S flip-flop.

2.4.3 Timing Diagrams

The behavior of a clocked flip-flop is determined by examining the control inputs at the time that the clock input is going through its specified transition. This can most easily be done with the aid of a sketch showing the various signals as functions of time. Such

Cl	R	S	$Q+$
↓	0	0	$Q-$
↓	0	1	1
↓	1	0	0
↓	1	1	–

(*a*)

R Q
Cl
S $\overline{Q}$

(*b*)

FIGURE 2.19
The clocked R-S flip-flop: (*a*) Transition table; (*b*) Logic symbol.

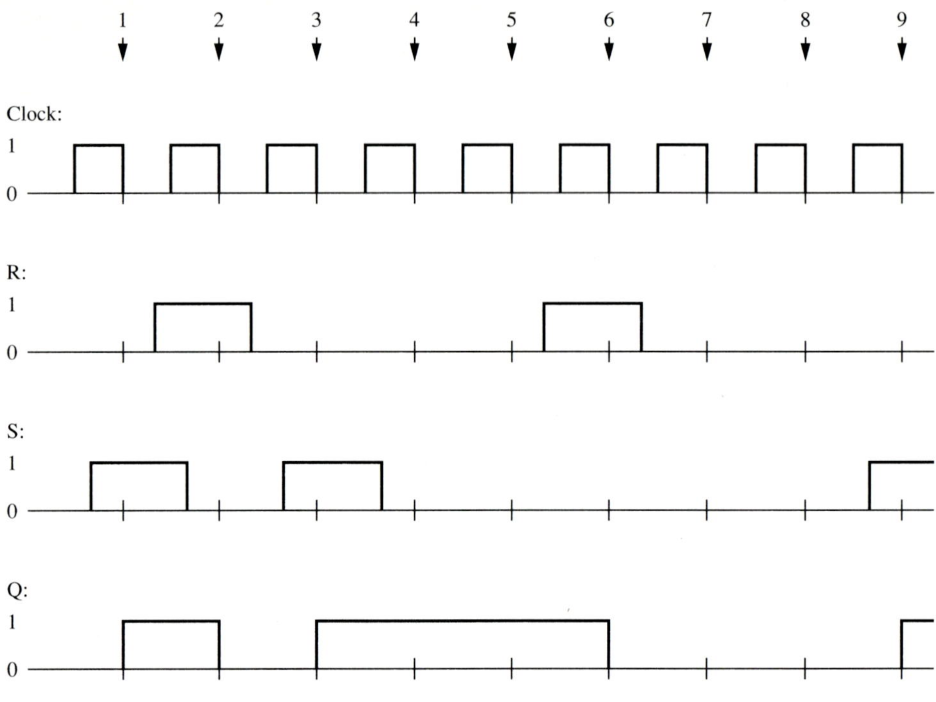

FIGURE 2.20
Typical timing diagram.

a sketch is called a *timing diagram*. A typical timing diagram for a negative-edge-triggered R-S flip-flop is shown in Figure 2.20. In this example the clock signal is shown as a periodic signal alternating regularly between 0 and 1. Although this is not always the case within a system, it is a commonly used representation in illustrations.

When preparing timing diagrams one should **always** start by indicating on the diagram which edges of the clock signal are critical. Figure 2.20 shows arrows on the trailing edge of the clock since the flip-flop is negative-edge-triggered. The next step is to sketch in the input signals, showing exactly when they change. For the purpose of this illustration arbitrary choices were made for R and S to simulate some externally generated signal. Of course, R and S are not permitted to change during the time that the clock is going through its critical change nor may they both be 1 at such a time.

The final step is to sketch the output based on the input values at the times of the clock transitions. Since the circuit is sequential, the initial value for the output must be known or assumed. The common convention is to assume an initial value of 0. The sequence of outputs to be shown on the timing diagram is then determined by examining the inputs at each indicated instant and extending the new output to the next indicated instant.

In the example of Figure 2.20, at point 1 the value of $RS = 01$ will set the output to 1. It will remain at that value until point 2 when $RS = 10$ will reset it to 0. At point 3, the value of $RS = 01$ will set the output to 1. At points 4 and 5, $RS = 00$ calls for no change in the output and so it remains at 1. At point 6, the output is reset by $RS = 10$. The output will remain at 0 through points 7 and 8 since $RS = 00$ at both points. It will then change to 1 at point 9 where $RS = 01$.

Although it serves here as an introductory example of a clocked flip-flop, the clocked R-S flip-flop is not commonly used. More popular types are the J-K *type* and the *D-type* or *data-type* flip-flops. Neither of these comes in an asynchronous or unclocked form. Their behavior *requires* the presence of a clock input.

2.4.4 The J-K Flip-Flop

The behavior of the J-K flip-flop shown in Figure 2.21 somewhat resembles that of the clocked R-S type, with J acting like S and K like R. That is, $JK = 00$ results in no change, $JK = 01$ clears or resets the output, and $JK = 10$ sets the output. Unlike the R-S flip-flop, however, both inputs to the J-K flip-flop are allowed to be 1 at the time of an appropriate clock edge. This combination causes the output to *toggle* or change state from its prior value to the complement of that value.

Figure 2.22 shows an example of a timing diagram for a J-K flip-flop. Notice the toggling action taking place at points 6 and 9 in this diagram. Unlike R and S, which stand for reset and set, the letters J and K are not abbreviations and so have no inherent meaning. As a mnemonic aid to keeping their effects in mind, the expressions Jet Set and Klear may be of value.

One of the most commonly used flip-flops in digital systems constructed with small-scale or medium-scale integrated circuits is the negative-edge-triggered J-K flip-flop with active low asynchronous preset and clear inputs, shown in Figure 2.23. The J and K inputs present when the clock input changes from 1 to 0 determine the new output in accordance with the transition table shown in Figure 2.21. The PRE and CLR inputs are asynchronous, dominant, and active low. That is, whenever PRE = 0 the flip-flop is set, regardless of the condition of the J, K, and Cl inputs; and whenever CLR = 0 the flip-flop is cleared regardless of the condition of the J, K, and Cl inputs. The condition of PRE = 0 simultaneous with CLR = 0 leads to an unstable output and should be avoided. MSI circuits are available that contain from one to four flip-flops of this type.

Cl	*J*	*K*	*Q*+
↓	0	0	*Q*–
↓	0	1	0
↓	1	0	1
↓	1	1	$\overline{Q}$–

(*a*)

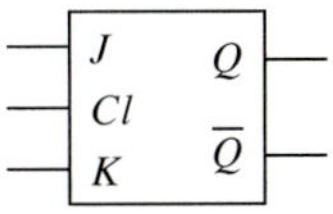

J Q
Cl
K $\overline{Q}$

(*b*)

FIGURE 2.21
The J-K flip-flop: (*a*) Transition table; (*b*) Logic symbol.

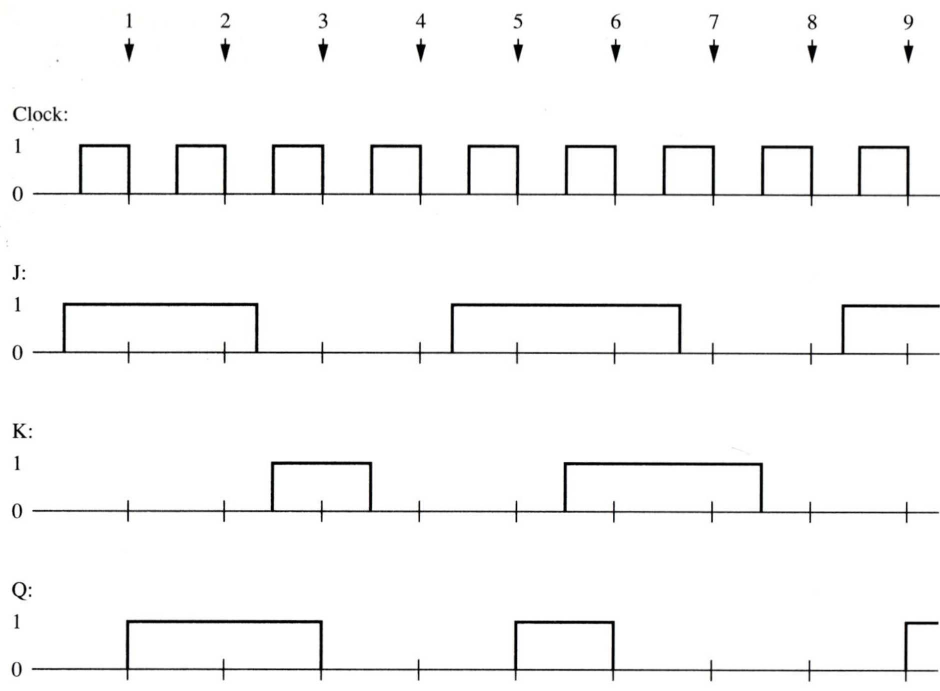

FIGURE 2.22
Typical timing diagram for a J-K flip-flop.

2.4.5 The D-Type Flip-Flop

The data or D-type flip-flop shown in Figure 2.24 is commonly used to capture and retain the value of a single bit for future reference. The output of a D-type flip-flop remains unchanged until the appropriate clock transition occurs, at which point the flip-flop captures the binary signal present at input D. This value is retained until the next appropriate clock edge. With a D-type flip-flop the clock often remains unchanged for relatively long periods of time, changing only when the system must capture a new bit value.

A *register* is a group of D-type flip-flops with a common clock signal used to capture and retain a set of related bits. Registers will play a major role in the description of the internal structure of computers in later chapters of this book. Because of their use in registers, D-type flip-flops are the most commonly used flip-flops in computer systems.

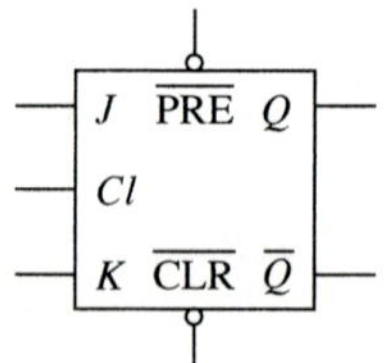

FIGURE 2.23
J-K flip-flop with asynchronous preset and clear.

Cl	*D*	*Q*+
↓	0	0
↓	1	1

(*a*)

D *Q*
Cl $\overline{Q}$

(*b*)

FIGURE 2.24
The data (D-type) flip-flop: (*a*) Transition table; (*b*) Logic symbol.

2.5 SEQUENTIAL LOGIC CIRCUITS

Sequential logic circuits are those in which the output is a function of some prior inputs to the circuit as well as the current inputs. Flip-flops are almost universally used as the devices which store the relevant past history of inputs to the circuit. In most computers the sequential circuits are synchronous. That is, their flip-flops are synchronous and the entire system operates in synchronism with a central clock. In the examples shown here, we shall assume that the clock signal simply alternates periodically between 0 and 1. In a real system, different types of clock signals will be present in different places, although they will always have critical edges that are in synchronism with the computer's central clock.

2.5.1 Registers and Memory

A common type of sequential logic circuit is the register described above. Figure 2.25 shows an eight-bit register constructed of D-type flip-flops with a common clock

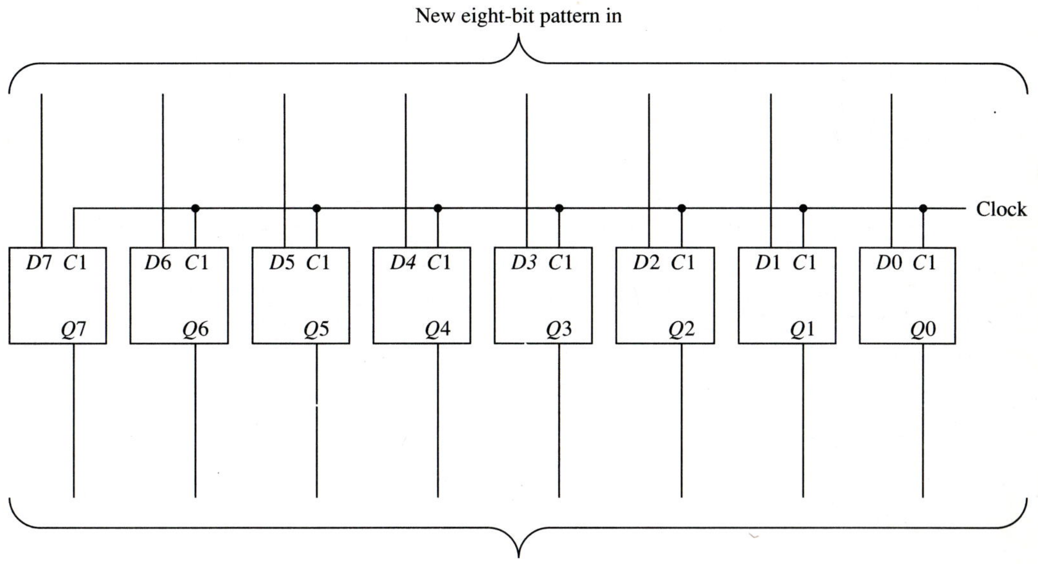

FIGURE 2.25
An eight-bit register.

input. A new eight-bit pattern of inputs can be captured or *latched* into the register by cycling the clock signal through one alternation from 0 to 1 and back. Notice that at any time after it is latched into the register, the eight-bit pattern is available to other parts of the system from the output terminals of the flip-flops.

The bit numbering convention shown in Figure 2.25 is the most common way to number bits in a group, that is: right to left, 0 through $n-1$, where n is the number of bits in the group. This is the convention that will be used throughout this book.

An array of registers is called a *memory.* This type of memory can be pictured as a multi-bin box into which bit patterns can be stored and from which patterns can be retrieved. Each individual bin in the box is a register of the sort shown in Figure 2.25. A memory box may contain thousands of such registers.

In order to make it possible to retrieve a pattern from a specific bin in a memory, the system must have a means of identifying or numbering the bins. Each bin's identification number is called its address and it is usually expressed as a binary pattern. Thus, each register or *location* in a memory has associated with it two specific bit patterns: the location address and the location content. The characteristics of flip-flop memories as well as other types will be examined in a later chapter.

2.5.2 Shift Registers

A register may be constructed so as to be able to shift its bit pattern to the left or to the right. Such registers are called *shift registers.* A shift register can be assembled from J-K flip-flops with outputs connected to neighboring inputs as shown in Figure 2.26. In this example, the bits enter the register one at a time from the left edge and are shifted to the right position during each cycle of the SHIFT input. At any time the bit values are available at the outputs of the individual flip-flops. A shift register configured like this is called a *serial-input/parallel-output* shift-register. The bits come in one at a time (in serial) and are all available at the same time (in parallel). Other configurations may allow the input of bit patterns through preset/clear terminals (parallel input) or may make only the last bit on one end available (serial output). Still another possibility is to configure the register so as to switch the direction of the shift with a control input. This requires many additional gates and results in a *bi-directional* shift register. Various combinations of these characteristics are available in MSI integrated-circuit shift registers.

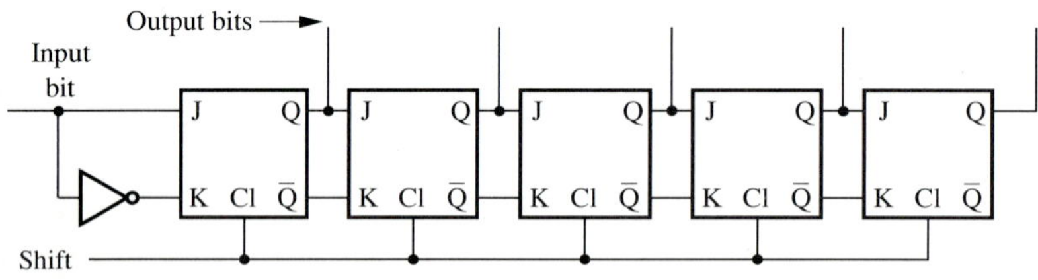

FIGURE 2.26
A five-bit shift register.

2.5.3 Counters

Another example of a sequential circuit is a *counter,* which is a group of flip-flops interconnected in such a way that the bit pattern stored in them changes during each cycle of the single input. The patterns are unique and return to some starting value (often all 0s) after a pre-determined number of input cycles.

Figure 2.27 shows a circuit which cycles through eight unique patterns and then repeats. It uses negative-edge-triggered J-K flip-flops with the J-K terminals permanently wired to toggle. Notice that the clock input for each stage is derived from the output of the previous stage. A circuit such as this is called a *ripple counter* since changes in the pattern must often ripple through several flip-flops before the pattern stabilizes.

The timing diagram for the ripple counter of Figure 2.27 is shown in Figure 2.28. Notice the rippling changes that occur on every even-numbered triggering edge. The ripple carries the farthest at points 4 and 8 where a change in C causes a change in B which in turn causes a change in A. This diagram also shows that the patterns through which the bits cycle are those that were used earlier to label the rows on a truth table (with A being the most significant bit). Counters that cycle through these patterns and recycle after 2^n counts are called *binary counters*. Because the output goes through the same pattern once in every n cycles of the input, a counter is often referred to as a *divide-by–n* circuit. Thus, the counter in Figure 2.27 could be called a divide-by-eight circuit. It could also be described as a three-bit ripple counter, or a divide-by-eight binary counter.

Each flip-flop in a counter has only two possible states, and so an m-stage counter can have, at most, 2^m different patterns. Therefore, a counter can count to a maximum of only 2^m where m is the number of flip-flops it contains. If the flip-flops in an m-stage binary counter have asynchronous clear inputs, these can be used to abort the count whenever some predetermined count pattern appears. By resetting the counter to the all-0 pattern, they can be used to build a counter which counts to less than 2^m.

Figure 2.29 shows the counter of Figure 2.27 modified to recycle to 000 after completing six unique cycles (000 through 101). The NAND gate senses when the pattern becomes $ABC = 110$. Actually, it senses the condition $AB = 11$, which is

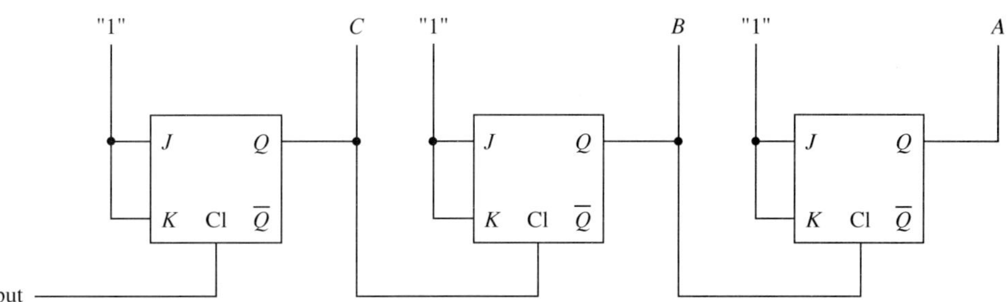

FIGURE 2.27
A three-bit ripple counter.

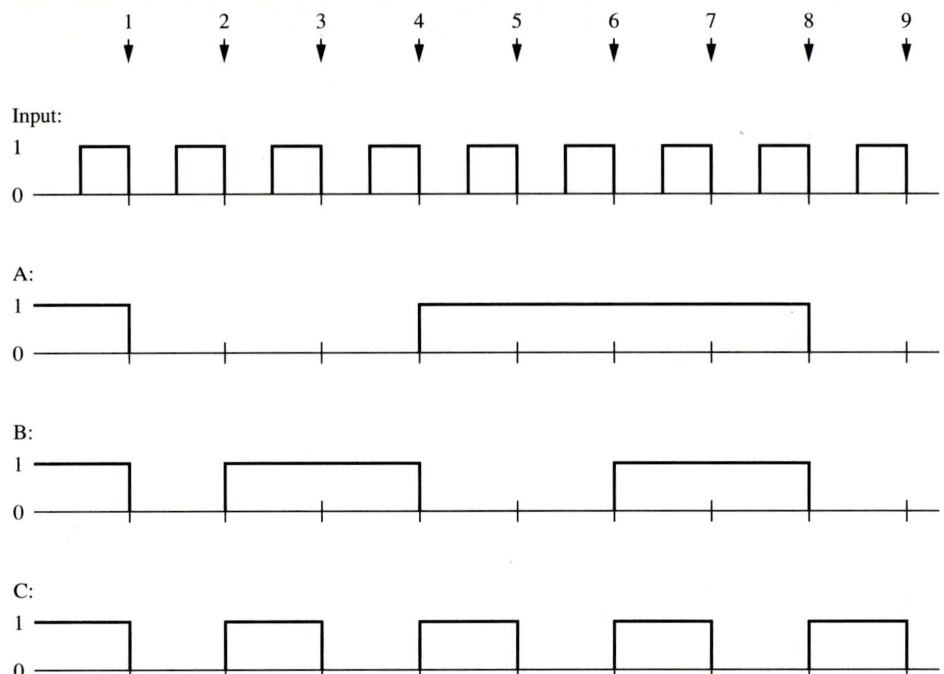

FIGURE 2.28
Timing diagram for the counter of Figure 2.27.

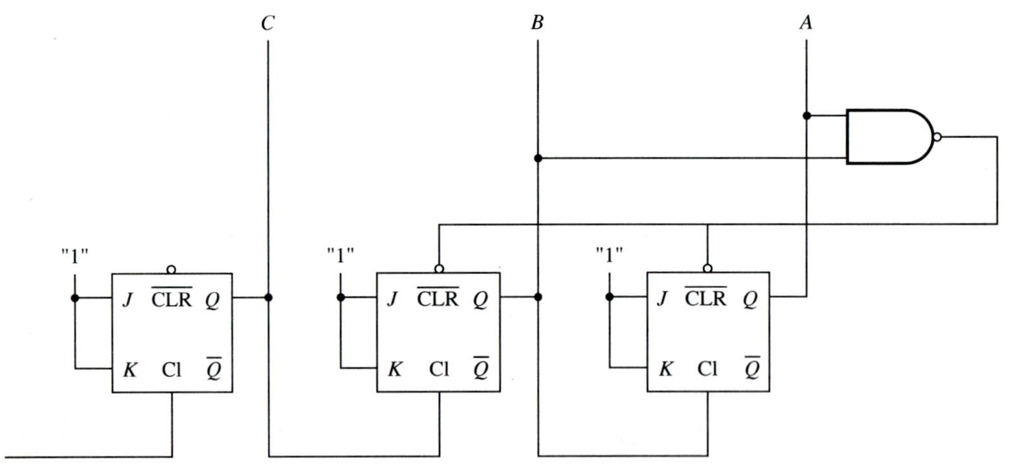

FIGURE 2.29
Three-bit counter modified to reset after six cycles.

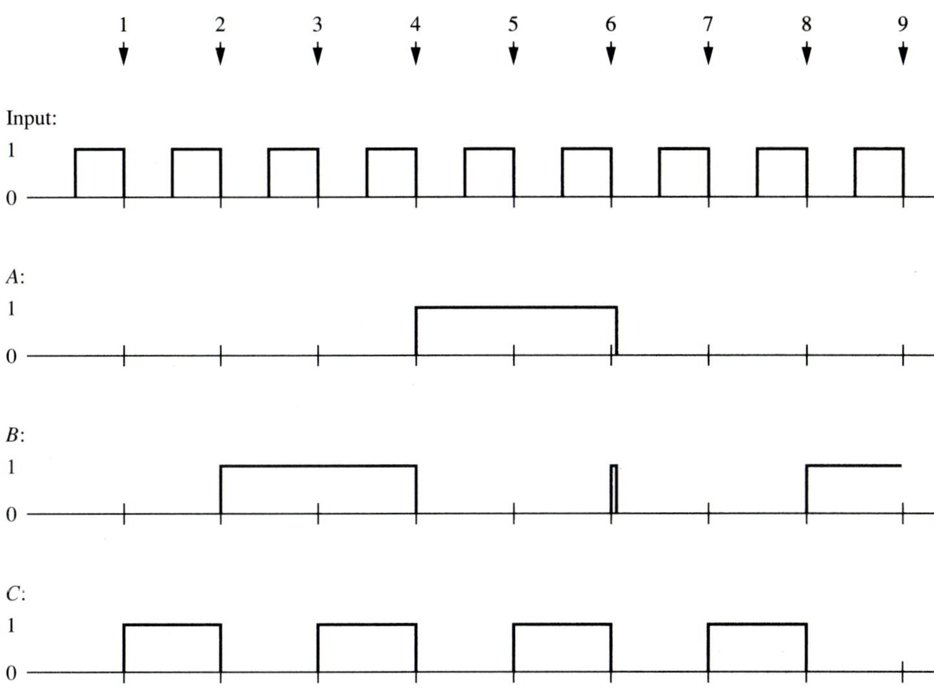

FIGURE 2.30
Timing diagram for the counter of Figure 2.29.

equivalent in this case. When the gate senses this condition it immediately resets flip-flops *A* and *B* through their asynchronous $\overline{CLR}$ inputs. The result is a divide-by-six counter that repeatedly cycles through the six binary numbers 000 through 101.

The timing diagram for the divide-by-six counter of Figure 2.29 is shown in Figure 2.30. This diagram exaggerates the presence of a momentary *glitch* in the output from this counter. The glitch is present because the pattern 110 must occur and remain for a long enough time for the NAND gate to reset flip-flops *A* and *B*. This resetting action then removes the 110 pattern that initiated it. Thus, its duration depends upon the speed with which the gate and the flip-flops respond.

Many other types of counters have been devised. One type has the input connected to each flip-flop, resulting in a so-called *synchronous* counter. This type does not use the asynchronous CLR input to reset and so it does not exhibit the momentary glitch of the example above. Still others use an entirely different sequence of patterns, so-called *creeping code* or *Grey code* counters. These and other types of counters will not be discussed in this book.

SUMMARY

The logical characteristics of the gates and flip-flops that constitute the building blocks of digital systems are quite simple. Their behavior in isolation may be readily understood with the aid of such tools as Boolean algebra, truth tables, transition tables, and timing diagrams. In addition, these tools can be of invaluable assistance in the analysis and design of systems incorporating such circuits.

When combined by the thousands, these simple structures may be used to construct incredibly complex systems. All computers from the simplest microprocessor that controls the operation of a microwave oven to the fastest and most complex supercomputer used to calculate the behavior of millions of galaxies in a theoretical model of the universe depend for their operation upon circuits such as these.

A basic knowledge of the behavior of logic circuits serves as a solid introduction to the field of computer engineering. Furthermore, such a basis is an asset in understanding the structure and operation of computers as well as their myriad applications.

REVIEW PROBLEMS

2.1. Prove the following theorems:

a. $AB + A\overline{B} = A$

b. $(A + B)(A + C) = A + BC$

c. $AB + \overline{A}B + A\overline{B} + \overline{AB} = 1$

d. $(A + B)(A + \overline{B}) = A$

e. $A(\overline{A} + B) = AB$

f. $(\overline{AB}) + B = 1$

2.2. Simplify each of the following by applying only one of the 12 rules. State which rule was applied.

a. $A\overline{B}C + \overline{(A\overline{B}C)}$

b. $\overline{A} + A\overline{B}$

c. $(\overline{A}B)\overline{(\overline{A}B)}$

d. $\overline{(A + \overline{B})}$

e. $\overline{B}(B + C)$

f. $AB(C + D) + AB\overline{(C + D)}$

2.3. Simplify the following expressions and express each in SOP form.

a. $ABC + A(B\overline{C} + \overline{B}C) + \overline{A}BC$

b. $\overline{B}(\overline{C} + A) + B\overline{C} + \overline{AB}$

c. $\overline{C}(AB + \overline{B}) + C(A + \overline{B})$

d. $\overline{A}(C + \overline{BC}) + AB$

e. $\overline{A}(D + \overline{B}C + \overline{BD}) + A(BD + \overline{CD}) + B\overline{C}$

f. $\overline{A}BD + \overline{AB}D + \overline{BCD} + \overline{B}C\overline{D}$

g. $A\overline{BC} + ABD + AC\overline{D} + A\overline{B}CD + AB\overline{CD}$

2.4. Draw logic diagrams to implement each of the following functions the way they are expressed. Use only inverters and AND and OR gates.

a. $W = AB + A\overline{CD} + CD$

b. $X = A(BC + \overline{CD}) + \overline{A}D$

c. $Y = \overline{\overline{A}B} + CD$

d. $Z = (A + \overline{B} + C)(\overline{A} + D)(B + \overline{C})$

2.5. Write the following Boolean function as a product of sums with no complements over AND and OR functions.

$$X = \overline{(\overline{A}B) + (BC) + (A\overline{BC})}$$

2.6. Write the function of problem 2.5 as a sum of products with no complements over AND and OR functions.

2.7. Construct truth tables for the logic diagrams shown below.

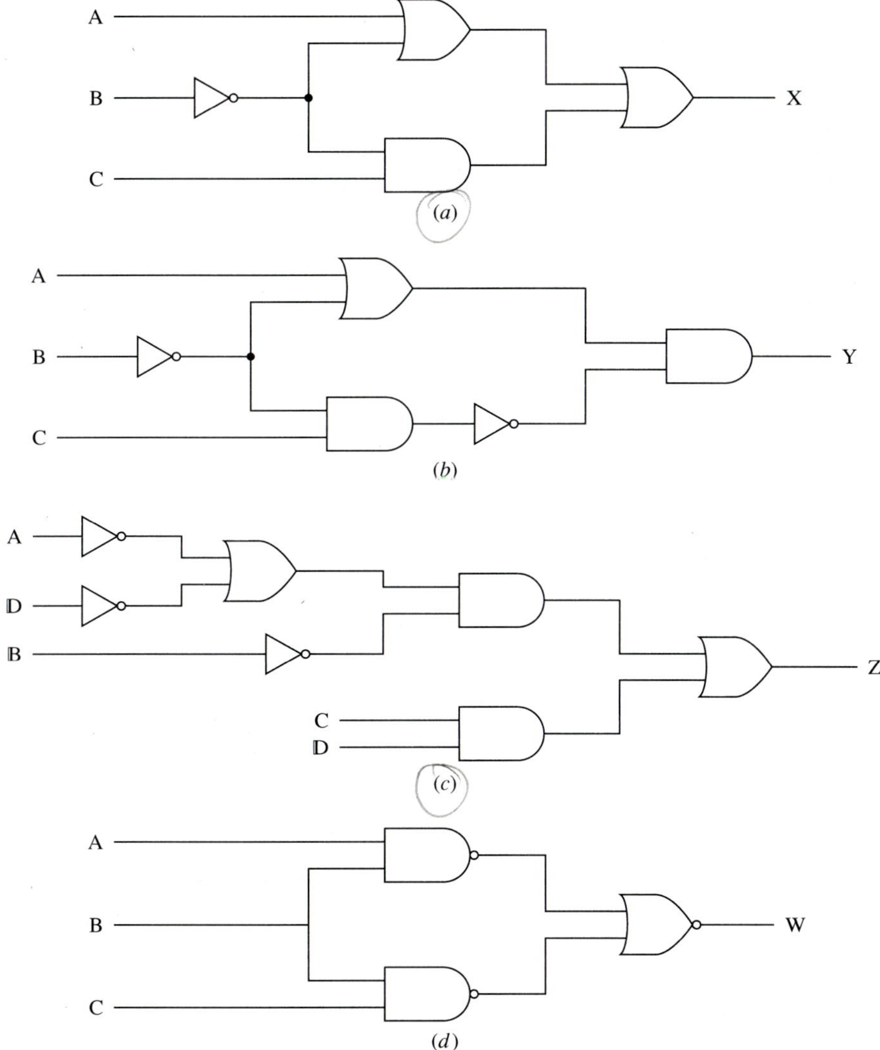

2.8. Draw logic diagrams for the two outputs C_o and S from a full adder using inverters and AND and OR gates. Simplify the diagrams as much as you can.

2.9. A three-input exclusive-OR gate has an output of 1 when an odd number of its inputs is 1. Construct a truth table for a three-input exclusive-OR gate and draw a logic diagram for it using the three basic gates.

2.10. A one-out-of-eight decoder circuit is shown below. For each of the following input signal conditions list the eight outputs (X0 through X7):

a. $A = 0, B = 1, C = 1$, Enable $= 1$ b. $A = 1, B = 0, C = 1$, Enable $= 0$
c. $A = 0, B = 0, C = 0$, Enable $= 1$ d. $A = 1, B = 1, C = 0$, Enable $= 1$

A(MSB) X0
B X1
C X2
Enable X3
X4
X5
X6
X7

2.11. Show how two one-out-of-eight decoders and an inverter may be used to construct a one-out-of-sixteen decoder. The final circuit will not have an enable input. Show how to add an enable input using two AND gates.

2.12. Generate the transition table for the following circuit. Specify X and Y for the inputs and $Q+$ for the output.

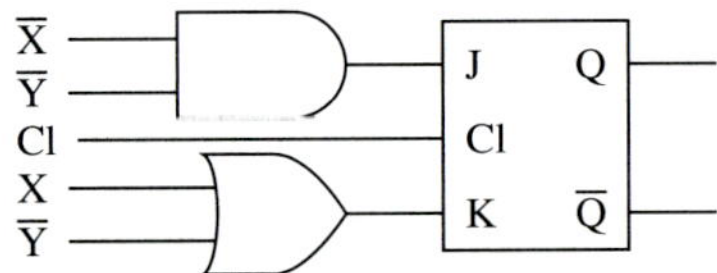

2.13. A pair of cross-connected NAND gates may be used as an R-S flip-flop with behavior similar to (but somewhat different from) the NOR gate R-S flip-flop introduced in this chapter. Draw a diagram of the NAND circuit and label the set and reset inputs. Describe how this NAND circuit would differ from the NOR circuit.

2.14. Add the necessary gates to a negative-edge-triggered D-type flip-flop to convert it into a J-K-type flip-flop. HINT: Start by constructing a table listing the D input required for each possible combination of J and K.

2.15. Sketch the timing diagram showing the output of a negative-edge-triggered J-K flip-flop whose inputs are shown below. The output is initially 0.

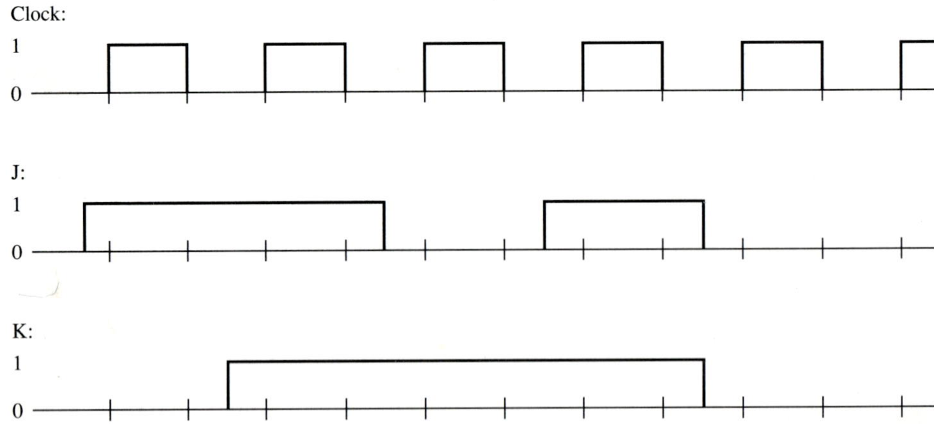

2.16. Draw timing diagrams for the outputs of the following circuits, each of which uses negative-edge-triggered flip-flops. Assume that all of the flop-flops start in the 0 state.

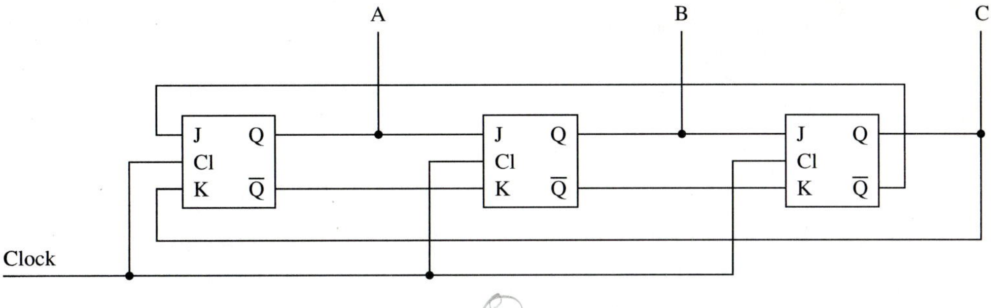

(*a*)

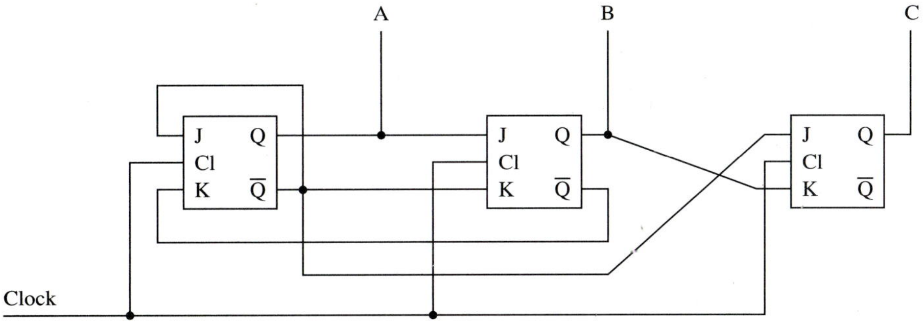

(*b*)

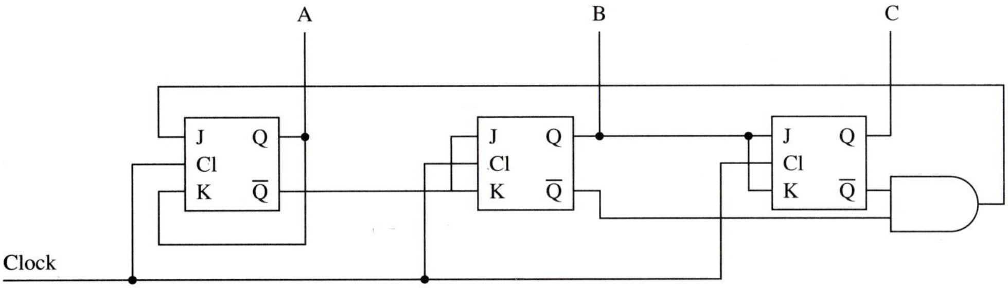

(*c*)

2.17. Modify the count-to-16 binary counter shown below to make it count to 10, i.e., to recycle from an output of 1001 to an output of 0000 on the succeeding clock cycle.

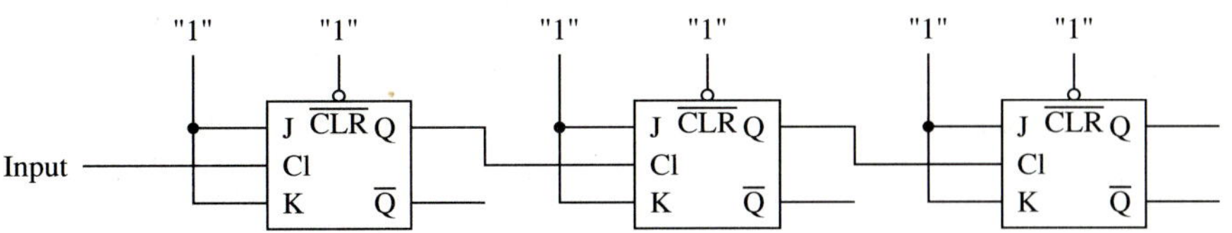

2.18. Show how to construct a data register similar to the one in Figure 2.25 using J-K-type flip-flops rather than D-type flip-flops.

2.19. Show how three J-K flip-flops can be interconnected to form a three-bit shift register which shifts right on a SHIFT signal with 0s coming in from the left. The preset/clear inputs will be used to load the register.

2.20. Modify the circuit of problem 2.19 to include a control signal ROT. When ROT is 0, the register is to behave as it was originally designed to do. When ROT is 1, the register is to *rotate* its contents right (shift one place right on each clock pulse with the right most bit coming back in from the left).

2.21. The crystal oscillator in a digital watch typically generates a train of alternating 1s and 0s at a precise rate of 32,768 cycles per second. Using divide-by-ten counters, divide-by-six counters, and divide-by-two-to-the-*n*th counters, show how to generate the following frequencies from this crystal oscillator. When using a divide-by-two-to-the-*n*th counter, specify the value of *n*.

a. one cycle per second
b. one cycle per ten seconds
c. one cycle per minute
d. one cycle per hour
e. one cycle per day

CHAPTER 3

BIT PATTERNS

The symbols "0" and "1" have been chosen arbitrarily to represent the two binary signals in computer circuits. Thus, for example, rather than describing a pattern of signal voltages on four wires as being +5 Volts, 0 Volts, 0 Volts, and +5 Volts respectively, one would describe them as 1001. Binary signal patterns provide the exclusive mechanism for storing information and conveying it from one place to another within a computer. This chapter describes many of the forms that these patterns may take and some of the ways in which they may be interpreted.

3.1 NUMBER SYSTEMS

Numbers constitute one of the primary types of information which may be represented by binary patterns. An understanding of the ways in which numbers can be represented by such patterns depends upon an understanding of number systems in general and of *non decimal positional number systems* in particular.

3.1.1 Positional Number Systems

In a positional number system the actual value which a numerical symbol has depends upon its position within the number. In a nonpositional number system such as the roman numeral system a symbol has the same value regardless of its position. Consider the symbol "7" in the number 17 and in the number 1735. In the first case it has a value of 7, but in the second, it has a value of 700 by virtue of its position. On the other hand, consider the symbol "V" in the numbers XV and LVIII. In each case it has a value of 5, even though its position is quite different in the two numbers.

Positional number systems are based upon an integer value called the *radix* or *base* of the system. The radix is the number of symbols that are available to be used to form a number in that system. For example, the decimal number system has a radix of 10 and uses 10 symbols (0 through 9) with which to form numbers. The binary number system has a radix of two and uses two symbols (0 and 1). In order to make it possible to keep track of position in a number, one of the symbols must represent a value of zero.

In general, the value of a specific symbol in a number is given by the product of its intrinsic value and the quantity R^n, where R is the value of the radix and n is the (integer) position of the symbol within the number. The position n is measured from a location called the *radix point* (in the decimal number system this is the decimal point). The first place to the left of the radix point has a position of $n = 0$, and each successive place to the left has a more positive position. The first place to the right of the radix point has a position of $n = -1$, and each successive place to the right has a more negative position.

The total value of a number is given by the following equation:

$$\begin{aligned} Q_R &= S_N R^N + S_{N-1} R^{N-1} + \cdots + S_0 R^0 + S_{-1} R^{-1} + \cdots + S_{-M} R^{-M} \\ &= \sum_{n=-M}^{N} S_n R^n \end{aligned} \tag{3.1}$$

where Q_R is the value of a number being represented in the base R, S_i is the symbol value of the symbol in position i, and the number has positions ranging from M places to the right of the radix point to $N + 1$ (counting $n = 0$) to the left of the radix point.

An example in the decimal system is:

$$\begin{aligned} 348.06_{10} &= 3 \times 10^2 + 4 \times 10^1 + 8 \times 10^0 + 0 \times 10^{-1} + 6 \times 10^{-2} \\ &= 300 + 40 + 8 + 0/10 + 6/100 \end{aligned}$$

3.1.2 Nondecimal Number Systems

In everyday human activities the decimal number system with its radix of 10 is commonly used. However, because of the binary nature of the signals, different systems are used when dealing with the internal workings of computers. The *binary system* (base 2), the *octal system* (base 8), and the *hexadecimal system* (base 16) are used with computers.

The importance of the binary system is probably apparent to you at this point. The octal and hexadecimal (*hex*) systems are useful because their radixes (8 and 16) are integer powers of 2 and this leads to a unique interrelationship between these systems and the binary system. This interrelationship will be discussed later after examining the number systems themselves.

When the base of a number system is less than 10, the symbol set used is a subset of the decimal symbols. Thus, in the binary system the symbols used are 0 and 1; in the octal system, 0 through 7. When the base is larger than 10, additional symbols must be added to the decimal set. The most common symbol set currently used in the hexadecimal system (base 16) consists of the decimal symbols 0 through 9 and A (for 10), B (11), C (12), D (13), E (14), and F (15). Examples of numbers in these non-decimal systems are (where the subscript indicates the base):

$$\begin{aligned} 101.11_2 &= 1 \times 2^2 + 0 \times 2^1 + 1 \times 2^0 + 1 \times 2^{-1} + 1 \times 2^{-2} \\ &= 4 + 0 + 1 + 0.5 + 0.25 \\ &= 5.75_{10} \end{aligned}$$

$$\begin{aligned} 523.4_8 &= 5 \times 8^2 + 2 \times 8^1 + 3 \times 8^0 + 4 \times 8^{-1} \\ &= 320 + 16 + 3 + 0.5 \\ &= 339.5_{10} \end{aligned}$$

$$\begin{aligned} \mathrm{A3D.2}_{16} &= \mathrm{A} \times 16^2 + 3 \times 16^1 + \mathrm{D} \times 16^0 + 2 \times 16^{-1} \\ &= 10 \times 256 + 3 \times 16 + 13 \times 1 + 2 \times 0.0625 \\ &= 2560 + 48 + 13 + 0.125 \\ &= 2621.125_{10} \end{aligned}$$

As shown in the above examples, conversion from any other base to decimal is accomplished by carrying out the arithmetic of equation 3.1. To convert from decimal to any other base, the integer and decimal parts must be dealt with separately. To convert from a decimal integer to any other base, observe the result of dividing the integer part of equation 3.1 by the radix:

$$Q_R = S_N R^N + S_{N-1} R^{N-1} + \cdots + S_0 R^0 \qquad \text{(3.1—integer part)}$$

$$Q_R/R = S_N R^{N-1} + S_{N-1} R^{N-2} + \cdots + S_1 R^0 + S_0 R^{-1} \qquad (3.2)$$

In equation 3.2, dividing the integer Q by the radix R generates a mixed number, one having both an integer part and a fractional part. But if two mixed numbers are equal then their fractional parts and integer parts must be separately equal. Thus, from equation 3.2, the fractional part of Q_R/R equals $S_0 R^{-1}$,or the remainder obtained when Q divided by R is equal to S_0.

Thus, to convert a decimal integer to any other base, divide it by the radix of the desired number system. The remainder is the least significant digit in the desired system. Discard the remainder and repeat the process to generate the other digits.

For example, to convert 1532_{10} to octal:

Division	*Remainder*	*Octal Digit*
1532/8 = 191	4	$S_0 = 4$
191/8 = 23	7	$S_1 = 7$
23/8 = 2	7	$S_2 = 7$
2/8 = 0	2	$S_3 = 2$

So 1532_{10} is equal to 2774_8.

To convert 1532_{10} to binary:

Division	*Remainder*	*Binary Digit*
1532/2 = 766	0	$S_0 = 0$
766/2 = 383	0	$S_1 = 0$
383/2 = 191	1	$S_2 = 1$
191/2 = 95	1	$S_3 = 1$
95/2 = 47	1	$S_4 = 1$
47/2 = 23	1	$S_5 = 1$
23/2 = 11	1	$S_6 = 1$
11/2 = 5	1	$S_7 = 1$
5/2 = 2	1	$S_8 = 1$
2/2 = 1	0	$S_9 = 0$
1/2 = 0	1	$S_{10} = 1$

So 1532_{10} is equal to 10111111100_2.

To convert 1532_{10} to hexadecimal:

Division	*Remainder*	*Octal Digit*
1532/16 = 95	12 (C)	$S_0 = C$
95/16 = 5	15 (F)	$S_1 = F$
5/16 = 0	5	$S_2 = 5$

So 1532_{10} is equal to $5FC_{16}$.

To convert a decimal fraction to any other base multiply it by the radix of the desired number system. The integer part of the result is then the most significant fractional digit in the desired system. Drop the integer part and repeat the process to generate the other digits. Since fractions are seldom used in microprocessor control systems, they will not be discussed any further in this book. Examples of the conversion of fractions from decimal to other systems are left for the problems at the end of this chapter.

3.1.3 The Binary Number System

The term *bit*, which is applied to each individual symbol in a binary pattern, is a contraction of the expression *binary digit*. The implication is that binary patterns are often used to represent numbers using the binary number system. Thus, the eight-bit pattern 01010101 can be said to represent the decimal integer 85 since $01010101_2 = 85_{10}$.

The first bit in any group of bits may be a 0 or a 1. For each of these possibilities, the second bit may be a 0 or a 1. For each of these four possibilities, the next bit may be a 0 or a 1. Thus, a group of n bits may have any one of 2^n different possible patterns.

TABLE 3.1
Integer powers of two (to be memorized)

n	2^n
0	1
1	2
2	4
3	8
4	16
5	32
6	64
7	128
8	256
9	512
10	1024 (1K)

The binary patterns within a computer are organized into groups, typically of eight bits or an integer multiple of eight bits each. A group of eight bits is called a *byte*, with a half of a byte referred to as a *nibble* (spelled *nybble* by some wits!). One byte is capable of 256 different patterns, one nibble, of 16.

Because of the importance of the binary number system it will be necessary to learn the integer powers of two up to 2^{10}. Table 3.1, which lists these integer powers of two, should be committed to memory. Perhaps this might best be done by working a large number of problems of the sort provided at the end of this chapter. Whether that approach or sheer rote memorization works best, the table must be memorized. This table will be as important when working with computers as are the addition and multiplication tables when dealing with decimal numbers.

The value of 2^{10} is 1024, which is so close to 1000 that it is universally recognized and given a special symbol K. Note that this is an upper-case letter in contrast with the symbol k which stands for the prefix kilo (1000) in the mks system of physical units. The symbol K is used in a similar manner to the way k is used. Thus, one may use the expression 8K bytes of memory to stand for 8×1024 or 8096 bytes of memory.

The value of 2^{10} is useful in determining nearby powers of two. Since $2^{10} = 1024$, 2^{11} must be twice that or 2048 and 2^9 must be one-half that or 512. Also note that 2^{14} is $2^4 \times 2^{10}$ which in turn is 2^4K or 16K or 16×1024. Similarly, the symbol M may be used to refer to the value $2^{20} = 2^{10}\text{K} = 1024\text{K}$. Often the prefix mega is used rather than M, as in the expression "two megabytes of memory".

3.1.4 The Octal and Hexadecimal Number Systems

The octal and hexadecimal number systems are important primarily because they provide shorthand ways of remembering and communicating binary patterns. This is a direct consequence of the fact that the radixes in these two systems (8 and 16) are integer powers of two.

Consider the binary pattern 101101011010. This pattern consists of a string of 12 symbols and as a consequence it cannot be conveniently retained in human short-term memory. Take the time right now to convert the binary number represented by this pattern into decimal and then from decimal into octal and then from decimal into hexadecimal. The values are 2906 in decimal, 5532 in octal and B5A in hexadecimal. That is:

$$101101011010_2 = 2906_{10} = 5532_8 = B5A_{16}$$

Now examine the original binary pattern. Convert each group of three bits, starting from the right, into the equivalent octal digit (0 through 7). The result will be 5532, which is the correct octal value. That is:

101	/	101	/	011	/	010	=	5 / 5 / 3 / 2
5		5		3		2		

Similarly, if each group of four bits starting from the right is converted into the equivalent hex digit (0 through *F*), the result will be the correct hexadecimal value of *B*5*A*:

1011	/	0101	/	1010	=	B / 5 / A
B		5		A		

This example shows the importance of the octal and the hexadecimal number systems. Each provides a convenient way for humans to communicate binary patterns to each other. In the example above, it is more convenient to describe the binary pattern 101101011010 as octal 5532 or hex B5A. Each of these forms requires fewer symbols to convey the same information. Of course, inside a computer the pattern would still be 101101011010—strictly a binary pattern.

When describing the internal behavior of computers it will be necessary to convert back and forth between binary patterns and their hexadecimal or octal equivalent. To do this readily the three-bit binary patterns for the octal symbols 0 through 7 and the four-bit binary patterns for the hex symbols 0 through *F* must be committed to memory. Then, when discussing the binary pattern 100001101010, for example, it can be described as octal 4152 or hex 86A. The forms 4152 and 86A are more suited to human short-term memory requirements and each can easily be converted to the binary pattern if necessary.

Of the two alternatives (octal and hex), hex is by far the more popular choice because it requires fewer symbols to represent a given binary pattern. The primary reason that the octal representation is used at all is because it was very popular in the earlier era of the twelve-bit mini-computer. Its use resulted in balanced four-digit representations for the twelve-bit binary patterns found in those computers.

Another important table to memorize, then, is the table of binary equivalents for the hex digits 0 through F (Table 3.2).

TABLE 3.2
Binary equivalents of hex digits (to be memorized)

Hex	Binary	Hex	Binary
0	0000	8	1000
1	0001	9	1001
2	0010	A	1010
3	0011	B	1011
4	0100	C	1100
5	0101	D	1101
6	0110	E	1110
7	0111	F	1111

3.2 ADDITION IN NONDECIMAL SYSTEMS

Arithmetic techniques for nondecimal number systems can be developed by carefully analyzing decimal arithmetic and extending the insights obtained therein to these other systems. In this book only the operations of addition and subtraction will be discussed, using unsigned numbers as well as an important signed-number representation.

3.2.1 Decimal Addition

When adding two decimal integers the two least significant digits are added first. If the sum exceeds 9 (the largest-valued symbol) the amount in excess of 10 (the radix) is written in the least significant position for the sum and a carry of 1 to the next position (the 10's position) is noted. The next pair of digits and this carry are then added together. The process is repeated until all of the digit/digit/carry triplets are added. Each time (after the first) that digits are added, three digits are added together (one from each number and the carry from the next less significant position). After each individual addition the carry out must be either 0 or 1.

3.2.2 Hexadecimal Addition

To extend the decimal addition process to hexadecimal numbers, try to add A6C5 to 3A87. First add 7 to 5. This sum does not exceed the largest symbol (F) so write the sum ($7 + 5 =$ decimal $12 =$ C) and note a carry of 0. Next add the digits 8 and *C* with this carry of 0. The sum (decimal 20) exceeds the largest symbol (F) and exceeds the radix (decimal 16) by four. So write the sum digit (4) and note a carry of one. Repeat these steps for A + 6 + 1 to get a sum of one and a carry of one. Then repeat again for the last triplet to complete the sum as shown below.

	0	1	1	0		(Carries to next place)	
		A	6	C	5	(Augend)	= 42,693
+		3	A	8	7	(Addend)	= 14,983
	0	E	1	4	C	(Sum)	= 57,676

In this example, the decimal equivalents are shown to the right of the hexadecimal values. The result can be verified by checking the addition in decimal.

Notice that when two four-digit numbers are added, a five-digit result is possible because of the carry out from the most significant position. In the above example this is emphasized by showing that carry out is a part of the final sum even though in this case its value is 0.

3.2.3 Binary Addition

Binary numbers can be added by using a similar procedure. The example shown below illustrates the addition of two binary numbers with the decimal equivalents on the right.

	0	0	1	1	1	1	0	1		(Carries)	
		1	0	1	0	1	1	0	1	(Augend)	= 173
+		0	0	0	1	1	1	0	1	(Addend)	= 29
	0	1	1	0	0	1	0	1	0	(Sum)	– 202

When the triplet sum is odd the sum bit for that position is 1 and when the triplet sum is even the sum bit is 0. When the triplet sum is 0 or 1 the carry bit from that position is 0 and when the triplet sum is 2 or 3 the carry bit is 1. With binary numbers the triplet sum can not exceed 3.

A combinational logic circuit can be designed to add binary numbers represented by binary signals. The adding circuit used to implement the repeated triplet addition must accept three binary inputs: the augend bit, the addend bit, and the carry bit, and must generate two binary outputs: the sum bit and the carry out to the next position. A circuit which can do this is the full-adder circuit described in Section 2.3.3.

An entire n-bit adder can be assembled from n full-adders as shown in Figure 3.1. Notice that this circuit implements the binary addition process directly by adding each triplet and passing on the carry out to the next triplet adder. An adder which operates in this fashion is called a *ripple-carry adder*.

Consider the example below and picture the result as it would be generated by the ripple-carry adder of Figure 3.1. The rightmost full adder (FA0) has inputs of 110 for ABC_i and generates the least significant sum bit together with C_o. FA0 passes its C_o(1 in this example) to C_i of FA1 where it is combined with AB of 01 to generate the next sum and carry bits. In this fashion, the carries are passed on to successive full adders, each of which generates one sum bit and a new carry bit to be passed on. The final sum requires a total of nine bits.

	1	1	1	0	0	0	1	1		(Carries)
		1	0	1	0	0	0	0	1	(Augend)
+		0	1	1	1	1	0	1	1	(Addend)
	1	0	0	0	1	1	1	0	0	(Sum)

The adder circuit shown in Figure 3.1 can add eight-bit operands. Every computer will have a specific *word size* which is the number of bits with which it represents numbers. In this example, the word size is eight bits but the resulting sum won't fit

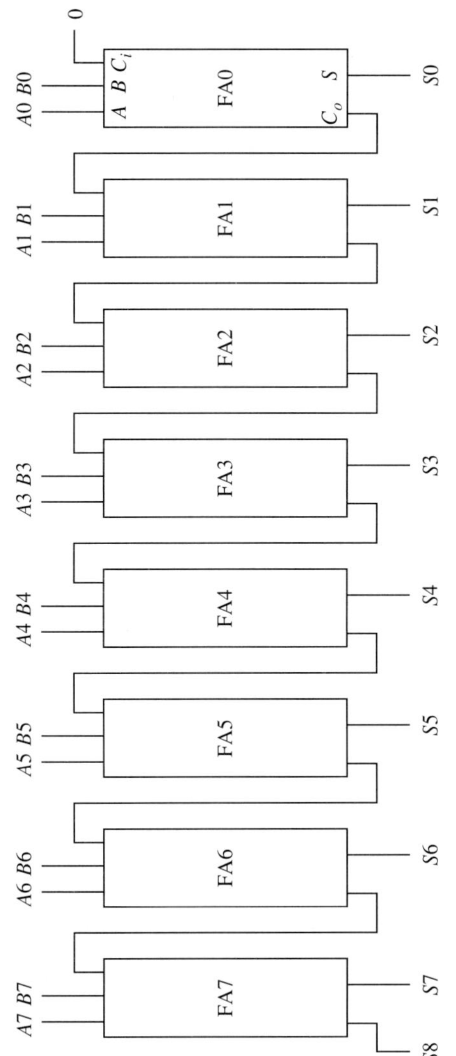

FIGURE 3.1
A ripple-carry adder.

into eight bits. This is called an *overflow* condition, and the result is said to overflow the capacity of the computer. Overflow during the addition of unsigned integers is indicated by a carry out of 1 from the most significant bit position.

The fact that the result of an operation overflows the capacity of the computer or that it does not must be recorded in some way so that the user (via the program) may take corrective action if necessary. This information is easily recorded after binary addition by retaining the most significant carry (regardless of its value) in a flip-flop which can later be accessed by the user. The carry out of the last bit position is called simply the *carry*; and the flip-flop which retains it is called the *carry flip-flop* or the *carry flag*.

3.3 BINARY SUBTRACTION

Computer hardware typically does not perform subtraction as such. Instead, subtraction is performed by changing the sign of the subtrahend and adding it to the minuend using whatever adder circuitry the computer has. In order for this approach to work properly numbers must be represented inside the computer in a special fashion.

3.3.1 Unsigned Integers

A group of n bits can have any one of 2^n different possible patterns. Thus, a group of n bits used to represent unsigned integers can represent integers ranging from 0 to $2^n - 1$. Unsigned integers are most commonly represented in a computer in binary form as described in Section 3.1.2. With eight bits, the patterns range from 00000000 to 11111111 (00 to FF in hex). These patterns represent the decimal integers 0 through 255. In sixteen bits the patterns range from 16 0s to 16 1s (0000 to FFFF) and represent 0 through 65, 535 (64K − 1). Integers represented in this fashion are said to be in *straight binary* or *unsigned binary* form.

3.3.2 Sign-Magnitude Notation

A simple way to represent a signed number is to affix one extra bit to the pattern and interpret it as a sign. This leads to the so-called *sign-magnitude* representation, where the sign bit is in the most significant (leftmost) position, and is interpreted to mean plus if it is 0 and minus if it is 1. The sign-magnitude representation finds limited use[1] in computers since it requires the inclusion of a separate subtracter circuit.

3.3.3 Two's Complement Signed Numbers

Instead, signed binary integers are commonly represented in what is called *two's complement* format. In this format the sign becomes an integral part of the num-

---

[1]See Section 3.4.3 for the use of sign-magnitude representation in floating point numbers.

ber and need not be kept track of separately. Also, the computer can subtract a number by simply changing its sign and adding it. The hardware which is used to perform binary addition can be used and will obtain correct results provided that the two's complement format is used for the operands. The primary motivation for using the 2's complement format is this fact that no special subtracter circuit is necessary.

Being able to understand and use the two's complement format requires the ability to perform the following four operations very quickly and accurately:

1. Determine the sign of a number.
2. Determine the magnitude of a number.
3. Change the sign of a number.
4. Determine the relative magnitudes of two numbers, i.e., determine which is larger in magnitude.

The sign of a two's complement number is determined by the most significant bit (the leftmost bit). Positive numbers begin with a 0; negative numbers with a 1.

Positive numbers are represented in straight binary form with a most significant bit of 0. That is, the magnitude of a positive integer in two's complement form is determined by adding the products of the weight of each position and the bit in that position. In the examples below, several positive numbers are shown in eight-bit two's complement form.

$$+85 = 01010101 = (+) + 1 \times 64 + 0 \times 32 + 1 \times 16 + 0 \times 8 + 1 \times 4 + 0 \times 2 + 1 \times 1$$

$$+54 = 00110110 = (+) + 0 \times 64 + 1 \times 32 + 1 \times 16 + 0 \times 8 + 1 \times 4 + 1 \times 2 + 0 \times 1$$

$$+24 = 00011000 = (+) + 0 \times 64 + 0 \times 32 + 1 \times 16 + 1 \times 8 + 0 \times 4 + 0 \times 2 + 0 \times 1$$

$$+1 = 00000001 = (+) + 0 \times 64 + 0 \times 32 + 0 \times 16 + 0 \times 8 + 0 \times 4 + 0 \times 2 + 1 \times 1$$

Notice that the leftmost or leading bit contributes 0 magnitude and represents the sign. Also notice that the smaller the positive number the more leading 0s it has.

The sign of a two's complement number is changed by complementing each bit (changing 1s to 0s and 0s to 1s) and then adding one to the result. This operation itself is often referred to as "taking the two's complement" of the original number. The following examples illustrate the operation by changing the signs of the positive numbers shown above.

$$-85 = -(01010101) = 10101010 + 1 = 10101011$$

$$-54 = -(00110110) = 11001001 + 1 = 11001010$$

$$-24 = -(00011000) = 11100111 + 1 = 11101000$$

$$-1 = -(00000001) = 11111110 + 1 = 11111111$$

Notice that the first bit conveys the sign of the number. Also notice that the smaller the magnitude of a negative number the more leading 1s it has.

In the following examples the signs of these same negative numbers are changed back to positive. Regardless of the direction of the change the process of changing the sign is the same, i.e., it is necessary to complement each bit and add one.

$$+85 = -(-85) = -(10101011) = 01010100 + 1 = 01010101$$

$$+54 = -(-54) = -(11001010) = 00110101 + 1 = 00110110$$

$$+24 = -(-24) = -(11101000) = 00010111 + 1 = 00011000$$

$$+1 = -(-1) = -(11111111) = 00000000 + 1 = 00000001$$

One way to determine the magnitude of a negative two's complement number is to change its sign and then evaluate the positive counterpart. An alternative is to assign to each bit position the same weight that it has in positive numbers but to include a weight of -2^{n-1} for the most significant bit position. This is the negative of the value which that bit position would have if the number were an unsigned binary number. The value of the number is then determined by adding up the products of the bit weights by the bit values. This method works for positive numbers as well as for negative ones. The examples below illustrate this method of evaluating both negative and positive two's complement numbers.

$$10101011 = 1 \times (-128) + 0 \times 64 + 1 \times 32 + 0 \times 16 + 1 \times 8 + 0 \times 4 + 1 \times 2 + 1 \times 1 = -128 + 43 = -85$$

$$11001010 = 1 \times (-128) + 1 \times 64 + 0 \times 32 + 0 \times 16 + 1 \times 8 + 0 \times 4 + 1 \times 2 + 0 \times 1 = -128 + 74 = -54$$

$$11101000 = 1 \times -(128) + 1 \times 64 + 1 \times 32 + 0 \times 16 + 1 \times 8 + 0 \times 4 + 0 \times 2 + 0 \times 1 = -128 + 104 = -24$$

$$11111111 = 1 \times (-128) + 1 \times 64 + 1 \times 32 + 1 \times 16 + 1 \times 8 + 1 \times 4 + 1 \times 2 + 1 \times 1 = -128 + 127 = -1$$

$$01010101 = 0 \times (-128) + 1 \times 64 + 0 \times 32 + 1 \times 16 + 0 \times 8 + 1 \times 4 + 0 \times 2 + 1 \times 1 = +85$$

$$10000000 = 1 \times (-128) + 0 \times 64 + 0 \times 32 + 0 \times 16 + 0 \times 8 + 0 \times 4 + 0 \times 2 + 0 \times 1 = -128$$

The number 1000000 (−128) is the largest magnitude negative number that can be represented in eight bits. It has no positive counterpart since the largest positive number is 01111111, which represents +127.

3.3.4 The Addition of Two's Complement Numbers

Signed numbers in two's complement form can be added in the same manner as unsigned numbers. Provided that there is no overflow, the sum will be in the correct two's complement form. The eight-bit examples below illustrate the addition of signed numbers in two's complement form in which there is no overflow. The numbers in parentheses are the decimal equivalents.

$$
\begin{array}{cccccccccc}
 & 0 & 0 & 1 & 1 & 0 & 0 & 0 & 0 & \\
 & 0 & 0 & 1 & 1 & 0 & 1 & 0 & 0 & (+52) \\
+ & 0 & 0 & 0 & 1 & 1 & 0 & 1 & 1 & (+27) \\
\hline
 & 0 & 1 & 0 & 0 & 1 & 1 & 1 & 1 & (+79)
\end{array}
$$

$$
\begin{array}{cccccccccc}
 & 0 & 0 & 0 & 1 & 1 & 0 & 0 & 0 & \\
 & 0 & 1 & 0 & 1 & 1 & 0 & 0 & 0 & (88) \\
+ & 1 & 0 & 0 & 0 & 1 & 0 & 1 & 1 & (-117) \\
\hline
 & 1 & 1 & 1 & 0 & 0 & 0 & 1 & 1 & (-29)
\end{array}
$$

$$
\begin{array}{cccccccccc}
 & 1 & 1 & 1 & 1 & 1 & 1 & 0 & 0 & \\
 & 0 & 1 & 1 & 0 & 1 & 1 & 1 & 0 & (+110) \\
+ & 1 & 0 & 1 & 1 & 1 & 1 & 0 & 0 & (-68) \\
\hline
 & 0 & 0 & 1 & 0 & 1 & 0 & 1 & 0 & (+42)
\end{array}
$$

$$
\begin{array}{cccccccccc}
 & 1 & 1 & 1 & 1 & 0 & 0 & 0 & 0 & \\
 & 1 & 1 & 0 & 1 & 0 & 0 & 0 & 0 & (+48) \\
+ & 1 & 0 & 1 & 1 & 1 & 1 & 1 & 1 & (-65) \\
\hline
 & 1 & 0 & 0 & 0 & 1 & 1 & 1 & 1 & (-113)
\end{array}
$$

The final carry out is not shown in these examples because it has no significance. In the first two examples the carry is a 0, while in the second two examples the carry is a 1. Yet in each of these four examples the result fits into eight bits and there is no overflow. The carry conveys no information as to the condition of overflow in the case of two's complement operands. This is in direct contrast to the case for unsigned binary operands.

Assume that the "natural" ordering of binary patterns is that of the unsigned binary numbers as shown in Figure 3.2. The two's complement system splits the range into two groups and moves the upper group down to the left of the origin to become the negative numbers while retaining the same ordering within each group.

The splitting of the system into negative and positive numbers is shown in Figure 3.3. In the eight-bit case, the original upper group of 10000000 through 11111111

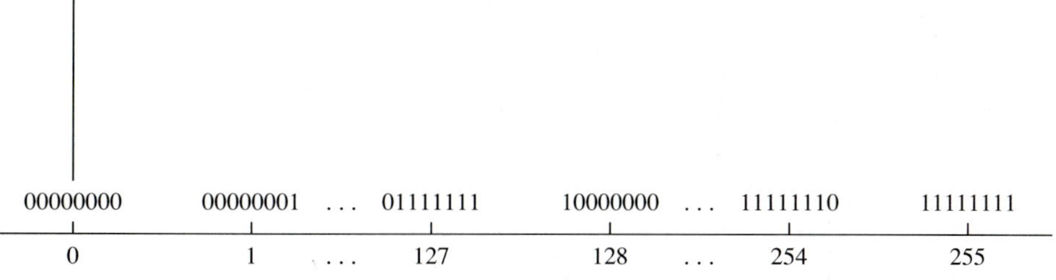

FIGURE 3.2
Graphical representation of unsigned binary numbers.

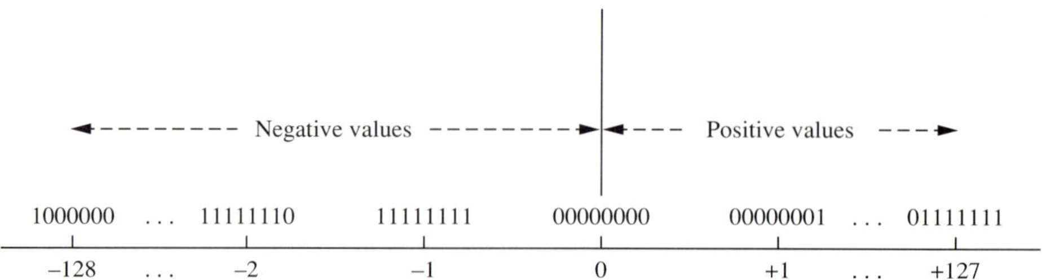

FIGURE 3.3
Graphical representation of two's complement numbers.

(80 through FF in hex or 128 through 255 in decimal) is moved to become the group of negative numbers (−128 through −1 in decimal). Thus, the two's complement system preserves the "natural" order of the patterns while using half of them to represent negative numbers. It is this ordering of the two's complement numbers which preserves the integrity of the addition operation and allows the standard binary addition process to generate correct answers.

Notice that whenever two unlike-signed numbers are added, overflow is impossible. This is illustrated by adding the numbers geometrically as shown in Figure 3.4. Moving to the right any allowed distance and then moving back to the left another allowed distance can not result in leaving the bounds of the system.

It is only when two positive numbers or two negative numbers are added together that overflow is possible. Figure 3.5 shows that if overflow occurs in either of these cases, the result will be that the sign of the sum is different than the (common) sign of the original operands. Thus, the overflow test for the addition of two's complement numbers might involve the comparing of these signs. However, a simpler test can be devised based upon detailed analyses of these cases.

Consider the case of adding two positive numbers and generating an overflow as shown below. The sign bits of the operands are both 0 but if there is overflow the sign bit in the sum must be 1. The only way this can occur is if the carry into the sign position is 1. Then, as a consequence, the carry out of the sign position will be a 0. Therefore, overflow is indicated when the two most significant carries are 01.

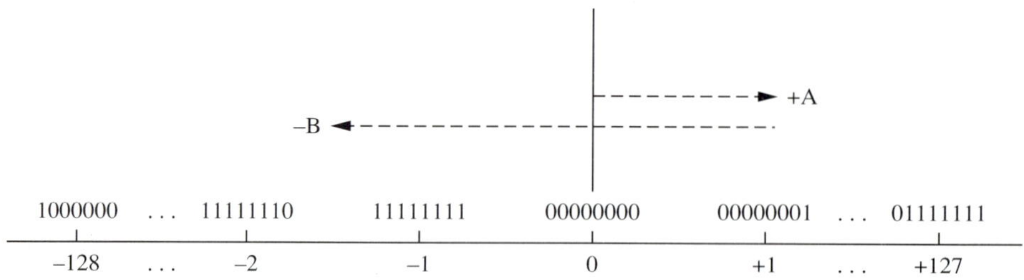

FIGURE 3.4
Addition of unlike-signed two's complement numbers.

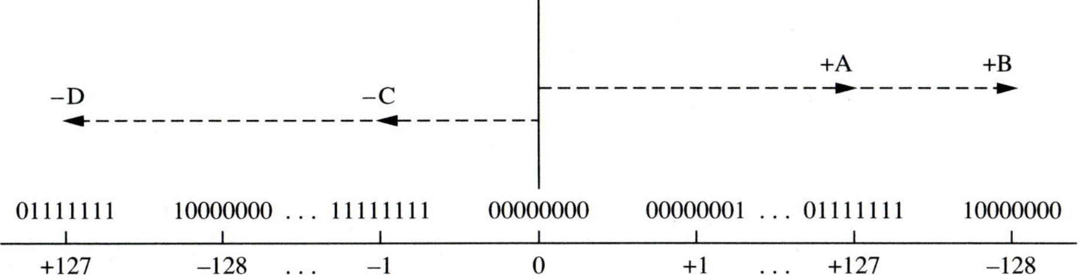

FIGURE 3.5
Overflow from two's complement addition.

		Sign Bit	
Carries:	0	1	· · ·
Augend:		0	· · ·
Addend:		0	· · ·
Sum:		1	· · ·

Overflow from adding two negative numbers is illustrated below. Here, the sign bits of the operands are both 1 and the sign bit of the sum is 0. The only way this can occur is if the carry into the sign position is 0 while the carry out of this position is 1. In this case overflow is indicated when the two most significant carries are 10.

		Sign Bit	
Carries:	1	0	· · ·
Augend:		1	· · ·
Addend:		1	· · ·
Sum:		0	· · ·

If the signs of the operands are unlike then a carry of 1 into the sign position will generate a carry out of 1, while a carry of 0 into the sign position will generate a carry out of 0. Therefore, the condition of no overflow is indicated whenever the last two carries are either 00 or 11.

In summary, overflow is indicated when the two most significant carries are 01 or 10; absence of overflow is indicated when they are 00 or 11. Thus, the exclusive-OR function of the last two carries may be used to detect the overflow condition. This is the way overflow is detected within a computer after the addition of two's complement numbers. The exclusive-OR of the last two carries is called the *overflow bit* and is saved in a flip-flop called the *overflow flag*.

Within the computer there is no distinction between a bit pattern which represents unsigned numbers and one which represents signed numbers. The circuits which perform the addition operation will save both the carry bit and the overflow bit. The user of the system knows which representation is intended and so the user must decide which of the two flags to consult in order to determine whether the result fits into the word size of the computer.

3.4 FLOATING POINT REPRESENTATION

Two important characteristics of a number system which uses a fixed number of digits are its range and its precision. The range of a number system refers to the largest and the smallest magnitude nonzero numbers which can be represented. The precision refers to the number of significant digits with which a number is represented.

3.4.1 Fixed Point Numbers

A *fixed point number* is one in which the radix point is fixed in place, whether it is specifically shown or implied. The signed and unsigned integers referred to in earlier sections of this chapter are examples of fixed point numbers with the position of the radix point implied at the right end of the number. In fixed point numbers, the range and the precision are simultaneously fixed by the position of the radix point and the number of digits.

Consider a 10-digit calculator. The range of integers which can be represented in ten digits is from 0 to (plus or minus) about 10 billion. Each number is said to have a precision of one part in 10 billion or a precision of 10 decimal digits. This precision is much higher than is often necessary in engineering or scientific calculations while the range is much smaller than is necessary. For example, it is not sufficient to calculate 15 factorial ($15 \times 14 \times 13 \times \cdots \times 1$). As a consequence, such a number system could not be used to represent the number of ways you could line up a set of pool balls along an edge of a pool table, not even approximately. The range of the system is also too small to represent many other useful and important quantities.

3.4.2 Floating Point Numbers

An alternative format for a number system divides the representation into two parts, the mantissa and the exponent. In this format, the location of the radix point moves about in the number depending on the value of the exponent, hence the term *floating point* representation. The precision of a floating point representation is determined by the number of digits allocated to the mantissa. The range is determined by the number of digits allocated to the exponent and the base used with the exponent. Thus, floating point numbers trade precision for an increased range. You are probably familiar with the floating point format known as *scientific notation* or with the exponential notation used in many calculators.

Consider the same 10-digit calculator mentioned above. A common floating point format for such a calculator uses a 7-digit mantissa with the decimal point one digit in from the left and a 2-digit signed integer exponent with a base of ten. In this format, each number has a precision of one part in 10 million, or a precision of 7 decimal digits. In exchange for this reduced precision, the floating point format has gained an integer range extending to about 10 to the hundredth power. Using this format, it is possible to determine that the value of 15 factorial is approximately 1.30764×10^{12}, so there are about 1.3 million million ways to line up a set of pool balls. The range with this format is even large enough to calculate the approximate number of grains of sand which could be crammed into the entire universe with no spaces in between![2]

3.4.3 Binary Floating Point Numbers

An example of an eight-bit binary floating point representation might be one which uses five bits for the mantissa and three bits for the exponent. Two numbers are represented in this format below. Note that separate signs are necessary for the mantissa and the exponent. Note also that the representation is not unique. Each example shows the numbers represented in four different ways using the same numbers of bits for the mantissa and exponent in each case.

$$+100.1 = +10.01 \times 2^{+01} = +100.1 \times 2^{+00} = +1001. \times 2^{-01} = +.1001 \times 2^{+11}$$

$$-1.010 = -1.010 \times 2^{+00} = -1010. \times 2^{-11} = -.001010 \times 2^{+11}$$

$$= -.1010 \times 2^{+01}$$

The last representation, in which the most significant bit of the fractional mantissa is a 1, is called the *normalized* form and is the form most commonly used. A binary floating point number is normalized when the mantissa is expressed as a binary fraction greater than or equal to 0.1 (decimal 1/2). If the mantissa is un-normalized after an arithmetic operation, it may be normalized by shifting it and changing the value of the exponent.

Most computer formats for floating point numbers express the mantissa in sign-magnitude form and the exponent as a two's complement integer. The most common base is two, with 16 used in some cases. It is common to add a positive constant to the exponent so that every exponent will be represented by a positive number. For example, a popular format uses exponents ranging from −64 to +63 which are expressed as ranging from 0 to 127 by adding 64 to each exponent. This so-called *biased exponent* simplifies some arithmetic operations.

Figure 3.6 shows three common floating point formats used in computers. Since the mantissa is always known to be a normalized fraction, the leading bit need not be shown. As a consequence, the mantissa is effectively one bit larger than the allocated space.

Floating point numbers are seldom used with microprocessors in control applications. When they are used in microprocessor-based personal computers, the arithmetic must often be carried out in the software or in special hardware accessories called *arithmetic co-processors*. Floating point operations are seldom supported by the processor itself. Therefore, this book will make no further mention of floating point formats or arithmetic operations.

[2]Using a value of 20 billion light years for the radius of the universe (approximately 1.89×10^{26}meters) and a (square) 0.5mm sand grain, the result is 2.27×10^{89} grains give or take a few.

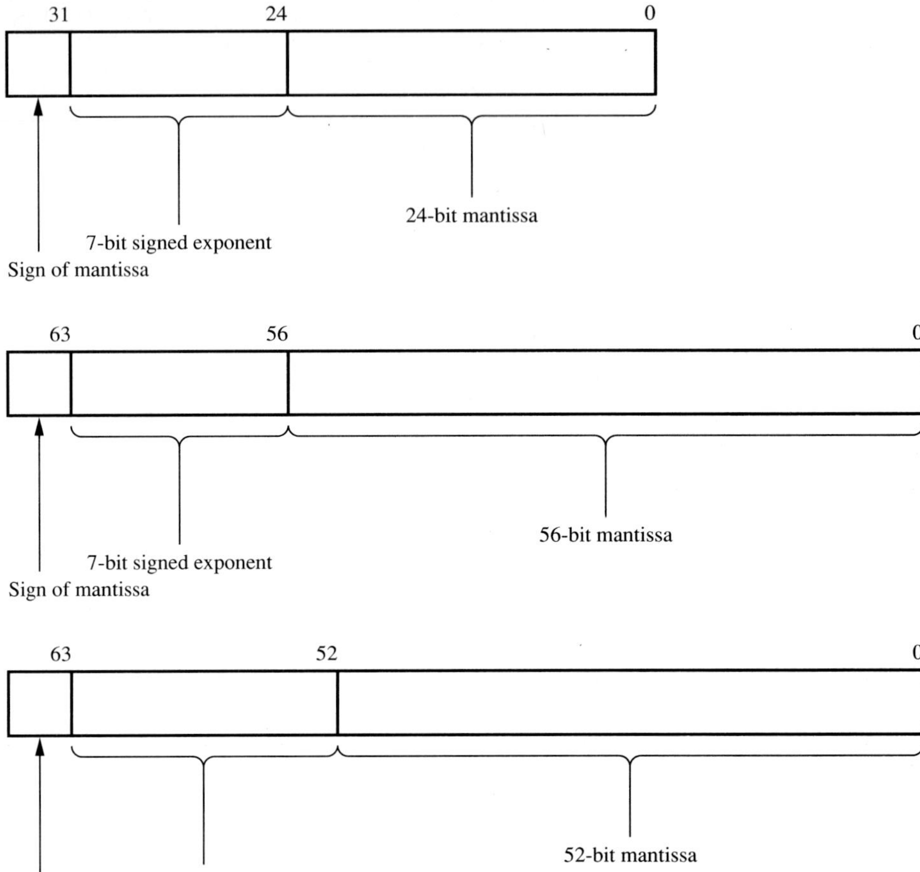

FIGURE 3.6
Floating-point formats.

3.5 BINARY-CODED DECIMAL

Most computers perform arithmetic with binary numbers. This means that the data provided by the user (which will naturally be in decimal form) must first be converted into binary form. After the necessary computations are performed, the results must be converted back into decimal form before returning them to the user. These number conversion tasks can be readily accomplished by short program segments. However, when a particular application includes a large quantity of numbers as input and output from the computer, these conversion routines can become time consuming. For such situations, most computers support some decimal arithmetic operations as well as binary ones.

In computers which support decimal operations, the operands are represented within the computer in decimal form. This means that each individual digit of each

TABLE 3.3
BCD codes for decimal digits

Decimal digit	BCD code
0	0000
1	0001
2	0010
3	0011
4	0100
5	0101
6	0110
7	0111
8	1000
9	1001

decimal number is represented in some sort of binary code. The arithmetic operations are designed to take place directly upon these coded digits with the results being generated in like-coded digits.

The simplest and most popular code for representing decimal digits within a computer is one known as *binary coded decimal* or *BCD*. Decimal numbers are represented in BCD by encoding each digit separately as a four-bit binary number. Table 3.3 lists the codes for the decimal digits. The BCD code is merely the binary equivalent of the individual digit. Thus, the decimal number 1295 would be encoded as 0001,0010,1001,0101 (1295 in hex also). Contrast this with the 16-bit unsigned binary representation of 1295 (0000,0101,0000,1111 or 050F in hex). In these examples the commas have been added in order to make the patterns easier to read; actually, each pattern within the computer includes only the binary symbols 0 and 1.

Smaller microprocessors provide decimal arithmetic support only for addition. Larger ones commonly support both addition and subtraction. In each case, the user has the option of doing the operation as if the operands were expressed in binary (unsigned or two's complement) or in decimal (BCD). When decimal is selected, the processor first calculates the result as if the operands were in binary form and then corrects it to reflect the decimal nature of the patterns.

Representing numbers in a computer in a decimal code such as BCD wastes much of the capacity of the machine. Of the 16 combinations which are possible with four bits (0000 through 1111) only ten are allowed (0000 through 1001). This means that the remaining codes can never be used. For example, a 16-bit register can contain any of the decimal integers 0 through 65,535 in unsigned binary form. However, the same register can contain only the integers 0 through 9,999 in BCD form. This is the reason that numbers are most often represented in binary internally rather than in a decimal code.

3.6 CHARACTER CODES

In addition to representing numerical values, the binary patterns within a computer may be used to represent letters of the alphabet, numerals, punctuation marks, and various other symbols. The two most commonly used standard codes for such characters are the *Extended Binary Coded Decimal Interchange Code* (*EBCDIC*—pronounced *eb-see-dick*) and the *American Standard Code for Information Interchange* (*ASCII*—pronounced *ass-key*). EBCDIC was devised by IBM and is used almost exclusively by IBM. ASCII was devised by a consortium of other manufacturers of computers and machines which generate or display symbols (keyboards, displays, printers, and the like) and is the code used in non-IBM equipment. Currently, many IBM systems, particularly those in the personal computer class, also use the ASCII code.

The ASCII code is listed in Table 3.4 in terms of the hex equivalents for the binary patterns. It is a 7-bit code and as such includes the 128 different patterns shown in the table. The first 32 patterns represent control characters which are used to identify parts of a message, to generate an audible signal, to turn equipment on or off, to return the printing carriage to the left end of the line of print, or to advance to a

TABLE 3.4
The ASCII code

	0	**1**	**2**	**3**	**4**	**5**	**6**	**7**
0	NUL	DLE	SP	0	@	P	‘	p
1	SOH	DC1	!	1	A	Q	a	q
2	STX	DC2	”	2	B	R	b	r
3	ETX	DC3	#	3	C	S	c	s
4	EOT	DC4	$	4	D	T	d	t
5	ENQ	NAK	%	5	E	U	e	u
6	ACK	SYN	&	6	F	V	f	v
7	BEL	ETB	’	7	G	W	g	w
8	BS	CAN	(	8	H	X	h	x
9	HT	EM	)	9	I	Y	i	y
A	LF	SUB	*	:	J	Z	j	z
B	VT	ESC	+	;	K	[	k	{
C	FF	FS	,	<	L	\	l	|
D	CR	GS	-	=	M	]	m	}
E	SO	RS	.	>	N	ˆ	n	˜
F	SI	US	/	?	O		o	DEL

NUL null (all zeros)
SOH start of header
STX start of text
ETX end of text
EOT end of transmission
ENQ inquiry
ACK acknowledgement
BEL bell
BS backspace
HT horizontal tabulation
LF line feed
VT vertical tabulation
FF form feed
CR carraige return
SO shift out
SI shift in
DLE data link escape

DC1 device control 1
DC2 device control 2
DC3 device control 3
DC4 device control 4
NAK negative acknowledgement
SYN synchronous idle
ETB end of transmitted block
CAN cancel (error in data)
EM end of medium
SUB start of special sequence
ESC escape
FS file separator
RS record separator
US unit separator
SP space
DEL delete

new line. The remaining patterns correspond, one-to-one, to the individual characters on an ASCII keyboard. Thus, when the following list is keyed into a computer:

Jones, R., 24
Smith, M., 19

the following binary string (shown in hex) will be transmitted:

4A 6F 6E 65 73 2C 20 52 2E 2C 20 32 34 (0D 0A) 53 6D 69 74 68 2C
20 4D 2E 2C 20 31 39 (0D 0A)

The string in this example includes a carriage return/line feed pair (0D/0A) marking the end of each line.

Notice that the hex patterns for the digits 0 through 9 are 30 through 39, respectively. This simplifies the task of converting between the patterns for decimal digits used outside the computer and the corresponding numbers stored inside the computer in BCD form.

The original seven-bit code has been extended to eight bits in which form it is known as the *extended ASCII code*. In this extended code the patterns listed in Table 3.4 start with an eighth (most significant) bit of zero and the other patterns start with an eighth bit of one. The additional patterns are used for graphical characters such as prompts and segments of line drawings, as well as for additional text characters which are not represented in the seven-bit code.

3.7 ERROR DETECTION

The original ASCII code (EBCDIC also) is a 7-bit code. Since modern computers work with bit groups which are integer multiples of 8, one bit is often available which is not used when encoding a character. This extra bit may be selected to be always 0 or always 1, in which case it is simply a wasted appendage to the pattern. An alternative is to make the eighth bit have a value such that the total number of 1s in the pattern (including the eighth bit itself) is either an even number or an odd number. When this is done, the pattern is said to have even or odd *parity*. Computer peripheral equipment that uses the 7-bit ASCII code can often be set to generate or to expect the eighth bit to be either one of these four options: always 0, always 1, odd parity, or even parity.

The advantage of using one of the parity options is that the pattern can be checked by counting the number of 1s in it. If the number of 1s does not satisfy the original parity choice, then this indicates that an error has occurred in one of the bits (or in an odd number of bits) and that the code is no longer valid. This parity checking procedure is used whenever it is important that the presence of an error be detected.

Consider the following examples of the use of parity to detect errors. The first row lists some characters and their corresponding 7-bit ASCII patterns from Table 3.4 in both hex and binary. The second row lists the correct odd-parity ASCII patterns which would be transmitted for these characters. The parity bit is included as the most significant bit in each pattern. Notice that each group of eight bits contains an odd number of 1s. The third row lists the patterns as they might be received after having been corrupted during transmission. A simple odd parity check shows that the second and fifth patterns have been changed during transmission.

M	o	n	e	y	M	o	n	e	y
4D	6F	6E	65	79	1001101	1101111	1101110	1100101	1111001
CD	EF	6E	E5	79	11001101	11101111	01101110	11100101	01111001
CD	AF	6E	E5	F9	11001101	10101111	01101110	11100101	11111001

In the above example notice that even though the receiver can be assured that the second and fifth bit-groups are incorrect, their original values cannot be reconstructed. A single parity bit can be used to detect the presence of a single error but it cannot correct that error. For example, the fifth pattern above was received as 11111001. With no additional information, the receiver can only narrow the original character down to one of the following (assuming only a one-bit error) where P stands for the parity bit:

P1111001 (79 → y)   P1110001 (71 → q)
P0111001 (39 → 9)   P1111101 (7D → })
P1011001 (59 → Y)   P1111001 (7B → {)
P1101001 (69 → i)   P1111000 (78 → x)

The parity scheme described above is capable of detecting single-bit errors. More complex codes have been devised which can detect the presence of multiple errors. Still others can even correct errors by determining the location of the bit or bits which are in error. Codes such as these are beyond the scope of this book.

SUMMARY

Some of the more common forms in which numerical information may be represented with binary patterns are unsigned binary, two's complement binary, floating point binary, and BCD. A thorough understanding of these forms is a necessary prerequisite to studying the internal behavior of computers. This understanding must include the ability to convert both unsigned and two's complement signed integers back and forth between decimal, hexadecimal, and binary representations easily and quickly. It also includes the ability to add such numbers in hexadecimal and binary and to determine the validity of the results.

The ASCII code is the most commonly used code for representing textual information. It will be useful to be able to recognize some of the codes for the more common symbols such as the digits and the carriage return and line feed. Although they assume more importance when signals leave a computer for the outside world, the concepts of parity and error detection are also useful in understanding many digital systems.

It is particularly important to realize that there is no sort of tag or other indication which accompanies a bit pattern inside a computer to state whether it represents a number in unsigned binary or in two's complement form or in BCD; or whether it is an ASCII code pattern with odd parity, no parity, or even parity; or whether it is part or all of a floating point number; or whether it is neither of these but instead is an instruction, a representation of a part of a photograph, or perhaps something else. The designer of the system must understand what each and every pattern is supposed to represent based upon such information as where it is in the system and at what specific time it is there. The designer must also then interpret and make use of the pattern accordingly.

REVIEW PROBLEMS

3.1. Convert the following unsigned integers to decimal:
- a. $(11011011)_2$
- b. $(1001010001110101)_2$
- c. $(62)_8$
- d. $(5714)_8$
- e. $(A3)_{16}$
- f. $(3C8E)_{16}$

3.2. Convert the following unsigned decimal integers to binary, octal, and hexadecimal:
- a. 187
- b. 913
- c. 4321
- d. 6532

3.3. Convert the following unsigned mixed numbers to decimal:
- a. $(100011.1011)_2$
- b. $(10110.0001)_2$
- c. $(3B.A)_{16}$
- d. $(D81.42)_{16}$

3.4. Convert the following unsigned mixed decimal numbers to binary and to hexadecimal:
- a. 27.1875
- b. 74.385
- c. 173.352
- d. 93.4

3.5. Write the following signed decimal integers in two's complement binary form (8 bits) and then write the two-digit hexadecimal equivalent:
- a. +17
- b. −43
- c. −116
- d. +94
- e. −94
- f. −1
- g. −2
- h. −3
- i. −4
- j. −5

3.6. Add each of the following pairs of unsigned hexadecimal integers directly in hex. Repeat the addition by first converting the integers to binary and then adding in binary. Indicate in each case whether an overflow has occurred.

a. 3C, 82
b. 89, 6A
c. 1234, 5678
d. A9E4, 3B87
e. 9D, 6F
f. 483C, B7C4
g. 8F, 39
h. 63, FF
i. 63, FE
j. 63, FD

3.7. Add each of the following pairs of signed hexadecimal integers by first converting to binary (8 bits) and then adding and converting the sum back to hexadecimal. Express each sum as an unsigned two-digit hexadecimal number. Also indicate in each case whether an overflow has occurred.

a. 52 + 1A
b. 13 + 3C
c. 2A + 4D
d. 63 + 3A
e. −13 + (−4D)
f. −2C + (−27)
g. −3C + (−2D)
h. 6D + (−23)
i. −7D + 1A
j. 5B + 27
k. 72 + (−3D)
l. −48 + (−5A)
m. −6D + 23
n. −72 + (−19)

3.8. Consider the following bit pattern: 100101010100.

a. If the bit pattern represents a BCD number, what is its decimal value?
b. If the bit pattern is an unsigned binary integer, what is its decimal value?
c. If the bit pattern is a 12-bit two's complement number, what is its decimal value?
d. Express this bit pattern as a hexadecimal number.
e. Express this bit pattern as an octal number.

3.9. Write the decimal number 1234

a. as a 16-bit binary number.
b. as a 4-digit hexadecimal number.
c. as a 16-bit BCD number.
d. as an 8-digit hex representation of even-parity ASCII.
e. as a 32-bit binary representation of odd-parity ASCII.

3.10. Design a BCD error detector. The inputs are to be A, B, C, and D with A as the most significant bit. The output is to be a 1 whenever the input pattern is not a legitimate BCD code. Show the truth table, simplified Boolean expression, and logic circuit.

3.11. Construct truth tables and write Boolean expressions for the seven outputs of the BCD to seven-segment display decoder shown below. Use the convention that a 1 will light the segment.

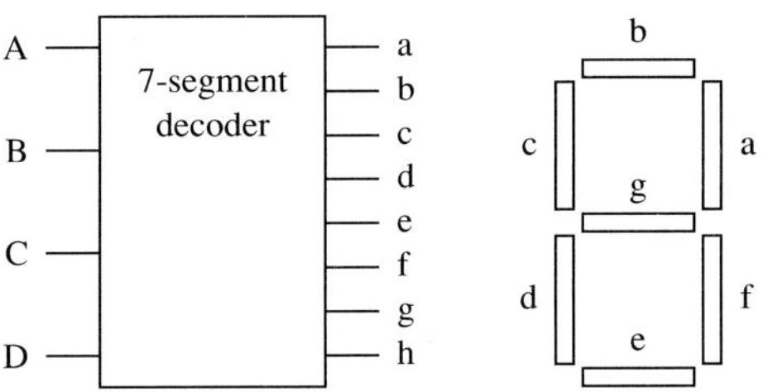

3.12. Encode the following sentence using the ASCII code. Express your result in hex. Include spaces, carriage returns, and line feeds.

"Less often used characters are the tilde (˜), the vertical slash (|), the reverse slash (\), the reverse apostrophe (‘), and the carat (ˆ)."

3.13. A particular ASCII keyboard has a user selectable four-position switch labeled 0, 1, ODD, EVEN. With the switch in the position marked ODD, a computer receives the following five patterns from the keyboard. Which patterns indicate the presence of bit errors?

a. 01101011
b. 10100101
c. 11011010
d. 11011011

3.14. In a particular system, ASCII characters are transmitted with odd parity. The following 2-digit hexadecimal numbers each represent one of the received patterns. What different ASCII characters could have been sent in each case, assuming at most a single bit-error? Include unprintable (control) characters as well as printable ones.

a. 53
b. 38
c. FF

CHAPTER 4

THE MODUS OPERANDI OF MICROCOMPUTERS

A computer was described briefly in Chapter 1 as a programmable, sequential, binary, electronic machine which can perform certain specific operations. This chapter will flesh out some of the details of that description and will examine the internal structure of a computer. The objective of this discussion is to develop a functional understanding of a computer. Although the hardware making up a computer is comprised of logic circuits of the type discussed in Chapter 2, these kinds of circuit details will not be included. Instead, the emphasis will be on the internal operation of computers at the register level.

4.1 THE BASIC ARCHITECTURE OF A COMPUTER

The block diagram of a generic computer system was first introduced in Chapter 1 (Figure 1.2). That diagram has been reorganized to emphasize the structure of a typical microprocessor-based computer system and is shown here as Figure 4.1. In this figure the control unit and the processor have been combined into a single unit known as the *central processing unit* or *CPU* (the microprocessor in this case). In addition, the various buses have been combined into three: the *address bus*, the *data bus*, and the *control bus*. In a microprocessor-based system, these three buses are the common interconnections between the three major parts of the system: the *microprocessor unit* or *MPU* (sometimes simply referred to as the *processor*), the *memory*, and the

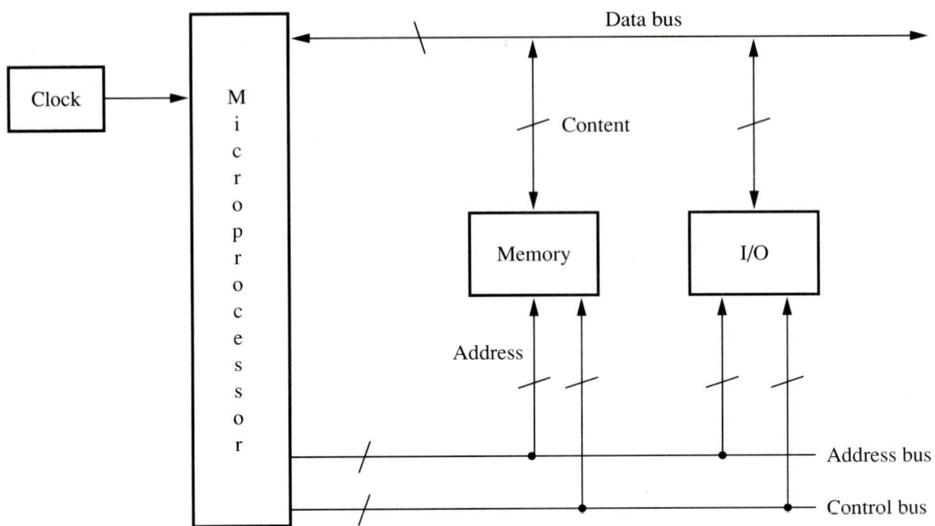

FIGURE 4.1
A typical microprocessor-based system.

input/output (I/O) circuits (sometimes referred to as the *interface circuits*), together with their associated *peripheral devices*.

The memory contains the storage locations for the program instructions, the data used in the program, and any results (intermediate or final) generated by the program. These items are stored in the memory in the form of binary signals in flip-flop-like circuits.

The central processing unit fetches instructions and data from the memory and processes them sequentially to generate intermediate results. It does this by sending interrogation signals to the memory and receiving the returned information by latching it into various registers. The CPU then manipulates the binary information in order to generate the results (also in binary form). It uses these results to generate signals representing necessary input or output information which it then sends to the I/O circuits.

The I/O circuits provide the interface between the internal parts of the system and the I/O devices or peripherals. These circuits modify the signals received from either the CPU or the peripherals and then send them on to their destination. The source signals may be modified by changing their voltage levels, power levels, or time duration to meet the requirements of the destination.

By definition, a microprocessor is implemented into a single integrated circuit. However, a single memory circuit or a single interface I/O circuit has insufficient capacity to provide for the total needs of any but the smallest systems. Typically, each of these two units would occupy several integrated circuits. However, each is shown as a single functional block in Figure 4.1.

The internal structure of the processor itself is made up of thousands of logic circuits of the types described in Chapter 2: AND gates, OR gates, inverters, flip-flops, counters, registers, and so forth. Fortunately, the general operation of a specific processor may be described with a limited subset of these components. The circuits of primary importance to such a discussion are the various registers which are directly accessible to the user of the system. These are used to retain various types of information on a temporary basis while the processor is executing a program. The structure, size, and nature of these registers comprise what is called the *architecture* of the processor, and they constitute the primary differences between various processors.

The architecture of most processors includes certain common types of registers. These registers are described below in terms of their interaction with each other and with the computer system's memory.

4.2 MEMORY AND THE READ/WRITE CYCLE

The memory used by a computer system to contain the data and the instructions as they are being executed is sometimes called *main memory* to distinguish it from *secondary memory* which is used to store programs and data in a more permanent fashion or to provide for program portability and off-computer storage. Secondary memory consists of devices such as disks or tape units which are usually treated as I/O peripheral devices by the rest of the computer system.

Main memory consists of an array of electronic circuitry capable of retaining binary patterns and providing these patterns to the central processing unit upon request. This sort of memory may also be called *solid-state memory* because it is commonly implemented electronically in the form of solid-state integrated circuits. This is the form of memory which will be referred to during the remainder of this discussion.

4.2.1 Memory Organization

The binary patterns retained in the memory circuits are organized into groups of bits, each typically containing eight bits (one byte) or an integer multiple of eight bits. Each group is identified by a binary number called the address of the group. Thus, the memory may be pictured as an array of byte-sized groups of bits where each group has two binary patterns associated with it: the pattern of the group itself (known as the *content*) and the pattern of the address of the group (known as the *location*). The two patterns are usually described by their hexadecimal equivalent, one byte being represented by two hex digits.

Figure 4.2 illustrates a typical memory structure for a small microprocessor-based system. Each word in memory contains eight bits and there are 64K words. In order to specify one of the 64K locations the address pattern must contain 16 bits. Thus, the addresses range from 0000 to FFFF in hex. The content of each location is itself an eight-bit pattern ranging from 00 to FF. Parentheses are used to distinguish between the address and the content of a memory location. Thus, the equation (123B) = 4F should be read as "the content of location 123B is equal to 4F".

Larger microprocessor systems may have memories containing several megabytes. A byte-addressable one M-byte memory would require an address pat-

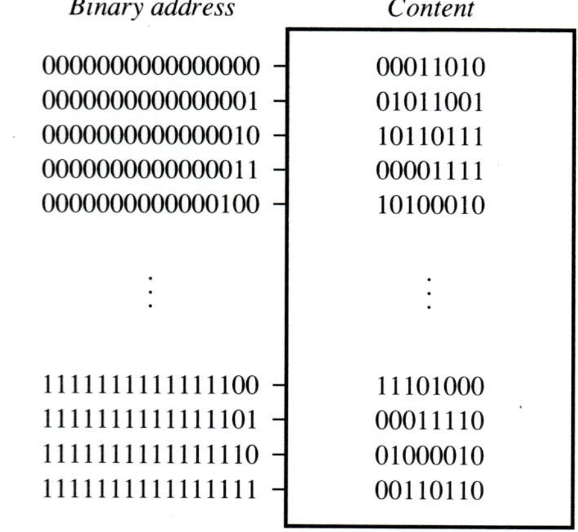

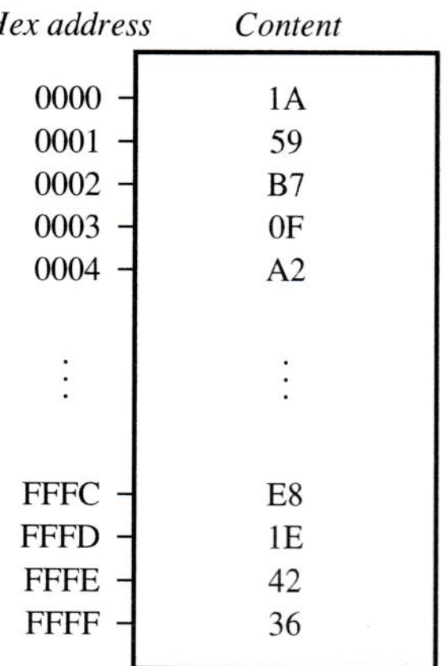

FIGURE 4.2
Memory array.

tern containing 20 bits and would have an address range from 00000 to FFFFF in hex. One additional address bit is required for each doubling of the memory size.

4.2.2 Basic Memory Types

Each location in the main memory of a computer is equally as accessible as any other. The memory is said to be a *random-access* memory. In this respect, it resembles the array of boxes in a post office lobby. In order to access one of the boxes one need simply go to that particular box. Contrast this type of memory with the *serial-access* memory which is typical of secondary memory devices such as tapes or disks. In those devices the location which is currently nearest to a read head is more readily available than another one farther away. This more nearly resembles the array of boxes along a rural postal route. One must pass by many of the boxes in sequence in order to get to a desired one.

Two primary classifications of random-access memory are *read-only* and *read-write* memory. Read-only memory, denoted by the acronym *ROM*, contains information in a more or less permanent form in which it is available for inspection by the MPU, but in which it cannot be readily changed. The contents of ROM are present even when the power is turned off. Thus, ROM is used to contain programs which must be present whenever the computer is first turned on. These programs are said to be "cast in concrete" because of their permanent nature. Another expression is that they are "burned" into memory because of one type of ROM in which links actually must be fused or burned out in order to insert the information.

Read-write memory is an array of flip-flop-like circuits which can be set or reset individually by data presented to them on the data bus. The contents of these locations can be readily changed by the processor under program control. The memory is said to be *volatile* since its contents are lost whenever the power is turned off, in contrast to the *nonvolatile* behavior of ROM. Read-write memory is denoted by the (mis)acronym *R*AM. The letters stand for random access memory, which is actually descriptive of all solid state memory and not just of read-write memory. As a result of long-time usage, however, the term RAM has come to be applied exclusively to read-write memory.

A computer system requires both ROM and RAM. ROM is necessary in order that some program may be up and running when the power is first turned on, even if it is simply a program to load another program into RAM from a disk. In typical control applications, all of the programs will be in ROM. It would be awkward to require the driver of a microprocessor-controlled automobile, for instance, to load the program from a disk before starting the engine.

RAM is necessary in a computer system in order that the system may have some place to store input data and the results of calculations. In a typical desktop computer the user's programs are executed from RAM. Before they can be executed they must first be loaded into RAM from their storage locations in secondary memory.

Although they are not normally implemented on the same integrated circuit, ROM and RAM are combined in a computer memory and share the same address space in an indistinguishable fashion. The system hardware is designed in such a way that certain blocks of addresses refer to ROM chips and others refer to RAM chips. The software must be written with this understanding on the part of the programmer. That is, the programmer must know which locations are available for the (read only) programs and which are the read-write locations which can be changed by the programs.

For the purpose of instruction, all programs must be installed in read-write memory, even though this may not be the norm in many microprocessor applications. Some instructional hardware is designed so as to simulate ROM for the user's programs, some is not. If not, then the user must make a special effort to differentiate between ROM and RAM locations in programs.

The assembler-simulator software packages which are available for use with this text[1] simulate the MC6809 and the MC68000 microprocessors on a personal computer. During the execution of a user's program each simulator acts as though the program is running from ROM and will not allow the program to write over any part of itself. Any required RAM space must be declared as such before the simulator will allow the user's program to change its contents.

4.2.3 Bus Cycles

When the processor is executing a program its primary operations consist of reading binary patterns from the memory locations where they are stored, manipulating these binary patterns, and writing the results back into other memory locations. The steps which the processor follows in reading from or writing to a location are collectively known as a *bus cycle* since the process is a cyclic one which makes use of the processor's address, data, and control buses. Bus cycles may be further identified as *read cycles* or *write cycles*. Examples of typical bus cycles are shown in the flow diagrams in Figures 4.3 and 4.4.

At the beginning of a read cycle (Figure 4.3) the processor signals the memory as to the address of the desired location and the direction of the transaction. It does this by placing the address on the lines of the address bus and by placing logic level one on a line in the control bus called the $R/\overline{W}$ line. Following this, the processor signals the memory through additional control lines that the address and the direction information are valid. After a short time delay to allow the memory to respond and to place the content of the specified location on the data bus, the processor latches the information from the data bus into one of its registers.

The read cycle is divided into four distinct parts or phases:

1. Send address and direction to the memory.
2. Signal valid information to the memory.
3. Wait for memory to respond.
4. Latch data and prepare for next cycle.

[1] ASSYM000 and ASSYM09. See the preface for information on how and where to obtain these programs.

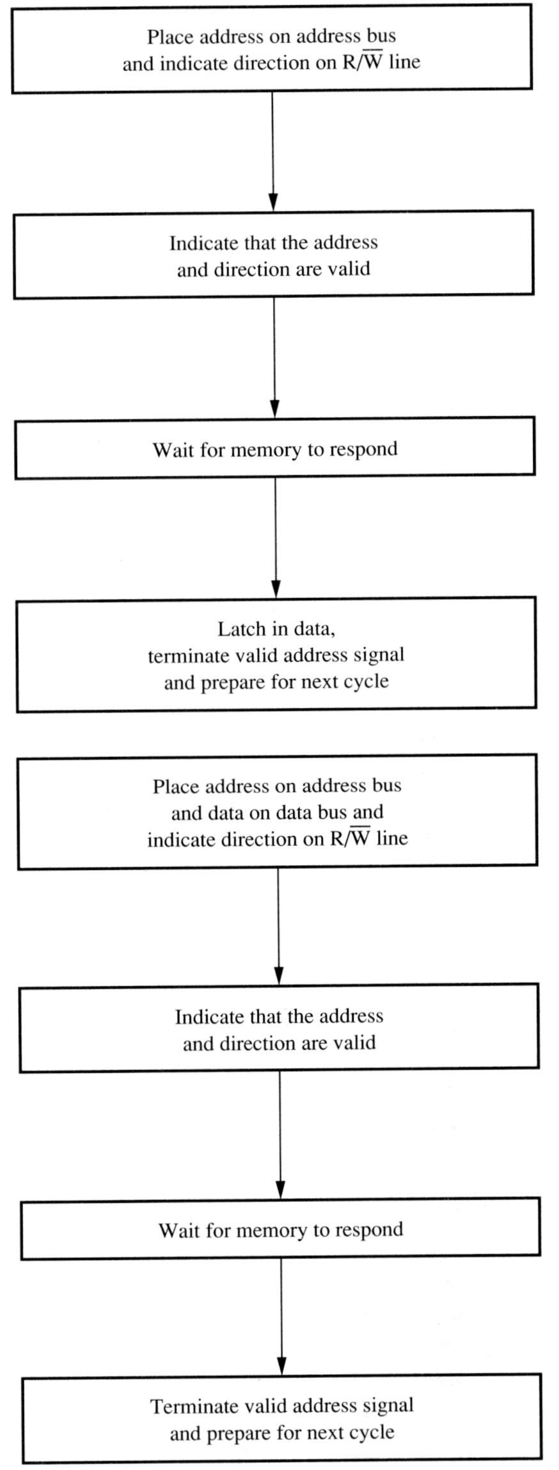

FIGURE 4.3
Read cycle.

FIGURE 4.4
Write cycle.

This four-phase cycle is common in many microprocessors and so the frequency with which bus cycles occur is often one-quarter of the frequency of the clock in the microprocessor. Thus, a microprocessor with a four MHz (four million cycles per second) crystal clock will typically read or write memory at a maximum rate of one MHz.

The write cycle (Figure 4.4) is similar to the read cycle except that the processor places the data on the data bus at the same time that it places the address on the address bus. The processor signals the direction of the transfer by placing logic level zero on the $R/\overline{W}$ line. The valid memory address signal (and valid data in this case) from the processor lasts long enough for the memory to prepare to write the data into the proper location. The trailing edge of this signal is then used by the memory to latch the data into the specified memory location.

The address space of the processor often includes I/O circuits as well as memory circuits. In that case, the processor uses these same procedures to communicate with I/O interface circuits. These circuits respond to the bus cycles in the same fashion as the memory circuits do.

The three types of information which flow between the processor and the I/O circuits or memory are address, data, and control. The three corresponding buses (see Figure 4.1) contain the conductors over which these signals flow. These three buses constitute the sole means which the processor has for communication with the other parts of the computer system.

4.2.4 Memory Contents

The nature and uses of the bit patterns which are stored in memory and which are provided to the processor during a read cycle vary widely. In some cases the patterns represent the *instructions* which specify the individual steps which the processor is to follow in a program. In other cases the patterns represent *data* which the processor needs to use while executing the program. Data patterns, in turn, may represent *signed* or *unsigned* binary *integers*, *BCD* numbers, binary *fractions*, *floating point* numbers, or *character codes* such as ASCII. The numbers may be complete in a single word in memory (*single precision*) or may take up two or more consecutive locations in memory (*multi-precision*).

For example, the pattern 01000011 (hex 43) may be an instruction to write all 0s into a particular register in an MC6809 system or to check the contents of a register against some limits in an MC68000 system. On the other hand, in either system it may represent the decimal integer 67 in binary form or the decimal number 43 in BCD or the ASCII code for the letter C. There is no identification tag accompanying the pattern 01000011 to state which of these representations is intended.

When the processor fetches an instruction from memory then the pattern fetched is interpreted as an instruction. When the processor is fetching data, then the pattern will be used as the type of data that is expected. This means that the programmer and the system designer must see to it that the proper pattern is fetched from memory at each point during the execution of the program.

An old acronym in computerese is *GIGO, garbage in garbage out*. In no situation is this adage more fitting than in this context. If the processor fetches data when it expects an instruction it will accept the data as an instruction and proceed to interpret and to execute the data as if it were an instruction.

The simulators available for use with this book attempt to save the user from some of the more straightforward problems of the type alluded to above. Instructions can be executed only from regions of memory described in the program as containing instructions. Data, when separate from the program, must be in areas of memory which have been previously defined as containing data. However, this sort of assistance is seldom provided in real systems as most beginners quickly (and painfully) discover.

4.3 THE PROGRAM COUNTER

The processor uses a register called a *program counter* to keep track of where it is in memory while it is fetching and executing instructions. This register contains a bit pattern corresponding to the address of the next instruction to be fetched from memory. The processor automatically increments the program counter after each new instruction is fetched. In addition, when a branch in the sequence of program execution occurs the processor loads the target address of the branch into this register.

The program counter must be able to point to any location in the memory space of the processor. Its size, therefore, is an indication of the addressing capability and the size of the address space of the processor. The MC6809 has a 16-bit program counter and so can access as many as 2^{16} (64K or 65,536) different locations in memory. This size of address space is typical of the popular eight-bit microprocessors. The MC68000 uses 24 bits of a 32-bit program counter and so can access up to 16M bytes in its byte-addressable memory. This size is typical of the current 16- and 32-bit microprocessors.

When the power is first turned on in a computer system the program counter is automatically loaded with a starting address in a manner which is specific for that particular processor, and the processor is started in the instruction fetch cycle (described below). This ensures an orderly start-up of the system.

4.4 THE FETCH/EXECUTE CYCLE

Unless it is in a halted state, the normal operation of a processor consists of a two-phase cycle. The processor fetches (reads) an instruction from the memory location pointed to by the program counter (automatically incrementing the program counter immediately afterward) and then it executes that instruction. It then fetches the next instruction and executes it. This fetch/execute cycle is repeated over and over again.

The instructions in most microprocessors have varying lengths. That is, some instructions in a processor's set occupy only a single location in memory while others may occupy two or more consecutive locations. The first word of the instruction (called the *operation word*, *operation code*, or *op-code*) contains a particular bit pattern which includes information as to how many additional words must be fetched in order to complete the instruction. As it fetches each word the processor increments the program counter in order to point to the next instruction word. Only after the complete instruction is fetched does the processor execute it.

During the execution of a particular instruction, the processor may need to refer to data contained in another memory location. In such a case the processor must use a register other than the program counter to hold the address of that location. The program counter is always reserved to point to the next instruction in memory and is never used to refer to locations containing data outside of the program area.

During the execute phase of the cycle the processor may read or write data to some memory location. It may read the bit pattern contained in a memory location, modify the bit pattern, and then write it back to the same location. It may fetch a bit pattern from an input device or move one to an output device. It may modify the content of one of its own internal registers (including the program counter). Or it may do nothing but idle away a few microseconds in order to establish a precise time interval. Whatever the processor does, after it has completed the execution it fetches the next instruction from the location pointed to by the program counter.

4.5 THE ACCUMULATOR

Many smaller microprocessors have what is known as an *accumulator architecture*. They are organized in such a way that arithmetic and logic operations are performed only on bit patterns stored in one or two special registers called *accumulators*. When addition is to be performed the augend must first be loaded into an accumulator and then an addend is added to it to generate the sum in the accumulator. Similarly, the minuend must be loaded into an accumulator prior to a subtraction operation and the difference replaces it after subtraction. The logic operations of AND, OR, and exclusive-OR are performed bit-by-bit between the bits in an accumulator and those in a target pattern in memory with the results replacing the original contents of the accumulator.

The accumulator often serves as a destination for input data and as a source for output data as well. It also serves as an intermediate resting point for data which is being moved from one location in memory to another. Thus, in contrast to the program counter which contains addresses the accumulator is used to contain data.

The number of bits of data which the processor manipulates at one time is called the *word size* of the processor and is one of the fundamental parameters describing its capability. The size of the accumulator(s) in an accumulator-based architecture is the word size of the processor. Thus, 8-bit microprocessors have 8-bit accumulators, 16-bit processors have 16-bit accumulators, etc. The MC6809 has two 8-bit accumulators and so is an 8-bit accumulator-based microprocessor.

4.6 DATA REGISTERS

The accumulator is a major bottleneck in an accumulator-based machine. Essentially every manipulation of which the processor is capable must be funnelled through one of the accumulators. As a consequence, this type of architecture is found primarily in smaller processors intended for control applications with limited computational requirements. Most larger more powerful processors have a *general register architecture* which includes a much larger set of general purpose registers for manipulating data. These registers are called *data registers*.

The general register architecture comprises a set of 8 or 16 or more data registers which serve to hold the operands and results of data manipulations. A data register serves a role similar to that of an accumulator in that it may be used in arithmetic/logic, input/output, and load/store operations. However, instructions may specify a data register or a memory location for either or both operands. In some processors, they may even specify a separate destination for the result.

The large number of possible sources and destinations for operands and results in a general register machine requires that its instructions contain many more bits than similar instructions with an accumulator architecture. As a consequence this type of architecture is restricted to microprocessors which have a larger word size and a more complex internal structure.

The MC68000 includes eight 32-bit data registers and has a 32-bit (internal) general register architecture. However, it includes only a 16-bit data bus and is known as a 16-bit microprocessor. The MC68020, which is a member of the 68000 family and has a similar architecture, includes a 32-bit data bus and is recognized as a true 32-bit microprocessor.

4.7 ADDRESS REGISTERS

When a program refers to a location in memory to retrieve or store an item of data, it often does so by first assembling the appropriate address in a register. It then directs the processor to use the contents of this register to identify and access the memory location. A register which is used for this purpose is called an address register. Note that the program counter is not commonly referred to as an address register since it has the specific function of pointing to the next instruction and may not be used for pointing to any location outside the program area.

Address registers are commonly used to contain addresses which must be changed while the program is running. They may be used to point to locations within a program loop where, each time around, the next consecutive location in memory is accessed. They may also be used to point to return addresses from subroutines. These addresses are commonly stored in RAM during the execution of the subroutine. In some processors the address registers may also serve as accumulators or data registers with somewhat limited arithmetic capabilities. For example, many processors support addition into address registers and such simple operations as incrementing or decrementing the value in an address register.

4.8 CONDITION CODE BITS

A fourth type of register found in microprocessors is really not a register at all but several unrelated bits which are often assembled into a single group for convenient reference only. The group includes bits which tell the processor something about the results of recent operations or something about the status of the processor hardware itself. They may be called *status bits* or *flags* or *condition code bits,* and the assemblage is called the *status register* or the *condition code register (CCR).*

The carry out from the most significant position after an addition or subtraction operation, the carry bit, is one of the condition code bits. Also present is a copy of the most significant bit of the result (the sign bit in two's complement numbers). An intermediate carry bit may be present in order to facilitate BCD arithmetic in some processors. A zero-test bit, commonly referred to as the Z bit, will also be included. All processors test most instruction results for zero. They perform the test by combining in a NOR gate all of the bits from the result. The output of the NOR gate, the Z bit, will be one only when all of the result bits are zero, i.e., when the result is zero. Often an overflow bit is included as a condition code bit to indicate overflow from two's complement arithmetic. Some processors also include a bit to identify the parity of the result of operations.

Different processors include different bits in the condition code register. However, those which are universally included are the carry, sign, and zero bits. Most processors also include the overflow bit. The register may include additional bits which are used to indicate the status of other parts of the system, such as the I/O circuits. Examples and uses of these bits will be discussed in a later chapter.

The processor refers to individual bits in the condition code register when executing a test and branch instruction. That is, the test is performed not on the actual result of an operation but on certain bits in the CCR. It is very important for the correct operation of a program that the programmer at the machine level be acutely aware of how the instructions affect the condition code bits and how these bits are used by the processor when executing branch instructions.

4.9 OTHER REGISTERS

Processors include many other registers in addition to those mentioned above. Whatever the source of the address, it must be placed into a *memory address register* in order to hold it on the address bus during a bus cycle. Whatever the content of a memory location being read, it must be latched into a *memory buffer register* when it first enters the processor. While it is being decoded prior to execution, the current instruction must be held in an *instruction register*. Other registers are used to count the parts of an instruction as they are read from memory, to keep track of the various phases of each bus cycle and of the fetch/execute cycle, to shift operands during certain arithmetic operations, and to facilitate many other operations.

Most of these registers are of consequence only in that they are absolutely necessary in order for the processor to work properly. None of them may be directly influenced by the programmer through the program. There are no specific instructions which direct the processor to change the contents of these particular registers. Understanding their behavior is of no consequence to the user of a microprocessor system and so they will receive no further mention here.

4.10 THE PROGRAMMING MODEL

The registers of primary interest in the design of the software and hardware for microprocessor-based systems are those which may be directly and specifically affected by the program instructions. Together with the memory space and any separate I/O space, these registers comprise what is known as the *programming model* for the processor.

The programming model should be the starting point in understanding any new processor. Unfortunately, many microprocessor manufacturers do not make this information as clear as it should be for the user. Often it is buried in a complex block diagram of the entire processor. However, you should always attempt to identify and to understand the programming model as the first step in learning about a new processor.

The programming model, when available, is commonly shown as a collection of registers identified by name (in abbreviated form) and size (identified by bit numbers), together with a representation of the maximum memory space with which the processor is capable of interacting. The bits in each register are numbered from 0 on the right (the least significant bit) to $n - 1$ on the left (the most significant bit). This is the conventional way to label the bits in any group for individual reference.

4.10.1 The Motorola MC6809 Programming Model

The programming model for the MC6809 microprocessor is shown in Figure 4.5. It consists of nine registers and the 64K bytes of combined memory and I/O space. The MC6809 has no I/O space separate from memory. Two of the registers, A and B, can be concatenated side by side in the order shown and referred to as register D. The bits in registers A and B are numbered from 0 to 7 but when referred to as register D, they are numbered from 0 to 15 as shown.

The program counter (PC) size of 16 bits establishes the address range for the processor as being from 0000 to FFFF hexadecimal for a total of 64K locations. This is shown in the memory space which is a part of the programming model. The model also shows that each word in memory includes eight bits or one byte.

The MC6809 includes two eight-bit accumulators, A and B, which identify it as an eight-bit processor. For certain operations the accumulators may be combined into a single 16-bit double accumulator, D. When combined in this way, register D can be used to implement 16-bit load, store, add, and subtract instructions.

Registers X, Y, S, and U are 16-bit address registers whose specific uses will be described in the next chapter. They are used to hold addresses and therefore to point to locations in memory which are of particular interest in a program. They may also be used to implement 16-bit load and store operations.

The eight-bit direct page register, DP, is a register that doesn't appear to be an address register because of its eight-bit size. It is actually a partial address register. The DP register is used to hold the most significant half of an address so that the program instructions need specify only the other half. This can reduce the space required when

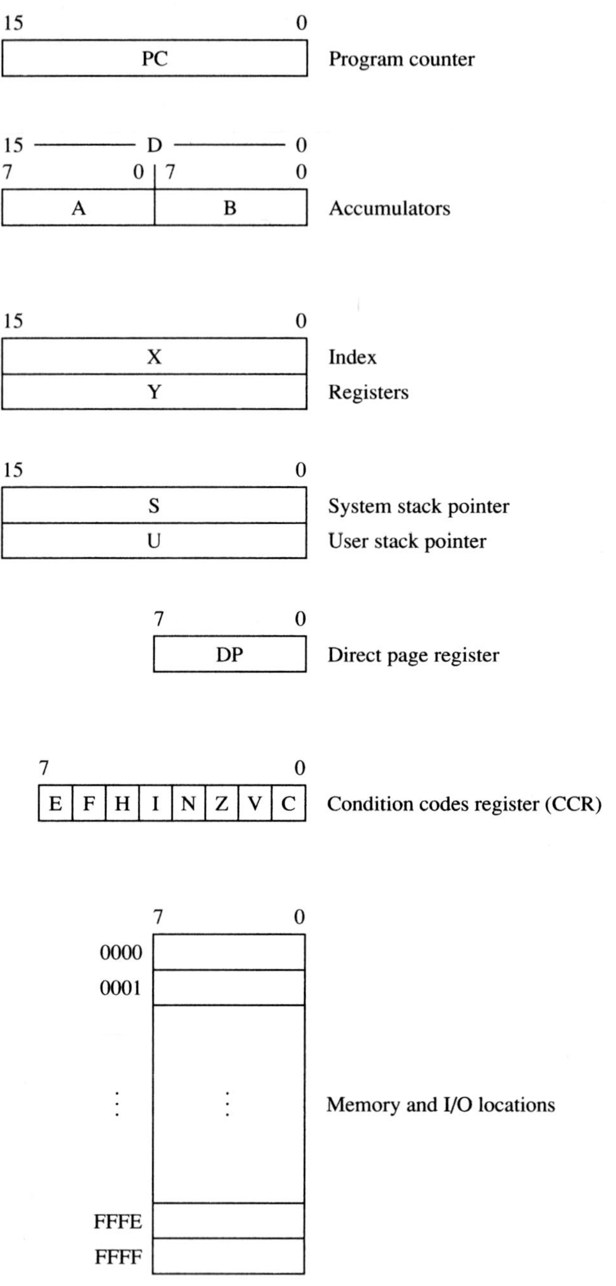

FIGURE 4.5
Programming model for the MC6809 microprocessor.

addresses of data must be explicitly stated in a program. The details of the operation of this register will be discussed in a later chapter.

The final register is the assemblage of bits called the condition code register, or CCR. Note that it includes the intermediate or half carry bit, H, used to support BCD addition; the sign or negative bit, N; the zero bit, Z; the overflow bit, V; and the carry bit, C. In addition, it includes several bits related to the interrupt system of the MC6809 which will be discussed in detail later along with I/O and interrupt systems.

4.10.2 A First Example Program for the MC6809

The program segment of Figure 4.6 will serve to illustrate the operation of the MC6809 processor from the point of view of its programming model. After the last byte of each instruction the column to the right of the memory content column lists the instruction in mnemonic form. The last two columns show the contents of two of the processor registers as the program is fetched and executed.

Assume that the bit patterns listed in Figure 4.6 in hex are in the memory locations specified and that location 100D is in RAM so that the processor may write into it. Assume also that the program counter contains the value 1000 and that the processor starts in the fetch cycle. The PC starts at 1000 but after fetching the first byte, it is incremented to 1001. The original content of register A is immaterial, since it will be overwritten by the first instruction.

Since the processor starts in the fetch cycle, it fetches the content of the location in memory to which the PC is pointing (1000 hex) by placing that address on the address bus and executing a read cycle. It then immediately increments the PC by one. The byte fetched from location 1000 is B6. The processor, expecting this to

			After Fetch (Execute)	
Address	*Content*	*Instruction*	*PC*	*A*
1000	B6		1001	–
1001	10		1002	–
1002	0B	LDA 100BH	1003	34
1003	BB		1004	34
1004	10		1005	34
1005	0C	ADDA 100CH	1006	8A
1006	B7		1007	8A
1007	10		1008	8A
1008	0D	STA 100DH	1009	8A
1009	3F	SWI	100A	8A
100A	08	Code Number	100B	8A
100B	34	Data		
100C	56	Date		
100D	00	Place For Result		

FIGURE 4.6
A simple MC6809 program segment.

be the first byte of an instruction, decodes it as such. Recall that it is the pattern of this op-code byte which determines whether the instruction requires one or more bytes. In this case, the decoding informs the processor that this is the first byte of a three-byte instruction and so it continues to fetch the remaining bytes, incrementing the PC immediately after fetching each one.

Having fetched the entire instruction, the processor proceeds to execute it. The three-byte instruction B6-10-0B (LDA 100BH) requires the processor to fetch the byte from memory location 100B (the H stands for hex) and to load it into register A. The processor executes a read cycle with the address 100B on the address bus and latches the value read out of this location (hex 34) into register A.

This instruction is typical of the complexity of instructions as they appear inside of a computer. A more complex higher-level instruction must be expressed in dozens of these simple machine language instructions when a higher-level language program is compiled for execution.

Having completed that instruction, the processor fetches the first byte of the next instruction from the location pointed to by the PC. The byte BB is fetched from location 1003 and the PC is automatically incremented to 1004. Decoding BB as an op-code, the processor discovers that it requires two more bytes and fetches them, leaving the PC with the value 1006.

This second three-byte instruction BB-10-0C (ADDA 100CH) requires that the processor add to the content of register A the value read out of memory location 100C. This requires another read cycle, this time to get the required operand from location 100C (hex 56). The processor then adds this value to the content of register A to generate the sum (hex 8A). This completes the second instruction.

The processor then fetches the third instruction (also three bytes long) leaving the PC pointing to location 1009. This instruction, B7-10-0D (STA 100DH), tells the processor to store the content of register A into memory location 100D. It does so by executing a memory write cycle to location 100D with 8A (from register A) on the data bus. Since the location 100D is in RAM, the value 8A will be written into it. Note that the processor has no way of knowing whether the writing actually takes place. If 100D were a ROM location, the processor would simply execute a write cycle which would have no effect on memory.

The fourth instruction is a one-byte instruction (3F or SWI) which acts as a call to the monitor system (somewhat like a simple operating system), and acts in conjunction with the subsequent code number (08) to end the program. All MC6809 programs which are run on the ASSYM09 simulator or on hardware using the ASSIST09 monitor must end with this pair of bytes. As a consequence of this simple eleven-byte program, the contents of memory locations 100B and 100C are added together and the sum is stored into location 100D.

In this example note that whenever a piece of information is moved about in the computer, the source does not get changed. When the processor loads the content of a memory location into a register, it simply makes a copy of the content into the register. When the processor adds the content of a memory location to a register, the original value remains in memory, intact. Of course, the destination does get changed, but only the destination, and not the source.

4.10.3 The Motorola MC68000 Programming Model

The programming model for the MC68000 microprocessor is shown in Figure 4.7. It consists of 19 registers and the 16 M-byte (2^{24} bytes or 2^{23} 16-bit words) combined memory and I/O space. The MC68000 has no I/O space separate from memory. Although the address registers and the program counter are 32 bits wide, the processor chip has a 24-bit address bus which uses only the lowest ordered bits of these registers. Thus, the processor is capable of addressing 2^{24} individual bytes. As emphasized in Figure 4.7, a byte may be accessed at any one of 16M locations, but a word (16-bits) may be accessed only at one of the 8M even-addressed locations. The internal structure and the instruction set of the MC68000 support 32-bit operations; however, its 16-bit data bus and its byte-addressing scheme limit memory accesses to 8 or 16 bits of data per cycle.

Although the processor is capable of accessing individual bytes of memory during the *execution* of instructions, the instructions themselves have lengths which are multiples of words (16 bits). Thus, the PC, which always points to instructions, must contain an even number (bit 0 is always 0) and is always incremented by two after each step of the instruction fetch.

The bank of eight data registers, D0 through D7, identifies the MC68000 as a general register machine. The data movement and arithmetic/logic instructions manipulate data in these registers or in memory locations. Most of those instructions can be specified to operate on 8-, 16-, or 32-bit pieces of data in the data registers. Eight-bit operations affect only bits 0 through 7, 16-bit operations affect bits 0 through 15, and 32-bit operations affect the entire register.

Registers A0 through A7 and A7′ are used to hold addresses of locations in memory which are of particular interest in a program. The contents of these registers may also be manipulated by the instructions in many ways as if they were data registers. Specific uses for these registers will be described in later chapters.

The status register (SR) is divided into two parts, the *user byte* and the *system byte*. The system byte will be discussed in a later chapter. The user byte (also referred to as the CCR) is directly affected by the execution of certain instructions. It includes the usual carry bit (C), overflow bit (V), zero bit (Z), and sign or negative bit (N). In addition, it includes the extend bit (X), a modified version of the carry bit which is used exclusively for multi-precision arithmetic operations. The remaining three bits in the user byte are not used and appear as 0s whenever the byte is read.

4.10.4 A First Example Program for the MC68000

To illustrate the way in which some of the MC68000 programming model resources function and interact, consider the program segment shown in Figure 4.8. The column to the right of the memory content column lists the mnemonic form of each instruction after the final word of that instruction. The last two columns show the contents of the PC and either register D0 or D7 after the word is fetched or the instruction is

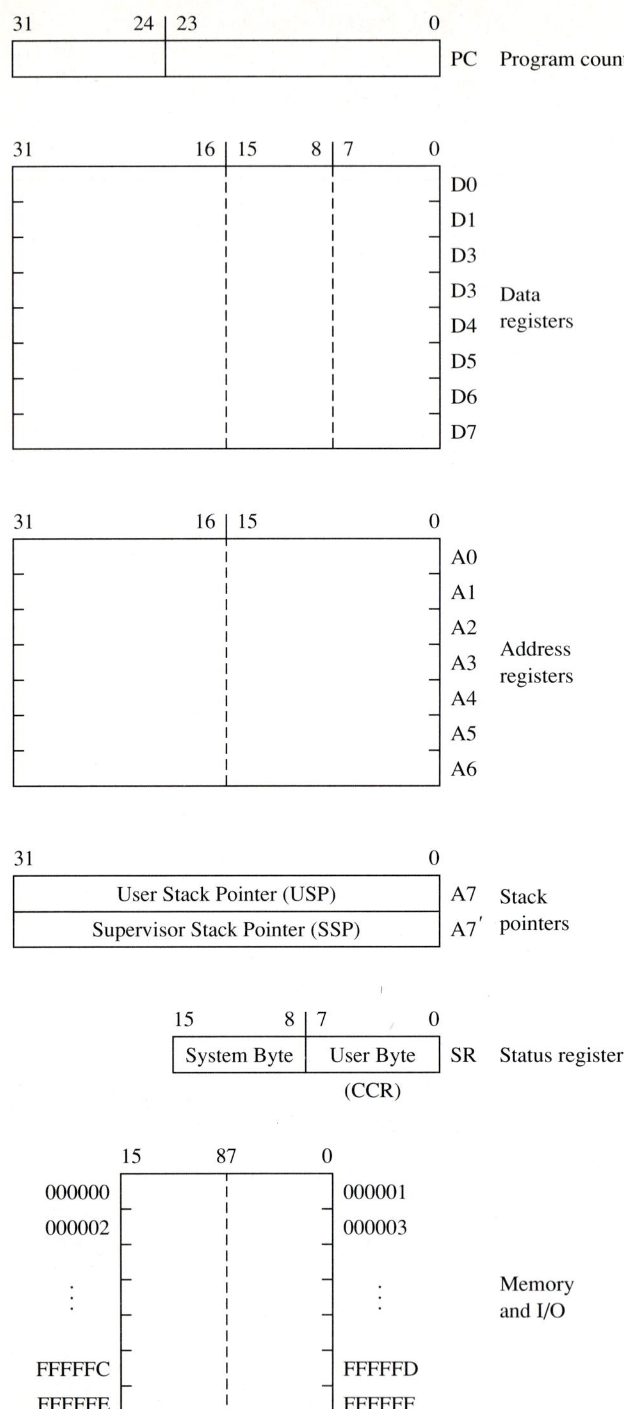

FIGURE 4.7
Programming model for the MC68000 microprocessor.

			After Fetch (Execute)	
Address	*Content*	*Instruction*	*PC*	*D0*
001000	3038		001002	--------
001002	1014	MOVE 1014H,D0	001004	----1234
001004	D038		001006	----1234
001006	1016	ADD 1016H,D0	001008	----68AC
001008	3E00		00100A	----68AC
00100A	1018	MOVE D0,1018H	00100C	----68AC
				D7
00100C	2E3C		00100E	--------
00100E	0000		001010	--------
001010	00E4	MOVE.L #228,D7	001012	000000E4
001012	4E4E	TRAP #14	001014	000000E4
001014	1234	Data		
001016	5678	Data		
001018	0000	Place for Result		

FIGURE 4.8
A simple MC68000 program segment.

executed. The dashes in the contents of the data registers indicate that the values present are immaterial because they either will not be affected by any instruction or they will be overwritten by the current instruction.

Assume that the bit patterns shown in hex in Figure 4.8 have been stored in the respective memory locations, and that the processor is started in the fetch cycle with the value 001000 (hex) in the lowest ordered 24 bits of the program counter. The PC starts at 001000, but after the first word is fetched it is incremented to 001002.

The processor starts in the fetch cycle and will therefore fetch the content of the word location in memory to which the program counter is pointing. It does this by placing the address 001000 on the address bus and executing a read cycle. It then automatically increments the program counter by two. The word fetched is 3038, and, since it is supposed to be the first word of an instruction, the processor decodes it as such. The decoding informs the processor that the instruction requires one more word, which it then fetches, automatically incrementing the PC by two.

Having completed fetching the instruction, the processor proceeds to execute it. The instruction, 3038-1014 (MOVE 1014H,D0), requires that the processor fetch the word from the memory location whose address is 1014, sign extended to 001014 (the H indicates hex). The processor is then to load that word into register D0. The processor does this by executing another read cycle, this time with the address 001014, and latching the value read (1234) into D0. Notice that this is a word (16 bits) transfer, so it does not affect the most significant half of D0. Notice also that the processor merely copies the value from the memory location into the register. The source (the memory location) does not change; only the destination changes.

As is typical in any computer at the machine level, this instruction has accomplished only a limited manipulation, involving only a small number of registers. Although they include a wider variety of more complex instructions, even larger processors are able to accomplish much less in one instruction than the operations called for in a typical higher-level instruction. A single higher-level instruction must often be broken down into dozens of these simple machine language instructions when a higher-level language program is compiled.

After completing the execution of the first instruction, the processor fetches the next word from the location pointed to by the program counter (001004) while automatically incrementing the PC to 001006. This word (D038), when it is decoded as an op-code, informs the processor that this second instruction also comprises two words. It then fetches the remainder of the instruction and proceeds to execute it, leaving the value of 001008 in the PC.

The second instruction, D038-1016 (ADD 1016H,D0), calls for the processor to add to the content of register D0 the word read out of location 1016 (sign extended to the 24-bit address 001016). This requires another read cycle to obtain the word from memory location 001016 (5678 hex). The processor adds this value to the content of D0 to generate the sum of 68AC, which then replaces the original content of the lower half of D0. Again, this word-sized operation has no affect on the upper half of D0.

The third instruction, fetched from locations 001008 and 00100A, is 3E00-0018 (MOVE D0,1018H). This instruction tells the processor to copy the content of register D0 into memory location 001018. It does so by executing a memory write cycle with the address 001018 and the data 68AC (from register D0). If the location 001018 is in RAM memory, the value 68AC will be written into it. If 001018 is in ROM, the processor would simply have executed a write cycle which had no effect. The processor has no way of knowing, during the execution of this instruction, whether the write cycle had the desired effect.

The fourth instruction (MOVE.L #228,D7) is a three-word instruction (2E3C-0000-00E4 in hex) used to prepare the system to terminate the program segment gracefully. It requires the processor to load the 32-bit pattern for the decimal number 228 (hex 000000E4) into register D7. When the final instruction (4E4E or TRAP #14) is executed, it acts as a call to the monitor or the operating system and, in conjunction with the value stored in D7, serves to end the program. All programs which use the ASSYM000 simulator software must end with these two instructions.

If you will be using some other means of writing and running programs you should determine how to stop the system you will be using. Note that if the processor were not stopped from fetching and executing instructions at this point in the program it would go on to fetch the next word (1234 from location 001014), which happens to be data, and interpret it as an op-code!

This 10-word example program would occupy a total of 26 bytes of memory, including data locations and a place for the result. When it is executed it causes the 16-bit words stored at locations 001014 and 001016 to be added and the sum to be stored in location 001018. Although it has many more complex instructions and modes of identifying data in memory, there is no simpler way for the MC68000 to accomplish this task.

SUMMARY

The basic functional blocks of a microprocessor system are the processor, the memory, and the I/O circuits with their associated peripherals. With the exception of the peripherals, the various parts are implemented in integrated circuits comprising combinational and sequential circuits of the types described in an earlier chapter.

A computer system's memory must include both read-write memory, called RAM, and read-only memory, called ROM, in order to serve the system properly. In addition, the I/O circuits are often intermingled with memory circuits, sharing the same address space. The order in which these resources are intermixed in a specific system is almost completely at the discretion of the hardware designer. The programmer must know which locations are implemented with which type of memory and which locations access I/O interface circuits if the programs are to work properly.

The content of a location in a computer's memory may be interpreted in many different ways. It may represent, among other things, one of the several parts of an instruction, a number or part of a number expressed in one of several different ways and with many possible degrees of precision, or a character expressed in one of several different codes. The way in which the processor interprets the content depends on where it is and what it is doing at the time. It is the responsibility of the programmer to ensure that the appropriate patterns are fetched from memory at the proper times.

Locations in the system memory or I/O interface circuitry are accessed by the processor through three buses, the address, data, and control buses. These buses represent the only means the processor has of accessing the program instructions and data. The two types of accesses, read cycles and write cycles, are intermixed during the execution of instructions by the processor.

The primary operation of the processor is a repetitive two-step cycle, the fetch/execute cycle. During the fetch part of the cycle the processor fetches an instruction word-by-word, starting with the op-code word. Once the entire instruction has been fetched the processor executes it and then repeats the fetch/execute cycle over and over again, keeping track of where it is in the program by means of a register called the program counter.

Other common registers which will be found in the programming models of almost any microprocessor are accumulators or the related data registers, address registers with differing capabilities and functions, and a condition code register with its several independent condition code bits.

Every processor includes a memory address register separate from those in the programming model to hold addresses on the bus during bus cycles, a memory buffer register to hold data on its way to and from memory, an instruction register to hold an instruction while it is being interpreted, counters, shift registers, etc. A detailed understanding of the structure and functioning of these registers is not a prerequisite for the proper design and use of microprocessor-based systems. The user of microprocessors should concentrate instead upon the programming model.

REVIEW PROBLEMS

4.1. The programming model for a particular microprocessor includes a 20-bit program counter (PC), four 20-bit index registers (W, X, Y, and Z), two 16-bit accumulators (A and B), a 12-bit direct-page register (DP) and four flags (N, Z, C, and V) as part of an 8-bit condition code register.

a. How many bits comprise the address bus?
b. How many bits comprise the data bus?
c. How many distinct memory locations can this processor access? Answer in K-locations and in exact decimal form.
d. What is the address range in hex?
e. What is the (single precision) range of unsigned binary numbers for this machine? Answer in decimal.
f. What is the (single precision) range of unsigned BCD numbers for this machine? Answer in decimal.
g. What is the (single precision) range of two's complement numbers for this machine? Answer in decimal.
h. How many pages does the memory contain? Answer in decimal.
i. How many words comprise a page of memory? Answer in decimal.
j. Describe the conditions under which each bit in the CCR will be a 1 and under which cach will bc a 0.

4.2. How many bits must a processor's program counter have in order to be able to access 512K (one-half of a MB) locations? one MB? 32 MB? 1024 MB?

4.3. Currently popular personal computers have either a 16- or a 32-bit word size. Several popular mainframes have a 64-bit word size. Compare these computers as to the range of both signed and unsigned integers (unsigned and signed binary numbers) which can be represented in single precision, the range of (unsigned) single precision BCD decimal numbers which can be represented, and the number of packed ASCII characters which may be represented in a single word. All conclusions should be expressed in decimal form.

4.4. Draw a flowchart describing the basic fetch/execute cycle of a processor.

4.5. Draw a logic diagram showing how eight D-type flip-flops can be used to construct an eight-bit register. The register is to be loaded from a bus consisting of eight signal leads during any clock cycle that a control signal named LD is at logic level one.

4.6. Draw a logic diagram showing how the overflow flag (V) can be implemented. The inputs to the circuit are the appropriate carries from the adder, a V-update signal (VU), and the clock signal.

4.7. Draw a logic diagram showing how a zero flag (Z) can be implemented. The inputs to the circuit are each of the eight result bits (R0-R7), a Z-update signal (ZU), and the clock signal.

4.8. Write a program in MC6809 machine language (hex) to add three numbers together. The program is to start in memory location A100 and is to add the numbers in locations 8B00, 8B01, and 8B02. It is to store the sum in location A300. List the program by showing the addresses and the contents of the memory locations which contain the program instructions. Then list the locations which will contain the data which will be used or generated by the program.

4.9. Write a program in MC68000 machine language (hex) to add three numbers together. The program is to start in memory location 00A400 and is to add the word-sized numbers in locations 006B00, 006B02, and 006B04. It is to store the sum in location 006D00. List the program by showing the addresses and the contents of the memory locations which contain the program instructions. Then list the locations which will contain the data which will be used or generated by the program.

CHAPTER 5

INSTRUCTIONS AND ADDRESSING MODES

In its basic operation the central processing unit alternates between fetching instructions and executing instructions. The instructions cause the processor to manipulate the contents of specific programming model registers and of memory and I/O locations. Certain types of instructions, namely load/store, arithmetic/logic, and input/output, must identify specific registers and/or locations for the processor in order that it may locate operands or store results properly. Test/branch instructions must also identify the branch target locations in the program. The ways in which these addresses and registers are specified are known as the addressing modes for the processor. This chapter examines the various classes of instructions which processors must be able to execute, and some of the basic categories of addressing modes. It then introduces the specific addressing modes used with MC6809 and MC68000 processors.

When learning about a new processor, one must learn first the programming model and then the available addressing modes. Thus, this chapter introduces the second major set of important details about the MC6809 and the MC68000 microprocessors.

5.1 TYPES OF INSTRUCTIONS

The computer was defined in Chapter 1 as a programmable, sequential, binary, electronic machine which can do certain basic types of operations: load/store, arithmetic/logic, test/branch, and input/output. Although the instructions which direct these operations in the central processing unit vary widely from processor to processor, certain common characteristics are found in all processor instruction sets. Some of these are described below, together with a few specific examples. The instructions used with the two processors discussed in this book, the MC6809 and the MC68000, will be examined in more detail in later chapters.

5.1.1 Load/Store Instructions

Load/store operations are those which move data between a register in the processor and a memory location (or another register). They are often collectively referred to as *data movement* instructions. The two terms *load* and *store* are often confused and should be carefully distinguished from each other. Figure 5.1 illustrates the difference. Note that an alternative (British) name for the memory is the "store," and that the store operation puts data into the store or stores it away. In these data movement operations the data is not altered in any way. The processor moves the data from the source to the destination.

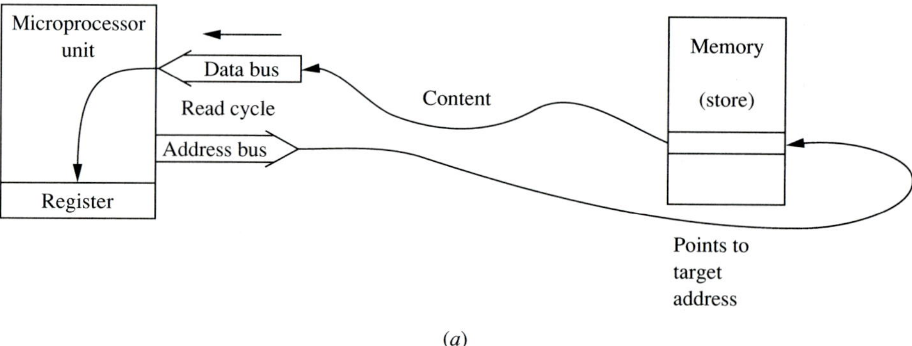

(*a*)

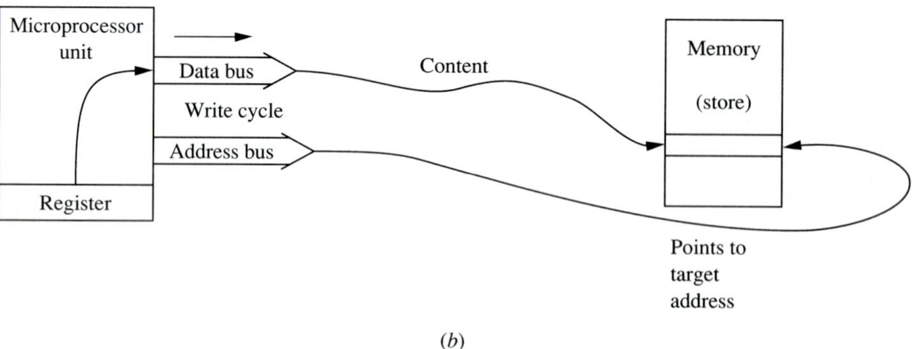

(*b*)

FIGURE 5.1
Load and store operations: (*a*) load, (*b*) store.

One of the universal characteristics of instruction execution is that the source does not get changed, only the destination. Thus, in a load operation the processor copies data into a register, and in a store operation the processor copies data from a register into a memory location.

Examples of load/store instructions in the MC6809 are LDA, STA, LDB, STB, LDD, STD, and so forth. The address of the memory location involved in the instruction must be included in the instruction. This can be done in any of several different ways, which will be examined in Sections 5.2 and 5.3.

Examples of load/store instructions in the MC68000 are MOVE (for either direction of data movement), MOVEM (for moving the content of several registers into or out of memory with a single instruction), and EXG (for exchanging register contents). These instructions and others like them must include information identifying the source and destination. Methods of doing this will be discussed in Sections 5.2 and 5.4.

5.1.2 Arithmetic/Logic Instructions

Arithmetic/logic operations provide the primary data-processing capabilities of the computer. The minimum arithmetic operations required are those of addition and subtraction. Many of the smaller microprocessors provide only these two basic operations together with increment and decrement (add or subtract one) capabilities. Larger microprocessors may include both signed and unsigned integer multiplication and division functions.

All processors implement the basic logic operations of AND, OR, and exclusive-OR on a bit-by-bit basis between two operands. They also include the 1's complement operation (the NOT function) on a single operand.

With operations requiring two operands, smaller microprocessors usually require that one of the operands must be in a destination register initially, while the other may be in another register or in memory. Their instructions may identify at most a single operand in memory, as shown in Figure 5.2*a*. They support such operations as adding or ANDing to processor registers as illustrated but not to memory locations.

Larger microprocessors permit either the source or the destination to be in memory. Their instructions may identify both operands as being in memory, as shown in Figure 5.2*b*. They support such operations as adding or ANDing to memory locations as well as to registers.

Still larger and more complex processors may even allow the user to specify a destination in memory separate from either operand, as shown in Figure 5.2*c*. However, this degree of complexity is not available with current microprocessors. In any case, the source operands always remain unchanged; only the destination changes.

Some examples of two-operand arithmetic/logic instructions in the MC6809 are ADDB, SUBA, SUBD, ANDA, and EORA (exclusive-OR). Each of these requires one operand to be in an accumulator. The memory address of the other operand is included in the instruction in one of the ways to be described. With some two-operand arithmetic instructions the operands must be in two registers. In the MUL instruction, for example, the operands must be in the two accumulators, A and B.

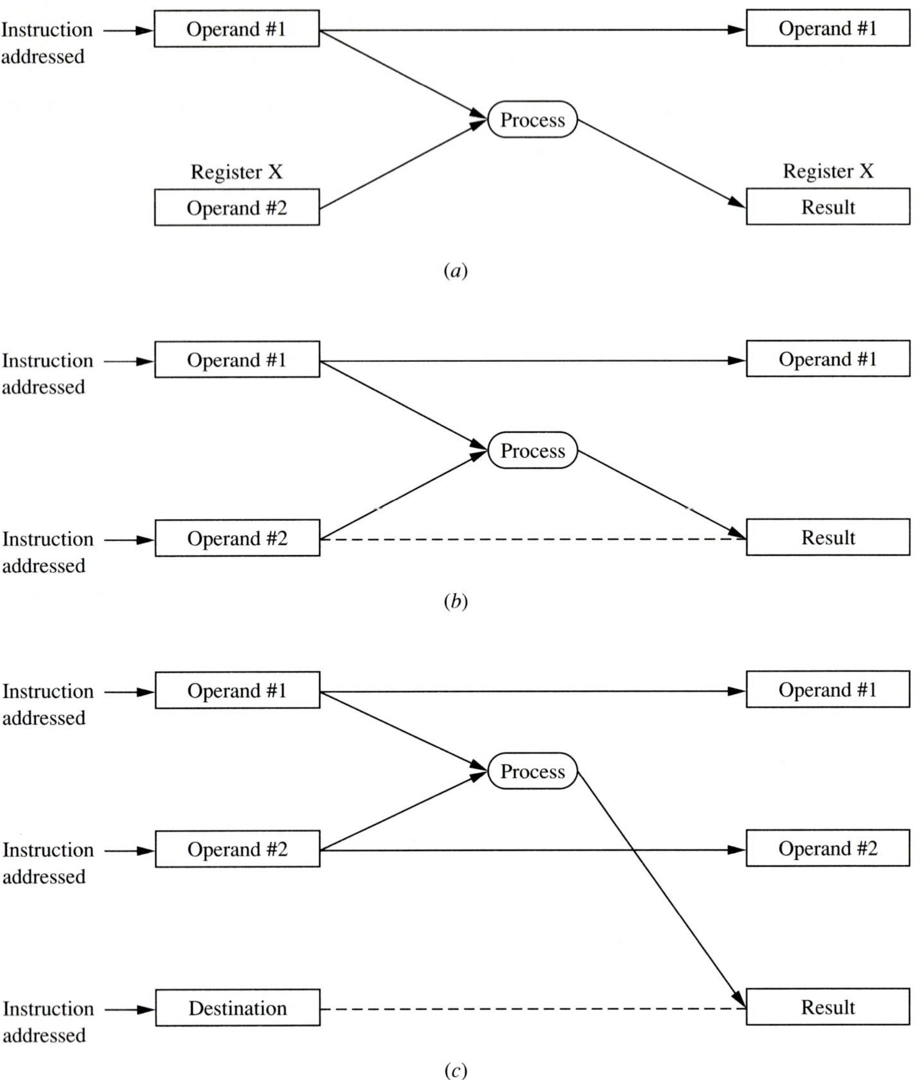

FIGURE 5.2
Instruction formats: (*a*) single address, (*b*) double address, (*c*) triple address.

Some two-operand arithmetic/logic instructions in the MC68000 instruction set are ADD, AND, OR, SUB, and EOR. All of the two-operand instructions in the MC68000 must specify the source and the destination. With a few exceptions, these may both be registers or memory locations or one of each.

Among the single-operand arithmetic/logic operations are increment and decrement operations, the 1's and 2's complement, and various shift and *rotate* operations. These operate directly upon the specified operand to modify it. Thus, the operand location is both the source and the destination for the operation.

Examples of one-operand instructions in the MC6809 include COMA (complement A), ASLB (arithmetic shift left B), INC (increment a memory location whose address is identified in the instruction), and NEGA (2's complement or negate A). The MC68000 includes the instructions CLR (clear), NEG (change sign of), NOT (complement), and EXT (extend the sign bit to double the number of bits in an operand).

5.1.3 Test/Branch Instructions

Test/branch operations provide the decision-making capabilities so important in computer programs. The test must often be performed on the result of some prior arithmetic/logic operation. It determines whether the result was zero or nonzero, positive or negative, or some other binary choice involving bits in the condition code register. During the execution of a test/branch instruction the processor examines the appropriate condition code bits to determine the result of the test. Depending upon the result, the processor may or may not branch to a remote location for the next instruction. For one outcome the next instruction will be fetched as normal from the original location indicated by the program counter. For the other outcome the content of the program counter is first changed and then used to fetch the next instruction. The result in the latter case is a branch in the sequence of instructions.

Examples of test/branch instructions common to both the MC6809 and the MC68000 are BCC (branch if carry is cleared), BEQ (branch if equal to 0), BMI (branch if minus), and BRA (branch always). Of course, the address to which the branch will go must also be identified in the instruction.

5.1.4 Input/Output Instructions

Every computer must communicate with the outside world in some way, and instructions which support this function are called *input/output* or *I/O* instructions. Although they support input/output operations in other ways, microprocessors typically have very limited I/O instructions. They will often be as simple as "input a byte to a register" or "output a byte from a register".

Neither the MC6809 nor the MC68000 has any I/O instructions. Instead, each requires that the user implement I/O devices as if they were memory locations with regular memory addresses. Any memory reference instruction, therefore, becomes an I/O instruction when it refers to one of those addresses.

5.2 ADDRESSING MODES

Most of the instructions must refer to the address or content of a specific memory location. These so-called *memory reference instructions* must somehow identify the address of the location as a part of the instruction encoding. The manner in which this *target address* or *effective address* is identified within the instruction is called the *addressing mode*. This definition has been extended to include the specification of operands in processor register banks as well.

In addition to understanding the programming model, the designer must be thoroughly familiar with the addressing modes used in a processor and with how they are specified, particularly in the mnemonic form. This is the second major learning task a designer faces when encountering a new processor.

This section describes the more common addressing modes used in microprocessors. The names used here are more or less accepted terms for broad and general classes of addressing modes. The manufacturer's literature for each microprocessor may use somewhat different terminology in describing the specific addressing modes that it uses. Later in this chapter the actual modes used in the MC6809 and the MC68000 processors will be described, using the standard Motorola terminology.

5.2.1 Direct Addressing

When the instruction explicitly states the location of an operand or a destination (either in memory or in a processor register), the addressing mode is known as *direct addressing*. The op-word for the instruction includes a group of bits which identifies this mode of addressing. The effective address itself is included in the subsequent words of the instruction (*post-words*). If the specified location is a register, the register identification number may fit into the op-word itself with no need for post-words.

Two subclassifications within the direct addressing mode are often recognized. When the location is in memory the mode may be referred to as *absolute addressing*. When the location is a processor register it may be referred to as *register direct addressing*. Figure 5.3 illustrates the two modes. In part *a* the instruction specifies the address of the operand; in part *b* the instruction specifies the register containing the operand.

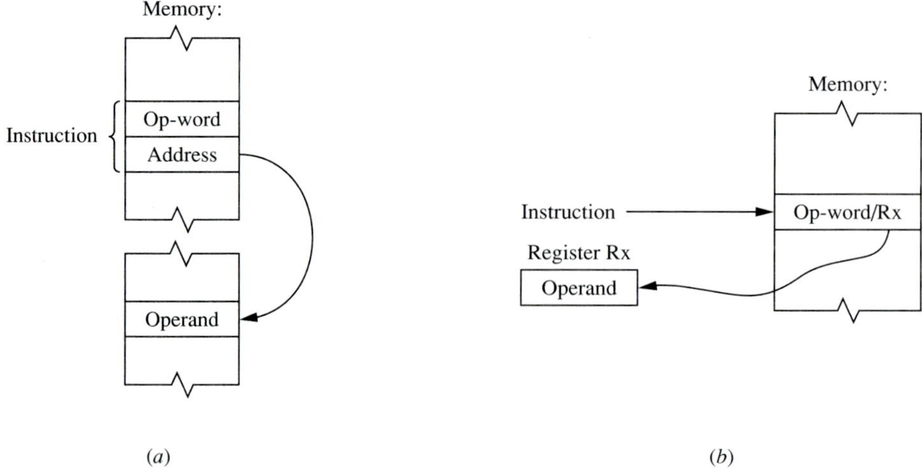

FIGURE 5.3
Direct addressing: (*a*) absolute addressing, (*b*) register direct addressing.

Several instructions in each of the sample programs at the end of Chapter 4 use the direct addressing mode. These are shown here in mnemonic form.

From the MC6809:	From the MC68000:
LDA 100BH	MOVE 1014H,D0
ADDA 100CH	ADD 1016H,D0
STA 100DH	MOVE DO,1018H

Notice that each of these instructions includes the address of the operand or the destination. In fact, the MC68000 examples each include two "direct addresses", one in memory and one in the register bank (D0). The MC6809 examples also include a second specification, that of accumulator A. Within an accumulator machine, however, one operand must always be in an accumulator, and so this specification is considered to be a part of the basic instruction itself and not an addressing mode.

With direct addressing an operand may be in any location in memory. Including the complete memory address may result in quite a lengthy instruction. Some processors allow an abbreviated expression of the address with some simple rule to generate the complete address. One such approach allows a partial address in the instruction but has the processor append 0's to the leading edge during execution to obtain the complete address. Another approach is to sign-extend the abbreviated address to obtain the complete address. (Normally, only one method will be used in any one processor.) The second of these two methods is the one permitted with the MC68000 and shown in the above examples. In each of these, the address of the memory location was abbreviated to 16 bits (1014, 1016, and 1018). During program execution the processor sign-extends each value to 24 bits (001014, 001016, and 001018).

Direct addressing is used when the memory address or the selected register is to be fixed in the program. The content may or may not change while the program is executed, but the place stays the same. The instruction "directly" and specifically identifies the place. This addressing mode is commonly used to specify the locations of variables used within a program.

5.2.2 Immediate Addressing

In many cases an instruction requires a constant quantity, a bit pattern which will never change no matter when or how often the instruction is executed. A convenient way to store a constant is to include it inside the instruction so that it becomes an integral part of the program itself. This mode of including a bit pattern as a part of an instruction is called the *immediate addressing* mode. The op-word for the instruction includes a group of bits which identifies this mode of addressing, and the post-words include the bit pattern itself. Since the instruction is located in program memory the constant itself is also in program memory.

When using the immediate addressing mode the instruction does not state explicitly the location of the operand; rather, it explicitly states the operand itself. The example in Figure 5.4 illustrates this mode. Note that the operand becomes an integral part of the instruction.

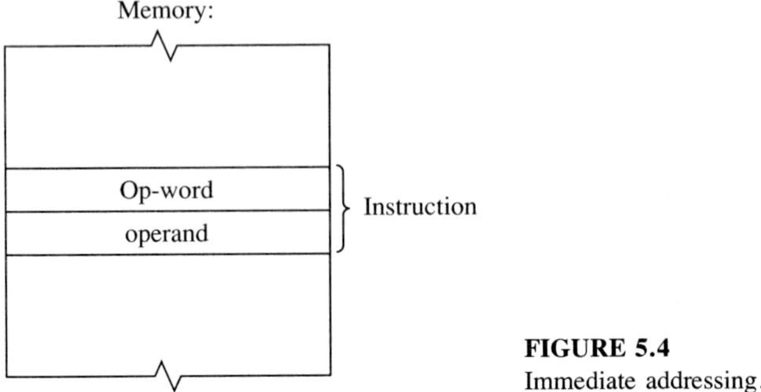

FIGURE 5.4
Immediate addressing.

As can be seen in Figure 5.4, the effective address (of the operand) is within the program area and not within a data area. A program should not modify itself as it is executed; in control applications this is not even possible since the program memory is ROM. Therefore, immediate addressing may be used only to *read* a pattern out of memory, not to *write* one into memory. Instructions which write into memory are not allowed to use the immediate addressing mode.

Just as some processors include an option to abbreviate a direct *address*, so also do some processors include an option to abbreviate an immediate *operand*. During execution the processor either appends leading 0's or sign-extends the constant to obtain the full immediate operand. In some cases the use of this option may even allow the constant to fit within the op-word itself.

Immediate addressing is used when a particular constant value is to be fixed within the program itself. The value is found in memory "immediately" after the instruction code word and may never change at any time.

5.2.3 Indirect Addressing

In the *indirect addressing* mode the instruction tells the processor neither the address of the operand nor the operand itself. Instead, it tells the processor where to go to find the address of the operand. The instruction may explicitly state either the address of a location in memory or the name of a processor register, but the binary number which is found there is not the operand. Instead, it is the effective address, the address of a location in memory to which the processor must go to find the operand. The result is that the processor must take one extra step in order to locate the operand. Hence, this mode is sometimes called *deferred* addressing.

The op-word for the instruction includes a group of bits which identifies this mode of addressing, and the (indirect) address is specified in one or more additional post-words. If the instruction names a processor register as the source of the effective address, then the register identification number may fit into the op-word itself.

The form of this mode in which the address of the operand or the destination is found in a memory location is often separately identified as the *memory indirect* addressing mode; if it is found in a processor register it may be referred to as the *register indirect* addressing mode. When the latter form is used, an address register rather than a data register must be specified. Both forms are illustrated in Figure 5.5.

Indirect addressing is used when a program must operate upon different data values under different circumstances. For example, a program may need to operate upon successive values in a list during a program loop, or it may need to branch to one of 10 different places depending upon which of 10 keys is struck, or it may use a table look-up procedure to find the square root of a number which will be provided when the program is running. In each of these cases the effective address must be constructed or deduced while the program is being executed. The address cannot be directly included in a program instruction. Instead, the program itself must create the address in memory or in a register during execution. Indirect addressing allows the program to use this address in succeeding instructions by referring to it "indirectly" through its location.

Figure 5.6 compares and contrasts the first three addressing modes. Note that in the immediate mode the instruction includes the operand, in the direct mode it includes the address of the operand, and in the indirect mode it includes the address of the address of the operand.

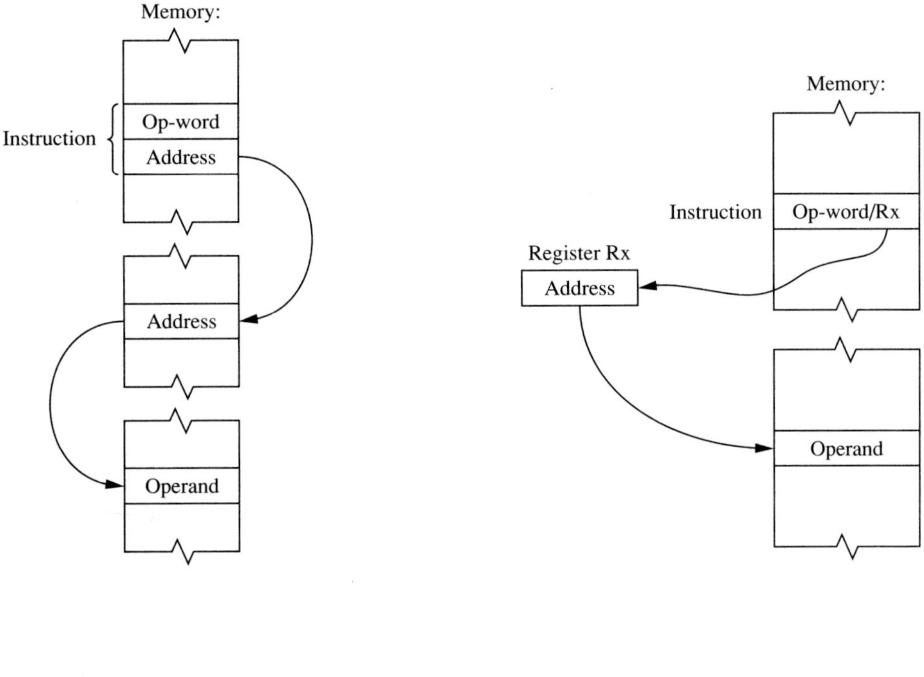

FIGURE 5.5
Indirect addressing: (*a*) memory indirect, (*b*) register indirect.

a. Immediate:

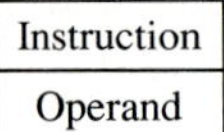

b. Direct:

c. Indirect:

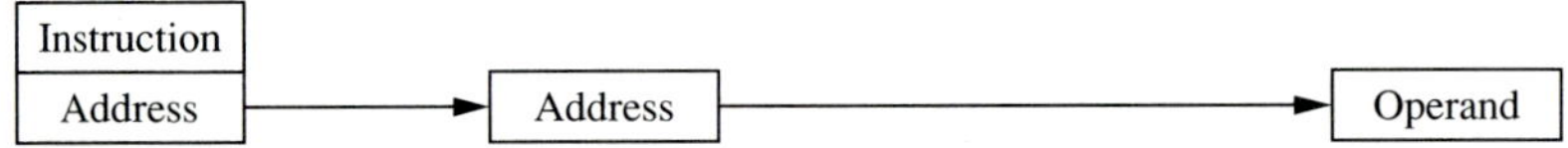

FIGURE 5.6
Comparison of immediate, direct, and indirect addressing.

5.2.4 Multi-Component Addressing Modes

Each of the following related addressing modes requires that the processor assemble two or more components together during the execution of the program in order to create the effective address. In each case the effective address itself is that of a memory location. However, at least one of the components is found in a processor register.

Instructions which use *indexed addressing* specify two registers, often by coding within the op-word itself. During program execution the processor temporarily adds the contents of these registers to generate the effective address. One of the registers is an address register and it is said to hold the *base address*. The other is commonly a data register, and is referred to as the *displacement* or *index* register.

Based addressing is a similar mode wherein the instruction specifies an address register and a fixed constant (an *offset* or *displacement*). The register designation often fits within the op-word and the offset usually requires post-words. In this mode the content of the register is the base and the constant is the displacement. During execution the processor adds the constant and the value in the register to generate the effective address.

In microprocessors, the distinction between these modes has been blurred and various authors use the terms quite loosely. Thus, based addressing is sometimes known as "indexed addressing," indexed addressing is occasionally called "address register indirect with index," and one even sees references to the "relative based

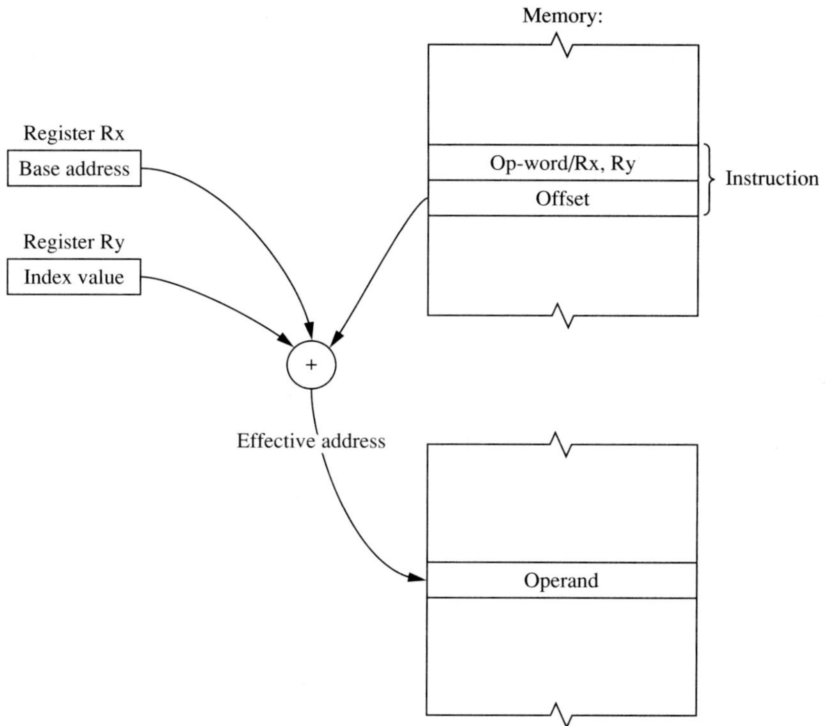

FIGURE 5.7
"Indexed/based/offset" addressing.

indexed" mode! The general structure of this type of addressing mode is illustrated in Figure 5.7. The instruction shown depicts a mode which specifies both a base register and an index register as well as a fixed offset.

These modes provide methods whereby a program may operate upon successive data values in a list during a program loop. The base register gives the processor the address of the start of the list. The displacement or index is the distance into the list. The primary requirement is that one of the components (either the index or the base) may be changed under program control. In that way the program may refer to successive locations in the list while executing a program loop and yet not modify *itself*. During the execution of the loop the program can change the index or base register contents, thereby causing the indexed instruction to refer to successive locations in the list.

Another similar mode is *relative* or *PC-relative addressing*. In this mode the instruction specifies the offset or the distance from the address in the program counter (PC) to the effective memory address. This mode allows the processor to access locations during program execution by simply adding the (signed) offset to the address in the PC. The addition is temporary; the content of the PC remains unchanged (unless the effective address is the target of a branch instruction). This mode is illustrated in

Figure 5.8. As shown in this figure, during the execution of the instruction the PC has already advanced to the next instruction. This fact must be accounted for when the offset is calculated and the instruction is coded.

The relative addressing mode permits the writing of "position-independent code," programs which will be properly executed by the processor regardless of where they are located in memory. The entire program (together with any necessary data) may be picked up from one region of memory and moved to another with no adverse effect. In order to be location-independent a program may not refer to any specific location by address. All references to memory must be through the use of relative addressing. Examples will be shown in a later chapter.

The final multi-component mode to be described here is *paged addressing*. In this mode the instruction includes only *some of the bits* of the address of the operand in a post-word. The processor obtains the rest of the address bits from a *page register* during the execution of the instruction. The page register contains the upper part of the effective address (referred to as the *current page of memory*), and the post-word contains the lower part. The processor concatenates the two parts of the address, the

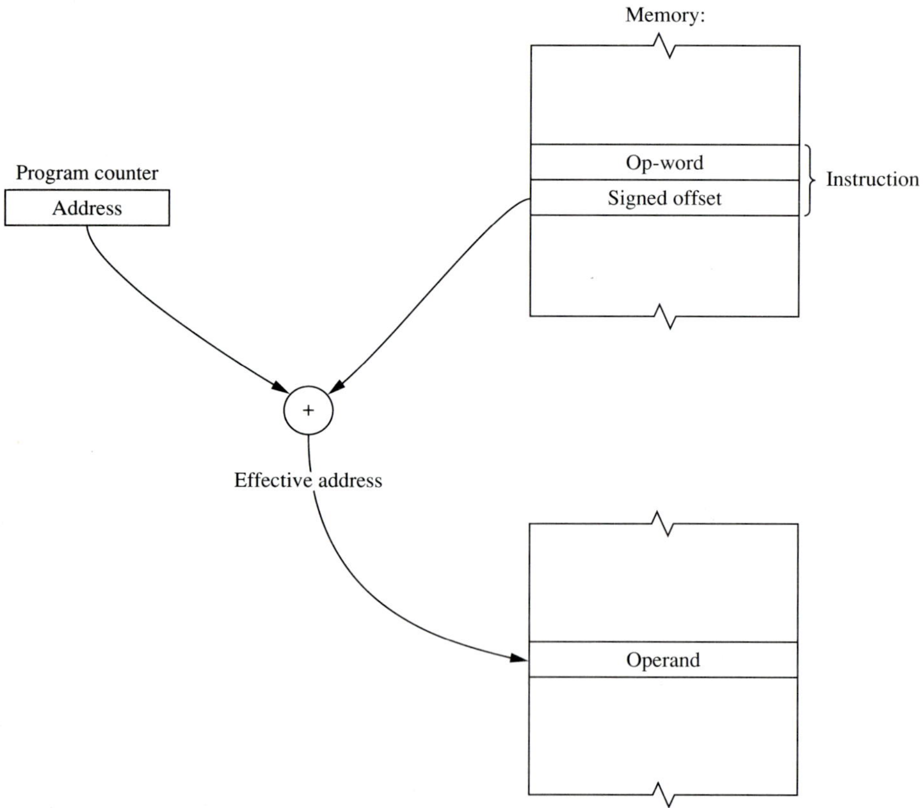

FIGURE 5.8
(PC) Relative addressing.

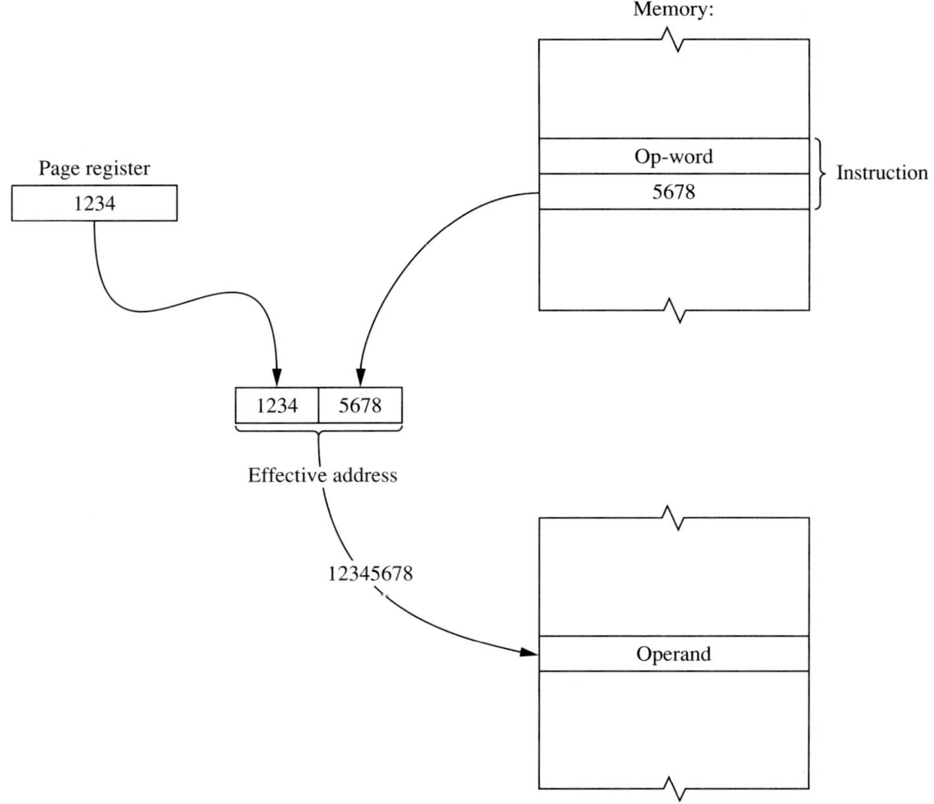

FIGURE 5.9
Paged addressing.

current page number and the location on the page which is contained in the post-word of the instruction. This mode is illustrated in Figure 5.9. Paged addressing reduces the number of words which an instruction must use to address memory directly. It is practical only in processors in which the address size is an integer multiple of the word size.

5.2.5 Implied or Inherent Addressing

Certain instructions allow no choice of register or location but always cause the processor to refer to the same registers. One example is the multiply instruction in the MC6809 which always assumes that the operands are in accumulators A and B. Another is the return from subroutine instruction in both the MC6809 and the MC68000 which automatically uses one specific address register as a pointer to the return address stored in memory. Such instructions may be said to have no addressing mode or to use *implied addressing* or *inherent addressing*.

Instructions in accumulator-based machines which use only processor registers and do not refer to memory locations are often said to be in this category as well.

The programmer has no addressing options with these instructions. Examples in the MC6809 are ABX (add B to *X*), CLRA (clear A), and TSTA (test A).

Finally, there are certain types of instructions which really do not refer to any operands, locations, or registers at all. Examples are those which halt the processor permanently or temporarily and those which do nothing but take some time to be fetched and executed (no-operation or NOP). These are usually grouped together with the others under the label of inherent addressing.

5.3 THE MC6809 ADDRESSING MODES

This section describes in detail the addressing modes used in the Motorola MC6809 microprocessor, their formats within program memory, and how they are specified in mnemonic form. The terminology is that used in the manufacturer's literature.

The MC6809 includes five addressing modes: extended, immediate, direct, relative, and indexed[1]. In addition, the indexed mode has a large variety of options. In each case the addressing mode together with the instruction operation is encoded in the first byte of the instruction (in some cases the first two bytes). This byte is called the *operation code* or *op-code* and is the code listed in the various programming aids provided by the manufacturer.

Because of the large number of instructions and addressing modes, the instructions vary in length from one to five bytes. When the processor fetches the op-code from memory it decodes it to determine how many additional bytes must be fetched to complete the instruction. Each two-byte op-code starts with the hex byte 10 or 11. Thus, when the first byte fetched is 10 or 11 the processor fetches the second byte to complete the op-code fetch and to allow the determination of the instruction length.

The op-codes for the MC6809 instructions are listed in the programming aid tables found in Appendix A. However, writing instructions by looking them up in such tables is impractical except perhaps as an emergency procedure while debugging a program. This section shows some examples of encoded instructions only as aids in describing the operations of the processor. Chapter 6 outlines a more feasible way to prepare machine language programs for the MC6809 using only the mnemonic formats.

The basic addressing modes are illustrated in Figure 5.10 and are described in the following sections.

5.3.1 Extended Addressing in the MC6809

Extended addressing is the term Motorola uses for absolute addressing (memory direct) in the MC6809. In this mode, the instruction includes the complete two-byte address of the target location. Thus, extended address instructions are all three or four bytes

[1]In some of its literature Motorola refers to a sixth mode, inherent. As described in Section 5.2.5, this mode requires no specification on the part of the programmer and so will not be discussed here.

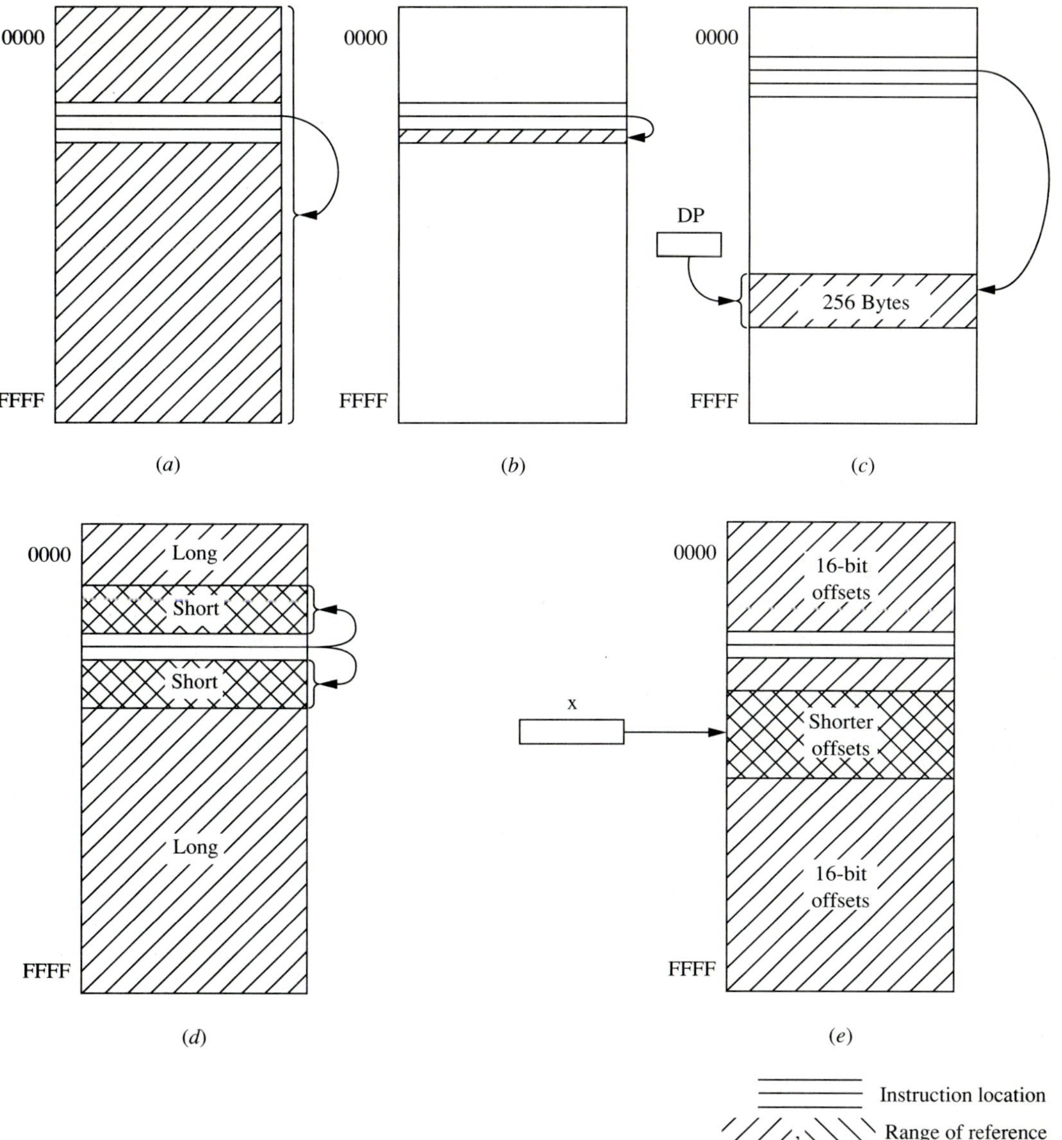

FIGURE 5.10
MC6809 addressing modes: (*a*) extended, (*b*) immediate, (*c*) direct, (*d*) relative (branches only), (*e*) indexed.

long, one or two bytes for the op-code and two for the address. The range of extended addressing is the entire memory space of the processor as illustrated in Figure 5.10*a*.

Figure 5.11 shows two examples of the format for extended addressing. The first example is the instruction to load accumulator A from hex location 1234 (LDA 1234H in mnemonic form). The op-code, B6 (obtained from Appendix A), is followed by the two-byte address, 1234. This identifies the address of the operand as 1234 hex.

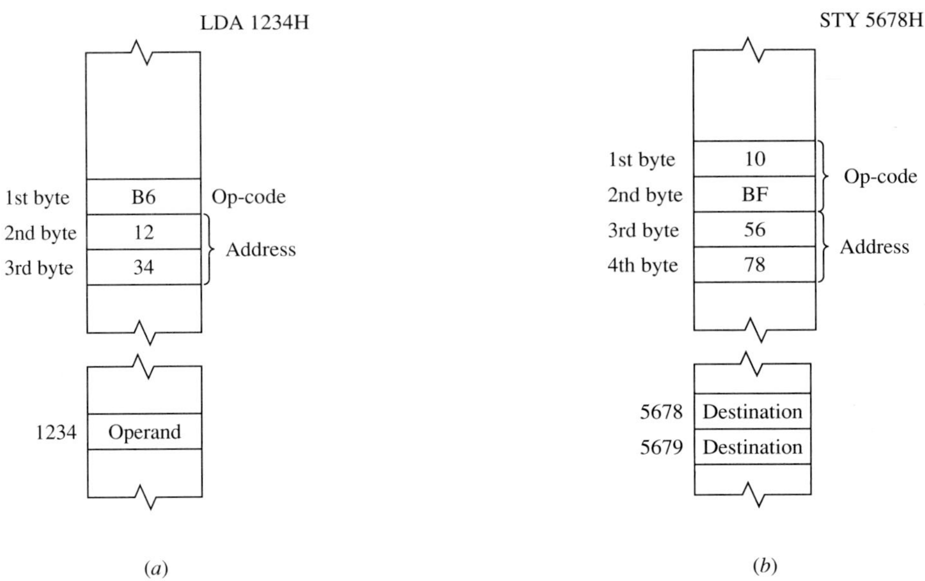

FIGURE 5.11
MC6809 extended addressing mode: (*a*) example 1, (*b*) example 2.

The second example is the instruction to store the content of the 16-bit register Y in location 5678 and 5679. The two-byte op-code, 10-BF, is followed by the address of the destination, 5678. Since double bytes are always stored in consecutive memory locations, the instruction must identify only the first location. The processor automatically generates the address of the second location. Thus, the mnemonic form (STY 5678H) includes only the address 5678. In each of these examples the address could have been any value within the range from 0000 to FFFF.

5.3.2 Immediate Addressing in the MC6809

In immediate addressing the instruction includes the operand within its own coding so that it becomes an integral part of the program itself. The range of immediate addressing is, of course, limited to only those locations inside the instruction immediately following the op-code as illustrated in Figure 5.10*b*.

Some instructions require two bytes of data and some require only one. Thus, we have single-byte-data immediate addressing and double-byte-data immediate addressing. The processor determines which to execute from the op-code itself. The format for the immediate addressing mode for both cases is illustrated in Figure 5.12. The first example is an instruction to AND the bit pattern represented by 7F with the content of accumulator B. The op-code for ANDB immediate, C4, is immediately followed by the data byte, 7F. The immediate addressing mode is specified in the mnemonic form by the use of the number sign, #. The mnemonic (ANDB #7FH) should be read as "AND B with the number 7F (hex)".

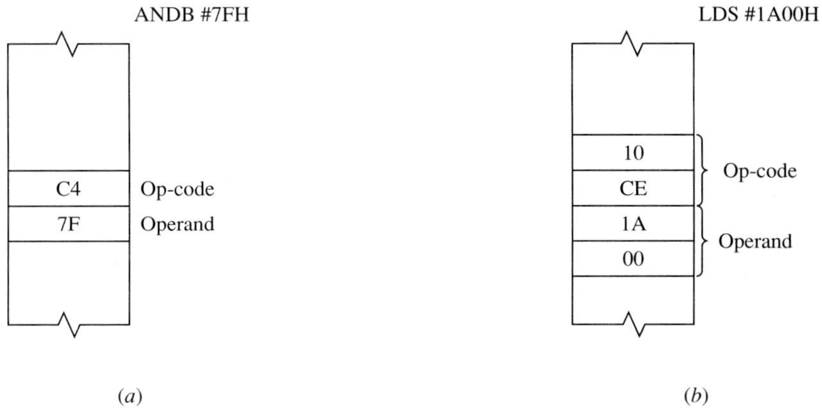

FIGURE 5.12
Immediate addressing in the MC6809: (*a*) example 1, (*b*) example 2.

In the example given in Figure 5.12*b*, the instruction is to load the system stack pointer, register S, with the number 1A00, LDS #1A00H in mnemonic form. The op-code for the instruction in the immediate mode is a double byte, 10-CE. This is followed by the double-byte number 1A00.

With immediate addressing the target location or the location of the data is actually within the instruction and not in some other region of memory. To avoid the possibility for self-modifying programs, the MC6809 does not support immediate addressing with any instruction type which will modify the target location. Thus, instructions such as clear a location, store into a location, increment a location, and so forth, do not permit immediate addressing.

5.3.3 Direct Addressing in the MC6809

Paged addressing is implemented in the MC6809 under the label of "direct" addressing. It is illustrated in Figure 5.10*c*. In this mode only the lower half of the address of the target location is included within the instruction. The upper half is obtained by the processor from the direct page register (DP) during execution. Of course, if this addressing mode is to be used, the DP register must first have been loaded with the upper half of the desired address. However, once this upper-half address has been loaded into the DP register it remains there until it is changed by the program.

An instruction using direct addressing must specify only half of the address, and so requires fewer bytes than it would if it used the extended mode. Consequently, it is fetched and executed more quickly. This mode can access any one of the 256 (decimal) different locations which are on the same direct page of memory, i.e., those which have the same upper half-address.

Because the page number is infrequently changed and because it affects all of the instructions which use the direct addressing mode, changing the page number in the MC6809 is a roundabout procedure. There is no instruction to load the DP

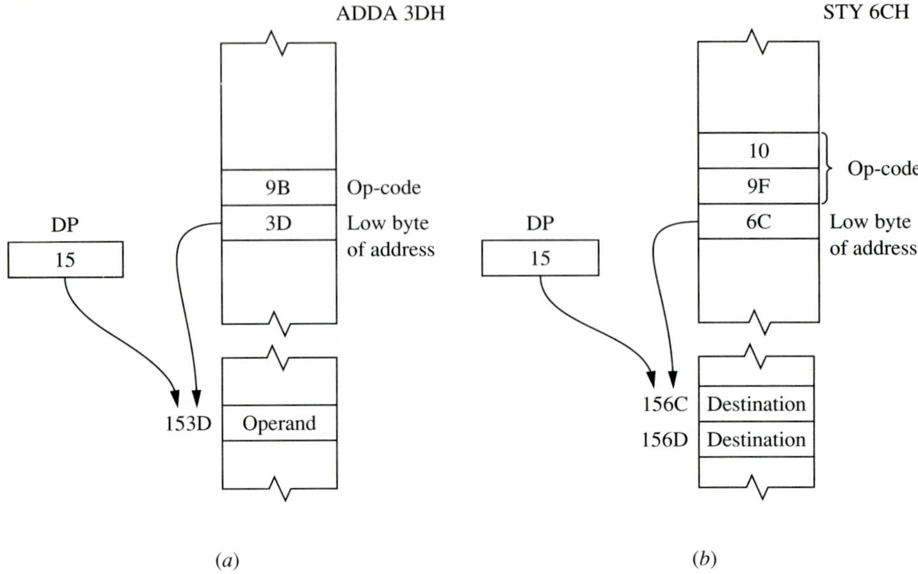

FIGURE 5.13
Direct addressing in the MC6809: (*a*) example 1, (*b*) example 2.

register. Instead, the desired page number must be loaded into an accumulator and then transferred into the DP register by another instruction.

Examples of the direct addressing mode are shown in Figure 5.13. In the mnemonic form direct addressing looks like extended addressing. The two are distinguished only by their op-codes. The first example is the instruction ADDA 3DH (add the content of location 3D on the direct page to the content of accumulator A and leave the result in accumulator A). The op-code, 9B, is followed by the on-page address, 3D. When the instruction is executed the processor creates the address for the operand by concatenating the value in the DP register, 15, with the value 3D. It then fetches the operand from location 153D and adds it to accumulator A.

The example in Figure 5.13*b* is an instruction to store the content of the Y register into the memory locations whose addresses are 6C and 6D on the direct page. As always, the instruction must identify only the first destination address, in this case 6C. The two-byte op-code for the instruction and the addressing mode is 10-9F. This op-code is followed by the on-page address, 6C. During execution the processor forms the effective address 156C and stores the content of register Y into locations 156C and 156D.

The program segment which was used as an example in Chapter 4 has been rewritten to incorporate the direct addressing mode and appears here as Figure 5.14. This program will add together the data found in locations 0B and 0C on the direct page and store the result in location 0D. For it to execute properly, the DP register must first be loaded with hex 10, the page number corresponding to the region of memory where the values are located and the result is to be stored.

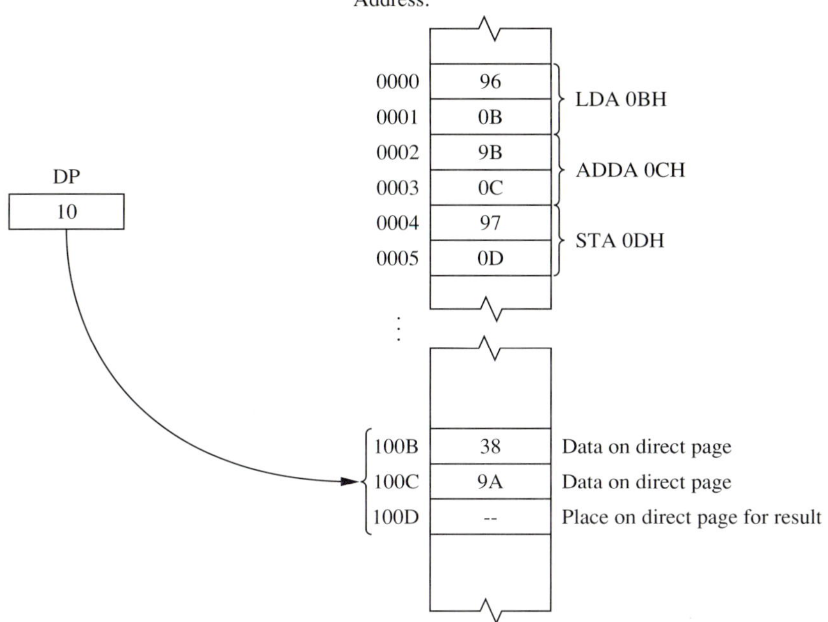

FIGURE 5.14
MC6809 program segment in the direct addressing mode.

5.3.4 Relative Addressing in the MC6809

The PC-relative addressing mode is implemented in the MC6809 under two different names. "Relative addressing" is used with branch instructions and "PC-relative addressing" is an option listed under the indexed addressing mode. The modes have identical effects during execution, but they must be identified and coded differently. This section will discuss only the relative addressing mode as it applies to branch instructions. The option under the indexed mode will be described in Section 5.3.5.

The target address of each of the branch instructions is identified by specifying an offset value to be added to the content of the program counter. The offset value is a part of the instruction and is treated by the processor as a 2's complement number. It may be a single byte (regular branch) or a double byte (long branch). The two are distinguished by the op-codes for the instructions. The coding of this addressing mode is complicated by the fact that when the instruction is executed, the content of the program counter is the address of the next instruction in the sequence (after the branch instruction). Thus, the offset value must be calculated not from the branch instruction itself, but from the next instruction in the sequence.

Two examples of the format for the branch instructions are shown in Figure 5.15. The first is a regular conditional branch, branch if not equal to 0 (BNE). During execution, if the Z-bit in the condition code register is cleared (if the preceding

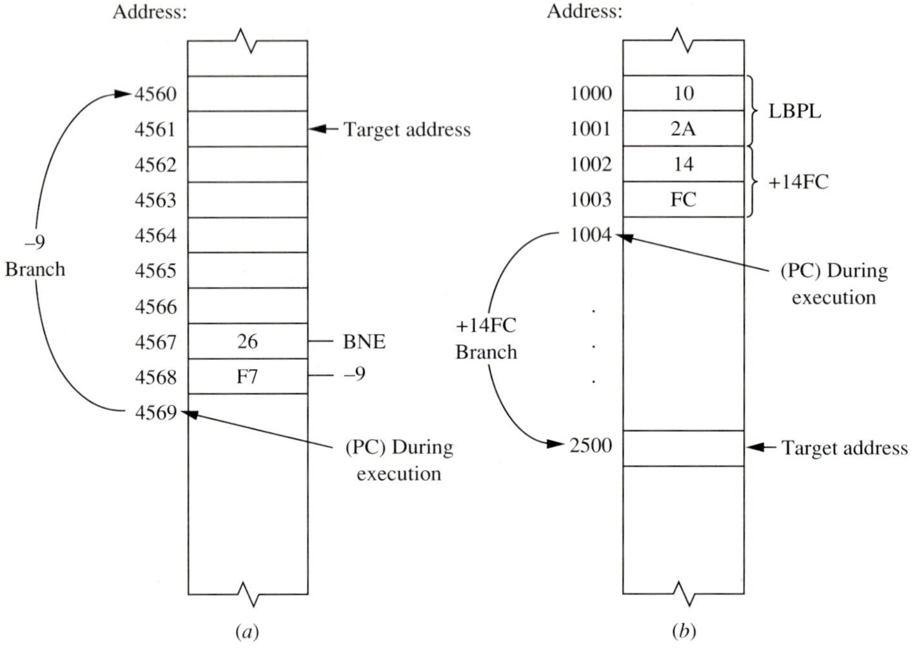

FIGURE 5.15
Relative addressing in the MC6809: (*a*) short branch, (*b*) long branch.

operation did not result in a 0) the processor will branch by adding the offset value of −09 to the content of the program counter.

The op-code for BNE is 26. The offset of −09 in 2's complement form is F7 (hex). Hence, the coding for this two-byte instruction is 26 F7. If this instruction starts at location 4567 then the branch target address is 4560. That is the sum of the value in the program counter at the time of execution, 4569, and the offset of -09.

Although the offset is expressed as a single byte in the instruction coding, the processor must add a two-byte sign-extended version of the offset to the content of the program counter in order to generate the target address. Notice also that the offset can range only from −128 decimal to +127 decimal since that is the range of an eight-bit 2's complement number. If the distance to the target address is farther, then a different form of the instruction must be used (the long branch form).

Each branch instruction has both a regular form, as in the preceding example and a long form which allows a double-byte offset. Figure 5.15*b* shows the long form of an instruction to branch if positive, LBPL, which is to branch to location 2500 hex if the N-bit is clear. The op-codes for most of the long branch instructions are two bytes long. In this case, the op-code is 10-2A. The target address is 1500 (hex) locations away from this instruction, and so the offset is 14FC. This value is obtained by subtracting the size of the branch instruction (four bytes) from the distance. This can be understood by noting that when the instruction is executed the program counter will already have been incremented by four and so the remaining distance to the target is 14FC.

The range for the relative addressing mode is shown in Figure 5.10*d*. The long form of a branch instruction allows branching to any location in memory since the value obtained in the calculation will wrap around if it exceeds the largest address of FFFF. Thus, although the range of the long branch offset value is −32,768 (decimal) to +32,767, the effective location of the target address is anywhere in memory.

5.3.5 Indexed Addressing in the MC6809

One MC6809 addressing mode, called indexed addressing by Motorola, includes register indirect, memory indirect, indexed, and based addressing as described in Section 5.2.4 as well as several optional modifications of these. This mode is by far the most complex mode in the MC6809 processor.

In its basic form, indexed addressing provides a means for the processor to access different memory locations with the same instruction at different times by combining the value in a selected address register, called an index register, with other components as specified by the various options. With this mode the index register may be thought of as a pointer to a target location in memory. The address of the location is called the *effective address*. The options modify the way in which the pointer is used to determine the effective address.

Any one of four registers, X, Y, S, or U, may be specified as the index register for an instruction executing in the indexed mode. In addition, the program counter (PC) may be specified in a few options. In addition to the register to be used the programmer must select one of 24 different options governing this mode. The result is a rich variety of indexed addressing options that span the entire range of the address space for the machine. The various options will be described by a series of examples.

The example illustrated in Figure 5.16 shows the basic mode where the effective address is the unmodified content of the index register. The indexed addressing mode is

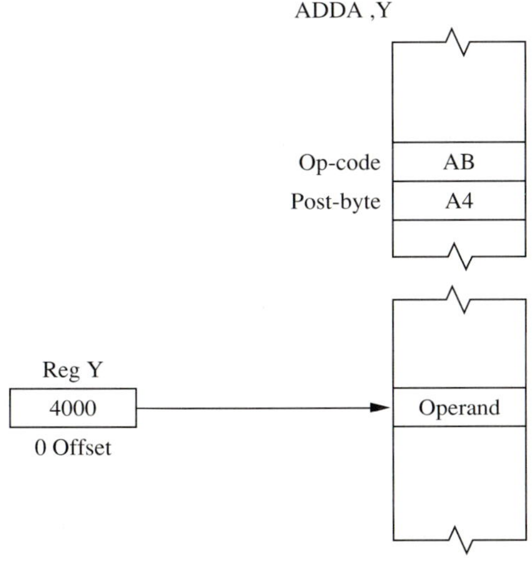

FIGURE 5.16
MC6809 indexed addressing, no-offset option.

indicated in the mnemonic form by the presence of a comma followed by the choice of index register. This example (add to accumulator A the content of the location being pointed to by register Y) is written as ADDA ,Y. When the instruction is executed the processor uses the content of register Y as the effective address for fetching the operand.

The op-code for the instruction ADDA using the indexed addressing mode is found from the tables in Appendix A to be AB. The option in this example, no offset, is found from Table F-2 in Appendix A to require a second byte (postbyte) of 1RR00100 in binary, where RR is a two-bit code specifying the index register used, in this case Y. The register code (from the same aid) is found to be 01. The final binary value, 10100100, (A4 in hex) is the postbyte of the two-byte instruction ADDA ,Y.

Other options in the indexed addressing mode allow the inclusion of an offset from the value in the index register. The offset may be specified in one of six different ways from the regular index registers and two ways from the PC. The six regular choices are: a 5-bit, 8-bit, or 16-bit constant offset, an offset which is taken from accumulator A, an offset from accumulator B, or a double-byte offset taken from the double register D (which is the concatenation of A and B). The two options with the PC are an 8-bit or a 16-bit constant offset. Any constant offset value, whether 5, 8, or 16 bits, is included in the postbytes as part of the instruction.

Figure 5.17 illustrates the use of a five-bit constant offset. The instruction (SUBB 0CH,U) is indexed with an offset of 0CH. The op-code for SUBB indexed is E0. The offset of 0C hex will fit into the five-bit option, for which the programming aid shows the postbyte to be 0RRnnnnn. This includes a code for the register (RR = 10 for register U) and room for the five-bit (signed) offset (nnnnn = 01100 for +0C hex). Thus, the second byte of the instruction is 4C.

When this instruction is executed the processor will temporarily add the value of 0C and the content of register U to generate the effective address. It will then pick

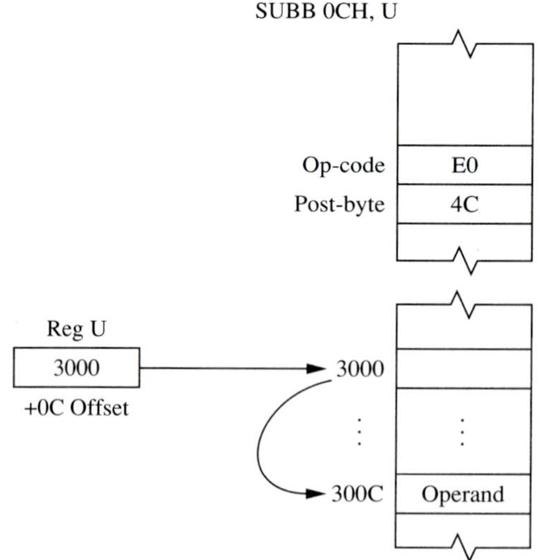

FIGURE 5.17
MC6809 indexed addressing, five-bit offset option.

up the operand from that address and subtract it from accumulator B. After execution the content of register U will not have been changed from its original value.

If the offset does not fit into five bits, then one of the longer constant options must be selected. In some instances, the offset is not known ahead of time by the programmer but will be calculated when the program is executed. In that case one of the accumulator offset options must be selected. Whatever the number of bits in the offset and regardless of whether the offset is a constant in the instruction or a number in an accumulator, it is always treated by the processor as a 16-bit sign-extended (2's complement) value when it is used.

The program counter relative option uses the address in the program counter during execution as the base address with a constant offset specified in the instruction. The offset may be either 8 or 16 bits long. This option extends the relative addressing mode described in Section 5.3.4 to all of the indexed instructions. The mode is indicated in mnemonic form by the letters PCR in place of the index register letter, for example, LDA 40H,PCR.

5.3.6 Auto Increment/Decrement Options in the MC6809

While repeating a program loop the processor must often change a pointer to an adjacent address in memory on each pass through the loop. In this way an array of data may be accessed one value at a time during each subsequent pass. It may be necessary to increment or decrement the value in the pointer, depending upon the direction in which the array is being scanned. The values in the array may be single bytes or double bytes, and so the pointer may need to be changed by 1 or 2 during each pass.

Four of the indexed addressing mode options automatically increment or decrement the selected index register while also using it to point to a location in memory. In the mnemonic form these options are indicated by the presence of plus or minus signs. Two of the options first use the index register as a pointer and then increment its value. The other two first decrement the value in the index register and then use it as a pointer. They are known as the auto increment and auto decrement options. To emphasize the sequence of the activities, these options may be referred to as *post-inc* (increment after using) and *pre-dec* (decrement before using). Note that no offset may be specified when an auto increment/decrement option is selected.

Two examples of auto increment/decrement options are shown in Figure 5.18. Part *a* is the instruction LDA ,X+, load A indexed with X post-inc by one. The coding includes the op-code of A6 for LDA indexed and the postbyte of 80 obtained from the formula for post-inc by one (from Appendix A), 1RR00000 with RR = 00 for register X. When it is executed, this instruction will load A with the target byte found in memory at the address contained in register X and then increment X by 1.

Figure 5.18*b* is the instruction STY ,− − U. When it is executed the processor will first decrement the index register U by 2. Following that, it will store the upper half of the two-byte register Y into the new location indicated by register U and the lower half into the next subsequent location. Pre-decrementing by 2 opens up two new slots

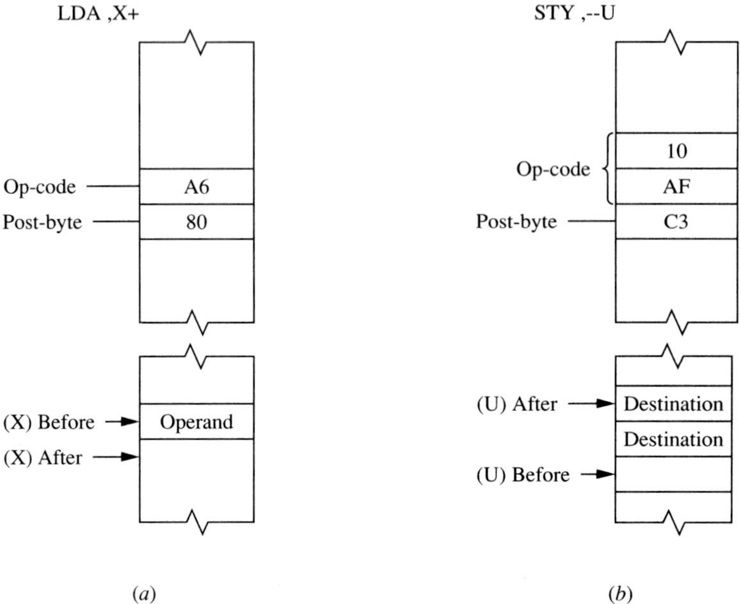

FIGURE 5.18
MC6809 indexed addressing, auto increment/decrement options: (*a*) post-increment, (*b*) pre-decrement.

in memory where the double-byte value in Y can be stored in accordance with the instruction. The coding of this instruction should be evident from the programming aid.

As a consequence of the increment/decrement option, not only does the instruction accomplish its primary task of manipulating the targeted operands, it also modifies the content of the selected index register. Thus, this option combines two basically different operations into a single instruction.

5.3.7 The Indirect Options in the MC6809

The remaining indexed mode options include memory indirect addressing and several forms of multi-component indirect addressing. In the Motorola literature, they are referred to as the indirect options in the indexed mode.

With a few exceptions, each indexed option mentioned in preceding sections is also available in an indirect form. When this form is selected, the programmer is saying that the address in the index register (combined with any associated offset) is not the effective address of the target. Instead, it is the address of a location in memory where the effective address will be found. Thus, the pointer points to an address for the target.

Figure 5.19 shows an example of the indirect option. The instruction is to clear the location whose address is found in the location pointed to by register X. Of course, register X points to a single location in memory, while addresses, being double bytes,

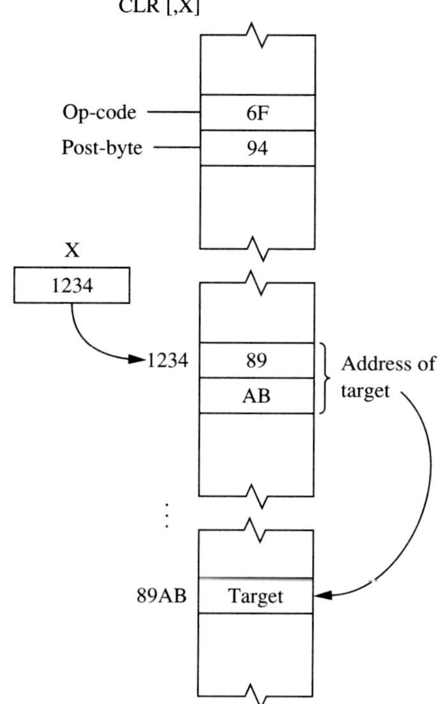

FIGURE 5.19
MC6809 indexed addressing, indirect option.

occupy two locations in memory. As usual it is necessary only to identify the first address. The processor will automatically locate the second. The sample instruction is written as CLR [,X]. The comma and the register letter identify the indexed mode while the square brackets indicate the indirect option. The instruction coding follows the same procedure as in earlier examples.

A single postbyte does not include a sufficient number of bits to include an encoding for the option of a five-bit offset with indirection, so this option is not available. Also, since the calculated address must point to a *pair of locations* in memory which contain a *two-byte* address, auto increment/decrement by 1 with indirection makes no sense. Therefore, these choices are also absent.

One option is available in the indirect form which does not have an indexed non-indirect form: the memory indirect mode, called the *extended indirect addressing option* by Motorola. Although it is listed as an indexed mode option it is actually an indirect version of the extended addressing mode. The mnemonic for it does not resemble those for the other indexed options. Instead, it looks like extended addressing with the address enclosed within brackets. However, instructions using this mode must be encoded with the indexed addressing op-code and the appropriate postbytes.

An example of the extended indirect option is shown in Figure 5.20. The instruction is intended to cause an unconditional branch to a location in memory whose address will be found in locations 789A and 789B. It is called the jump instruction and, unlike the branch instructions, it is available in extended, direct, and indexed

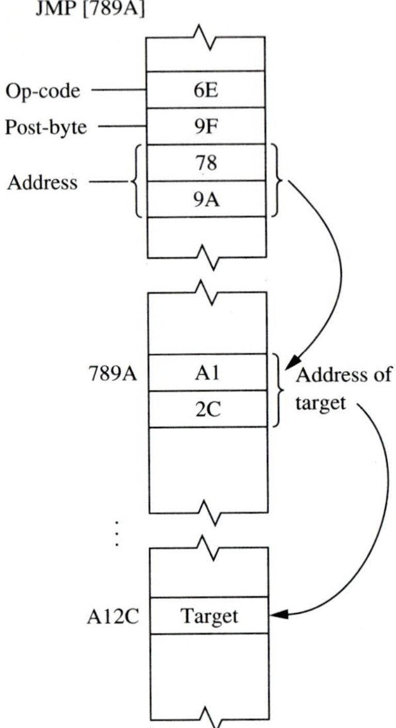

FIGURE 5.20
MC6809 extended indirect addressing option.

modes. The mnemonic form is JMP [789A]. Since the mode is an option under the indexed mode the op-code is that for JMP indexed, 6E. The extended indirect option is specified by the postbyte of 9F. Following this comes the address 789A, which is the location in memory where the upper half of the effective address is to be found. This instruction, then, is a four-byte instruction.

When the instruction is executed the processor fetches the contents of 789A (A1) and 789B (2C). It concatenates these two bytes to form the target address A12C. This address is then loaded into the PC to effect the jump. Notice that if this were the instruction JMP 789A (extended mode, not indirect), the address 789A would itself be loaded into the PC.

Some of the options under the indexed addressing mode have not been illustrated in this section. However, they are self-evident variations of those which have been. Many of them will be encountered in programming examples in later chapters.

5.4 THE MC68000 ADDRESSING MODES

This section describes the addressing modes used in the Motorola MC68000 microprocessor, their formats within program memory, and how they are specified in the instruction mnemonics.

Motorola's literature lists 14 different addressing modes used with the MC68000. One of these, the implied mode, is not discussed here since it requires no specification on the part of the programmer. The remaining 13 are grouped into seven categories in this chapter: absolute, immediate, register direct, address register indirect, address register indirect with auto increment/decrement, address register indirect with offset/index, and PC relative.

Instructions occupy one to five consecutive (16-bit) words in memory. The addressing mode is encoded in the first word, the op-word, which also identifies the total number of words in the instruction and the operation it is to implement. The remaining words, called extension words, further specify the operands when necessary.

The op-words for the MC68000 are listed in tables found in Appendix C. However, writing instructions by looking them up in such tables is impractical with a processor of this complexity. This section shows some examples of encoded instructions only in order to assist in describing the functioning of the processor. Chapter 6 outlines a more feasible way to prepare machine language programs for the MC68000 using only the mnemonic formats.

Although the MC68000 is described as a 16-bit processor and has a 16-bit data bus, it can access memory on the byte level. That is, every byte in the memory space has its own 24-bit address. Instructions may refer to a single byte, a double-byte word, or a quadruple-byte long word. Figure 5.21 shows how these various-sized elements are arrayed in memory. The figure shows eight consecutive bytes in memory which may be accessed as eight bytes, four words, or two long words. The most significant byte is B0 and it comes first in memory. The most significant word is W0 and it comes first and includes bytes B0 and B1. The most significant long word is LW0 and it comes first and includes bytes B0 through B3 as well as words W0 and W1. Bytes may be accessed at any location, but words and long words may be accessed only at even addresses as shown. Any attempt by an instruction to perform a word or long word access at an odd address will interrupt the program.[2]

[2]See Chapter 12 for a discussion of the MC68000 interrupt system.

Memory:

Even Addresses			Odd addresses
n	LW0, W0, B0	---, --, B1	$n + 1$
$n + 2$	---, W1, B2	---, --, B3	$n + 3$
$n + 4$	LW1, W2, B4	---, --, B5	$n + 5$
$n + 6$	---, W3, B6	---, --, B7	$n + 7$

FIGURE 5.21
MC68000 data formats.

With most instructions the programmer must select the desired data size by including an extension after the mnemonic (.B .W or .L). If such an extension is not included, the default size is word. When the data is specified as being in an address register, the byte option is not allowed. The choice of size is encoded in two bits which are a part of the op-word for the instruction.

When the destination is a data register or a memory location, only the lowest-ordered bits as determined by the specified data size are modified. However, when the destination is an address register the entire register is modified, word-sized operands being sign-extended to 32 bits.

Most of the examples of addressing modes shown here use the MOVE instruction, which may be used to move any operand from anywhere to anywhere else. To keep the examples as simple as possible, the destination used in most cases is data register D1 and the data size is word. Thus, these examples show how the various addressing modes can specify the 16-bit source operand to be loaded into the low half of D1.

5.4.1 Absolute Addressing in the MC68000

The MC68000 includes two forms of absolute addressing, long and short. The long form requires two extension words (32 bits) after the op-word to specify the 24-bit address (the most significant 8 bits have no effect). The short form specifies a 16-bit address in a single extension word. During execution it is sign-extended to 32 bits (24, effectively). The absolute short addressing mode is the mode which was used in the short sample program segment discussed in Chapter 4.

Figure 5.22 shows an example of the absolute long mode. The instruction is to load register D1 with the (word) content of location 123456 hex. The mnemonic form is MOVE.W 123456H,D1 including the optional .W extension. The source and

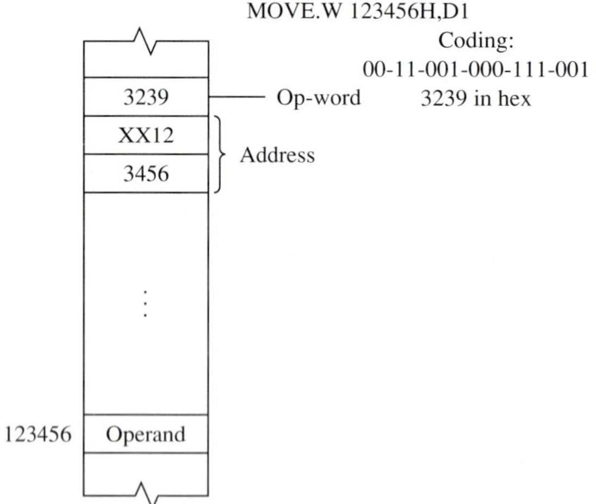

FIGURE 5.22
Absolute long addressing in the MC68000.

destination identifiers are listed in the order *from, to* (from location 123456 to register D1). The op-word is found from the tables of Appendix C to be

00 − size − destination − source (effective address)

The size code for word is 11, the destination code for register D1 is 001,000 (register number, mode), and the source or effective address code for absolute long is 111,001 (mode, register in the table). Combining these yields 00 11 001 000 111 001, which is 3239 in hex. This op-word is followed by the two-word extension which provides the absolute address. In Figure 5.22 the symbol X represents nibbles which are of no consequence in the program but which would normally be made equal to 0.

This example illustrates the details of the coding of the op-word into binary (or hex) form. With a processor as complex as the MC68000, this *hand-coding* process is not feasible. The only reasonable approach to this necessary task of encoding the instructions is to use a computer. Chapter 6 describes one way to employ a computer in this task. The details of instruction encoding will not be discussed for the remaining examples. However, the figure for each example includes the encoding.

In mnemonic form the same instruction with a 32-bit operand would be specified by MOVE.L 123456H,D1. When this instruction is executed the processor loads the word from location 123456 into the upper half of D1 and the word from location 123458 into the lower half of D1.

5.4.2 Immediate Addressing in the MC68000

Immediate addressing requires that the instruction include the operand as an integral part of itself (in extension words). Thus, this addressing mode refers to locations immediately following the op-word. To avoid self-modifying code, the MC68000 does not allow the choice of immediate addressing for any destination effective address.

An example of immediate addressing is shown in Figure 5.23, where the instruction is to move the 16-bit word 789A into the low half of D1. Immediate addressing in Motorola processors is indicated in the mnemonic form by the use of the number symbol #. The example MOVE #789AH,D1 implies a word length operand by the lack of an extension and should be read as "move the word-sized number 789A hex into register D1". The op-word is 323C, which is followed by the single extension word which contains the operand itself (in this case 789A).

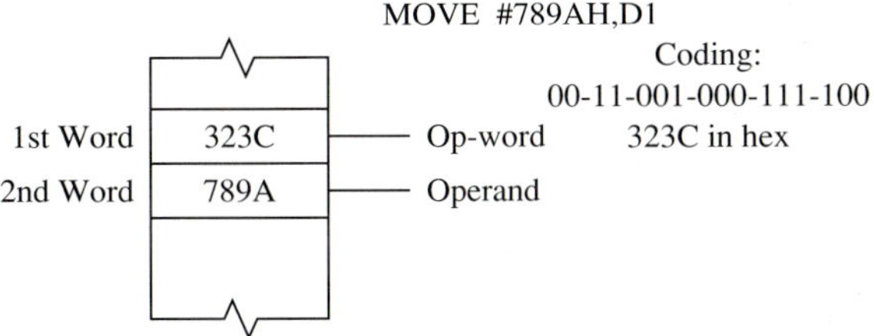

FIGURE 5.23
Immediate addressing in the MC68000.

Instruction	*Binary coding*	*Hex code word*
a. MOVE D5,D1	00-11-001-000-000-101	3205
b. MOVE A3,D1	00-11-001-000-001-011	320B
c. MOVEA D1,A3	00-11-011-001-000-001	3641

FIGURE 5.24
Register direct addressing in the MC68000.

5.4.3 Register Direct Addressing in the MC68000

In the register direct modes the operand is in a processor register. The MC68000 lists two addressing modes under this category, data register direct and address register direct. Three examples of instructions using these modes are shown in Figure 5.24. Each one includes only an op-word with no extensions.

The instruction in each of the first two examples in Figure 5.24 is to copy the 16-bit operand from the source register into the destination register D1. Example *a* uses data register D5 for the source; example b uses address register A3 for the source.

When the *destination* for a MOVE instruction is an *address register* then a different mnemonic, MOVEA, is used, although the instruction format is the same. Example c in Figure 5.24 shows an instruction which will move the sign-extended lower half of the contents of data register D0 into the 32-bit address register A3.

5.4.4 Address Register Indirect Addressing in the MC68000

The address register indirect mode calls upon the processor to use an address register as a pointer to a target memory location. The pointer register must contain the address of the target location at the time the instruction is executed. This mode must specify one of the address registers (not a data register) as a pointer. Register indirect addressing in the MC68000 includes many options which will be discussed in later sections. These options are listed in Motorola's specifications as separate addressing modes and are encoded as such.

Three examples of instructions using the register indirect mode of addressing to specify a source or destination are shown in Figure 5.25. The register indirect mode is indicated by including the pointer register designation within parentheses. Each is encoded with a single op-word and no extensions.

The first instruction shown in Figure 5.25 should be read as "move the (word) content of the memory location pointed to by register A3 into data register D1". This is

Instruction	*Binary coding*	*Hex code word*
a. MOVE (A3),D1	00-11-001-000-010-011	3213
b. MOVE D1,(A3)	00-11-011-010-000-001	3681
c. MOVE (A3),(A6)	00-11-110-010-010-011	3C93

FIGURE 5.25
Address register indirect addressing in the MC68000.

an example of a load instruction where data is moved into the processor from memory. The second example, "move the (word) from D1 into the memory location pointed to by A3," is an example of a store operation, where data is moved into memory from the processor. The third example is a rarity among microprocessors, a memory-to-memory move which bypasses the programming model registers. Its operation is to move the content of a location pointed to by A3 into the location pointed to by A6.

5.4.5 Address Register Indirect with Auto Increment/Decrement in the MC68000

Arrays of data are normally stored in sequential locations in memory. When operating on arrays, the processor often traverses a program loop during which it must change the address in an address register in order to "point to" subsequent array elements. In this way the array may be accessed one element at a time during each pass through the loop. It may be necessary to increment or decrement the address, depending upon the direction in which the array is scanned. The address may need to be changed by 1, 2, or 4, depending upon whether the array consists of bytes, words, or long words.

The MC68000 includes addressing modes which automatically increment or decrement an address register used as a pointer during the execution of the instruction. The auto increment mode first uses the register as a pointer in the instruction and then increments its value. The auto decrement mode first decrements the value in the register and then uses it as a pointer. To emphasize the sequence of activities the modes are referred to as *address register indirect with postincrement* and *address register indirect with predecrement*, often abbreviated *post-inc* and *pre-dec*. In the mnemonic form the modes are indicated by the use of a plus or minus sign.

The amount of increment or decrement is automatically selected by the processor during execution to reflect the data size specified in the instruction: 1 for byte, 2 for word, and 4 for long word. The one exception to this is when the pointer is register A7. In that case a byte operand will result in an increment or decrement of 2 in order to keep the register pointing to a word boundary. This is necessary because of the special use of A7 as a stack pointer, as will be described in Chapter 8.

Two examples illustrating the auto increment/decrement modes are shown in Figure 5.26. The first example is the instruction MOVE D1,(A3)+, move the word in D1 to memory, address register A3 indirect with postincrement. When this single word instruction is executed the processor moves a word from D1 into the location pointed to by A3 and then increments the content of A3 by 2.

The example in Figure 5.26b is the instruction MOVE.L D1,−(A3) ("move the long word in D1 to memory, address register A3 indirect with predecrement"). When it is executed the processor first decrements the content of register A3 by 4. This opens up four new bytes in memory where the long word in D1 is subsequently stored in accordance with the instruction.

As a consequence of using the increment/decrement modes not only does the instruction accomplish its primary task of manipulating the targeted operands, it also modifies the content of the selected address register. Thus, these modes combine two basically different operations into a single instruction.

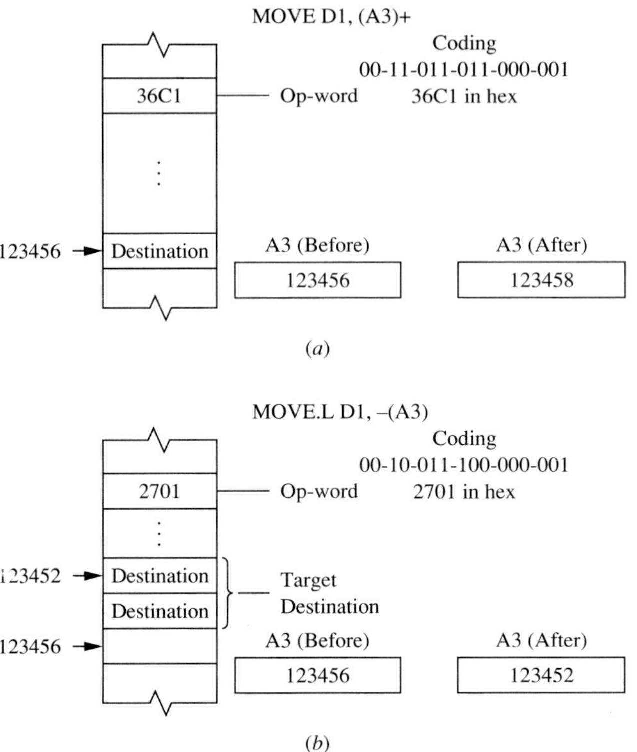

FIGURE 5.26
Auto increment/decrement modes in the MC68000: (*a*) post-increment, (*b*) pre-decrement.

5.4.6 Address Register Indirect With Offset/Index in the MC68000

Based addressing, as defined in Section 5.2.4, builds upon the address register indirect mode by allowing the programmer to specify a fixed offset value to be temporarily added to the content of the register in order to generate the target address. It is available in the MC68000 where it goes by the name *address register indirect with displacement*. The displacement or offset value is a 16-bit signed number which occupies a single extension word within the instruction. When the instruction is executed the processor temporarily adds a sign-extended 32-bit version of the displacement, together with the contents of the specified address register, to generate the target address. The content of the address register is not changed by the instruction.

An example of this mode is shown in Figure 5.27. The displacement value of 4000 hex is specified in the mnemonic form by writing it just ahead of the lead parenthesis indicating the register indirect mode: MOVE D1,4000H(A3). The displacement must be an even number when the operand size is word or long word so that the target address will also be an even number.

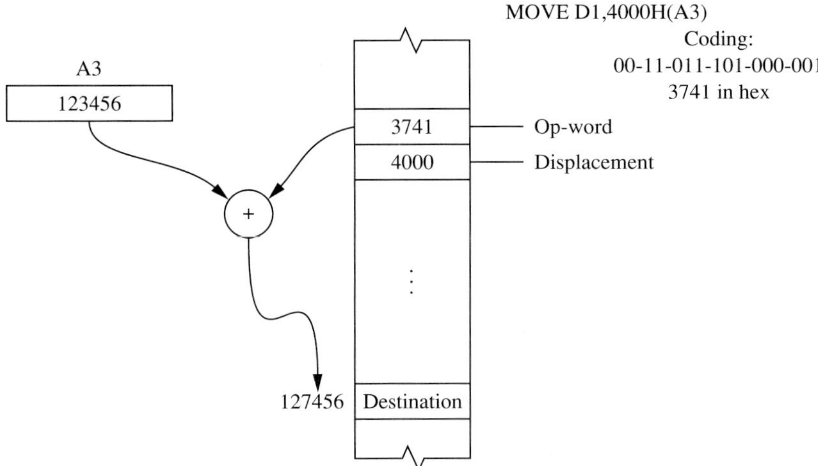

FIGURE 5.27
MC68000 address register indirect addressing with displacement.

A combined indexed and based addressing mode is available in the MC68000 under the name *address register indirect with index*. This mode allows the programmer to specify both a constant offset and a processor register to be used as an index register. When this mode is used, the processor adds three numbers together to generate the target address. These include the 32-bit content of the specified address register, the 8-bit displacement contained within the instruction (sign-extended to 32 bits), and the 32-bit long word or the low-ordered 16-bit word (sign-extended to 32 bits) in the address or data register which the instruction has specified as the index register.

The mode is indicated in the mnemonic by following the indirect address register number with a comma, followed by the selected index register and the appropriate extension (.W or .L), followed by the closing parenthesis (for example A6,A2.L).

The instruction MOVE D1,7AH(A3,D5.L) is shown in Figure 5.28*a*. The extension word includes all the necessary index and displacement information, including the eight-bit offset value of 7A. An instruction which uses this mode for both the source and the destination would require two extension words, one for the source and one for the destination.

The calculation of the target address during the execution of the example instruction is shown in Figure 5.28*b*. Registers A3 and D5 are assumed to contain the values 22222200 and 33338800, respectively. The processor generates the target address of 5555887A by adding these together with the offset of 7A from the instruction. It then stores the content of D1 in that location. Neither the content of A3 nor that of D5 is changed by the instruction.

Note that if the instruction had an operand specification of D1,7AH(A3,D5) (no extension on D5 which defaults to a word-sized index) then the target address would be 2221AA7A, as shown in Figure 5.28*c*. This is obtained by adding together the content of A3 (22222200), the sign-extended word content of D5 (FFFF8800), and the sign-extended displacement (0000007A).

MOVE D1,7AH(A3,D5.L) Coding: 00 - 11 - 011 - 110 -- 000 - 001 = 3781
MOVE.W A3 Mode Mode D1

Extension word coding: 0 -- 101 -- 1 -- 000 -- 0111 - 1010 = 587A
D/A D5 W/L 000 7 A

(*a*)

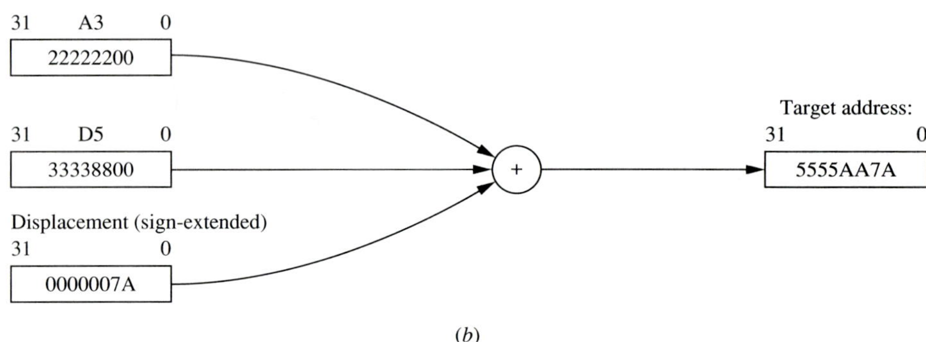

(*b*)

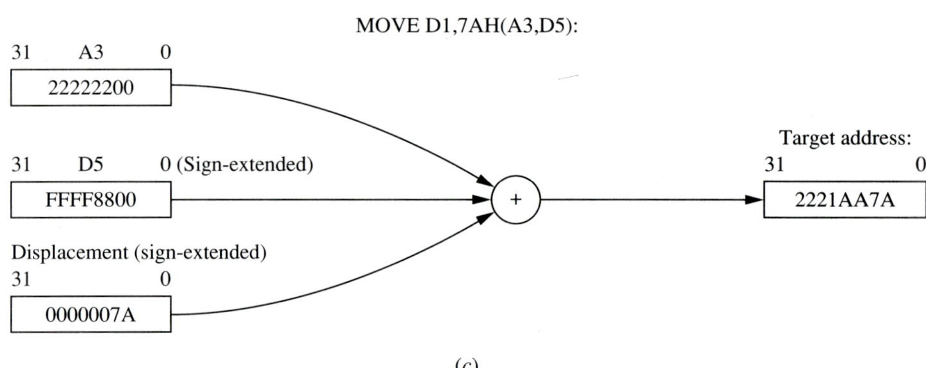

(*c*)

FIGURE 5.28
MC68000 address register indirect addressing with index: (*a*) coding, (*b*) target address generation, (*c*) target address for word-length index.

5.4.7 Program Counter Relative Addressing Modes in the MC68000

The PC-relative addressing mode is implemented in the MC68000 under two different names: "program counter with displacement" and "program counter with index." These two modes are similar to the two address register indirect modes: "address register indirect with displacement" and "address register indirect with index." The program counter is used instead of a specified address register as the base register to which the displacement and/or index register contents are temporarily added to calculate the target address.

These modes are specified in the mnemonic in the same format as are the address register modes, but with the letters PC in the parentheses rather than an address register name. Thus, the instruction MOVE D1,2000H(PC) would store the content of D1 into the memory location whose address is found by adding the offset value of 2000 hex to the content of the program counter. Note that at the time this two-word instruction is executed the program counter is pointing to the next instruction, which is two words down in memory. Thus, the offset is from the location of the *subsequent* instruction.

The mode with displacement includes a 16-bit signed displacement; the mode with index specifies both a register (data or address) and an 8-bit signed displacement. These requirements are the same as those for the two above-named address register indirect modes.

A similar mode, sometimes referred to as *relative addressing*, is used only with certain branch instructions. This mode includes the option of two different displacement sizes (and no index register). The target address of the branch is identified in the instruction by specifying a displacement value to be added to the content of the program counter. The displacement, which may be a single byte or a 16-bit value, is sign-extended by the processor during program execution. The target address obtained when the instruction is executed will wrap around if it exceeds the largest system address of FFFFFF or if it goes lower than the lowest address of 000000. As with other instructions using the PC-relative modes, the offset value must be calculated not from the location of the branch instruction itself, but from the beginning of the next instruction in sequence.

Including the displacement in the mnemonic form for a branch instruction would require the programmer to calculate the displacement value. To simplify the programming task the programmer will instead write a branch instruction in mnemonic form by *naming* the target destination address for the branch and writing that *name* instead of the displacement in the instruction. The displacement is calculated and included in the code at a later time when the program is translated into binary form (usually by a computer).

When the instruction is coded an 8-bit displacement can be included in the op-word as the final (least significant) byte, resulting in a single-word instruction. A 16-bit displacement is specified by making the least significant byte of the op-word equal to 0. This condition tells the processor to expect the word following the op-word to be an extension word containing the 16-bit displacement. This results in a two-word instruction.

The example in Figure 5.29*a* is an instruction to branch (unconditionally) to the instruction at the location named LOOP (BRA LOOP in mnemonic form). The instruction is in location 4568 and the op-code for BRA is 60. The displacement from the following instruction at 456A back to LOOP at 4560 is −0A, which is F8 in 2's complement form. Hence, the coding for this instruction is 60F8 and includes no extension words.

The processor executes the instruction by adding to the content of the program counter the displacement value of F8 specified in the instruction, sign-extended to FFFFF8. This new address, which is loaded into the program counter (004560), is the location from which the next instruction will be fetched.

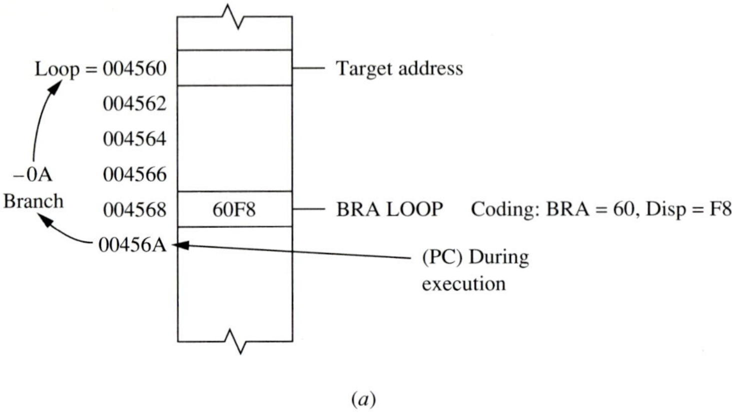

(*a*)

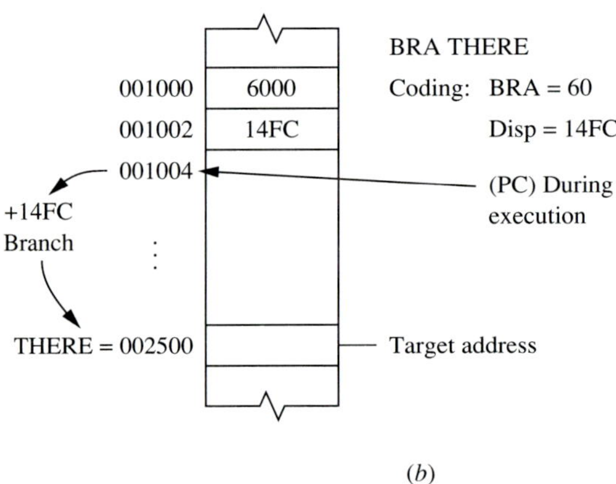

(*b*)

FIGURE 5.29
(PC) Relative addressing in the MC68000: (*a*) eight-bit displacement, (*b*) sixteen-bit displacement.

Although the offset in this example is expressed as a single byte in the instruction coding, the processor must add a 32-bit (24 effective bits) sign-extended version of the offset to the content of the program counter in order to generate the target address. Notice also that the offset can range only from −128 decimal to +127 decimal since that is the range of an eight-bit 2's complement number. If the distance to the target address is farther, then more bits must be used to specify the displacement.

The example in Figure 5.29*b* illustrates this case. The instruction is to branch to the location named THERE (BRA THERE). Notice that the instruction is in the same format as the one in Figure 5.26*a*. Only the codings for the two instructions differ.

Assuming that the instruction starts in location 1000 hex and that the target address is 2500 hex, the distance is too great to fit into a single byte. Therefore, the encoding must specify a displacement of 0 in the op-word and include a 16-bit (signed) displacement in a single extension word. No other options exist. The op-code for BRA is 60, so the op-word is 6000. The target address is 1500 (hex) locations after this instruction, and so the displacement included in the extension word is 14FC. This value is obtained by subtracting the size of the instruction (four bytes) from the distance. This can be understood by noting that when the instruction is executed the program counter will already have been incremented by 4 and so the remaining distance to the target is 1500 − 4 = 14FC.

Even with the larger displacement, the addressing mode allows branching only to locations within the range of −32,768 (decimal) to +32,767 from the immediately following instruction. When a branch to a greater distance is necessary, a different instruction with the option of other addressing modes must be used. The MC68000 instruction set includes such an unconditional branch, called a jump instruction (JMP in mnemonic form), which allows the use of other addressing modes which are capable of reaching any location in memory.

SUMMARY

The addressing modes for a processor determine how the instructions may specify the address of a target location, whether as a place from which to fetch an operand, a place to put the result of an operation, or the destination of a branch instruction. Addressing modes may be grouped into several broad categories with many possible options and minor variations.

Immediate addressing includes the operand itself within the instruction. Direct addressing includes the location of the operand in the instruction by naming the register or stating the address. Indirect addressing includes the location of the address of the operand in the instruction by naming the place (register or memory location) where the address of the target location may be found.

Multi-component addressing modes are based on an indirect address in an address register (or the program counter), and generate the target address by adding to this base a constant (displacement) specified in the instruction, or the content of a particular register (index) specified in the instruction. The addition is used to generate the effective address, not to change the content of the register (except with auto increment/decrement options). Only when a displacement is used with the program counter to calculate the target address for a branch does the addition actually change the content of the register.

The second major item to learn about a new processor, after the programming model, is the set of addressing modes available for use with it. The names of the addressing modes and the terminology used to describe them are unique to that processor. Although they may be similar from one processor to another, there is enough dissimilarity to require an effort on the part of the user to ferret them out of the literature for that particular processor.

REVIEW PROBLEMS

5.1. Name the general addressing mode corresponding to each of the following descriptions:

a. The instruction itself contains the data.

b. The instruction refers to no specific data or location in memory or processor register.
c. The instruction contains the memory address of the location where the data is to be found.
d. The instruction refers to a register that contains the address of the memory location containing the data.
e. The instruction refers to the register that contains the data.
f. The instruction includes a constant that must be added to the content of a register to determine the address of the memory location which contains the data.
g. The instruction includes the value of the distance to the target address from the current location.
h. The instruction specifies two registers whose contents must be added to determine the address of the memory location which contains the data.

5.2. Name the MC6809 addressing mode corresponding to each of the following descriptions:
a. The instruction itself contains the data.
b. The instruction includes the exact memory address of the data.
c. The instruction refers to no specific data or location in memory.
d. The instruction refers to a register which specifies the location which contains the data.
e. The instruction contains only one-half of the address of the location which contains the data.
f. The instruction includes the value of the distance to the target address from the current location.

5.3. Write the name of the MC6809 addressing mode specified in each of the following instructions:
a. ASL $1234
b. CMPS $1234,X
c. RORA
d. SBCB #$34
e. JMP $1234
f. ADDD #$1234
g. INC $34
h. NEG ,X+
i. SEX
j. BRA $1234

5.4. Name the MC6809 indexed addressing mode option corresponding to each of the following descriptions:
a. The address of the data is a location whose offset from an index register is specified in the last two bytes of the instruction.
b. The address of the data is contained in the location whose offset from the program counter is specified in the last two bytes of the instruction.
c. The address of the data is contained in an index register which is to be incremented by 2 after it is used.
d. The address of the data is a location whose offset from an index register is contained in accumulator B.
e. The address of the data is contained in a location in memory whose entire address is included in the instruction.

5.5. Write the name of the MC6809 indexed addressing mode option which is specified in each of the following instructions:

a. ADDB $1234,S
b. COM [B,Y]
c. BITA ,−U
d. SUBD [,X++]
e. LDX 105,PCR
f. STB ,X
g. JMP [1234H]
h. ROL D,U

5.6. Name the MC68000 addressing mode corresponding to each of the following descriptions:
a. The instruction itself contains the data.
b. The instruction includes the exact memory address of the data.
c. The instruction refers to no specific data or location in memory.
d. The instruction specifies the address of the data which is in one of the lowest or highest 32,767 locations in memory.
e. The instruction refers to a register which contains the address of the memory location which contains the data.
f. The instruction includes the value of the distance to the target address from the current program counter address.
g. The instruction specifies two registers whose contents are to be added together with a displacement value in order to determine the address of the memory location which contains the data.
h. The instruction specifies a data register which contains the data.

5.7. Write the name of the MC68000 addressing mode specified in each of the following instructions:
a. CLR 123456H
b. SWAP D4
c. ASR (A6)
d. CLR 48H(A3,D2)
e. JMP 1234H(PC)
f. LSL (A4)+
g. TRAP #7
h. RESET
i. NEG.L −(A1)
j. MOVEA A5,A0

5.8. Name the MC68000 addressing mode corresponding to each of the following descriptions:
a. The address of the data is a location whose offset from an address register is specified in the last two bytes of the instruction.
b. The address of the data is contained in the location whose offset from the program counter is specified in the second word of the instruction.
c. The address of the data is the sign-extended version of the number in the last word of the instruction.
d. The address of the data is a location whose offset from an address register is partly specified in the last byte of the instruction and partly contained in register D5.
e. The entire address of the data is included in the instruction.
f. The address of the data is contained in an address register which is to be incremented by 2 after it is used.

CHAPTER 6

ASSEMBLY LANGUAGE PROGRAMMING

In order for a computer to be able to execute a program, the program must first be present in binary form within the computer's memory. However, writing a program directly in binary form is completely out of the question. The solution to this conflict is for the programmer to write a program in a more suitable language and then to use a special computer program to translate it into the binary machine code necessary for the target computer.

This chapter introduces one choice of a programming language, assembly language. It first describes the basic aspects of Motorola assembly languages in general. Following this, it introduces some specific details of the MC6809 and the MC68000 assembly languages, including the more commonly used instruction mnemonics.

As noted earlier, the first step in learning about a new processor is to identify and study its programming model, and the second step is to learn which addressing modes are available, what names they are called in that processor, and how they are identified in the assembly language. The third step is to learn the general aspects of the instruction set, what kinds of instructions exist, how involved they are, some of their assembly language mnemonics, limitations as to addressing modes, and so forth. This chapter addresses this third step with respect to each of the target microprocessors.

The instructions available with processors can be grouped into four broad categories: load/store or data movement instructions, arithmetic/logic instructions, test/branch instructions, and input/output instructions. When learning a new processor it is best to try to categorize the instructions accordingly. Once the more common instructions become familiar, an alphabetical listing can more easily be consulted to determine the pertinent details. Such is the approach taken in this chapter.

6.1 COMPUTER LANGUAGES

When preparing software for a microprocessor system, the designer must first select the particular language in which to write the programs. Three classes of computer languages exist: machine languages, assembly languages, and higher-level languages. Of these, only the last two are normally used by a programmer in preparing programs.

6.1.1 Machine Language

A computer is a binary machine. The signals used by the various parts of the machine to communicate with each other must be in binary form. Therefore, the program and any data used in it must be present in memory in the form of binary electronic values. A program shown in binary form (or in hex for ease of reading) so as to reflect these values is said to be in *machine language*. Machine language is the most basic and elementary form in which any program can exist. All of the encoded instructions shown in earlier chapters in this book are examples of machine language.

6.1.2 Assembly Language

Before it can be executed a program must reside in memory in machine language. The few examples we've seen so far should have convinced you that it is a hopeless task to try to write a program in machine language. The programmer would need to know all of the op-word and postbyte or extension-word codes as well as all of the addresses of locations which contain the data or which are to serve as destinations for results. These codes and addresses would then have to be very precisely and carefully brought together to construct the program. Just keeping all of the necessary information in mind would be a nearly impossible task.

One step away from using machine language would be to write the program using mnemonics rather than op-codes for the instructions. This would be a limited improvement since it would still be necessary to remember the myriad of addresses for the constants, variables, tables of data, branch targets, etc. A major improvement would be to include some convenient way to keep track of these elements. *Assembly language* provides this by allowing the user to refer to numerical addresses and constants by name, that is, to use mnemonics for addresses and data as well as for instructions. The programmer still must thoroughly understand the programming model, addressing modes, and instruction of the target processor, but the use of assembly language will greatly reduce the bookkeeping necessary to keep track of all of the memory resources of the program.

Since every program must eventually be in machine language and since no one ever writes a program in machine language, it follows that there must always be two

			Address	*Content*
	ORG	5000H		
	LDB	#SIZE	5000	C614
	LDX	#VEC1	5002	8E1000
	LDY	#VEC2	5005	108E2000
	LDS	#VEC3	5009	10CE3000
LOOP	LDA	,X+	500D	A680
	ADDA	,Y+	500F	ABA0
	STA	,S+	5011	A7E0
	DECB		5013	5A
	BNE	LOOP	5014	26F7
	SWI		5016	3F
	FCB	8	5017	08
SIZE	EQU	20		
VEC1	EQU	1000H		
VEC2	EQU	2000H		
VEC3	EQU	3000H		
	END			
	(*a*)		(*b*)	

FIGURE 6.1
Source and object programs: (*a*) source program, (*b*) object program.

versions of each program. The original version prepared by the programmer is called the *source program*. The machine language version which must be loaded into the computer memory is called the *object program*.

Figure 6.1 shows an example of a short segment of an assembly language program. Part *a* is the source program and part *b* is the object program. Observe the word/symbol/mnemonic orientation of the source code as opposed to the strictly binary form of the object code (shown here in hex).

The conversion from the source program into the object program is the sort of procedure for which a computer is particularly well suited. The usual procedure, therefore, is for the programmer to write the source program in whatever language is suitable and then to submit it in machine-readable form to a computer. There, a program translates it into the machine code object program. If the source program is written in some higher-level language such as FORTRAN or Pascal then the translation program is called a *compiler*. If it is written in assembly language then the translation program is called an *assembler*.

6.1.3 Assembly Language versus Higher-level Languages

Most programmers are capable of writing a relatively constant number of program statements per day regardless of the programming language used. An assembly language program requires on the order of ten times as many statements as an equivalent higher-level language program. Thus, programming in a higher-level language is much more efficient than programming in assembly language. However, assembly language may be a suitable choice in some cases.

One reason for using assembly language in a particular application is to reduce memory requirements. A good assembly language programmer can usually write a program that occupies less space in memory than does a corresponding higher-level program after it is compiled. Having access to all of the instructions of the target computer, the assembly language programmer can readily optimize the program. The programmer can use the minimum amount of memory necessary to implement the specific application at hand. For example, if a counter is needed to count up to 100, the programmer can allocate a single byte of memory for it. In a higher-level implementation, a compiler might automatically reserve a much larger memory space for any counter in anticipation of larger count values.

A second reason for the use of assembly language is that all of the resources of the target computer system are readily available to the programmer. The input/output devices are directly accessible, the interrupt system can be manipulated, stacks can be modified at will, and so forth. As a consequence, assembly language programs generally run faster than their higher-level counterparts. And so, even in applications where a higher-level language is used for the bulk of the system programs, certain segments of the code may be written in assembly language. In many simple control applications it is not unusual for all of the programming to be done in assembly language.

6.1.4 Characteristics of Assembly Languages

Although assembly languages are processor-dependent they do have some common characteristics. All assembly languages use mnemonics to specify the processor instructions and certain supporting operations required of the assembler itself. Unfortunately, although all assemblers for a specific processor will use the same instruction mnemonics, there is no universal set of instruction mnemonics common to all processors. Nor is there a common set of mnemonics for the other support features of assemblers. Thus, two different assemblers for the same processor, say the MC6809, may not use identical mnemonics to specify an ASCII string. An assembly language programmer must know the instruction set mnemonics for the target processor as well as the support mnemonics for the specific assembler that will be used to assemble the program.

All assembly languages include a set of directives which are used by the programmer to issue commands to the assembler itself. These are called *pseudo-instructions* since they resemble instructions in format although they are not instructions. They are also known as *assembler directives*, since they are commands or directives issued to the assembler. For example, the *origin* directive, whose mnemonic is (universally) ORG, may be used to specify the origin or starting address of a section of the program. Thus, the statement ORG 1234 would tell the assembler to translate the subsequent instructions, using 1234 as the starting address for the first instruction.

All assemblers provide for the use of *symbolic labels* which may be affixed to constants and memory addresses. These labels may be used as substitutes for the numbers with which they are identified. The use of labels rather than absolute numbers is a powerful programming tool. It is much easier to recall that a string of ASCII characters which constitute a message to be printed, for example, starts in location MSSG rather than in location A92D. In addition, if the location MSSG must later be changed to A930, the instructions will require no changes since they refer not specifically to *A92D* but to MSSG. A branch target address, too, is easier to implement in the program when the programmer need not be concerned with its actual value or its distance but may refer to it by name. Of course, each label must be defined by the programmer at some point, but it may be referred to from anywhere within the program.

All assemblers include certain assembler directives which can allocate memory locations for data storage and convert and store data into memory. For example, the directive "form a constant byte" (FCB in some assemblers, DC.B for define constant.byte in others) may be used to cause the assembler to place a constant value into a memory location. Constants may be specified in one of several different bases with decimal, hexadecimal, octal, and binary being common options. The assembler converts each constant into the appropriate binary pattern which then becomes a part of the object program.

The set of rules regarding the proper form for statements in the assembly language is called the *syntax* of the assembler. The syntax for most assemblers divides each statement into four fields: from left to right, the *label*, *mnemonic* or *operation*, *operand*, and *comment* fields. Different assemblers specify different means of delimiting the fields in order to separate and identify them. Some use a colon after the label and so the absence of a colon denotes the absence of a label. Others require that all labels must start in column one; if there is no label then the statement must start in a later column. Some require that comments be preceded by a semi-colon, others require a space. The programmer must therefore become familiar with the syntax for the particular assembler used.

An assembler typically scans the source program twice while translating it into machine code. During the first pass it counts bytes and locates all of the label definitions, which it places into a table along with the corresponding numerical values. During the second pass it uses this label table or *symbol table* to generate the machine code. The first pass is necessary in order to allow labels to be referred to before they are defined (forward referenced). This feature is particularly important in branches where the target address may be defined by being a label on a later instruction. One-pass assemblers have been written, but the code they generate is less efficient.

6.2 MOTOROLA ASSEMBLY LANGUAGES

The two assembler-simulator programs available for use with this book are named ASSYM09 and ASSYM000 for the MC6809 and the MC68000, respectively. This section describes some of the features common to most Motorola assemblers, with the emphasis on those which are included in ASSYM09 and ASSYM000. If you use a different assembler you must determine its idiosyncrasies before you can use it to assemble your programs successfully.

6.2.1 The Character Set

The following characters are recognized by the assemblers:

1. The alphabet A through Z
2. The integers 0 through 9
3. Four arithmetic operators: + − * /
4. Characters used as special prefixes:
   a. # specifies the immediate addressing mode
   b. $ specifies a hexadecimal number
   c. % specifies a binary number
   d. @ specifies an octal number
5. Characters used as delimiters:
   a. * or ; in column 1 specifies a comment line
   b. * or ; or space separates comment from operand
   c. a space separates operation from label and operand from operation; this is also the standard delimiter between operand and comment in Motorola assemblers
   d. Comma separates multiple operands
6. Characters with special meanings in certain places:
   a. * in operand stands for present location in memory
   b. " in operand stands for beginning and end of a string of ASCII characters
   c. Letters used as suffixes in numbers:
      i. B denotes a binary number
      ii. D denotes a decimal number
      iii. H denotes a hexadecimal number
      iv. O or Q denotes an octal number
7. A comment may include any printable character.

6.2.2 Program Statements

A source program is composed of a sequence of statements, one per line. These statements must be written into an ASCII file with an editor program. When the assembler program is executed it will prompt the user for the name of the source code file and then pick up a copy of it from the computer system. The statements in that file must comply with the syntactic description which follows.

A source statement includes between one and four fields. From left to right these are:

(1) label (2) operation (3) operand (4) comment

A label is required with some statements involved in the definitions of symbols; otherwise it is optional. The use of labels on branch destinations, although optional, will greatly reduce the programming effort and opportunity for error. The operation or mnemonic must be included in every statement except those which are purely comment. An operand may or may not be required, depending upon the nature of

```
Label   Operation  Operand(s)  Comment
*
*
*THE FIRST EXAMPLE IS AN MC6809 PROGRAM
*
        ORG        1000H       6809 PROGRAM STARTS IN LOCATION 1000
START   LDA        FIRST       PICK UP FIRST OPERAND
        ADDA       SCND        ADD SECOND OPERAND
        STA        SUM         STORE THE RESULT
        SWI                    RETURN TO MONITOR
        FCB        8           MONITOR CODE
        BRA        START       START AGAIN
FRST    BCB        34H         DATA AREA
SCND    FCB        56H
SUM     FCB        0
        END
*
*
*THE SECOND EXAMPLE IS AN MC68000 PROGRAM
*
        ORG        446000H     ;68000 PROGRAM STARTS IN 446000
START   MOVE.W     FRST,D0     ;PICK UP FIRST OPERAND
        ADD.W      SCND,D0     ;ADD SECOND OPERAND
        MOVE.W     D0,SUM      ;STORE THE RESULT
        MOVE.L     #228,D7     ;PREPARE TO RETURN TO MONITOR
        TRAP       #14         ;RETURN TO MONITOR
        BRA.W      START       ;START AGAIN
FRST    DC.W       1234H       ;DATA AREA
SCND    DC.W       5678H
SUM     DS.W       1
        END
```

FIGURE 6.2
Motorola assembler syntax.

the operation. The comment is always optional and may be included in any statement. Comments are intended for the convenience of the programmer and to facilitate proper documentation of the program.

The standard delimiter or field separator in Motorola assemblers is the space. Thus, in the absence of a label the statement must start with a space. A space must separate label from operation, operation from operand, and operand from comment. However, ASSYM09 and ASSYM000 both also allow the use of the asterisk or the semicolon to separate the operand from a comment. This delimiter and the colon after a label are popular alternatives to the space, particularly in non-Motorola assemblers. Figure 6.2 lists a short program in the proper format for each of the assemblers.

6.2.3 The Label Field

Labels always start in the first column of the statement line. If a label is not used in a particular statement, that statement must begin with a space. Except when it is used with the assembler directives EQU or SET (described below) to define a constant, a label corresponds to a numerical address in the computer. The address is either the starting address of the instruction in the statement or the address of the location where the assembler directive in the statement calls for data storage. The label provides a convenient means for the programmer to refer to that address within the operand field of other statements in the program. The programmer need only use the identical symbols.

The following rules apply to labels:

1. A label consists of one or more alphanumerical characters. ASSYM09 will accept a maximum of six characters, ASSYM000 will accept a maximum of 16 characters.
2. The first character of a label must be alphabetic.
3. A label must begin in the first column of the statement.
4. Each label used in a program must be unique.

Although the above rules are quite unrestrictive, it is good practice to follow the following "unwritten rules" in devising labels:

1. Use labels which are meaningful in the context of the program, i.e., SPEED rather than X7.
2. Avoid using a label which duplicates any mnemonic of the assembly language. Some assemblers specifically exclude these as labels and their use can be confusing.
3. Do not use labels which are too similar to each other. Although the assembler can distinguish between PART1 and PARTI or between IIIIII and IIIII, a human reader will have difficulty.

6.2.4 The Operation Mnemonic Field

The operation mnemonics recognized by an assembler include the executable instructions of the respective processor and a set of assembler directives. Each instruction mnemonic, together with its addressing mode and operands, is translated by the assembler into the appropriate machine code. Certain of the assembler directives result directly in the generation of binary code as part of the object program. Others simply control the assembly process and do not call for any binary code.

The instruction mnemonics used with the MC6809 and the MC68000 processors will be introduced in Sections 3 and 4 of this chapter. Many of the assembler directives are common to both processors and so they will be introduced as a group immediately below.

6.2.5 Assembler Directives

The following list describes some of the more common Motorola assembler directives and includes an example of each. Those implemented in the ASSYM09 assembler are indicated with an asterisk. Those in ASSYM000 are indicated with the @ symbol.

ORG*@ Defines **ORiG**in of the code. Tells the assembler where in memory to start assembling code

	ORG	1000H	*sets the starting address of the subsequent code to be 1000H*

EQU*@ Permanently defines the value of the label to be **EQU**al to the value of the operand. A label is required.

CR	EQU	0DH	*makes the label "CR" equal 0DH*

SET* Temporarily defines the label until the next time it appears in a SET. A label is required.

PI	SET	3141	*makes the label "PI" equal 3141*
PI	SET	3	*changes the label "PI" to a new value of 3*

EXTERN@ Imports the value of a label from another module so that the current module may reference it. The other module must also declare the label(s) as global (see GLB).

	EXTERN	TIME,SIZE	*import the values of TIME and SIZE from another module*

GLB@ Makes a label available to be exported to another module, which will be linked with the current one before they are executed (see EXTERN).

	GLB	TIME,SIZE	*declares that the labels TIME AND SIZE may be used in another module and that their values are defined in the current module*

END*@ The last statement in the source program. It tells the assembler to start the assembly process.

	END		*tells the assembler "I'm finished; start assembling code."*

FSH* **F**orces the 8-bit (**SH**ort) offset in MC6809 indexed mode. This is a non-standard directive implemeted in ASSYM09 which uses neither a label nor an operand.

	FSH		
	LDA	OFFSET,Y	*forced by preceding statement to be implemented with the 8-bit option*

ABS_SHORT@
ABS_LONG@

Changes the *default* absolute addressing mode in the MC68000 to either short (16 bits) or long (32 bits). This is a nonstandard directive implemented in ASSYM000 which uses neither a label nor an operand.

ABS_SHORT		(or no directive)
CLR	$1234	*uses absolute short mode since the address fits in 16 bits (address is implemented in instruction as $1234)*
ABS_LONG		
CLR	$1234	*forced by preceding statement to be implemented with the absolute long addressing mode (address appears in instruction as $00001234)*

SETDP

Informs the assembler as to what value is in the DP register so it will know when to use the direct mode. Not implemented in ASSYM09. Not applicable in ASSYM000.

SETDP 2AH	
INC 2A46H	*forced by the earlier statement to be coded in the direct mode*

FCB*

Form **C**onstant **B**ytes. Stores the operand list in memory. May have a label to permit convenient reference to the list of constants. ASSYM09 requires a separate FCB statement for each byte.

LIST	FCB	1,53H,$64	*stores 01, 53, and 64 (hex) in memory starting at the current location and names the first location LIST*

FCC*

Form **C**onstant **C**haracters. Converts character strings (enclosed between any pair of identical characters for delimeters) into the corresponding ASCII codes and stores them in memory. May have a label.

STRNG	FCC qNow is the time.q	*converts the string "Now is the time." into ASCII, stores it into memory starting at the current location, and names that location "STRNG"*

FDB

Form **D**ouble **B**ytes. Stores the operand list in memory using two bytes per entry. May have a label. Not implemented in either ASSYM09 or ASSYM000.

FDB	12H,200AH	*stores the hex values 00 12 20 0A consecutively in mem-*

ory starting at the current address

RMB **R**eserve **M**emory **B**ytes. Reserves memory locations without placing any values in them. May have a label. Not implemented in either ASSYM09 or ASSYM000.

STOR RMB 15 — *reserves 15 consecutive locations starting at the current address which will be named STOR*

DC.X@ **D**efine **C**onstant. Stores the operand list in memory using one byte per operand if *X* is B, two bytes per operand if *X* is W, and four bytes per operand if *X* is L. May have a label. Operands may be expressed as an ASCII string enclosed within quotes.

DC.B $4C,100,"Do it." — *stores the hex values 4C, 64, 44, 6F, 20, 69, 74, 2E in memory starting at the current address*

LIST DC.W $4C,$1234,"Do it." — *stores the hex values 00, 4C, 12, 34, 00, 44, 00, 6F, 00, 20, 00, 69, 00, 74, 00, and 2E in memory starting at the current address which will be named LIST*

DS.X@ **D**efine **S**torage. Reserves memory locations without placing any values in them. May have a label. The operand tells how many bytes, double bytes, or quadruple bytes to be reserved depending upon whether *X* is B, W, or L, respectively.

ARRAY DS.L 15 — *reserves 60 consecutive bytes (15 long words of four bytes each) starting at the current address which will be named ARRAY*

EVEN@ Adjusts the assembler's location counter to the next even address if it is not already even. This directive may include neither a label nor an operand. It is used whenever the programmer wishes to ensure that the next line is assembled starting in an even location.

6.2.6 The Operand Field

The form of the operand will vary depending upon the operation mnemonic in the statement. The operand may convey addressing mode information; it may list data to be stored in memory locations by the assembler; it may provide an address for an

EQU or an ORG directive; or it may not be present because it is neither required nor allowed.

When any part of the operand conveys numerical information, it may be included in any one of several alternative ways. Numbers may be included directly in one of the supported number systems; they may be expressed in terms of the location of the current instruction plus an offset; they may be instruction labels or other address or constant labels; or they may be arithmetic expressions involving any of these. The following examples illustrate some of the possibilities:

Direct Numerical

a) Decimal:	1234 or 1234D Decimal is the default number system. Numbers with no other prefix or suffix are always interpreted as decimal.
b) Hex:	$1234 or 1234H Numbers must start with digits 0–9. A234H is invalid; it is interpreted as a label! Use $A234 or 0A234H.
c) Octal:	1234Q or @1234 or 1234O (letter O not digit 0)
d) Binary	01001001B or %01001001

Offset from Current Location

*+15	This number is the address of the current instruction op-word plus 15.
*−35	This number is the address of the current instruction op-code minus 35.

Note: The offset may be any value whatsoever. The assembler will do the calculation and insert the correct number into the instruction. This is not a run-time offset.

Constant Labels

HNDRD EQU 100	Defines the label HNDRD as 64 hex.
LDA #HNDRD	The immediate operand in the instruction is evaluated as 64 hex.

Address Labels

ORG $567A	Defines the origin.
CMD FCC "Do it!"	Defines the label CMD as the value 567AH.
CLR CMD,Y	The operand is evaluated as $567A,Y.

Arithmetic Expressions (using defined labels from above)

LDA #2*HNDRD	Coded as LDA #200 or LDA #$C8 (immediate addressing)
LDX CMD–$0A	Coded as LDX $5670

Some assemblers support logic operations between parts of the operand. ASSYM09 supports neither arithmetic nor logic operations, ASSYM000 supports only arithmetic operations.

Two of the above-listed operand formats should not be used, even though they are supported by most assemblers. The use of offsets from the current location requires the programmer to count the number of bytes in the offset. This task is contrary to the primary intent of assembly language and should be avoided. The use of arithmetic or logic expressions is very confusing as well and should also be avoided.

The assembler must complete the evaluation of symbols and expressions in two passes through the source program. Thus only one level of forward referencing is normally permitted in the use of symbols in the operand field. A chain such as

```
THOU EQU 10*HNDRD
HNDRD EQU 100
```

is valid, since the assembler can defer the evaluation of THOU until the second pass, by which time it would have evaluated HNDRD. However, a chain such as

```
THOU EQU 10*HNDRD
HNDRD EQU 10*TEN
TEN EQU 10
```

is not valid, as the assembler can not evaluate THOU in two sequential passes through the program. As is often the case, simple reordering of the statements will eliminate the problem. The general rule is that forward referencing is permitted, but to one level only.

6.2.7 The Comment Field

A comment may be included in any source statement at the option of the programmer. A statement may even be entirely comment, a choice which is indicated by starting the statement with an asterisk (*) or a semicolon (;). The comment, if present, may include any printable character. Comments do not affect the creation of the machine code during the assembly process. They are completely ignored by the assembler except that they are included in the program listing. Comments constitute an important part of the documentation of the program and serve to assist a reader in understanding the program.

6.3 THE MC6809 INSTRUCTION SET

The following sections introduce the more commonly used MC6809 instructions and describe some typical uses for them. More detailed applications will be presented in sample programs in the next chapter. Certain special instructions relating to stacks, subroutines, and the input/output and hardware interrupt system will be discussed in later chapters.

Refer to Appendix A for op-code details. The entire instruction set is also described in narrative form in Appendix B. The manufacturer's literature[1] should be consulted for complete details.

---

[1]MC6809-MC6809E Microprocessor Programming Manual, available from Motorola Inc.

6.3.1 The MC6809 Data Movement Instructions

This section includes instructions which allow bit patterns to be moved without being modified in any way. It includes instructions for moving data within the processor as well as between memory and processor registers.

The basic instructions to move data between memory and the processor are LD? (load) and ST? (store), where ? represents the processor register involved. Examples are LDA, LDX, STD, and STS. These instructions use any one of three of the MC6809 addressing modes: direct, extended, or indexed. The load instructions may also use the immediate mode. These instructions are used primarily to initialize registers and to store results into memory.

A useful variation of load/store is the clear instruction, which loads or stores a specific value of 0. This instruction clears every bit in a designated accumulator (CLRA or CLRB) or in a memory location (CLR followed by the appropriate operand). This instruction is used to initialize running sums to 0 or to establish starting values for other varying quantities.

The two instructions, exchange (EXG) and transfer (TFR), move data between a designated pair of registers. EXG exchanges the contents of the two registers; TFR transfers the content of the first register into the second register. The assembly language operand in each case consists of any pair of registers. The only restriction is that the two registers designated must be of the same size. Figure 6.3 compares the exchange and transfer operations.

Load effective address (LEA?) is an instruction which calculates an address and then loads it into the double register (S, U, X, or Y) designated in the mnemonic. It must use the indexed addressing mode and one of several allowed options. When the effective address is calculated as called for in the option selected, it is not used to find an operand but is loaded into the double register. Figure 6.4 shows several examples of the LEA instruction.

The LEA instruction allows the programmer to take advantage of the arithmetic capabilities that the processor must have in order to carry out the complex calculations required to evaluate the effective address. Thus, LEAX D,X provides a 16-bit add capability (add content of D to content of X and load the result into X). The content of either accumulator may be added to any of the 16-bit address pointer registers

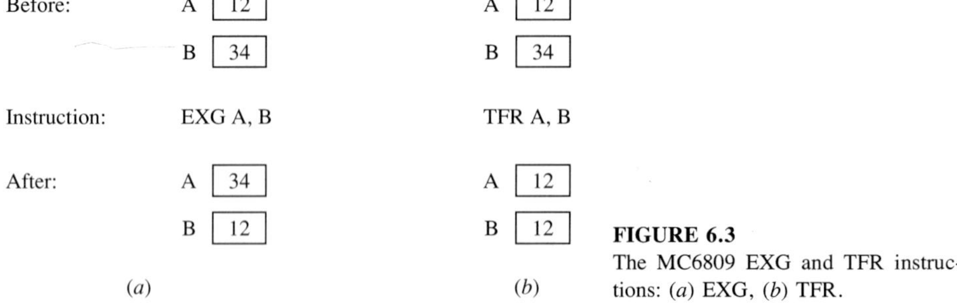

FIGURE 6.3
The MC6809 EXG and TFR instructions: (*a*) EXG, (*b*) TFR.

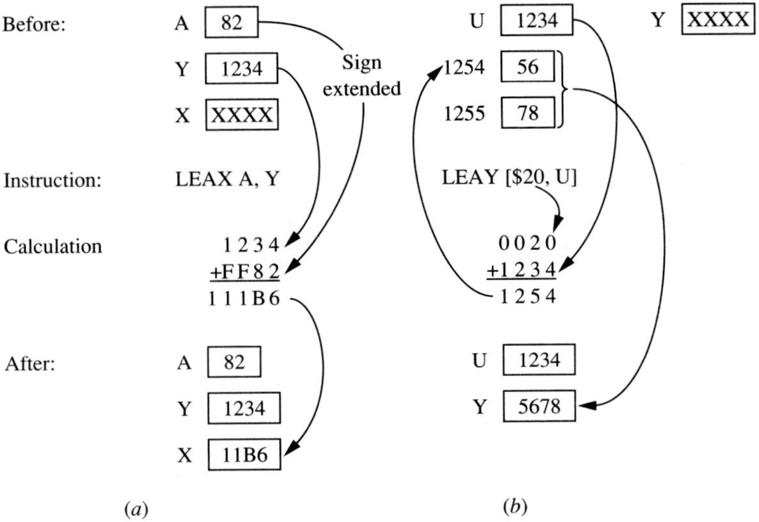

FIGURE 6.4
Examples of the MC6809 LEA instruction: (*a*) register offset, (*b*) indirect.

(LEAS A,S: add sign-extended content of A to content of S and load result into S). LEAU 16983,U can increment U by 16983 (add 16983 to U and load the result into U).

The LEA instruction is also useful when repeated reference must be made to the data at the effective address. It allows the programmer to call for the calculation of the effective address one time only and to load that address into an index register. Future references to data at that address can then be made with the more efficient 0-offset option. For example, LEAX D,Y loads into X the address which is calculated by adding together the content of registers D and Y. Subsequent instructions may refer to the data at that address by using the designation ,X as the operand, for example, LDA ,X or ADDB ,X.

The option of a constant offset from the program counter can be used to write position-independent code, in which a pointer to a table can be initialized using the *distance* from the instruction to the table as part of the instruction rather than the *absolute address* of the table (add the offset specified in the operand to the current value of the PC and load the result into a register).

Table 6.1 lists the MC6809 data movement instruction mnemonics, the permitted addressing modes, and the condition code bits which are affected when each instruction is executed. An asterisk in a column means that the bit is properly updated, while a dash indicates that the bit remains unchanged by the instruction. Appendixes A and B contain additional details for the entire instruction set.

6.3.2 The MC6809 Arithmetic Instructions

The instructions listed here perform arithmetic or arithmetic-related operations on the contents of registers or memory locations. Note that the LEA instruction may also be

TABLE 6.1
The MC6809 load/store instructions

Instruction mnemonic	Addressing modes					CCR bits				
	Imm	Dir	Ind	Ext	Inh	H	N	Z	V	C
CLRA-CLRB	–	–	–	–	X	–	0	*	0	0
CLR	–	X	X	X	–	–	0	*	0	0
EXG R1,R2	X	–	–	–	–	–	–	–	–	–
LD?	X	X	X	X	–	–	*	*	0	–
LEAS-LEAU	–	–	X	–	–	–	–	–	–	–
LEAX-LEAY	–	–	X	–	–	–	–	*	–	–
ST?	–	X	X	X	–	–	*	*	0	–
TFR R1,R2	X	–	–	–	–	–	–	–	–	–

used to perform arithmetic operations. It was included with the load/store instructions because the arithmetic is incidental to the addressing mode and is not the primary operation of the instruction.

The basic arithmetic instructions add or subtract the content of a memory location to or from the content of a specified accumulator. The mnemonics are ADD? and SUB?, where the designation may be A, B, or D. These instructions use any one of four of the MC6809 addressing modes: immediate, direct, extended, or indexed.

One variant, ABX, adds the content of register B (extended with 0s) to the content of register X and leaves the result in register X. It uses the inherent mode (no reference to memory). Although this is the only arithmetic/logic instruction which specifically adds an 8-bit register to a 16-bit register, either accumulator (sign-extended) may be added to any of the address pointer registers with the LEA instruction, LEAY B,Y for example.

Other variants add 1 to (increment, INC) or subtract 1 from (decrement, DEC) the value in the designated accumulator or the value in a memory location identified in one of the addressing modes. Examples are INCA, DEC 1234H, and INC ,X. These instructions are used primarily to increment counters used in a program. Although there is no counterpart instruction to increment any of the double registers, the LEA instruction may be used to do so. For example, LEAX −1,X will decrement register X.

Several instructions include the carry bit in the arithmetic in order to make it possible to extend the precision of the machine beyond eight bits. The add and subtract with carry instructions (ADCA, ADCB, SBCA, and SBCB) add or subtract the content of the specified memory location to or from the content of the designated accumulator. They then add to or subtract from that result the content of the carry flag in the condition codes register. This instruction supports multi-precision operations by providing a means to couple to a higher byte-result the carry from a lower byte-result of a multi-precision operation. Figure 6.5 shows an example of double-precision addition using the ADC instruction. Figure 6.6 shows an example of double-precision subtraction.

The decimal adjust accumulator instruction (DAA) is used to adjust the value in A to the correct BCD code. This instruction is the sole support available for BCD

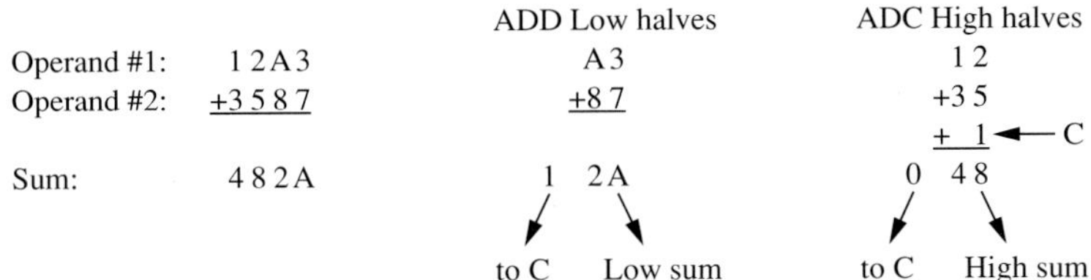

FIGURE 6.5
Double-precision addition in the MC6809.

arithmetic in the MC6809. It works properly only immediately after the execution of an ADDA or an ADCA instruction in which both operands were BCD values.

The compare instruction (CMP?) subtracts a value in the memory location identified in one of the addressing modes from the designated register (A, B, D, S, U, X, or Y), shown here as ?, but then discards the result after using it to update the condition code bits. This instruction is used to make numerical comparisons of the register content with the value in memory without changing the value in the register.

A similar instruction is the test instruction (TSTA, TSTB, or TST followed by an addressed operand), which subtracts 0 from the value in a designated location or accumulator. It is used to update the condition code register bits to reflect the actual target value, whether it is positive or negative, zero or nonzero.

The negate instruction (NEGA, NEGB, or NEG operand) changes the sign (2's complement) of the value in the designated accumulator or memory location. The sign-extend instruction, SEX, sign-extends the value of accumulator B into accumulator A as shown in Figure 6.7. It converts an 8-bit signed number in B into a 16-bit signed number in D (A concatenated with B) by copying the sign bit from B into every bit position in A.

The MC6809 includes a single unsigned multiply instruction (MUL) which multiplies the content of accumulator A by the content of accumulator B and loads the 16-bit product into the double register D (A concatenated with B). It uses the inherent mode and has no other options as to operands or destination.

The instructions "arithmetic shift left" and "arithmetic shift right" can be used to perform simple multiply and divide operations. Arithmetic shift left (ASL) shifts

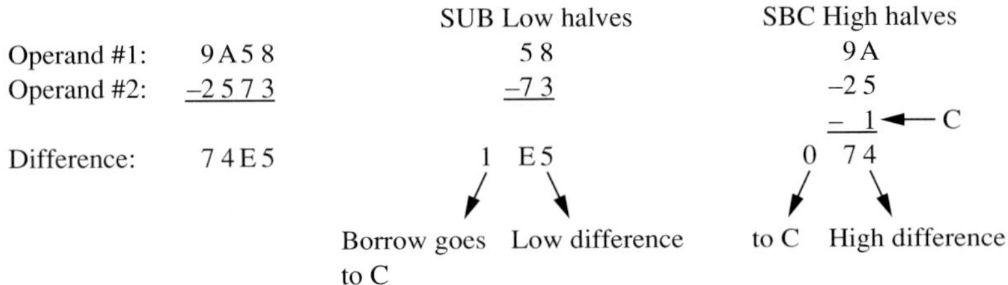

FIGURE 6.6
Double-precision subtraction in the MC6809.

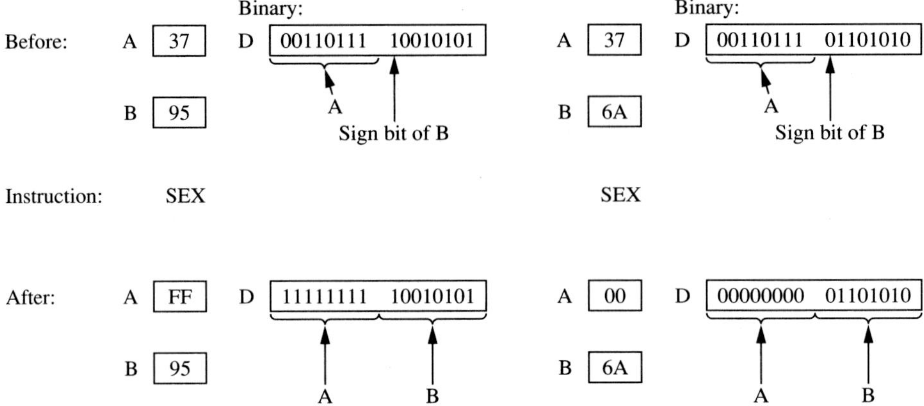

FIGURE 6.7
The MC6809 sign-extend instruction.

left by one bit the pattern in an accumulator or a memory location while bringing a 0 in from the right. The leftmost bit shifts into the carry as shown in Figure 6.8. This operation results in doubling the value. It is used in arithmetic operations but may also be used to isolate a bit into the carry or the sign position, where it may be readily tested by a test/branch instruction.

Arithmetic shift right (ASR) shifts the pattern right by one bit while bringing a copy of bit 7 (the sign bit) into the leftmost position. The rightmost bit shifts into the carry. This operation results in dividing the value by 2 while preserving the sign. Note, also, that the carry contains the remainder from the division.

Table 6.2 lists the MC6809 arithmetic instructions, the permitted addressing modes, and the condition code bits which are affected when each instruction is executed. An asterisk in a column means that the bit is properly updated, while a dash indicates that the bit remains unchanged by the instruction. Appendixes A and B contain additional details for the entire instruction set.

6.3.3 The MC6809 Logic Instructions

The instructions listed in this section perform logic operations or other bit-level manipulations on the contents of registers or memory locations. Any of three logic operations, AND, OR, and EOR (exclusive-OR), may be performed between the in-

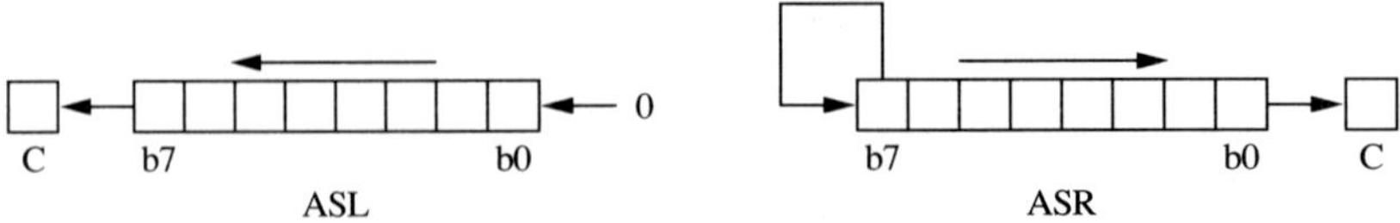

FIGURE 6.8
The MC6809 arithmetic shifts.

TABLE 6.2
The MC6809 arithmetic instructions

Instruction mnemonic	Addressing modes					CCR bits				
	Imm	Dir	Ind	Ext	Inh	H	N	Z	V	C
ABX	–	–	–	–	X	–	–	–	–	–
ADCA–ADCB	X	X	X	X	–	*	*	*	*	*
ADDA–ADDB	X	X	X	X	–	*	*	*	*	*
ADDD	X	X	X	X	–	–	*	*	*	*
ALSA–ASLB	–	–	–	–	X	?	*	*	*	*
ASL	–	X	X	X	–	?	*	*	*	*
ASRA–ASRB	–	–	–	–	X	?	*	*	–	*
ASR	–	X	X	X	–	?	*	*	–	*
CMPA–CMPB	X	X	X	X	–	?	*	*	*	*
CMPD,S,U,X,orY	X	X	X	X	–	–	*	*	*	*
DAA	–	–	–	–	X	–	*	*	0	*
DECA–DECB	–	–	–	–	X	–	*	*	*	–
DEC	–	X	X	X	–	–	*	*	*	–
INCA–INCB	–	–	–	–	X	–	*	*	*	–
INC	–	X	X	X	–	–	*	*	*	–
MUL	–	–	–	–	X	–	–	*	–	b7
NEGA–NEGB	–	–	–	–	X	?	*	*	*	*
NEG	–	X	X	X	–	?	*	*	*	*
SBCA–SBCB	X	X	X	X	–	b7	*	*	*	*
SEX	–	–	–	–	X	–	*	*	0	–
SUBA–SUBB	X	X	X	X	–	?	*	*	*	*
SUBD	X	X	X	X	–	–	*	*	*	*
TSTA–TSTB	–	–	–	–	X	–	*	*	0	–
TST	–	X	X	X	–	–	*	*	0	–

dividual bits of the specified accumulator and those of the content of an identified memory location. The result is left in the accumulator. The corresponding mnemonics are ANDA, ANDB, ORA, ORB, EORA, and EORB. Two other instructions, ANDCC and ORCC, require an immediate operand, which is combined in the appropriate manner with the bits of the condition code register with the result remaining in that register.

The AND operation is commonly used to *clear* certain bits in the accumulator or the CC register (those bits in positions where the other operand contains a 0). The OR operation is used to *set* certain bits, those in positions where the other operand contains a 1. The EOR operation *complements* selected bits in an accumulator, namely those in bit positions where the other operand contains a 1. Figure 6.9 illustrates these basic logic operations.

An instruction related to the AND instruction is the bit test instruction (BITA and BITB), which ANDs the content of the memory location with the content of the designated accumulator but discards the result after using it to update the condition code bits. It is used to isolate and test certain bits in an accumulator without changing its content.

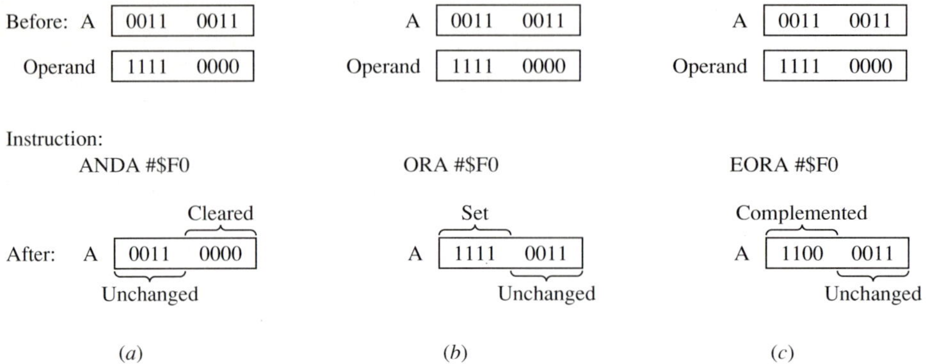

FIGURE 6.9
The basic MC6809 logic operations: (*a*) AND, (*b*) OR, (*c*) (*EOR*).

The remaining logic instructions operate on the individual bits in a pattern contained in either a designated accumulator or a specified memory location. The complement instruction (COM) complements each bit in the specified pattern. The logic shift/rotate instructions operate as shown in Figure 6.10.

The logic shift left instruction (LSL) is identical to the arithmetic shift left (ASL). Even the op-codes are the same! It simply provides an alternate mnemonic so that the programmer may indicate in the source program that the application is nonarithmetical. The logic shift right instruction (LSR) shifts the pattern right by one bit while bringing a 0 in from the left. This operation is used to move bits around in a word or to isolate a bit into the carry position where it may be readily examined.

The rotate left instruction (ROL) shifts the pattern left while bringing the carry bit into the rightmost position and moving the leftmost bit into the carry, thus rotating the pattern together with the carry one place left. The rotate right instruction (ROR) performs the same operation in the opposite direction. These operations are used to move bits around in the word or to isolate bits into the sign position or the carry while still retaining all of the bits in their original order.

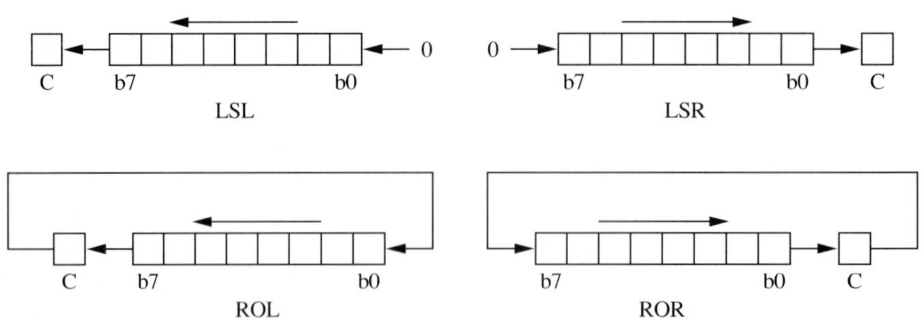

FIGURE 6.10
The MC6809 logic shift/rotate instructions.

TABLE 6.3
The MC6809 logic instructions

Instruction mnemonic	Addressing modes					CCR bits				
	Imm	Dir	Ind	Ext	Inh	H	N	Z	V	C
ANDA–ANDB	X	X	X	X	–	–	*	*	0	–
ANDCC	X	–	–	–	–					
BITA–BITB	X	X	X	X	–	–	*	*	0	–
COMA–COMB	–	–	–	–	X	–	*	*	0	1
COM	–	X	X	X	–	–	*	*	0	1
EORA–EORB	X	X	X	X	–	–	*	*	0	–
LSLA–LSLB	–	–	–	–	X	–	*	*	*	*
LSL	–	X	X	X	–	–	*	*	*	*
LSRA–LSRB	–	–	–	–	X	–	0	*	–	*
LSR	–	X	X	X	–	–	0	*	–	*
ORA–ORB	X	X	X	X	–	–	*	*	0	–
ORCC	X	–	–	–	–					
ROLA–ROLB	–	–	–	–	X	–	*	*	*	*
ROL	–	X	X	X	–	–	*	*	*	*
RORA–RORB	–	–	–	–	X	–	*	*	–	*
ROR		X	X	X	–	–	*	*	–	*

Table 6.3 lists the MC6809 logic instructions, the permitted addressing modes, and the condition code bits affected when each instruction is executed. Appendixes A and B contain additional details for the entire instruction set.

6.3.4 The MC6809 Test/Branch Instructions

This section describes those instructions which may cause the sequence of execution to branch to a different region of the program. The majority of these instructions in the MC6809 use the relative addressing mode: the address to which the program may branch is included as an offset from the next sequential instruction after the branch. In keeping with Motorola's terminology, these will be referred to as "branch" instructions.

In addition to the "branch" instructions, the MC6809 includes an unconditional branch instruction called the jump (JMP) instruction. This instruction causes a branch in the execution of the program to the location whose address is identified in one of three addressing modes: direct, extended, or indexed. This branch instruction is used whenever the programmer wishes to use one of these addressing modes to identify the target address for an unconditional branch.

The "branch" instructions use the relative addressing mode. The offset specified in the machine code may be a single-byte or a double-byte. The latter is indicated in the source program by the initial letter of L (long) in the mnemonic. In assembly language it is most convenient to write the destination address of a branch as a label. The task of calculating the necessary offset from the program counter is then left up to the assembler program.

A conditional branch is taken if the condition is satisfied. The decision is based upon the value of certain bits in the condition code register at the time the branch instruction is executed. Some of the numerical conditions (greater than, less than or

TABLE 6.4
The MC6809 branch instructions

Instruction mnemonic	Word description Branch if:	Test
(L)BCC	carry bit is clear	C = 0
(L)BCS	carry bit is set	C = 1
(L)BEQ	equal (to 0)	r = m (Z = 1)
(L)BGE	greater than or equal	r > m (signed)
(L)BGT	greater than	r > m (signed)
(L)BHI	higher than	r > m (unsigned)
(L)BHS	higher than or the same	r > m (unsigned)
(L)BLE	less than or equal	r < m (signed)
(L)BLO	lower than	r < m (unsigned)
(L)BLS	lower than or the same	r < m (unsigned)
(L)BLT	less than	r < m (signed)
(L)BMI	minus	N = 1
(L)BNE	not equal (to 0)	r ≠ m (Z = 0)
(L)BPL	plus	N = 0
(L)BRA	always	always branch
(L)BRN	never	never branch
(L)BSR	always (branch to subroutine)	always
(L)BVC	no overflow	V = 0
(L)BVS	overflow	V = 1

equal, and so forth) refer to the result of a preceding subtraction (or compare) instruction in which the content of a memory location has been subtracted from the content of an accumulator. The result of such an operation must be interpreted differently depending on whether the patterns are assumed to represent signed or unsigned numbers.

The 19 MC6809 branch instructions, each with a long and a short form, are listed in Table 6.4. Each word description should be preceded by the words "branch if," and the branch will be taken if the result of the test listed in the table is true. The symbols r and m refer to a preceding subtraction or compare instruction in which the content of a memory location (m) is subtracted from the content of an accumulator (r). The results of the number tests involving r and m will be properly determined even in cases where the result itself may overflow the machine, that is, the tests involve the appropriate carry or overflow bits.

The branch never instruction (BRN) may be used to reserve a place for a branch to be added to a program at some future time or to temporarily replace a branch in order to facilitate the debugging of a program. The branch always (BRA) and the branch to subroutine (BSR) are unconditional branches. Subroutines will be discussed in Chapter 8. The other branches include a rich set of condition tests capable of meeting almost any branch requirement with a single instruction.

6.3.5 The MC6809 No-operation Instruction

An instruction available with most microprocessors is one which does nothing. In the MC6809 it is the no-operation instruction (NOP). When it is executed it causes no activity other than the normal PC increment to take place. No data is moved, no arithmetic operation is performed, no bits are changed, no branch is taken. It may be used to reserve some space in a program so that during the debugging process it will be available for any temporary patching that may be required. Another common use is to insert an incremental amount of time delay into a segment of a program. Although the instruction causes no operation to take place, it does occupy a location in the program, and fetching and executing it takes some time (two cycles).

6.4 THE MC68000 INSTRUCTION SET

The following sections describe many of the MC68000 instructions, stating what they do and listing some uses for them. More detailed applications will be presented in sample programs in the next chapter. Instructions which relate to the stacks and subroutines as well as those which deal with the I/O and hardware interrupt systems will be discussed in detail in later chapters. See the programming aid in Appendix C for operation word details in tabular form and see appendix D for narrative descriptions of the instructions. The manufacturer's literature[2] should be consulted for complete details.

Most instructions involving the movement or manipulation of data specify the data size with an extension on the mnemonic, .B for single byte, .W for two-byte word, or .L for four-byte long word. The default size is word. Figure 6.11 shows how these options modify the effect of an instruction which writes 0s into a data register. The byte option affects only the lowest 8 bits, the word option affects only the lowest 16 bits, and the long word option affects all of the bits.

The MC68000 addressing modes are grouped into four classes depending on the type of operand involved. *Data modes* include those which refer to data operands as opposed to address operands. *Memory modes* refer to operands that are found in memory as opposed to those found in registers. *Alterable modes* are those referring to operands that may be modified or written over during the execution of the program. *Control modes* refer to operands that are addresses used in program control (targets

[2]MC68000 Microprocessor User's Manual available from Motorola, Inc.

	(a)	(b)	(c)
Before:	D5 1A2B3C4D	D5 1A2B3C4D	D5 1A2B3C4D
Instruction:	CLR.B D5	CLR.W D5 or CLR D5	CLR.L D5
After:	D5 1A2B3C00	D5 1A2B0000	D5 00000000

FIGURE 6.11
The MC68000 size extensions: (*a*) byte, (*b*) word, (*c*) long.

TABLE 6.5
MC68000 addressing mode classes

Addressing mode	Addressing classes				Assembly language Operand format
	Data	Mem	Alt	Contr	
Absolute short	X	X	X	X	XXXX
Absolute long	X	X	X	X	XXXXXX
Immediate	X	X	–	–	#XXX
Data register direct	X	–	X	–	Dn
Address register direct	–	–	X	–	An
Address register indirect (ARI)	X	X	X	X	(An)
ARI with post-increment	X	X	X	–	(An)+
ARI with pre-decrement	X	X	X	–	−(An)
ARI with displacement	X	X	X	X	d(An)
ARI with index	X	X	X	X	d(An,Rm)
PC Rel with displacement	X	X	–	X	d(PC)
PC Rel with index	X	X	–	X	d(PC,Rn)

for subroutine calls or branches, for instance). Table 6.5 lists the classes into which the 12 addressing modes are grouped. Each of the instructions described in the following sections allows the programmer to select the operands from within a restricted set of these classes. The classes may also be combined into even more restrictive groups. For instance, the group of data-alterable modes includes those in the data mode class and in the alterable mode class. For information on the allowed addressing modes, consult the tables at the end of each section, in Appendix C, or in the user's manual for the processor.

Many of the instructions include two operands. When this is the case, the first is referred to as the source operand and the second is known as the destination operand. The actual address of each operand as determined by the mode chosen from within the set of options is referred to as the *effective address* or *ea*.

6.4.1 The MC68000 Data Movement Instructions

This section includes instructions for moving bit patterns without modification of any sort. Most of the data movement instructions have no effect on the condition code bits. The few exceptions are indicated in the table at the end of this section.

The basic data movement instruction in the MC68000 is the move instruction (MOVE). The MOVE instruction and its variations are used primarily to initialize registers and to store results into memory. They cause the data specified in the source to be moved to the place specified in the destination.

Variations of the MOVE instruction include move *to* CCR and move *to* status register (SR), which restrict the source to one of the data modes. Others are move *from* SR, move *to* the user's stack pointer USP (register A7) from an address register or vice versa, and move an address (MOVEA in mnemonic form). Move multiple registers (MOVEM) transfers words or long words between the registers listed in the instruction and *consecutive* locations in memory starting with the effective address. Move peripheral data (MOVEP) transfers word or long word data between a data register and *alternate* bytes of memory. Move quick (MOVEQ) moves a sign-extended copy of an eight-bit immediate operand into a data register. Many assemblers will automatically select the MOVEA or MOVEQ instruction whenever an operand meets the restrictions.

The clear instruction (CLR) moves 0s into every bit of the byte, word, or long word destination. This instruction is used to initialize running sums to 0 or to establish starting values for other varying quantities.

Exchange (EXG) interchanges the entire contents of two registers (the allowed size is long only). The operands must be two registers from the set D1 through D7 and A1 through A7, for example EXG D1,A4.

SWAP is an instruction which interchanges the 16-bit halves of the data register specified in the operand. By definition, it is restricted to word size. This instruction is used to provide access to the more significant of the two words in a data register by moving it to a position where it can be accessed with a word-length operation.

Load effective address (LEA) loads the destination address register with the complete 32-bit effective address obtained from the address calculation as required by the source. This instruction is often used when repeated reference must be made to the data at the effective address. It allows the programmer to call for the calculation of the address one time only and to load it into an address register. Future references to data at that address can then be made with the more efficient address register indirect addressing mode.

As shown in Figure 6.12, the instruction LEA 25H(A5,D3.L),A2 loads into A2 the address which is calculated by adding together 25H, the content of A5, and the

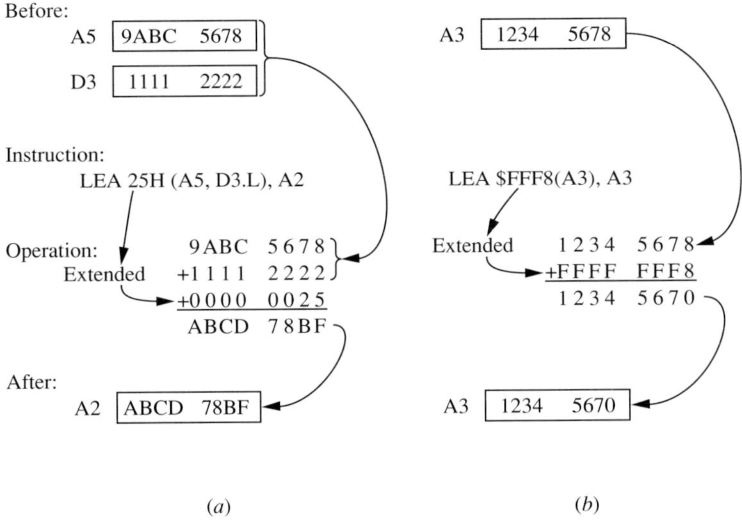

FIGURE 6.12
The MC68000 LEA instruction: (*a*) with index, (*b*) with displacement.

content of D3. Subsequent instructions may refer to the data at that address by using the address register indirect designation (A2) for the operand. The LEA instruction can also be used to increment or decrement an address by using the displacement mode with the source. The second example in Figure 6.12 shows an instruction which adds −8 (FFFFFFF8) to A3.

The allowed operand sizes and addressing modes for the data movement instructions are summarized together with the affected condition code bits in Table 6.6.

6.4.2 The MC68000 Arithmetic Instructions

The primary function of the instructions in this section is to perform arithmetic operations on the contents of registers or memory locations. Although the LEA instruction may also be used to perform arithmetic operations as shown in Figure 6.12, it is included with the data movement instructions because the arithmetic is incidental to the addressing mode and is not the primary function of the instruction.

The add and subtract instructions (ADD and SUB) add or subtract the source operand to or from the destination operand and store the result in the destination. In order to make it possible to extend the precision of arithmetic operations beyond 32 bits (long word), two instructions include the extend bit (X) in the operation. The add-extended (ADDX) and subtract-extended (SUBX) instructions add or subtract the operands. The extend bit (X) from the CCR is then added to or subtracted from the result. These instructions provide the means to couple the intermediate results from two lower-precision operations into a final higher-precision result.

TABLE 6.6
MC68000 data movement instruction limitations

Instruction mnemonic	Allowed operand size	Allowed modes/classes		CCR bits				
		Source	Destination	N	Z	V	C	X
EXG Rx,Ry	L only	Dn or An	Dn or An	–	–	–	–	–
CLR <ea>	B, W, L		Data alt	0	1	0	0	–
LEA <ea>,An	L only	Control	An	–	–	–	–	–
MOVE <ea>,<ea>	B, W, L	All	Data alt	*	*	0	0	–
MOVE <ea>,CCR	W only	Data	CCR	*	*	*	*	*
MOVE <ea>,SR	W only	Data	SR	*	*	*	*	*
MOVE SR,<ea>	W only	SR	Data alt	–	–	–	–	–
Move An,USP	L only	An	USP	–	–	–	–	–
MOVE USP,An	L only	USP	An	–	–	–	–	–
MOVEA <ea>,An	W, L	All	An	–	–	–	–	–
MOVEM list,<ea>	W, L	Dn list	Control alt or −(An)	–	–	–	–	–
MOVEM <ea>,list	W, L	Control or (An)+	Dn list	–	–	–	–	–
MOVEP Dx,d(Av)	W, L	Dn	d(An)	–	–	–	–	–
MOVEP d(Ax),Dy	W,L	d(An)	Dn	–	–	–	–	–
MOVEQ #<data>,Dn	L only	Imm	Dn	*	*	0	0	–
SWAP Dn	W only		Dn	*	*	0	0	–

All of the CCR bits are updated to reflect the result of this operation, except that Z is cleared if the result is non-0 but otherwise remains unchanged. This allows testing for 0 results after multi-precision operations as shown in the short program segment below. In line 1 the Z-bit is set so that if the final double-precision sum is 0 that condition will be retained. The operands are stored in registers D0-D1 and D2-D3 in the order high to low. The final sum appears in registers D2-D3, after which the Z-bit may be tested.

```
(1) MOVE      #$FF,CCR    SET Z-BIT
(2) ADD.L     D1,D3       ADD LOW HALVES
(3) ADDX.L    D0,D2       ADD HIGH HALVES
```

The MC68000 includes several varieties of the add and subtract instructions. Add/subtract address (ADDA/SUBA, word or long word only) allows any source operand but requires an address register for a destination. Add/subtract immediate (ADDI/SUBI) uses an immediate source operand and any data-alterable destination. Add/subtract quick (ADDQ/SUBQ) includes a small immediate operand (8 bits) and any data-alterable destination. Although the quick versions allow only a limited range of operands, they are single-word instructions which are executed very quickly. They replace the increment and decrement instructions more commonly found in microprocessors. Many assemblers will automatically select the ADDQ/SUBQ or the ADDA/SUBA variations whenever the operands meet the restrictions.

Compare (CMP) is an instruction which subtracts the source operand from the destination operand and discards the result after using it to update the condition code bits. It is used to make numerical comparisons of the operands without changing either value. CMPA should be used when the destination is an address register, CMPI should be used when the source is an immediate operand, and CMPM should be used for memory-to-memory comparisons. Many assemblers will automatically make the appropriate selection.

Negate (NEG) changes the sign (2's complement) of the destination value by subtracting it from 0 and storing the result in the destination location. Negate with extend (NEGX) subtracts the value and the extend bit from 0 and stores the result.

The test instruction (TST) subtracts 0 from the value of the operand. This instruction is used to update CCR bits N and Z to reflect the value of the operand, whether it is positive or negative, 0 or non-0. The related instruction, test and set (TAS), operates only on a byte-sized operand in a similar fashion but it also sets the highest bit in the operand byte. The test and set operation is indivisible and may not be interrupted. It is used to synchronize the operations of a multi-processor system.

Extend (EXT) sign extends the value of the operand in a designated data register from 8 to 16 bits (.W) or from 16 to 32 bits (.L). This instruction converts an 8-bit signed number into a 16-bit signed number or a 16-bit signed number into a 32-bit signed number by copying the sign bit from the original number into every extended bit position, as shown in Figure 6.13.

The instructions "arithmetic shift left" and "arithmetic shift right" can be used to perform simple multiply and divide operations. Arithmetic shift left (ASL) shifts the pattern in the destination to the left while bringing 0s to the right end. The last

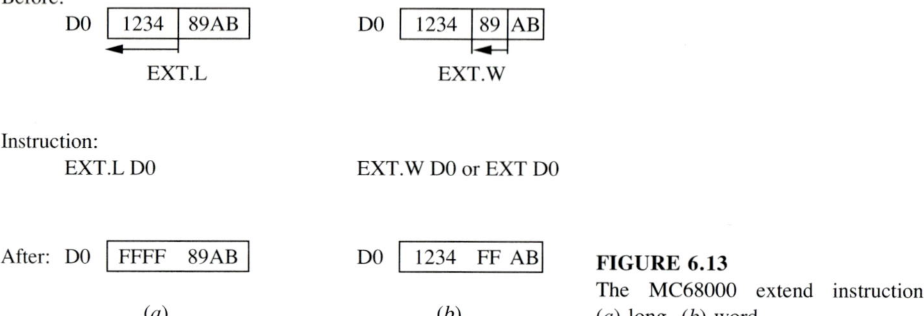

FIGURE 6.13
The MC68000 extend instruction: (*a*) long, (*b*) word.

bit shifted out shifts into the carry and the extend flags as shown in Figure 6.14. The overflow flag indicates whether any sign change has occurred. The number of bits shifted in a data register may be specified as an immediate source operand (ranging from 1 to 8), or may be contained in a data register designated as the source operand. In the latter case the shift count will be the remainder after the value is divided by 64 (the value *modulo* or *mod* 64). The content of a memory location may also be shifted by specifying it in a memory-alterable mode (one operand only). In that case the pattern will be shifted by one bit position only.

Each bit-shift to the left doubles the weight of each position in the original binary number, so the effect of this instruction is to multiply the destination value by an integer power of 2. It is used in arithmetic operations but may also be used to isolate a bit into the carry or the sign position where it may be readily tested by a test/branch instruction.

Arithmetic shift right (ASR) shifts the pattern right while bringing a copy of bit 7 (the sign bit) into the leftmost position. The rightmost bit shifts into the carry and extend flags. This operation results in dividing the value by an integer power of 2 while preserving the sign. Note, also, that the carry contains the remainder from the division.

Decimal arithmetic is supported by two instructions, add and subtract decimal extended (ABCD and SBCD). These instructions add or subtract the (single-byte only) operands along with the extend bit, as in the case of the extended binary operations. However, both operands must be valid eight-bit BCD numbers and the BCD result is stored in the destination location.

The sign of a single-byte BCD operand may be changed with the instruction NBCD, negate decimal extended. The sign of the destination operand is changed

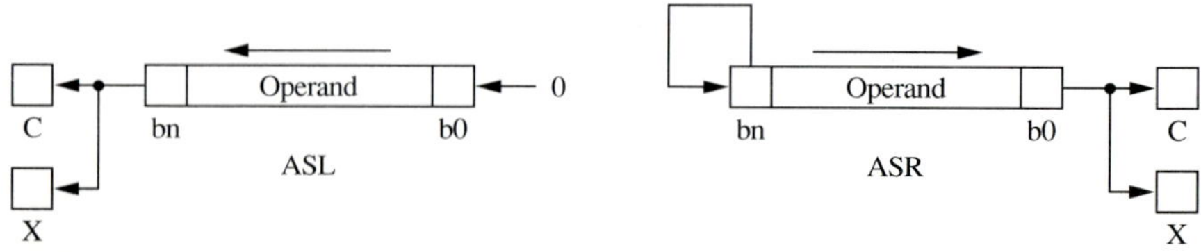

FIGURE 6.14
The MC68000 arithmetic shifts.

by subtracting it and the extend bit from 0 and storing the result in the destination location.

Two versions each of the multiply and divide instructions provide both signed and unsigned operations, word size only. The multiply instructions (MULS and MULU) multiply two 16-bit operands and load the 32-bit product into a destination data register. The divide instructions (DIVS and DIVU) divide the 32-bit destination operand by the 16-bit source operand and load the quotient into the lower half of a destination data register and the remainder into the upper half.

Table 6.7 lists the various forms of the arithmetic instructions, together with the allowed operand sizes and addressing modes and the affected condition code bits.

TABLE 6.7
MC68000 arithmetic instruction limitations

Instruction mnemonic	Allowed operand size	Allowed modes/classes		CCR bits				
		Source	Destination	N	Z	V	C	X
ABCD Dx,Dy	B only	Dn	Dn	?	*	?	*	*
ABCD −(Ax),−(Ay)	B only	−(An)	−(An)	?	*	?	*	*
ADD <ea>,Dn	B, W, L	All	Dn	*	*	*	*	*
ADD Dn,<ea>	B, W, L	Dn	Alt mem	*	*	*	*	*
ADDA <ea>,An	W, L	All	An	–	–	–	–	–
ADDI #<data>,<ea>	B, W, L	Imm	Data alt	*	*	*	*	*
ADDQ #<data>,<ea>	B, W, L	Imm	Alt	*	*	*	*	*
ADDX Dx,Dy	B, W, L	Dn	Dn	*	*	*	*	*
ADDX −(Ax),−(Ay)	B, W, L	−(An)	−(An)	*	*	*	*	*
ASd Dx,Dy	B, W, L	Dn	Dn	*	*	*	*	*
ASd #<data>,Dn	B, W, L	Imm	Dn	*	*	*	*	*
Asd <ea>	W only	–	Mem alt	*	*	*	*	*
CMP <ea>,Dn	B, W, L	All	Dn	*	*	*	*	–
CMPA <ea>,An	W, L	All	An	*	*	*	*	–
CMPI #<data>,<ea>	B, W, L	Imm	Data alt	*	*	*	*	–
CMPM (Ax)+,(Ay)+	B, W, L	(An)+	(An)+	*	*	*	*	–
DIVS <ea>,Dn	W only	Data	Dn	*	*	*	0	–
DIVU <ea>,Dn	W only	Data	Dn	*	*	*	0	–
EXT Dn	W, L	–	Dn	*	*	0	0	–
MULS <ea>,Dn	W only	Data	Dn	*	*	0	0	–
MULU <ea>,Dn	W only	Data	Dn	*	*	0	0	–
NBCD <ea>	B only	–	Data alt	?	*	?	*	*
NEG <ea>	B, W, L	–	Data alt	*	*	*	*	*
NEGX <ea>	B, W, L	–	Data alt	*	*	*	*	*
SBCD Dx,Dy	B only	Dn	Dn	?	*	?	*	*
SBCD −(Ax),−(Ay)	B only	−(An)	−(An)	?	*	?	*	*
SUB <ea>,Dn	B, W, L	All	Dn	*	*	*	*	*
SUB Dn, <ea>	B, W, L	Dn	Alt mem	*	*	*	*	*
SUBA <ea>,An	W, L	All	An	–	–	–	–	–
SUBI #<data>,<ea>	B, W, L	Imm	Data alt	*	*	*	*	*
SUBQ #<data>,<ea>	B, W, L	Imm	Alt	*	*	*	*	*
SUBX Dx, Dy	B, W, L	Dn	Dn	*	*	*	*	*
SUBX −(Ax),−(Ay)	B, W, L	−(An)	−(An)	*	*	*	*	*
TAS <ea>	B only	–	Data alt	*	*	0	0	–
TST <ea>	B, W, L	–	Data alt	*	*	0	0	–

6.4.3 The MC68000 Logic Instructions

This section includes instructions whose primary functions are to perform logic operations or other bit-level manipulations on the contents of registers or memory locations. Three logic operations, AND, OR, and exclusive-OR, may be performed between the individual bits of a source operand and those of a destination operand. The result is loaded into the destination location. The corresponding mnemonics are AND, OR and EOR.

Variations of these instructions include operations with an immediate source and either a standard destination, the condition code register (CCR), or the status register (SR). The mnemonics are ANDI, ORI, and EORI. Many assemblers will automatically select the proper form whenever the operands meet the restrictions.

The AND operation is commonly used to *clear* certain bits in the destination (those bits in positions where the other operand contains a zero). The OR operation is used to *set* certain bits in the destination (those bits in positions where the other operand contains a one). The EOR operation is commonly used to *complement* selected bits in the destination, namely those in bit positions where the other operand contains a 1. The logical complement instruction (NOT) complements every bit in the destination operand. Figure 6.15 illustrates these basic logic operations.

The logic shift and rotate instructions are similar in format to the arithmetic shift instructions. They shift the bits in the destination pattern and the X and C bits in the CCR, as shown in Figure 6.16. These operations are used to move bits around in the pattern or to isolate bits in the sign position or the carry while still retaining all of the bits in their original order.

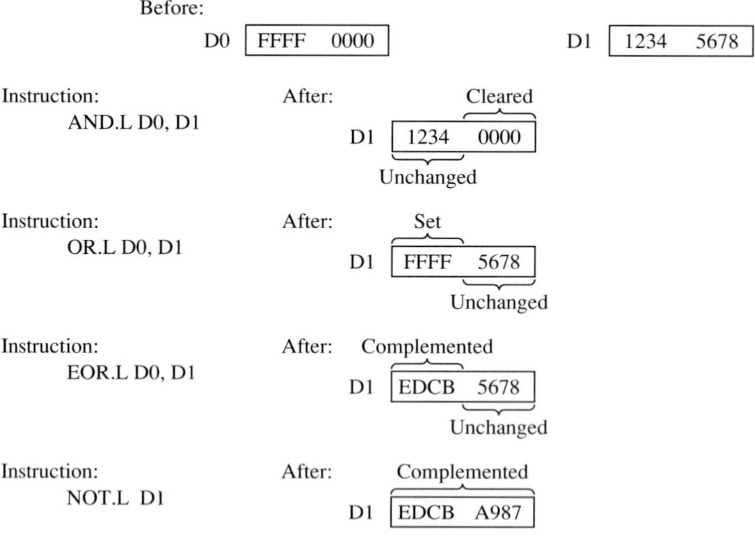

FIGURE 6.15
The basic MC68000 logic operations.

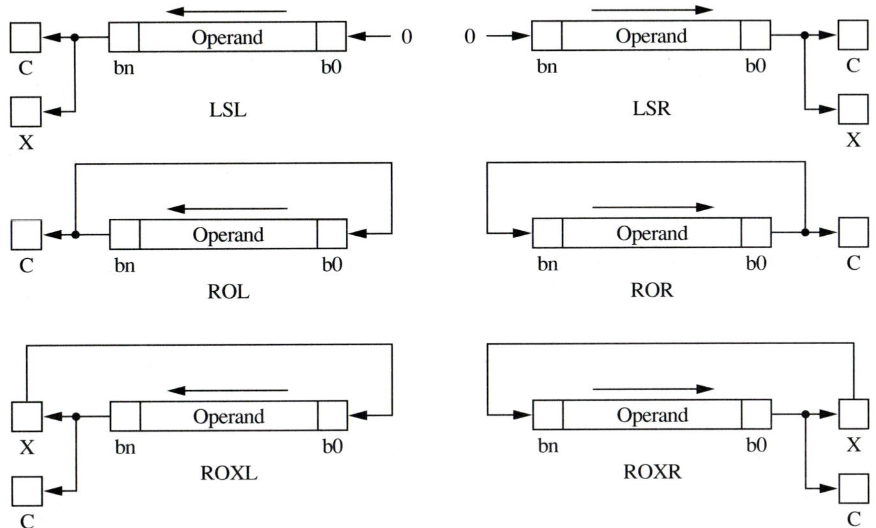

FIGURE 6.16
The MC68000 logic shift/rotate instructions.

The logic shift left instruction (LSL) shifts the pattern left while bringing a 0 in from the right. The bits shifted out from the most significant position go to both the carry and the extend flags. This instruction is identical in its effect to the arithmetic shift left (ASL), except that it does not change the *V* bit. It provides an alternate mnemonic to ASL so that the programmer may indicate in the source program that the application is nonarithmetic. The logic shift right instruction (LSR) shifts the pattern right while bringing a 0 in from the left. The rightmost bits shift into the carry and the extend.

The rotate left instruction (ROL) shifts the pattern left while bringing the most significant bit into the carry and also back into the least significant position, thus *rotating* the target data pattern. The rotate right instruction (ROR) shifts the pattern right while bringing the least significant bit into the carry and also back into the left-most position, moving the rightmost bit into the carry. The extend bit is not modified during either instruction.

The rotate with extend instructions (ROXL and ROXR) include the extend bit in the rotation of the pattern, thus rotating a 9-, 17- or 33- bit pattern. In other respects, including the shifting of the end bit into the carry, these instructions are identical to the rotate instructions.

Four instructions allow the programmer to focus on an individual bit in the destination operand. The instructions test the bit's value, use its value to update the Z-bit, and then change the bit's value. If the specified bit is initially 1, Z will be cleared; if it is 0, Z will be set. The instructions are: test a bit and clear it (BCLR); test a bit and set it (BSET); test a bit and change it (BCHG), which complements the bit; and test a bit (BTST), which leaves the bit unchanged. Size is long and bit numbering is modulo 32 on data register operands, but size is byte and bit numbering is modulo 8 on memory location operands.

Table 6.8 lists the various forms of the logic instructions together with the allowed operand sizes and addressing modes and the affected condition code bits.

6.4.4 The MC68000 Test/Branch Instructions

Two conditional branch instructions in the MC68000 use a special addressing mode known as program counter relative. In keeping with Motorola's terminology, one of these will be referred to as the branch instruction, with the generic mnemonic of Bcc. The other is the test, decrement, and branch instruction, with the generic mnemonic of DBcc.

In the program counter relative addressing mode, the address to which the program may branch is included in the machine code for the instruction as an offset

TABLE 6.8
MC68000 logic instruction limitations

Instruction	Allowed	Allowed modes/classes		CCR bits				
mnemonic	operand size	Source	Destination	N	Z	V	C	X
AND <ea>,Dn	B, W, L	Data	Dn	*	*	0	0	–
AND Dn,<ea>	B, W, L	Dn	Alt mem	*	*	0	0	–
ANDI #<data>,<ea>	B, W, L	Imm	Data alt	*	*	0	0	–
ANDI #xxx,CCR	B only	Imm	CCR	*	*	*	*	*
ANDI #xxx,SR	W only	Imm	SR	*	*	*	*	*
BCHG Src,<ea>	B, L	Dn, Imm	Data alt	–	*	–	–	–
BCLR Src,<ea>	B, L	Dn, Imm	Data alt	–	*	–	–	–
BSET Src,<ea>	B, L	Dn, Imm	Data alt	–	*	–	–	–
BTST Src,<ea>	B, L	Dn, Imm	Data alt	–	*	–	–	–
EOR Dn,<ea>	B, W, L	Dn	Data alt	*	*	0	0	–
EORI #<data>,<ea>	B, W, L	Imm	Data alt	*	*	0	0	–
EORI #xxx,CCR	B only	Imm	CCR	*	*	*	*	*
EORI #xxx,SR	W only	Imm	SR	*	*	*	*	*
LSd Dx,Dy	B, W, L	Dn	Dn	*	*	0	*	*
LSd #<data>,Dn	B, W, L	Imm	Dn	*	*	0	*	*
LSd <ea>	W only	–	Mem alt	*	*	0	*	*
NOT <ea>	B, W, L	–	Data alt	*	*	0	0	–
OR <ea>,Dn	B, W, L	Data	Dn	*	*	0	0	–
OR DN, <ea>	B, W, L	Dn	Alt mem	*	*	0	0	–
ORI #<data>,<ea>	B, W, L	Imm	Data alt	*	*	0	0	–
ORI #xxx,CCR	B only	Imm	CCR	*	*	*	*	*
ORI #xxx,SR	WE only	Imm	SR	*	*	*	*	*
ROd Dx,Dy	B, W, L	Dn	Dn	*	*	0	*	–
ROd #<data>,Dn	B, W, L	Imm	Dn	*	*	0	*	–
ROd <ea>	W only	–	Mem alt	*	*	0	*	–
ROXd Dx,Dy	B, W, L	Dn	Dn	*	*	0	*	*
ROXd #<data>,Dn	B, W, L	Imm	Dn	*	*	0	*	*
ROXd <ea>	W only	–	Mem alt	*	*	0	*	*

from the next sequential instruction after the branch. This offset or displacement is a signed 8- or 16-bit integer; the instruction mnemonic is the same for either size. When programming in assembly language the destination address of a branch is most conveniently written as a label. This approach leaves to the assembler the complex task of calculating the offset distance to the target and including it in the machine code.

The "cc" in the Bcc mnemonic represents the condition to be tested by the processor. If the condition is satisfied at the time the instruction is executed, the branch is taken by adding the offset to the content of the program counter. If the condition is not satisfied then the next instruction in memory after the Bcc is executed. The mnemonics listed as cc in the table will become the last two letters of the instruction. Thus the instructions *branch if equal* and *branch if plus* will be found in Appendix C under the listing Bcc, but their assembly language mnemonics are BEQ and BPL, respectively.

The result of the specified conditional test is based upon the value of certain bits in the condition code register at the time the branch instruction is executed. The tests and their assembly language mnemonic forms are listed in Table 6.9. Each condition listed in the table must be true for the instruction to result in a branch.

Some of the numerical conditions (greater than, less than or equal, and so forth.) refer to the result of a preceding subtraction (or compare) instruction. For those cases, the letters *s* and *m* in Table 6.9 stand for subtrahend and minuend (s − m). As noted in the table, some of these conditions refer to signed (2's complement) results, while others designate unsigned results.

The instruction "test condition, decrement, and branch" (DBcc) first tests for the condition. If it is satisfied (true) then no further action is taken. If the condition is false,

TABLE 6.9
The MC6800 conditional tests

Instruction mnemonic (cc)	Word description Do if:	Test
CC	carry bit is clear	C = 0
CS	carry bit is set	C = 1
EQ	equal (to 0)	s = m (Z = 1)
F	false (never do it)	always false
GE	greater than or equal	m > s (signed)
GT	greater than	m > s (signed)
HI	higher than	m > s (unsigned)
LE	less than or equal	m < s (signed)
LS	lower than or the same	m < s (unsigned)
LT	less than	m < s (signed)
MI	minus	N = 1
NE	not equal (to 0)	m ≠ s (Z = 0)
PL	plus	N = 0
T	true (always do it)	always true
VC	no overflow	V = 0
VS	overflow	V = 1

then the lower word in the data register specified in the instruction is decremented by 1, and if the resulting value is −1 no further action is taken. If the resulting value is not −1 then the branch is taken. This instruction provides a construct that is useful for implementing a loop that must be traversed a specific number of times, but that may also be terminated when the condition is satisfied. The form DBF may be used when only the decrement result is to be tested and no auxiliary condition.

The short program segment of Figure 6.17 shows two ways to use the DBcc instruction at the end of a loop. The first uses a DBF instruction to force execution to take place 10 times by testing only the decremented register which is used as a counter (D1). The second allows an early termination if the N-bit in the condition code register is 1. Note that the counter in each case must be initialized to one less than the number of times the loop is to be traversed, since the terminating branch back to the beginning of the loop will continue to be taken until the count is at −1.

The unconditional branch instruction BRA (branch always) also uses the program counter relative addressing mode. Thus, its target destination must be within 64 K-bytes in order that the offset value may fit into 16 bits. The jump instruction (JMP) allows the use of other addressing modes (control class only), and so can target any location in the memory space. Like the BRA, it branches unconditionally.

The conditional set instruction (Scc) will test for the specified condition but will affect no branch. If the condition is true the byte specified in the destination is set (made all 1s); if the condition is not true the byte is cleared. This instruction is used to record the condition at the present time for future reference.

6.4.5 The MC68000 Input/Output Instructions

As mentioned earlier, the MC68000 microprocessor has no input/output space to which I/O instructions may refer. Instead, I/O devices must be included in the system as if they were ordinary memory locations. With this sort of an implementation, known as *memory-mapped I/O*, any memory reference instruction becomes an I/O instruction when the target address is a location where there is an I/O device. Thus, in order to transfer 16 bits of data between the processor and an I/O device, one could execute a word-sized move instruction with the device's address as the effective address of either the source or the destination.

```
1.          MOVE   #9,D1     COUNTER TO DO LOOP 10 TIMES
2.  LOOP    ...              BODY OF THE LOOP
            ...
            ...
3.          DBF    D1,LOOP   DECREMENTS COUNTER AND REPEATS LOOP
                             UNTIL VALUE IN D1 IS −1
            [or]
3.          DBM              AS ABOVE BUT EXIT PREMATURELY IF
                             RESULT OF LAST OPERATION IS NEGATIVE
```

FIGURE 6.17
The use of DBcc to terminate a loop.

Two MC68000 instructions used exclusively with I/O devices are the software reset and the move peripheral data instructions (RESET and MOVEP). RESET causes the reset line from the processor to be asserted, resetting all external devices to predetermined internal states. MOVEP is used to transfer data between the processor and eight-bit peripheral devices. Eight-bit devices are designed to occupy several consecutive bytes in the memory space, and yet they must be connected to either the low half or the high half of the data bus. The move peripheral data instruction (MOVEP) may be used to transfer a group of two or four bytes between the processor and such a peripheral. This instruction transfers a word or long word between a data register and alternate bytes of memory, starting at the effective address and incrementing by 2. If the effective address is even, this instruction communicates with devices connected to the high half of the data bus; if odd, to the low half. This is the *only* MC68000 instruction which allows the use of odd addresses with word or long word operands.

6.4.6 Miscellaneous MC68000 Instructions

Most microprocessors include an instruction which does nothing. In the MC68000 it is the no-operation instruction (NOP). When it is executed it causes no activity other than the normal PC increment to take place. No data is moved, no arithmetic operations are performed, no bits are changed, no branch is taken. It is often used to reserve some space in a program so that during the debugging process it will be available for any temporary patching that may be required. It is also used to insert an incremental amount of time delay into a segment of a program. Although the NOP instruction causes no operation to take place it does occupy a word in the program, and fetching and executing it takes some time (four cycles).

The processor may be stopped with the instruction "load status register and stop" (STOP). This instruction includes an immediate word which the processor loads into the status register. It then stops fetching and executing instructions with the program counter pointing to the instruction following the STOP. The processor will resume normal operations when an interrupt, trace, or hardware reset occurs. These conditions will be discussed along with the interrupt system in Chapter 11.

SUMMARY

Although assembly language programming no longer plays a major role in computer system design, it still finds some applications. Learning the basics of assembly language programming is one of the best ways to become familiar with the structure and capabilities of processors in general and microprocessors in particular. This chapter discussed the applications for assembly language programming as well as the general concepts of assembly language syntax, with particular emphasis on the Motorola assembly languages.

After identifying and studying a processor's programming model and then learning about its addressing modes, the next step to take is to learn about its instruction set. To dive right in and attempt to study the instructions in alphabetic order by mnemonic is hopelessly confusing. Rather, the instructions should be approached in categories. The intent should be to get a flavor for what kinds of basic operations the processor can perform in the major areas of data movement, arithmetic, logic, test/branch, and input/output. This chapter introduced most of the MC6809 and MC68000 instructions found in these basic categories.

REVIEW PROBLEMS

6.1. Write one or more Motorola assembler directives to do each of the following:

a. Tell the assembler to store the ASCII code for the message "DO IT NOW!" into memory starting at location 003000H, with location 003000H assigned a symbolic name of MSG.

b. Tell the assembler to store the constants 10, 20, 30, 40, 50, and 60 into consecutive memory locations starting at the current location, and to assign the name TENS to the address of the first constant.

c. Tell the assembler to store the constants 100, 200, 300, 400, 500, and 600 into consecutive memory locations using two bytes each starting at the current location, and to assign the name HNDS to the address of the first constant.

d. Tell the assembler that wherever it finds the symbolic name FREQ in the program it is to substitute the value 60.

e. Tell the assembler to assemble the subsequent lines of the program starting at location $4000.

6.2. List as many pairs of MC6809 or MC68000 assembly language instructions as you can which, when executed, will have exactly, or very nearly, the same effect. In cases where the effects are not exactly the same, describe the differences.

6.3. Write an instruction or series of instructions in MC6809 assembly language to accomplish the following:

a. Put the number 12H into A and the number 34H into B.

b. Store all ones (FFH) in memory locations 1234H and 1235H.

c. Multiply the unsigned number in A by 120 and store the result in locations $1234 and $1235.

d. Clear bits 0, 2, 4, and 6 in accumulator B, leaving the others unchanged.

e. Load the number 1234H into the program counter.

f. Divide the number in accumulator B by 2 and place the remainder in the carry bit.

g. Add the BCD number in location 1234H to the BCD number in A and store the result in location 1234H.

h. Decrement the content of register X by 1.

i. Add the content of accumulator A to the content of register Y, and put the result into register X.

j. Add $12 to the content of the program counter if the carry bit is set.

k. Load A with 00 if B contains a positive number or with $FF if B contains a negative number.

l. Set the N- and Z-bits to correctly reflect the content of accumulator B.

m. Set the two most significant bits of accumulator A, leaving the others unchanged.

n. Clear the two least significant bits of accumulator A, leaving the others unchanged.

o. Complement bits 2 through 5 of accumulator A, leaving the others unchanged.

6.4. Determine the hex content of the specified registers after the execution of each of the following MC6809 instructions. Use the following initial conditions for each of the parts of this problem. Be sure to return to the same initial conditions before answering each part.

Processor register values:

(A) = 33H	(B) = 88H	(DP) = 40H	(CC) = 0FH
(X) = 1008H	(Y) = 2000H	(S) = 5008H	(U) = F008H
(PC) = 1000H			

Memory location values:

(0020,1,2,3H) = A0,B0,C0,D0H	(0040,1,2,3H) = 10,28,33,44H
(1028,9,A,BH) = 55,66,77,88H	(1048,9,A,BH) = 50,44,BB,CCH
(1004,5,6,7H) = 10,20,30,40H	(1008,9,A,BH) = 50,60,70,80H
(2000,1,2,3H) = 90,A0,B0,C0H	(4040,1,2,3H) = D0,E0,F0,00H

Part	*Instruction*	*Register(s)*
a.	LDD $40 (direct)	D
b.	LDD [$0040]	D
c.	LDX $40,X	X
d.	LDA ,Y++	A, Y
e.	LDY ,--X	X, Y
f.	LDD [$40,X]	D, X
g.	MUL	D
h.	ADCB $20,X	B, CC
i.	SBCB $0040	B, CC
j.	ORA ,X++	A
k.	CMPA #$88	A, CC
l.	SEX	D
m.	LEAY $40,X	Y
n.	SUBD $20,X	D
o.	ASLA	A
p.	ASRB	B
q.	EORA ,Y	A
r.	RORB	B
s.	LEAX A,Y	X
t.	LEAY −10,S	Y

6.5. Write a *single* MC6809 assembly language instruction which will accomplish each of the following with as few additional effects as possible.

a. Load register B with the content of the memory location whose symbolic name is MSG.
b. Load register Y with the address whose symbolic name is MSG.
c. Add the content of register D to the content of register S and place the result into register X.
d. Double the value of the unsigned number in the memory location whose symbolic name is MPD.
e. Complement the four most significant bits of register B.
f. Set the four least significant bits of register A.
g. Set or clear the Z-bit to reflect the value of the least significant bit in register A, but do not change the content of A.

h. Load register Y with the content of the memory locations specified by register X, and then post-increment register X appropriately.
i. Change the sign of the 2's complement number that is in a memory location whose address is 100 higher than the address in register Y.
j. Immediately after the instruction CMPA VAL, branch to the location whose symbolic address is HISIGN if the signed number in VAL is greater than the signed number in A.
k. Immediately after the instruction CMPA VAL, branch to the location whose symbolic address is HIGH if the unsigned number in VAL is greater than the unsigned number in A.
l. Decrement register S by 2.
m. Load the program counter with the defined symbolic address THERE.
n. Do nothing (change no flag or register other than the PC), but use some instruction other than NOP.
o. Clear the location whose address is to be found in memory at a location whose address is in register Y.
p. Subtract the value 1234H from the content of register S.

6.6. The questions below refer to the following MC6809 assembly language program in Figure P6.6 which sorts a list of unsigned binary numbers into decreasing order.

```
1.           ORG   $1000
2.  START    CLR   FLG     CLEAR INTERCHANGE FLAG
3.           LDX   #LIST   POINT TO LIST
4.           LDB   ,X+     FIRST ELEMENT = LENGTH OF LIST
5.           DECB          NUMBER OF PAIRS = LENGTH-1
6.           STB   COUNT   COUNTER FOR RUN THROUGH LIST
7.  PASS1    LDA   ,X+     GET ELEMENT i
8.           CMPA  ,X      COMPARE TO i+1
9.           BHS   CONT    IN ORDER, GO ON
10.          LDB   ,X      OUT OF ORDER, INTERCHANGE THEM
11.          STA   ,X
12.          STB   -1,X
13.          CLR   FLG     RECORD THE INTERCHANGE
14.          COM   FLG     BY SETTING FLAG BITS
15. CONT     DEC   COUNT   COUNT THAT PAIR. FINISHED?
16.          BNE   PASS1   NO, GO BACK FOR NEXT PAIR
17.          TST   FLG     YES. ANY INTERCHANGES?
18.          BNE   START   YES. REPEAT THE ENTIRE PROCESS
19. HERE     BRA   HERE    NO. LIST IS SORTED
20. *
21. *
22.          ORG   $2000   RAM STORAGE AREA
23. FLG      RMB   1
24. COUNT    RMB   1
25. *
26.          ORG   $3000   DATA AREA
27. LIST     FDB   $30
28.          RMB   $30
29.          END
```

FIGURE P6.6

a. What is the hex content of the location LIST?
b. What is the hex value of the address START?
c. Which line is the last instruction to be executed by the program?
d. What is the hex value of the address PASS1?
e. Which lines contain assembler directives?
f. Which line tells the assembler to assemble the program starting in a specific location?
g. Which lines define values for labels or symbolic addresses (either directly or implicitly)?
h. Which line terminates the first pass of the assembler through the program?
i. Encode the instruction in line 2.
j. Encode the instruction in line 3.
k. How many numbers will the program sort (as it is written)?
l. Which line causes the assembler to set aside a certain area of memory into which the user can insert the numbers to be sorted?

6.7. Upon entering the routine BRANCH the hex contents of accumulator A (or the lowest byte of D1) and memory location VALUE are as shown in the following table for several different cases. Determine the symbolic address to which the program in Figure P6.7 will branch during the routine for each case.

MC6809 ROUTINE

```
BRANCH  SUBA VALUE
        BGT  HERE
        BGE  THERE
        BLE  EVRYWR
        BRA  NOWR
```

MC68000 ROUTINE

```
BRANCH  SUB.B VALUE,D1
        BGT   HERE
        BGE   THERE
        BLE   EVRYWR
        BRA   NOWR
```

Case	*A-D1*	*VALUE*
a.	82	E8
b.	7E	7E
c.	F3	79
d.	72	8E

6.8. Repeat problem 6.7 for the version(s) of the routine BRANCH in Figure P6.8.

MC6809 ROUTINE

```
BRANCH  SUBA VALUE
        BHI  HERE
        BHS  THERE
        BLS  EVRYWR
        BRA  NOWR
```

MC68000 ROUTINE

```
BRANCH  SUB.B VALUE,D1
        BHI   HERE
        BEQ   THERE
        BLS   EVERYWR
        BRA   NOWR
```

6.9. Repeat problem 6.7 for the version of the routine BRANCH in Figure P6.9

MC6809 ROUTINE

```
BRANCH  SUBA VALUE
        BGT  HERE
        BHI  THERE
        BLT  EVRYWR
        BLO  NOWR
        BRA  ICI
```

MC68000 ROUTINE

```
BRANCH  SUB.B VALUE,D1
        BGT   HERE
        BHI   THERE
        BLT   EVERYWR
        BNE   NOWR
        BRA   ICI
```

6.10. Write an instruction or series of instructions in MC68000 assembly language to do the following operations:

a. Put the number 1234H into the lower half of D0, leaving the upper half unchanged.
b. Store all 1s (FFH) in memory locations 001234H, 001235H, 001236H, and 001237H.
c. Multiply the unsigned number in D0 by 1200 and store the result in locations $56781A through 56781D.
d. Clear bits 0, 2, 4, 6, 8 and 10 in register D5, leaving the others unchanged.
e. Load the number 123456H into the program counter.
f. Divide the unsigned number in register D3 by 2 and place the remainder in the carry bit.
g. Add the BCD number in location 123456H to the BCD number in the lower byte of D1 and store the result in location 123456H.
h. Decrement the entire content of register D5 by 1.
i. Add the content of register D1 to the content of register A5 and put the result into register A6.
j. Store the value $FF in the location whose address is in register A3 if the carry bit is set.
k. Clear all of the bits in D1 if D2 contains a positive number or set them if D2 contains a negative number.
l. Set the N- and Z-bits to correctly reflect the content of the memory location whose address is 300 higher than the value in register A1.
m. Set the two most significant bits of register D4, leaving the others unchanged.
n. Clear the two least significant bits of register D4, leaving the others unchanged.
o. Complement bits 2 through 5 of register D4, leaving the others unchanged.

6.11. Determine the hex content of the specified registers after the execution of each of the following MC68000 instructions. Use the following initial conditions for each of the parts of this problem. Be sure to return to the same initial conditions before answering each part.

Processor register values:

(D1) = 11111111H	(D3) = 33333333H	(D6) = 66666666H
(A1) = 00001008H	(A2) = 00002000H	(A3) = 00005008H
(A4) = 0000F008H	(CCR) = 1FH	

Memory location values:

(0020,1,2,3H) = A0,B0,C0,D0H	(0040,1,2,3H) = 10,28,33,44H
(1028,9,A,BH) = 55,66,77,88H	(1048,9,A,BH) = 50,44,BB,CCH
(1004,5,6,7H) = 10,20,30,40H	(1008,9,A,BH) = 50,60,70,80H
(2000,1,2,3H) = 90,A0,B0,C0H	(4040,1,2,3H) = D0,E0,F0,00H

Part	*Instruction*	*Register(s)*
a.	MOVE.B $40,D3	D3
b.	MOVE $40,D3	D3
c.	MOVEA $2000,A1	A1
d.	MOVE.L (A2)+,D1	D1,A2
e.	MOVE.W −(A1),D1	D1,A1

Part	*Instruction*	*Register(s)*
f.	MOVE 2040(A2),D1	D1
g.	MULU D1,D3	D1,D3
h.	ADDX D3,D6	D6,CCR
i.	SUBX D3,D6	D6,CCR
j.	OR.B (A1)+,D6	D6,A1
k.	CMPI #$8888,D3	D3,CCR
l.	EXT.L D6	D6
m.	LEA $40(A1),A3	A3
n.	SUB.B $20(A1),D6	D6,CCR
o.	ASL #3,D6	D6
p.	ASR D1,D6	D6
q.	EOR D6,D3	D3
r.	ROR.B #1,D1	D1,CCR
s.	LEA.L (A2,D3),A1	A1
t.	ROXL #5,D6	D6,CCR

6.12. Write a *single* MC68000 assembly language instruction which will do each of the following with as few additional effects as possible.

a. Load register D0 with the long word which starts in the memory location whose symbolic name is MSG.

b. Load register A3 with the 24-bit address whose symbolic name is MSG.

c. Add the content of register D1 to the content of register A6 and place the result into register A2.

d. Double the value of the unsigned number in the memory location whose symbolic name is MPD.

e. Complement the six most significant bits of register D2.

f. Set the six least significant bits of register D2.

g. Set or clear the Z-bit to reflect the value of the least significant bit in a location named QU8, but do not change the content of QU8.

h. Load entire register A4 with the content of the memory locations specified by register A3 and then post-increment register A3 appropriately.

i. Change the sign of the two-byte 2's complement number which is in a memory location whose address is 100 higher than the address which is in register A5.

j. Immediately after the instruction CMP VAL,D5, branch to the location whose symbolic address is HISIN if the signed number in VAL is greater than or equal to the signed number in D5.

k. Immediately after the instruction CMP VAL,D5, branch to the location whose symbolic address is HIGH if the unsigned number in VAL is greater than or equal to the unsigned number in D5.

l. Decrement register A4 by 7.

m. Load the program counter with the defined symbolic address THERE.

n. Do nothing (change no flag or register other than the PC), but use some instruction other than NOP.

o. Clear the single memory location whose address is 100 higher than the sum of the entire content of D3 and A5.

p. Subtract the value 1234H from the content of register A3.

6.13. The following questions refer to the MC68000 assembly language program in Figure P6.13 which sorts a list of double-byte unsigned binary numbers into increasing order.

```
1.           ORG    $001000
2.   START   CLR    FLG          CLEAR INTERCHANGE FLAG
3.           MOVEA  LIST,A1      POINT TO LIST
4.   INIT    MOVE   (A1)+,D0     FIRST ELEMENT = LENGTH OF LIST
5.           SUBQ   1,D0         NUMBER OF PAIRS = LENGTH-1
6.   PASS1   MOVE   (A1)+,D1     GET ELEMENT i
7.           CMP    (A1),D1      COMPARE TO i + 1
8.           BLS    CONT         IN ORDER, GO ON
9.           MOVE   (A1),D2      OUT OF ORDER, INTERCHANGE THEM
10.          MOVE   D1,(A1)
11.          MOVE   D2,-1(A1)
12.          CLR    FLG          RECORD THE INTERCHANGE
13.          NOT    FLG          BY SETTING FLAG BITS
14.  CONT    SUBQ   #1,D0        COUNT THAT PAIR. FINISHED?
15.          BNE    PASS1        NO, GO BACK FOR NEXT PAIR
16.          TST    FLG          YES. ANY INTERCHANGES?
17.          BNE    START        YES. REPEAT THE ENTIRE PROCESS
18.  HERE    BRA    HERE         NO. LIST IS SORTED
19.  *
20.  *
21.          ORG    $004000      RAM STORAGE AREA
22.  FLG     RMB    1
23.  COUNT   RMB    1
24.  *
25.          ORG    $002000      DATA AREA
26.  LIST    DC.W   $30
27.          DS.W   $30
28.          END
```

FIGURE P6.13

a. What is the hex content of the location LIST?
b. What is the hex content of the location LIST + 1?
c. Which line is the last instruction to be executed by the program?
d. What is the hex value of the *address* INIT?
e. Which lines contain assembler directives?
f. Which line tells the assembler to assemble the program starting in a specific location?
g. Which lines define values for labels or symbolic addresses (either directly or implicitly)?
h. Which line terminates the first pass of the assembler through the program?
i. Encode the instruction in line 2.
j. Encode the instruction in line 3.
k. How many numbers will the program sort (as it is written)?
l. Which line causes the assembler to set aside a certain area of memory into which the user can insert the numbers to be sorted?

CHAPTER 7

ELEMENTARY PROGRAM EXAMPLES

The assembly language program segments presented in this chapter illustrate some of the features of the MC6809 and the MC68000 instruction sets. They are written in the assembler syntax described in Chapter 6. Following a brief discussion of the intended illustration, sample implementations for each processor are shown.

The first group of examples shows the use of the instructions which support multi-precision addition and subtraction. Next come various methods for accessing tables in memory, basic ways to construct program loops, the use of decimal support instructions, and position-independent coding. The final series of programs deals with various individual bit-by-bit operations. Included here are segments to convert ASCII hex characters into binary for internal representation in the computer, as well as segments to convert integers from decimal form (both in BCD and in ASCII code) into binary, and vice versa.

7.1 MULTIPLE PRECISION ARITHMETIC

Motorola processors store multi-precision numbers (addresses as well as data) sequentially in memory with the highest ordered byte at the lowest address (referred to as the *big endian* convention). Note that this is the address first encountered when scanning through memory in the usual direction.

Programs which add or subtract such multi-precision numbers must start with the least significant parts (LSPs) and work toward the other end. The basic approach is to combine the LSPs with an ADD/SUB instruction to generate the LSP of the result and the carry/borrow out of this part. This single bit is automatically stored in the C-bit (or X-bit) in the condition code register. The more significant parts are then combined together with the carry/borrow from the preceding combination by using the add with carry (or extend) or subtract with carry (or extend) instructions.

7.1.1 Double-Precision Addition With the MC6809

The program shown in Figure 7.1 will add two double-precision numbers and store the double-precision sum in memory. The program defines the locations and the values of the two operands and the location for the sum. Lines 1 through 5 ask the assembler to insert the values of the two double-precision operands into memory starting at location 8000 (hex) and to label them as shown. Lines 6 and 7 ask the assembler to set aside two labeled locations into which the program will store the result. Notice that these "data" locations are separated from the program area by the two ORG statements.

Line 8 tells the assembler to start the subsequent coding (from line 9 on) in location 1000. Line 9 actually contains the first MC6809 instruction in the program; lines 1–8 contain assembler directives.

The instruction in line 9 loads the lower byte of the first operand into A. Notice that it uses the extended addressing mode with a symbolic operand, which will be evaluated as 8001H. Lines 10 and 11 compute the lower half of the sum and store it. Line 12 loads the higher half of the first operand into A. Notice that lines 11 and 12 must preserve the value in the carry bit in the CCR unchanged in order that the addition process may be chained between the two halves of the operands. The programming aid in Appendix A shows that this is indeed the case. The carry bit is not affected by load or store operations. This is true in all processors which use the carry to support multi-precision arithmetic. Line 13 completes the chaining of the addition between the halves of the operands, and line 14 stores the result.

The assembler will encode line 15 as 20 FE, "unconditionally add FE (−2) to the content of the program counter"; that is, it treats the label as a destination and calculates the necessary offset.

```
1.          ORG   $8000
2.  HI1     FCB   5A      FIRST OPERAND IS IN 8000 AND 8001
3.  LO1     FCB   96
4.  HI2     FCB   93      SECOND OPERAND IS IN 8002 AND 8003
5.  LO2     FCB   8B
6.  HISUM   FCB   0       SUM WILL BE STORED IN 8004 AND 8005
7.  LOSUM   FCB   0
8.          ORG   $1000
9.  DPSUM   LDA   LO1     START OF PROGRAM
10.         ADDA  LO2     ADD LOW BYTES
11.         STA   LOSUM   STORE LOW HALF OF SUM
12.         LDA   HI1
13.         ADCA  HI2     ADD HIGH BYTES WITH CARRY FROM LOW
14.         STA   HISUM   STORE HIGH HALF OF SUM
15. HERE    BRA   HERE    LOOP TO HALT THE PROGRAM
```

FIGURE 7.1
MC6809 double-precision addition program segment.

```
14.         SWI
15.         FCB   8
```

FIGURE 7.2
Returning to the ASSIST09 monitor.

The instruction in line 15 will be executed repeatedly. This is one way to end the program. The MC6809 has no HALT instruction to stop the processor when a program has ended, and so a loop like this would be one way to prevent the processor from going any farther. Actually, a HALT instruction and the subterfuge used here are both poor ways to end a program. If the processor stops, then what? The only resort is to restart the system with an abort button or some other hardware input.

In most applications the user neither wants nor expects the processor to stop operating. Instead, upon completing one task, the user expects some sort of assistance in starting a new task. A program which assists the user in this manner when dealing with assembly language or machine language programs is called a *monitor*. One monitor program commonly used with 6809-based systems is *ASSIST09*. To return to ASSIST09 the user's program must end with the instruction SWI, followed by the next location in memory containing the value 08. ASSYM09, the assembler/simulator provided for use with this text, responds to this pattern also. Thus, line 15 in Figure 7.1 should more properly have been replaced by lines 15 and 16 as shown in Figure 7.2.

Try to assemble this program and to execute (or simulate its execution) with whatever system you may have available for running MC6809 programs. Execute the program one instruction at a time and observe the changes which occur in the pertinent registers and memory locations.

7.1.2 Double-Precision Addition With the MC68000

Although the MC68000 is a 16-bit processor, it is capable of adding or subtracting full 32-bit operands. Thus, double-precision addition/subtraction involves 64-bit operands. The program shown in Figure 7.3 will add two double-precision numbers and store

```
1.            ORG     $68000
2.   HI1      DC.L    5A9632A5H   ;FIRST OPERAND IS IN 68000-68007
3.   LO1      DC.L    9693A43CH
4.   HI2      DC.L    1234ABCDH   ;SECOND IS IN 68008-6800F
5.   LO2      DC.L    8B56F832H
6.   HISUM    DS.L    1           ;SUM WILL BE STORED IN 68010-6801F
7.   LOSUM    DS.L    1
8.            ORG     $61000
9.   DPSUM    MOVE.L  LO1,DO      ;START OF PROGRAM
10.           ADD.L   LO2,D0      ;ADD LOW BYTES
11.           MOVE.L  D0,LOSUM    ;STORE LOW HALF OF SUM
12.           MOVE.L  HI1,D1
13.           ADDX.L  HI2,D1      ;ADD HIGH BYTES WITH CARRY FROM LOW
14.           MOVE.L  D1,HISUM    ;STORE HIGH HALF OF SUM
15.  HERE     BRA.W   HERE        ;LOOP TO HALT THE PROGRAM
```

FIGURE 7.3
MC68000 double-precision addition program segment.

the double-precision sum in memory. The program defines the locations and values of the two operands and the location for the sum.

Lines 1 through 5 in Figure 7.3 ask the assembler to insert the values of the two double-precision operands into memory starting at location 68000 (hex), and to label them as shown. Lines 6 and 7 ask the assembler to set aside two labeled locations into which the program will store the result. Notice that these "data" locations are separated from the program area by the two ORG statements.

Line 8 tells the assembler to start the subsequent coding (from line 9 on) in location 61000. Line 9 actually contains the first MC68000 instruction of the program. The earlier lines all contain assembler directives.

The instruction in line 9 loads the lower part of the first operand into D0. Notice that the source is defined in the absolute addressing mode with a symbolic operand, which will be evaluated as 68004H. Lines 10 and 11 compute the lower half of the sum and store it, while line 12 loads the higher half of the first operand into D1. Notice that lines 11 and 12 must preserve the value in the extend bit unchanged in order that the addition process may be chained between the two parts of the operands. This is indeed the case; the extend bit is not affected by move instructions. Line 13 completes the chaining of the addition between the two parts of the operands, and line 14 stores the result. Notice that by using two registers (D0 and D1) for the addition, the entire eight-byte sum also remains within the processor. Should any additional manipulation be required, this sum need not be reloaded into the processor.

The assembler will encode line 15 into a single word (two bytes) as 60FE, "unconditionally add FE (-2) to the content of the program counter." That is, it treats the label as a destination and calculates the necessary offset which it then includes as part of the instruction.

The effect of line 15 is that the processor will continue fetching and executing the same instruction over and over. Although the MC68000 has a STOP instruction which can stop the processor, it is not normally available to the user, and so a loop like this would be one way to end a program. Actually, a STOP instruction and this substitute are both poor ways to end a program. If the processor stops, the only resort is to restart the system using the methods described with the HALT instruction.

In most applications the processor is not expected to stop operating. Instead, upon completing one task, the user expects some sort of assistance in starting a new task. A series of programs which assist the user in this manner constitute the *operating system* of the computer. Operating system support functions are provided in the ASSYM000 program (on the disk available for use with this book) with the instruction TRAP #14. Whenever this instruction is encountered, the simulator will examine register D7 and will interpret the value found there as a command to provide a specific function. The code to stop the user's program and return to the display mode is 228 or 229. Thus, line 15 in Figure 7.3 should more properly have been replaced by lines 15 and 16 as shown in Figure 7.4.

Try to assemble this program and to execute (or simulate its execution) with whatever system you may have available for running MC68000 programs. Execute the program one instruction at a time and observe the changes which occur in the pertinent registers and memory locations.

```
1.              ORG      $12000        ;PROGRAM AREA
2.   START      LEA      BCDS(PC),A0   ;A0 POINTS TO THE LIST
3.              CLR.W    D0            ;CLEAR 2 BYTES FOR RUNNING SUM
4.              MOVE.W   #19,D2        ;INITIALIZE COUNTER (D2)
5.   LOOP       ANDI     #0,CCR        ;CLEAR C AND X
6.              MOVE.B   (A0)+,D1      ;PICK UP A BCD VALUE
7.              ABCD.B   D1,D0         ;ADD IT TO THE RUNNING SUM
8.              BCC.W    ENDLP         ;CARRY OUT OF BYTE SUM = 1?
9.              ADD.W    #$100,D0      ;YES, ADD 1 TO NEXT BYTE
10.  ENDLP      DBF.W    D2,LOOP       ;FINISHED?
11.             LEA      SUM(PC),A1    ;YES, POINT A1 TO PLACE FOR SUM
12.             MOVE.W   D0,(A1)       ;STORE DOUBLE-BYTE SUM
13.             MOVE.L   #228,D7       ;CODE TO END PROGRAM
14.             TRAP     #14           ;CALL TO OPERATING SYSTEM
15.  *
     * DATA AREA FOLLOWS PROGRAM
     *
16.  SUM        DS.W                   ;SUM WILL GO HERE
17.  BCDS       DC.B     $21           ;LIST OF BCD NUMBERS
18.             DC.B     $85
                  :
```

FIGURE 7.11
MC68000 relocatable BCD addition program segment.

to the PC to obtain the address to be loaded into A0. Line 11 also uses this option to load A1 with the address of the final sum. Referring to memory addresses in this fashion rather than with absolute or immediate values is the key to making the program relocatable. In the MC68000, displacements from any address register including the PC are limited to 16 bits. Thus, relocatability can only be accomplished when all of the relative addresses are within −32K or +32K − 1 of the referring instructions.

ASSYM000 will not permit a direct verification of relocatability since all programs must be entered from the assembler. However, ASSYM000 may be used to assemble the program twice with different origin statements each time. If this is done and the machine language listings are compared, they will be found to be identical even though the program and its data areas are in entirely different regions of memory.

The three lines labeled 15 represent a multi-line comment. The data area immediately follows the program area in memory with no gap in order to simplify the process of checking out the relocatability of the code. There could be any sized gap and the data could be anywhere in memory within the range mentioned above. Relocatability would not be affected providing that when the program is moved the data area moves with it, maintaining the same relative spacing.

7.4 BIT PICKING AND BIT PACKING

The program segments discussed in this section illustrate some of the instructions that can be used to move bits around within a word or to alter selected bits. They make use of the logic operations to clear bits (AND with 0), set bits (OR with 1), or complement bits (EOR with 1). They also illustrate the use of the shift instructions and several conditional branches.

Two of the program segments convert hex digits represented by their ASCII codes into unencoded hex. The ASCII codes for the digits 0 through 9 are 30 through 39, those for the digits A through F are 41 through 46. The segments assume that the characters represented are from this set of 0 through F. A simple series of tests could be included in the program to verify this.

The segments are not complete, many of the labels used are not defined, nor has any attempt been made to make the program segments relocatable. Try to expand these examples by including labels and data and then assembling and running them. Then try to rewrite them to make them relocatable.

7.4.1 MC6809 Examples of Bit Manipulations

The program segment shown in Figure 7.12 repacks two hex digits represented by their ASCII codes into a single byte containing the two hex digits. The characters are in locations defined elsewhere as MSCH (most significant character) and LSCH (least significant character). The unencoded hex result is written into the location TEMP, which has been defined elsewhere.

The "stripping" operation in lines 4, 10, 16, and 18 is called masking. Bits 4 through 7 are said to be masked out. Note that the mask (operand pattern) is entered in binary in order to show the reader exactly which bits are affected. This is good

```
1.  START  LDA  MSCH          GET MORE SIGNIFICANT DIGIT
2.         CMPA #$40          IS IT IN THE SET A-F?
3.         BHI  LTTR          YES. GO TO LTTR
4.  NMBR   ANDA #%00001111    NO. STRIP OFF LEADING HALF
5.  ALIGN  LSLA               MOVE INTO UPPER NIBBLE POSITION
6.         LSLA
7.         LSLA
8.         LSLA
9.         BRA  GTLS          GO TO GET LESS SIG DIGIT
10. LTTR   ANDA #%00001111    STRIP OFF LEADING HALF
11.        ADDA #9            CONVERT 1-6 INTO A-F
12.        BRA  ALIGN
13. GTLS   LDB  LSCH          GET LESS SIGNIFICANT DIGIT
14.        CMPB #$40          IS IT IN THE SET A-F?
15.        BHI  LTTR2         YES. GO TO LTTR2
16. NMBR2  ANDB #%00001111    NO. STRIP OFF THE LEADING HALF
17.        BRA  COMB          AND COMBINE
18. LTTR2  ANDB #%00001111    STRIP OFF LEADING HALF
19.        ADDB #9            CONVERT 1-6 INTO A-F
20. COMB   STB  TEMP          COMBINE NIBBLES
21.        ORA  TEMP
              .
              .
              .
```

FIGURE 7.12
MC6809 ASCII hex to unencoded hex program segment.

practice. An operand should be shown in the number system which most clearly illustrates its specific use in that situation.

The segments in Figure 7.13 illustrate some other bit manipulations which are possible. The effects are described in the comments. The bit numbers referred to are the standard ones: bits 0 through 7, right to left. The first four operations obtain a boolean result bit-by-bit in register A. The other two operations illustrate the use of the BIT (bit test) instruction. This instruction does not alter the value in the designated accumulator. It updates the N- and Z-bits in the CCR to reflect what the result *would have been* if the operand had been ANDed with the content of that accumulator.

7.4.2 MC68000 Examples of Bit Manipulations

The MC68000 assembly language program segment shown in Figure 7.14 repacks four ASCII characters representing hex digits into a single word in register D0 containing

```
    *              CLEAR BITS
    *
1.  START  LDA     PATTERN      PICK UP INITIAL PATTERN
2.         TFR     A,B          COPY INTO B FOR LATER USE
3.  OP1    ANDA    #%00101101   CLEAR BITS 1,4,6,7 ONLY
    *
    *              SET BITS
    *
4.  OP2    TFR     B,A          GET PATTERN AGAIN
5.         ORA     #%00101101   SET BITS 0,2,3,5 ONLY
    *
    *              COMPLEMENT BITS
    *
6.  OP3    TFR     B,A          GET PATTERN AGAIN
7.         COMA                 COMPLEMENT ALL BITS
    *
8.  OP4    TFR     B,A          GET PATTERN AGAIN
9.         EORA    #%00101101   COMPLEMENT BITS 0,2,3,5 ONLY
    *
    *              TEST A SINGLE BIT AND BRANCH
    *
10. OP5    TFR     B,A          GET PATTERN AGAIN
11.        BITA    #%00000100   SET Z-BIT OF CCR IF BIT 2 IS 0
12. *                           ELSE CLEAR Z. DON'T CHANGE A
13.        BEQ     THERE        GO TO THERE IF BIT 2 IS 0
    *
    *              TEST SEVERAL BITS AND BRANCH
    *
14. OP6    TFR     B,A          GET PATTERN AGAIN
15.        BITA    #%00101101   SET Z IF BITS 0,2,3,5 ARE ALL 0
    *                           ELSE CLEAR Z. DON'T CHANGE A
16.        BNE     THERE2       GO TO THERE2 IF ANY BIT
    *                           0,2,3,5 IS SET
```

FIGURE 7.13
MC6809 individual bit manipulations.

```
1.  START   MOVEA  #CODES,A0        ;USE A0 FOR POINTER
2.          MOVEQ  #3,D1            ;USE D1 FOR COUNTER
3.          CLR.W  D0               ;CLEAR WORD SPACE FOR RESULT
4.  GETDIG  MOVE.B (A0)+,D2         ;PICK UP DIGIT
5.          CMPI.B #40,D2           ;IS IT IN THE SET A-F?
6.          BHI.W  LTTR             ;YES. GO TO LTTR
7.  NMBR    ANDI.B #%00001111,D2    ;NO. STRIP OFF LEADING HALF
8.  ALIGN   LSL.W  #4,D0            ;SHIFT RESULT TO MAKE ROOM
9.          OR.B   D2,D0            ;COMBINE DIGIT WITH RESULT
10.         BRA.W  GTNXT            ;PREPARE TO GET NEXT DIGIT
11. LTTR    ANDI.B #%00001111,D0    ;STRIP OFF LEADING HALF
12.         ADDI.B #9               ;CONVERT 1-6 INTO A-F
13.         BRA.W  ALIGN
14. GTNXT   DBF.W  D1,GETDIG        ;FINISHED?
15.                                 ;YES, CONTINUE ON WITH PROGRAM
                   .
                   .
                   .
```

FIGURE 7.14
MC68000 ASCII hex to unencoded hex program segment.

the four unencoded hex digits. The encoded digits are assumed to be located in memory sequentially (highest-ordered digit first), starting in the location whose address is defined elsewhere as CODES.

Register A0 is used as a pointer to the encoded digits while they are picked up from memory and converted to hex. Register D1, which is used to count the four ASCII codes, is initialized to 3 because the loop GETDIG starting in line 4 is entered at the beginning and ends with a DBF instruction.

The "stripping" operation in lines 7 and 11 is called masking. Bits 4 through 7 are said to be masked out. Note that the mask (source pattern) is entered in binary in order to show the reader exactly which bits are affected. This is good practice. An operand should be shown in the number system which most clearly illustrates its specific use in that situation.

The alignment operation in lines 8 and 9 first moves the destination pattern (the word in D0) four bits to the left, leaving four 0s on the right end. It then combines the current four bits (from the low byte of D2) into the pattern with the OR operation. Note that the four least significant bits in D0 are 0s and the four most significant bits in the lowest byte of D2 are also 0s at the time when the OR operation is performed.

The segments in Figure 7.15 illustrate some other bit manipulations. The effects are described in the comments. The bit numbers referred to are the standard ones: bits 0 through 7, right to left. The first four operations obtain a boolean result bit-by-bit in register D0. The last operation illustrates the use of the BTST (bit test) instruction. This instruction does not alter the value in the destination. It updates the Z-bit in the CCR to reflect the condition of the bit whose number is specified in the source.

```
    *              CLEAR BITS
    *
1.  START  MOVE.B  PATRN,D0          ;PICK UP INITIAL PATTERN
2.         MOVE.B  D0,D1             ;COPY INTO D1 FOR LATER USE
3.  OP1    ANDI.B  #%00101101,D0     ;CLEAR BITS 1,4,6,7 ONLY
    *
    *              SET BITS
    *
4.  OP2    MOVE.B  D1,D0             ;GET PATTERN AGAIN
5.         ORI.B   #%00101101        ;SET BITS 0,2,3,5 ONLY
    *
    *              COMPLEMENT BITS
    *
6.  OP3    MOVE.B  D1,D0             ;GET PATTERN AGAIN
7.         NOT.B   D0                ;COMPLEMENT ALL BITS
    *
8.  OP4    MOVE.B  D1,D0             ;GET PATTERN AGAIN
9.         EORI.B  #%00101101        ;COMPLEMENT BITS 0,2,3,5 ONLY
    *
    *              TEST A BIT AND BRANCH
    *
10. OP5    MOVE.B  D1,D0             ;GET PATTERN AGAIN
11.        BTST    #2,D0             ;SET Z-BIT OF CCR IF BIT 2 IS 0
    *                                ;ELSE CLEAR Z. DON'T CHANGE D0
12.        BEQ     THERE             ;GO TO THERE IF BIT 2 IS 0
```

FIGURE 7.15
MC68000 individual bit manipulations.

7.5 CONVERSION BETWEEN DECIMAL AND BINARY (HEX)

The program segments shown here illustrate methods of converting a single-byte decimal integer (BCD) into a binary integer and vice versa. In the case of conversion from BCD to binary, the tens and units digits are first isolated and then converted by multiplying the tens digit by 10 and adding the units digit to the product.

The conversion from binary to BCD is complicated by the possibility of overflow beyond a single-byte BCD representation. This will occur whenever the hex equivalent of the binary number exceeds 63 (equivalent to 99 in decimal). The routines shown will return FF as the decimal value when overflow occurs. They could easily be modified to return a correct double-precision BCD result when the hex value exceeds 63.

7.5.1 MC6809 BCD/Binary Conversion Routines

The program segment in Figure 7.16 converts a single-byte BCD integer assumed to be in a location whose address has been defined elsewhere as DECNUM into binary, and stores the result into a location whose address has been defined as BINNUM. The

```
1.   START  LDA   DECNUM       PICK UP NUMBER
2.   TENS   ANDA  #%11110000   MASK OUT UNITS, GET TENS DIGIT
3.   ALIGN  LSRA               MOVE INTO LOWER POSITION
4.          LSRA
5.          LSRA
6.          LSRA               TENS DIGIT IS NOW IN A
7.   CNVT   LDB   #10          WEIGHT OF TEN'S POSITION
8.          MUL                CONVERT TO BINARY
9.          STB   TEMP         SAVE CONVERTED TENS DIGIT
10.  UNITS  LDA   DECNUM       PICK UP NUMBER AGAIN
11.         ANDA  #%00001111   MASK OUT TENS, GET UNITS DIGIT
12.         ADDA  TEMP         ADD IN TENS VALUE
13.         STA   BINNUM       SAVE RESULT
```

FIGURE 7.16
MC6809 to binary program segment.

routine uses a location named TEMP (defined elsewhere) for temporary storage. The value in DECNUM is assumed to be a valid BCD integer. A simple routine could be devised to check this assumption.

The tens digit is first isolated and shifted into the units position in lines 2 through 6. It is then converted to binary by multiplying it (in binary) by 10 in line 8. The converted value appears in register B (the lower half of the product register D), and is then stored in location TEMP. The units value (which is already in binary—actually BCD) is isolated in line 11 and added to the 10s value in lines 10 through 12.

The program segment of Figure 7.17 encodes the binary integer found in location BINNUM into BCD and stores the result into location DECNUM. If the decimal value

```
1.   START   LDA   BINUM    PICK UP NUMBER
2.   TEST    CMPA  #99      GREATER THAN 99 (DECIMAL)?
3.           BHI   TOOBIG   YES, INDICATE OVERFLOW
4.   OKAY    CLRB           NO, START CONVERSION
5.   TENS    SUBA  #10      TAKE OUT A TEN
6.           BLO   ALIGN    NO MORE TENS, ALIGN THE TENS
7.           INCB           COUNT THE TEN
8.           BRA   TENS
9.   ALIGN   LSLB           MOVE TENS DIGIT INTO POSITION
10.          LSLB
11.          LSLB
12.          LSLB
13.          STB   TEMP     SAVE BCD TENS DIGIT
14.  UNITS   ADDA  #10      RESTORE UNITS VALUE
15.          ORA   TEMP     COMBINE IN THE TENS DIGIT
16.          STA   DECNUM
17.          BRA   FINIS
18.  TOOBIG  LDA   #$FF     OVERFLOW CODE
19.          STA   DECNUM
20.  FINIS   ...
```

FIGURE 7.17
MC6809 binary to BCD program segment.

exceeds two digits, overflow is indicated by storing FF in location DECNUM. It, too, uses one temporary memory location named TEMP.

The test and branch for overflow take place in lines 2 and 3. If overflow occurs (number greater than 99 decimal) the program branches to TOOBIG (line 18), where the value of FF hex is stored in DECNUM.

The conversion starts in line 4 by clearing register B, which is used to count the number of 10s in the integer. During the loop in lines 5 through 8, successive values of 10 are subtracted out of the original integer and counted. When the subtraction is found to be unsuccessful by the test in line 6, the loop is terminated. At that point, register B contains the number of 10s which were successfully subtracted out, and register A contains the leftover value minus 10.

In lines 9 through 13 the 10s digit in register B is shifted left to occupy its proper position for the final BCD result and then saved in TEMP. The units value is restored in line 14 and combined with the 10s digit in line 15. The final result is stored away in line 16. The branch in line 17 is to go around the overflow case (TOOBIG) in lines 18 and 19.

7.5.2 MC68000 BCD/Binary Conversion Routines

The program segment in Figure 7.18 converts a single-byte BCD number assumed to be in a location whose address has been defined elsewhere as DECNUM into binary and leaves the result in register D0. The routine uses register D1 for temporary storage. The value in DECNUM is assumed to bc a valid BCD number. A simple routine could be devised to check this assumption.

Register D0 is cleared in line 1 in anticipation of the need for 0s in the leftmost byte of the lower word during the subsequent alignment shifting process. The 10s digit is isolated and shifted into the units position in lines 4 and 5. It is then converted to binary by multiplying it (in binary) by 10 in line 6. The converted 10s value appears in register D0. The copy of the decimal number which was saved in line 3 is manipulated in line 7 to isolate the units value (which is already in binary—actually BCD), which is then added to the 10s value in line 8.

The program segment of Figure 7.19 encodes the binary integer (one byte) found in location BINNUM into BCD and leaves the result in the lowest byte of register D0. If the decimal value exceeds two digits, overflow is indicated setting the result in

```
1. START  CLR.W   D0
2.        MOVE.B  DECNUM,D0        ;PICK UP NUMBER
3.        MOVE.W  D0,D1            ;SAVE A COPY
4. TENS   ANDI.B  #%11110000,D0    ;GET TENS DIGIT
5. ALIGN  LSR.W   #4,D0            ;MOVE INTO LOWER POSITION
6. CNVT   MULU.W  #10,D0           ;CONVERT TO BINARY
7. UNITS  ANDI.B  #%00001111,D1    ;GET UNITS DIGIT
8.        ADD.B   D1,D0
```

FIGURE 7.18
MC68000 BCD to binary program segment.

```
1.  START   CLR.L   D0
2.          MOVE.B  BINUM,DO   ;PICK UP NUMBER
3.  TEST    CMPI.B  #99,D0     ;GREATER THAN 99 (DECIMAL)?
4.          BHI.W   TOOBIG     ;YES, INDICATE OVERFLOW
5.  OKAY    DIVU.W  #10,D0     ;CALCULATE TENS, UNITS
6.  ALIGN   LSL.B   #4,D0      ;MOVE TENS DIGIT INTO PLACE
7.          MOVE.B  D0,D1      ;SAVE TENS DIGIT
8.          SWAP.W  D0         ;GET UNITS DIGIT INTO PLACE
9.          OR.B    D1,D0      ;COMBINE TENS AND UNITS
10.         BRA.W   FINIS
11. TOOBIG  MOVE.B  #$FF,D0    ;OVERFLOW CODE
12. FINIS   . . .
```

FIGURE 7.19
MC68000 binary to BCD program segment.

D0 to FF. The program uses the lower word of D1 for temporary storage and modifies the content of the upper word of D0 as well.

The entire long word comprising the content of D0 is first cleared. This is necessary because during a subsequent divide operation the entire content of D0 will be treated as the 32-bit dividend. In line 2 the binary integer to be converted is picked up in the low byte of D0. The test and branch for overflow takes place in lines 3 and 4. If overflow occurs (number greater than 99 decimal) the branch is taken to TOOBIG (line 11) where the value of FF hex is stored in the low byte of D0.

If there is no overflow, the conversion starts in line 5 by dividing the integer by 10. The quotient of this operation appears in the lower half of D0 and the remainder, in the upper half. The quotient is the number of 10s in the integer and hence is the 10s digit of the BCD result. The remainder is the units digit. These digits each occupy only the least significant four bits of their respective words in D0, since each is nine or less. In lines 6 through 9 they are moved into their correct relative positions within the low byte of D0.

In lines 6 and 7 the 10s digit in the low half of D0 is shifted left to occupy its proper position for the final BCD result and then saved in D1. The units value is swapped into the low half of D0 in line 8 and the 10s digit combined with it in line 9. The branch in line 17 is to go around the overflow case (TOOBIG) in line 11.

SUMMARY

Besides the idiosyncrasies of the assembler, the microprocessor applications designer must be familiar with the specific operating system or monitor used with the target system. Various systems offer different support functions to the user and each has its own method of requesting such support from within the user's programs.

The assembler that you use to generate code together with the hardware or simulator software that you use to test and debug programs will determine what types of modifications you must make to the examples presented here in order to run them. In addition, some of these examples are only partially complete. They should be written in more complete form and then debugged and run in a single-step mode. This will help to solidify your understanding of the processor operation.

REVIEW PROBLEMS

Write an assembly language program to meet each of the following specifications. In the listing include any data which may be necessary to run the program. Assemble and debug the program with ASSYM09, ASSYM000, or whatever system you have available to you.

7.1. The program is to add two 6-digit BCD numbers which are stored in memory in three sequential bytes each. Your program should define the numbers and their locations with symbolic addresses and should store the six-digit sum in memory starting in a symbolically defined location.

7.2. The program is to reverse the order of a table of numbers in memory. Try to devise a way to do this without first copying the entire table elsewhere in memory. Use the table format described in the first sample program in this chapter. Use symbolic addresses throughout. After you have a program that works then try to make it relocatable.

7.3. The program is to build a table of numbers in memory. The table should start at an address named TABST and should include X values, where X is a single byte value stored in a location named SIZE. The table should consist of odd single-byte unsigned binary integers starting with 1 and in numerical order.

7.4. Repeat problem 7.3 but store a list of odd two-byte BCD integers starting with 0001 and in numerical order.

7.5. Many microprocessors do not support decimal subtraction. However, decimal subtraction may be accomplished with decimal addition if signed values are expressed in the *10's complement* system. This is the decimal counterpart of the 2's complement system. To change the sign of a 10's complement BCD number, subtract it from 99 (or 9999, or whatever is applicable) and then add 1. The subtraction may be carried out in hex since no borrow between digits is ever necessary. However, the addition of 1 must be a decimal operation. After calculating the 10's complement of the subtrahend, it must be added to the minuend (also a decimal operation). Use the 10's complement system to write a program to implement the subtraction of two 4-digit BCD numbers. Test the program by trying to subtract 0359 from 0842. Note that the largest positive 4-digit number would be 0999 (+999) and the largest-magnitude negative number would be 9000, which represents −1000.

7.6. The program is to multiply a double-precision multiplicand by a single-precision multiplier. Your program should define the numbers and their locations with symbolic addresses and should store the triple-precision product in memory starting in a symbolically defined location.

7.7. The program is to calculate the average of a table of single-byte unsigned binary integers. Use the table format described in the first example in this chapter with a maximum table size of 255 numbers.

7.8. The program is to reverse the order of the bits in a location. Your program should define the location with a symbolic address and place the result in the same location.

7.9. The program is to convert the 16 hex digits contained in a consecutive series of eight (single-byte) locations into ASCII codes and store them in 16 other consecutive single-byte locations. The codes are to have odd parity. Your program should define the hex digits and their locations with symbolic addresses and should store the final codes in memory starting in a symbolically defined location.

7.10. The program is to divide a signed integer by 2 and round the result. Your program should define the integer and its location with a symbolic address and should store the result in a symbolically defined location. Repeat for divide by 4.

7.11. The program is to change the sign of a double-precision signed integer. Your program should define the integer and its location with a symbolic address and should store the result in a symbolically defined location.

7.12. The program is to convert a 16-bit unsigned binary integer found in memory (in two consecutive bytes) into its six-digit BCD equivalent and store the result in a different area of memory (in three consecutive bytes).

7.13. The program is to convert a 16-bit unsigned binary integer found in memory (in two consecutive bytes) into its six-digit BCD equivalent and store the ASCII codes for the digits of the result in a different area of memory (in six consecutive bytes). Leading 0s in the result should be suppressed (replaced by spaces).

CHAPTER 8

SUBROUTINES AND STACKS

Modern microprocessors support one or more special structures in read-write memory known as stacks. These structures are used to retain register information whenever the processor interrupts its regular flow of fetching and executing instructions in their normal sequence. Examples of such instances occur whenever the program calls upon a subroutine or whenever some external device signals that it needs special attention. In addition, stacks may be used routinely to retain information in a convenient fashion for future reference. This chapter describes these unique structures and the details of their implementation in the two target processors.

8.1 SUBROUTINES

A subroutine is a specialized program module that may be called upon from elsewhere within the program, outside of the normal sequence of execution. The original intent was to allow the subroutine module to be coded only once but called upon many times during the course of execution of the program. The resulting reduction in program size was a major reason for the use of subroutines in earlier times when computer memory was expensive. Modern programming techniques, however, encourage the use of subroutines throughout a program, even in instances where they are called upon only once. This use of subroutines in so-called modular programming will be the subject of a later chapter. At this time we will merely note that most of the programs currently written include subroutines.

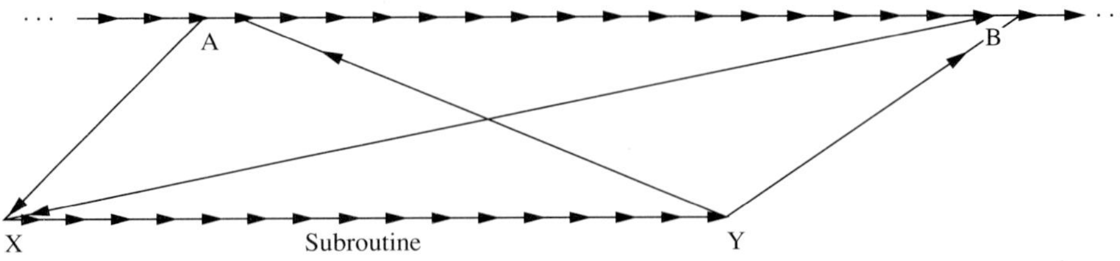

FIGURE 8.1
Subroutine execution.

Figure 8.1 shows how a subroutine fits into the structure of a program. The main program execution sequence is shown as the dashed horizontal line. At point *A* an instruction in the program calls upon the subroutine and so the processor must branch to it at point *X*. Upon the completion of the subroutine at point *Y*, the processor must branch back to just after point *A* in order to continue along the main sequence. Later, at point *B*, the subroutine is called upon again. Again the processor must execute the code between points *X* and Y. This time, however, the return to the main sequence must be to just after point *B*.

Thus, upon its completion, the subroutine in this example must branch to one of two different locations, to just after *A* or to just after *B*. None of the branch instructions described earlier is capable of that behavior. An entirely different type of branch instruction is necessary, one which can return the program back to the calling location, wherever it may have been. A special memory or register structure is also necessary in order to retain the address of that location. When executing the special return instruction, the processor must obtain the address from that structure and effect the branch back to the main sequence.

8.2 THE LAST IN FIRST OUT STACK

A simple structure to retain the return address from a subroutine would be a single register. Whenever a subroutine is called, the return address could be written into the register over the previous content. However, with only one register, no subroutine could ever call another subroutine, for then the first return address would be lost when it was written over by the second one.

A group of several registers could accommodate several subroutine calls of other subroutines (*nested subroutines*). A *last in first out* stack of registers (a LIFO stack) would be required. Upon completion of the innermost or most recently called subroutine, the last stored return address would be retrieved from the LIFO stack of registers. This process could then be repeated as often as necessary within the size limits of the register stack.

The implementation of a LIFO register stack is illustrated in Figure 8.2. Each register in the stack is numbered with an address. An auxiliary register called the stack pointer points to the last used register in the stack by holding the number of that register. When the current subroutine is completed, the processor uses the stack

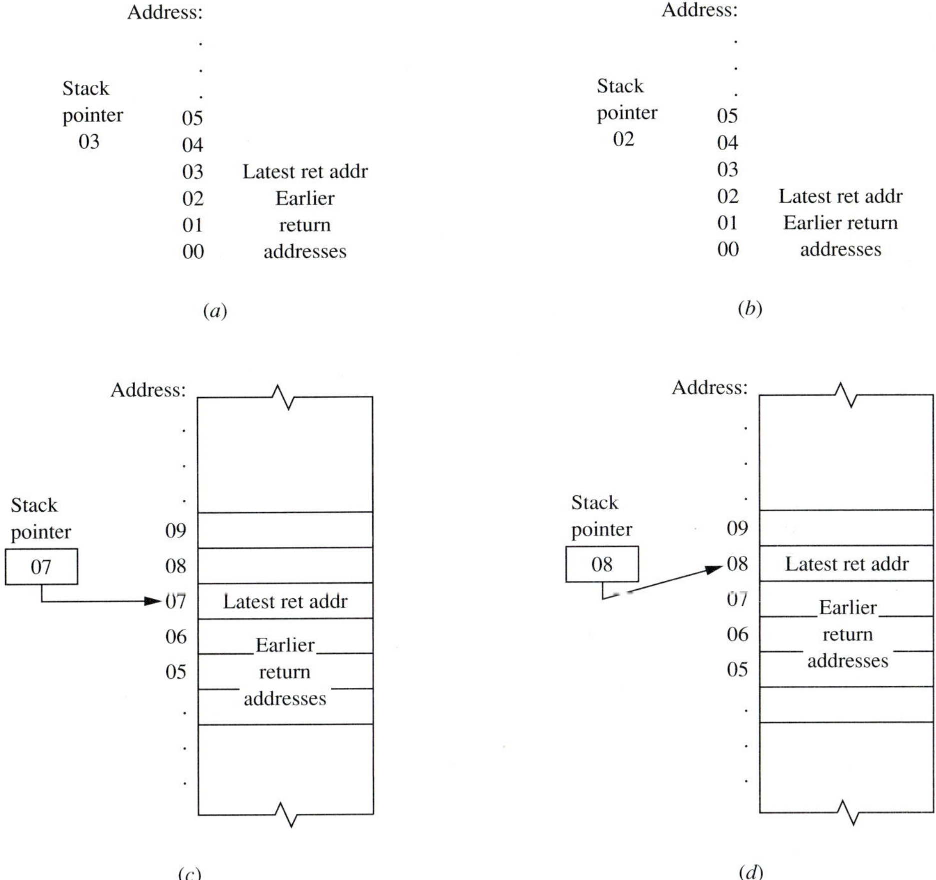

FIGURE 8.2
A LIFO register stack: (*a*) before a return, (*b*) after the return, (*c*) before a call, (*d*) after the call.

pointer to locate the register containing the required return address. After the processor retrieves the return address, the pointer is automatically changed to point to the next lower register in the stack in anticipation of the need for the next lower nested return address. This is shown in Figure 8.2*a* and *b*. When a new subroutine call is executed, the processor saves the new return address on the top of the stack. The stack pointer is automatically incremented to point to this next higher register in the stack, as shown in Figure 8.2*c* and *d*. Thus, the stack pointer changes its content whenever a new return address is saved (pushed) onto the stack or retrieved (pulled) from the stack. In this way the stack pointer always points to the top of the stack, the last written register.

Although stacks may be implemented with processor registers as in Figure 8.2, it is more common to implement them in read/write memory. The use of processor registers would result in a shorter access time, since no memory cycle time is involved in the push and pull operations. However, the number of registers in the stack would be limited. Implementing the stack in the memory space of the processor allows the system designer to provide whatever size stack is required. Indeed, it becomes feasible to provide two or more stacks; the processor need only include a separate stack pointer for each one.

Programs are executed from lower addresses toward higher addresses, and programmers customarily use read/write memory for storing arrays, variables, and temporary results in the same direction. Consequently, LIFO stacks in memory are implemented starting at the high end of a read/write memory space and filling toward the low end. This minimizes the possibility of the stack's inadvertently filling up and encroaching upon memory space used for other purposes.

Before a stack may be used in a program, its associated stack pointer must be loaded with the highest address of a block of read/write memory implemented in the system. From then on, the automatic behavior of the pointer during subroutine calls and returns will ensure proper operation of the stack. Of course, subroutine nesting must not be so deep that the stack fills into an area of memory used for other purposes. In addition, the program must not enter a subroutine in any way other than via a proper call to it. Nor may it exit a subroutine other than via a proper return. Violation of these rules could return the subroutine to the wrong location or could cause the stack to encroach upon a region of memory where it interferes with the proper execution of the program.

8.3 STACK APPLICATIONS

Although the primary application for a LIFO stack is to store return addresses during subroutine executions, it is such a versatile structure that it has found a variety of other uses. One method of controlling the transfer of data into or out of a computer uses an externally generated signal called an interrupt. Upon detecting the signal, the processor interrupts its current activity in order to attend to the external source of this signal. The status of the activity which was interrupted must be saved so that, after attending to the interrupt, the processor may resume where it left off. The stack provides a convenient place to store this status while servicing the interrupt. Thus, a processor may save the contents of the program counter, the condition code register, and other processor registers on the stack while it responds to an interrupt. Upon completing the interrupt service, the processor will then load these contents back into the original registers in order to resume the interrupted activity. The interrupt method of transferring information is discussed in detail in a later chapter.

The stack is also a convenient place to save data temporarily from within the program. Many processors provide a pair of instructions called *push/pull* or *push/pop*. When one of these instructions is executed the operand is pushed onto the stack or pulled off the stack. The operand is the content of a specified processor register or set of registers. Push/pull instructions have an advantage over other types of load/store instructions in that they require no addressing specification. They push onto the top of the stack or pull off of the top of the stack. The stack pointer automatically provides the address.

The push/pull instructions also provide a convenient means to transfer parameters to a subroutine. The calling program can push the parameters onto the stack and then call the subroutine. The subroutine can then access the parameters from the stack. Of course, if the same stack is used to save the return address from the subroutine call, then the called routine must skip over that address in the stack when retrieving the parameters.

To limit the overhead required in the calling program, subroutines should have a minimal effect upon the contents of processor registers. The subroutine should save on the stack the original content of any register it uses in performing its function. Then, at the conclusion of the subroutine, it should restore the content prior to the return. The push and pull instructions can readily be used for this.

The stack is also a convenient place for a subroutine to store intermediate results during its execution. Instructions accessing this temporary storage area need to include no absolute addresses. In addition, the storage area can be allocated to a routine when it is called and then deallocated upon its return, a process known as *dynamic allocation*. Dynamic allocation reduces the total memory requirement from what it would be if the space were permanently allocated to the routine. It also makes it possible for a routine to call itself, since any needed memory space will be made available upon each instance of the routine. For example, suppose a routine required one location to save a result temporarily and it saved the result in a specific location, say one named TEMP. If the routine then called itself, this second call of the routine would write over the value saved in TEMP during the first instance of the routine, thus destroying it. Dynamic allocation would eliminate this problem.

A subroutine which is structured to call itself is said to be recursive. Recursive programs are seldom written because they are often confusing and difficult to understand. They will not be discussed any further here.

Dynamic allocation of memory has another important application, however. It permits a routine to be interrupted by an input/output device and then to be called while that device is being serviced. In this situation, the routine is temporarily suspended in the middle of its execution and then restarted at the beginning and run to completion before continuing on with its suspended execution. A subroutine which may be interrupted and then called by the interrupt service routine is said to be reentrant. It is very useful to structure subroutines to be reentrant in any system which uses interrupts. This allows interrupt service routines to use any of the software resources of the system without interfering with the main program.

8.4 STACKS IN THE MC6809

The MC6809 directly supports two stacks, the system stack with its pointer, S, and the user stack with its pointer, U. The processor uses the system stack to save the return address during the execution of a subroutine call instruction. It also uses the system stack to store the current status while responding to an interrupt. Both stacks are available to the user for temporary storage as well, and both are supported by individual push and pull instructions.

If two stacks do not suffice for an application, the user may define up to two more by using the index registers X and Y as stack pointers. Registers may be stored in these stacks with the auto increment/decrement options. For example, to push the content of A onto the X stack use the instruction STA ,−X. To pull the content off the top of the Y stack into register B, use LDB ,Y+. Double-register pushes or pulls require the use of the option to increment/decrement by 2, for example LDD ,X++ or STU ,--Y.

The regular stacks should be used for temporary storage whenever possible since they are directly supported by the push and pull instructions. With their use, the size of the increment/decrement operation is taken care of automatically to accommodate the number and size of the registers.

The MC6809 instructions for calling subroutines are JSR, BSR, and LBSR. When executing the JSR instruction (jump to subroutine), the processor stores the current content of the program counter on the top of the system stack, with the stack pointer S changing automatically. This is the return address that will be used upon completion of the subroutine. It then loads the program counter with the target address. The target address is specified in one of the three standard addressing modes: direct, extended, or indexed. The branch to subroutine instruction (BSR) and the related long branch to subroutine instruction (LBSR) use relative addressing, specifying the target address in terms of its offset from the current program counter content. Otherwise, the result is the same as for the JSR instruction.

All subroutines must end with the instruction RTS (return from subroutine). This instruction pulls the two top bytes off the system stack and loads them into the program counter. The stack pointer (S) is incremented to point to the new top of the stack. If the programmer has not erred in the use of the stack, the value loaded into the program counter as the result of this instruction will be the proper return address.

The MC6809 includes another group of instructions that use the stacks, the push and pull instructions. These are load/store instructions that move data between processor registers and either the user or system stack. The operand for the instruction takes the form of a post-byte which is a coded list of the registers whose contents are to be pushed onto the stack or which are to be loaded from the stack. Hence the list of the registers to be pushed or pulled immediately follows the op-code for the instruction.

The push/pull instructions have four mnemonic forms, PSHS, PSHU, PULS, and PULU. The stack used is indicated in the final letter of the mnemonic. The operand is a list of one or more of the following registers: A, B, X, Y, DP, CC, PC, and the stack pointer, which is not used in the instruction. That is, PSHU A,B,S is acceptable but PSHU A,B,U is not. When the instruction is assembled the post-byte will be a simple coding of the registers in the operand list. A 1 in a particular bit position indicates that that register is on the list; a 0 indicates that it is not. The post-byte pattern is shown in Figure 8.3, which also shows the stacking order. Note that

PC	S/U	Y	X	DP	B	A	CC

First pushed (last pulled) — Last pushed (first pulled)

FIGURE 8.3
Post-byte for MC6809 PSH/PUL instructions.

the operand list is not an ordered list; the order in which the registers will be pushed or pulled from the stack is independent of the order in which they are specified in the operand. Note also that since one register which may be pulled is the program counter, the pull instructions may result in a branch in the program sequence. In fact, a pull instruction may be used as an alternative way to return from a subroutine (and simultaneously to restore registers).

Other MC6809 instructions which use the system stack are RTI (return from interrupt) and SWI, SWI2, and SWI3 (software interrupts). These instructions involve the interrupt system and so will be discussed in a later chapter.

8.5 EXAMPLES OF STACK OPERATIONS IN THE MC6809

The following sections describe some of the characteristics of the MC6809 stacks. They also include examples of MC6809 assembly language program segments which illustrate some of the more common stack manipulations.

8.5.1 Stack Pointer Initialization in the MC6809

Prior to the use of any stack the associated stack pointer register must be initialized to some address in read/write memory where the stack will have room to grow as it is used. Since the stack will fill toward lower addresses, this initial address should be toward the upper end of the available space. The regular load instructions LDS or LDU are used, usually in the immediate mode.

Support programs such as monitors and simulators often provide some special stack services. Thus, the ASSIST09 monitor initializes the system stack pointer for the user. However, it is poor practice to rely upon such services. If you get into the habit of doing these housekeeping tasks for yourself now, you are less apt to overlook them later.

The ASSYM09 simulator requires not only that the user perform the stack pointer initialization, but also that any stack space which will be used in the program be declared as such. If an attempt is made to execute any instruction which will write into either stack without having declared that area, the simulator will stop and display an error message.

The MC6809 assembly language program segment in Figure 8.4 shows the initialization of the system stack and its use in a subroutine call. The comments list the assembled starting address and machine code for each instruction.

In line 2 of Figure 8.4 the system stack pointer is initialized to 4000. When the subroutine DOIT (with a starting address of 1234) is called in line 2 the return

```
1.         ORG  $2000
2.  INIT   LDS  #$4000     $2000  10  CE  40  00
3.         JSR  DOIT       $2004  BD  12  34
4.  NEXT   LDA  #$64       $2007  86  64
```

FIGURE 8.4
MC6809 program segment to initialize and use a stack pointer.

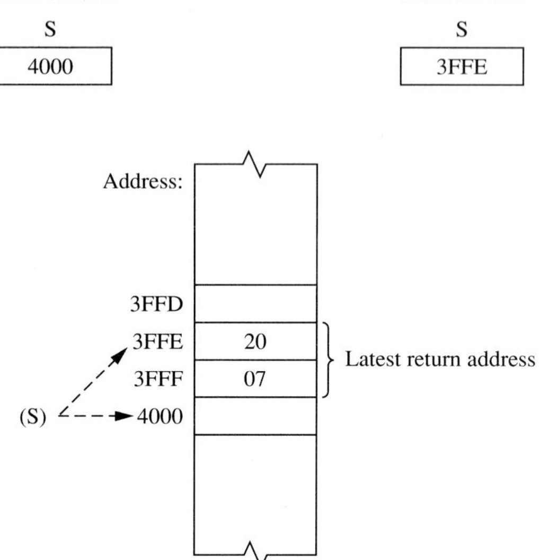

FIGURE 8.5
Stack pointer initialization n the MC6809.

address of 2007 will be saved on the stack, as shown in Figure 8.5. Note that the first used location in the stack will not be at the pointer address but at that address less 1. To have a stack start in location x, the pointer must be initialized to x+1. In this example, the top of read/write memory is location 3FFFH. To have the stack start there, the pointer is initialized to 4000H. Some processors maintain stacks with pointers to the first empty location in the stack; but in the MC6809 the pointers point to the last used location in the stack.

8.5.2 Parameter Passing in the MC6809

One way for the calling program to pass parameters to a subroutine is to pick up or create the parameters in processor registers and leave them there while calling the subroutine. The program segment shown in Figure 8.6 illustrates this approach. An alternative is to pass a starting address of a list of parameters stored in memory. This address can be passed in an index register or on a stack. Another approach is to push the parameters themselves onto the stack prior to calling the subroutine. When this approach is used with the system stack rather than the user's stack, the return address will be pushed on top of the parameters during the call. This requires that the subroutine reach down into the stack to access the parameters, as shown in the examples in Figure 8.7.

```
LDA  PARAM1     PASS PARAM1 IN A AND PARAM2 IN B
LDB  PARAM2
JSR  USEM
```

FIGURE 8.6
Passing parameters in MC6809 registers.

In the calling program:

```
LDA   PARAM1
LDB   PARAM2
PSHS  A,B        PUSH PARAM2 FOLLOWED BY PARAM1
LDA   PARAM3
LDB   PARAM4
PSHS  A,B        PUSH PARAM4 FOLLOWED BY PARAM3
JSR   USEM
```

In subroutine USEM:

```
LDA   4,S        GET PARAM1 INTO A
LDB   5,S        GET PARAM2 INTO B
```

Or:

```
LEAX 2,S         GET START ADDR OF PARAM LIST INTO X
LDA   ,X+        GET PARAM3 INTO A
LDB   ,X+        GET PARAM4 INTO B

      etc.
```

FIGURE 8.7
Passing parameters on the MC6809 stack.

Figure 8.8 illustrates the condition of the stack as the subroutine USEM shown in the program of Figure 8.7 would see it. Recall from an earlier discussion that the content of B will be pushed onto the stack before the content of A when both are pushed with the same instruction. Thus, PARAM4 will be deeper into the stack than PARAM3. PARAM1 and PARAM2 will be even deeper still since they were pushed in an earlier instruction. Thus, the subroutine instructions to retrieve these parameters must reach down into the stack with the offsets as listed in Figure 8.7.

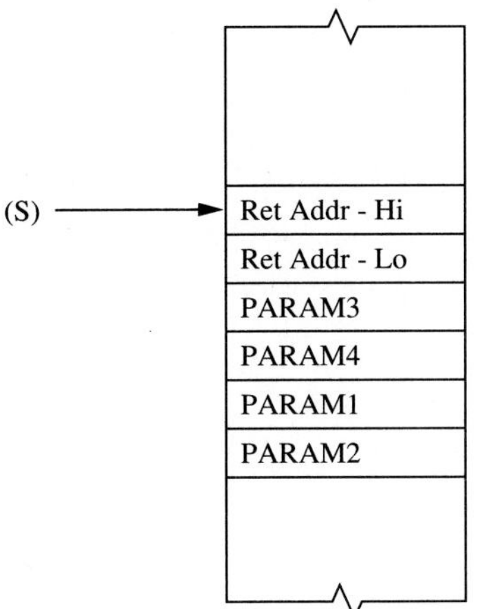

FIGURE 8.8
MC6809 parameter stacking order.

After using the stack for any purpose such as that just illustrated, the stack pointer should be returned to its original condition. This will ensure that no stack space is wasted by retaining unneeded data. In the example above, this would be accomplished in the calling program after the return either by pulling results off the stack (a total of four bytes) or by incrementing S by 4 (LEAS 4,S).

Another way to pass parameters is shown in the program segments of Figure 8.9. The calling program includes the parameters within itself as a list immediately following the subroutine call. Among these parameters could be addresses to other lists in memory as well. During the subroutine call, the processor stacks the address of the beginning of the parameter list as if it were the return address. The called subroutine locates the parameter list by referring indirectly to the top of the stack. Before the return, the subroutine must calculate the actual return address from the list length and its starting address.

In lines 1 through 6 of Figure 8.9 the subroutine call is followed by the parameter list. In line 8 the subroutine uses the stack pointer to find the top of the stack, fetches out the address saved there, and loads that address into an auxiliary pointer register, U. Register U now contains the address of the beginning of the parameter list. Throughout the subroutine, whenever a parameter is required, it can be fetched by using the appropriate offset from register U, as illustrated in lines 9 and 10.

The return address (NEXT in this example) is the address of the location immediately following the end of the parameter list. The parameter list is five bytes long. Thus, the return address is 5 plus the address in U. In line 11, this return address is constructed in register U. It is then written into the top of the stack (pointed to by S) in line 12 in preparation for the return in line 13.

In the calling program:

```
 1.          JSR   SBRTN    SUBROUTINE CALL
 2.  PLIST   FCB   PARAM1   START OF PARAM LIST
 3.          FCB   PARAM2
 4.          FCB   PARAM3
 5.          FCB   PARAM4
 6.          FCB   PARAM5
 7.  NEXT    LDA   #$64     NEXT INSTR AFTER RETURN
```

In the subroutine:

```
 8.  SBRTN   LEAU  [,S]     GET PLIST INTO U FROM STACK
 9.          LDA   ,U       GET PARAM1 INTO A
               :
10.          LDA   4,U      GET PARAM5 INTO A
               :
11.          LEAU  5,U      CALCULATE RETURN ADDRESS
12.          STU   ,S       WRITE IT INTO THE STACK
13.          RTS            RETURN
```

FIGURE 8.9
Listing parameters in an MC6809 calling program.

8.5.3 Allocating Memory Space Dynamically in the MC6809

The program segment in Figure 8.10 illustrates dynamic memory allocation. It shows various steps in a subroutine, including memory allocation, use, and deallocation. In line 1 of Figure 8.10 the first instruction in the subroutine moves the stack pointer, making six locations at the top of the stack available for temporary storage during execution. Some of these locations are used in the subroutine in lines 2 through 6. In line 8 the subroutine gives back the storage by incrementing the stack pointer. Note that the content of the stack pointer must not be changed at any time between the allocation and the deallocation of the memory. To do so could result in an interrupting service routine altering part of the stack. Thus, in all of the instances where this region is used in the subroutine, the locations are accessed with an offset from the stack pointer, leaving the content of the pointer unchanged.

8.5.4 Register Use in MC6809 Subroutines

When register contents are to be saved on the stack from within a subroutine that uses dynamic memory allocation, the order of the operations must be carefully considered. The example in Figure 8.11 illustrates the preferred order. In line 1 the first step in the subroutine saves the contents of the processor registers on the stack. Doing this before allocating the five-byte storage area (line 2) ensures that the register contents will be below the allocated area in the stack. Figure 8.12 shows the stack after the execution of line 2. The subroutine should use stack pointer offsets ranging from 0 to 4 when accessing the storage area. The subroutine must deallocate the storage area and restore the register contents just prior to the return, as shown in lines 5 and 6 of Figure 8.11. Note that these operations must be performed in an order opposite to that in which they were performed at the beginning of the subroutine (lines 1 and 2).

```
1.  SBRTN  LEAS  -6,S   ALLOCATE 6 LOCATIONS
                 :
2.         STD   ,S     SAVE D FOR LATER
                 :
3.         STA   3,S    SAVE A FOR LATER
                 :
4.         LDD   ,S     LOAD D WITH SAVED VALUE
                 :
5.         STX   4,S    SAVE X FOR LATER
6.         LDB   3,S    LOAD B WITH SAVED VALUE
                 :
7.         LEAS  +6,S   DEALLOCATE STORAGE
8.         RTS          RETURN
```

FIGURE 8.10
Dynamic memory allocation in the MC6809.

```
1.  SBRTN   PSHS  A,B,X,Y  SAVE REGISTER CONTENTS
2.          LEAS  -5,S     ALLOCATE 5 LOCATIONS
              :
3.          LDA   #64      USE REGISTER
              :
4.          STA   2,S      USE STORAGE
              :
5.          LEAS  +5,S     DEALLOCATE STORAGE
6.          PULS  A,B,X,Y  RESTORE REGISTERS
7.          RTS            RETURN
```

FIGURE 8.11
Register use in an MC6809 subroutine.

If the original order of saving register contents and allocating storage as shown in Figure 8.11 is reversed, then the register contents will be stacked on top of the storage area, as shown in Figure 8.13. In that case, the stack pointer offsets used to access the five locations in the storage area must run from 6 through 10. In other words, the pointer must dip below the stacked registers in order to access the storage area. The preferred order, shown in Figure 8.11 and illustrated in Figure 8.12, results in a subroutine that is easier to understand.

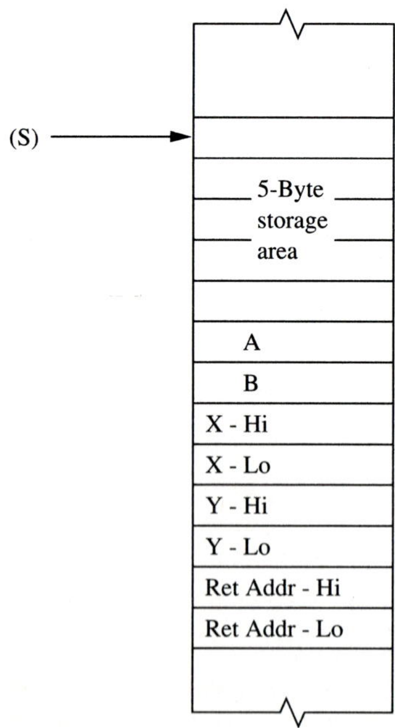

FIGURE 8.12
MC6809 example stack configuration.

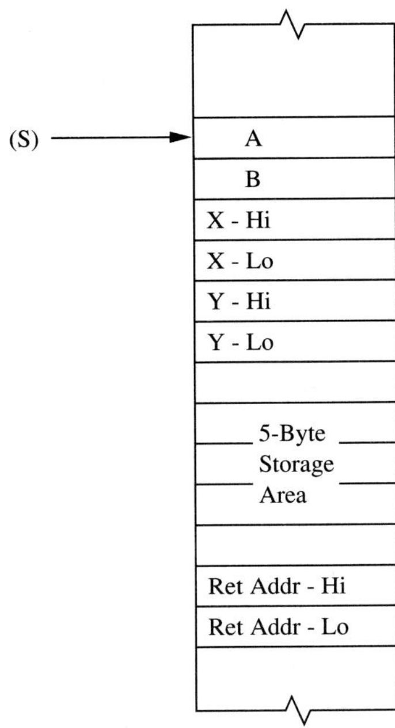

FIGURE 8.13
MC6809 stack configuration with reversed order of execution.

8.6 STACKS IN THE MC68000

In the MC68000 two address registers, A7 and A7′, share the title of *system stack pointer (SP)*. Only one of these is available to a program at any given time, depending on the current *privilege state* of the processor. In order to provide a means of implementing security restrictions in a system, the MC68000 operates in one of two privilege states, the *user* state and the *supervisor* state. While in the supervisor state, all of the system resources are available to a program, any of the instructions may be executed, and reference to register A7 will access register A7′, the supervisor stack pointer. While in the user state, certain of the system resources may be blocked from access, several of the instructions may not be executed, and reference to register A7 will access register A7, the user stack pointer. These privilege states will be described in detail in a later chapter.

When in the user state, the processor can perform operations *using* the system stack, *but it is not permitted to read from or write to either system stack pointer.* Only when it is in the supervisor state does the processor have access to the stack pointers themselves.

During a subroutine call the processor saves the return address in the system stack, either the user stack or the supervisor stack, depending on whether the system is in the user or supervisor state. When responding to an interrupt or when executing the interrupt-like trap instruction, the processor saves both the program counter and the status register contents on the supervisor stack, regardless of the state.

The user may define additional stacks for data storage by using the other address registers (A0 through A6) as stack pointers. A stack may be used to store data by using the address register indirect auto increment/decrement modes. Thus, to push the entire content of D0 onto the A4 stack, use the instruction MOVE.L D0,−(A4). To pull the word off the top of the A1 stack into register D3, use MOVE (A1)+,D3. Since the MC68000 has no ordinary push/pull instructions, this technique must be used to save or retrieve data from any stack, including the system stack (A7 or SP), if so desired. Note, however, that the processor will restrict the entry of data onto the system stack so that it is put in on a word boundary. Byte values are saved in the high half of the stack word with the low half remaining unchanged.

The MOVEM instruction (move multiple registers) may be used to push or pull several registers in a single instruction. When word length is selected, only the low order word is pushed; the low order word sign-extended to 32 bits is pulled. The instruction MOVEM A4/A6/D3-D5,−(A7) would save the (word) contents of registers A4, A6, D3, D4, and D5 on the system stack. The order in which the registers are pushed onto the stack is independent of the order in which they are specified in the instruction. The stacking order (push order) for MOVEM with the predecrement destination mode is as follows: address registers in reverse numerical order, and then data registers in reverse numerical order. Figure 8.14 shows the order in which the registers in the above instruction would be stacked.

The retrieving order (post-increment destination mode) is exactly the opposite. This results in the proper sorting out of the register contents after pulling them back off the stack. The instruction MOVEM (A7)+,A4/A6/D3-D5 will restore the registers

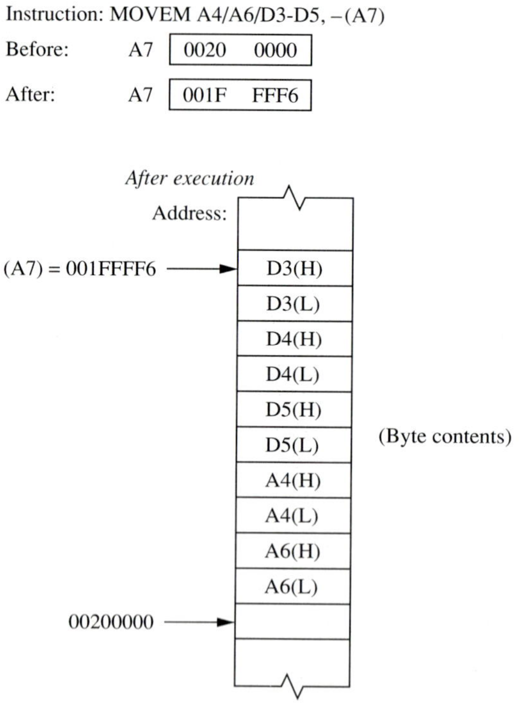

Instruction: MOVEM A4/A6/D3-D5, −(A7)

Before: A7 | 0020 0000 |

After: A7 | 001F FFF6 |

After execution

Address:

(A7) = 001FFFF6 → D3(H)

D3(L)

D4(H)

D4(L)

D5(H)

D5(L) (Byte contents)

A4(H)

A4(L)

A6(H)

A6(L)

00200000 →

FIGURE 8.14
Stacking order for MC68000 MOVEM instruction.

with the proper contents. This can be seen in Figure 8.14 by pulling the top values off the stack and into the registers in the following order: data registers first (low through high), then address registers (low through high)

The MC68000 instructions for calling subroutines are BSR (branch to subroutine) and JSR (jump to subroutine). When executing either one, the processor stores the current content of the program counter in the top four bytes of the system stack. This is the return address that will be used upon completion of the subroutine. The processor then loads the program counter with the target address, thus effecting the branch to the subroutine. The BSR instruction uses relative addressing, specifying the target address in terms of its (8- or 16-bit) offset from the current program counter content. As such, it may not be capable of reaching distant subroutines. JSR allow the use of any of the control modes of addressing and is thus capable of reaching a subroutine anywhere in the program.

All subroutines must end with either the instruction RTS (return from subroutine) or RTR (return and restore condition codes). RTS pulls the top four bytes off the system stack and loads them into the program counter. The system stack pointer (A7 or A7′) is incremented to continue to point to the top of the stack. If the programmer has not erred in the use of the stack, the value loaded into the program counter as the result of this instruction will be the proper return address. RTR is used when the subroutine has saved the condition codes on top of the return address in the stack in order to preserve the status of the calling program. RTR pulls the top word of the stack into the condition code register and the next two words into the program counter.

Among the other MC68000 stack instructions are PEA (push effective address), LINK (link) and UNLK (unlink). They will be described in the next section with specific examples of their use. The remaining instructions involving the system stack are RTI (return from interrupt), RTE (return from exception processing), and the various trap instructions. These involve the interrupt system and will therefore be discussed in a later chapter.

8.7 EXAMPLES OF STACK OPERATIONS IN THE MC68000

This section presents and describes several segments of assembly language programs that illustrate some of the characteristics and uses of stack manipulations in the MC68000.

8.7.1 Initialization of the MC68000 Stack Pointers

Prior to the use of any stack, the stack pointer register must be initialized to some address in read/write memory where the stack will have room to grow as it is used. Since stacks fill toward lower addresses, this initial address should be toward the upper end of the available space. Support programs such as monitors and simulators often provide some automatic initialization of the system pointers. It is poor practice, however, to rely upon this service. If you get into the habit of doing this kind of

```
1.          ORG       $200000
2.  INIT    MOVEA.L   #$00F00000,SP   200000  2E 7C 00 F0 00 00
3.          JSR       DOIT            200006  4E B9 00 00 12 34
4.  NEXT    MOVE      D0,D4           20000C  38 00
```

FIGURE 8.15
MC68000 program segment to initialize and use the supervisor stack.

housekeeping task for yourself now, you are less apt to overlook it when the support is not automatic.

The assembly language program segment of Figure 8.15 shows the initialization of the supervisor stack pointer and the indirect use of the stack with a subroutine call. The comments list the starting address and machine code for each assembled instruction. In line 2 the system stack pointer is initialized to 00F00000. As mentioned earlier, this instruction is privileged and can be executed only in the supervisor state. The result, therefore, is to initialize the supervisor stack pointer (A7′). If the user stack pointer is to be initialized, the destination must be referred to as USP and, again, the instruction will be privileged.

When the subroutine DOIT (with an assumed starting address of 001234) is called in line 3 of Figure 8.15, the return address of 20000C is saved on the stack, as shown in Figure 8.16. Note that the first used location in the stack will not be at the pointer address but that address less 1. To have a stack start in location X, the pointer must be initialized to $X + 1$. In this example, the top of read/write memory is assumed to be location 00EFFFFFH. To have the stack start there, the pointer is initialized to 00F00000H. Some processors maintain stacks with pointers to the first empty location in the stack; in the MC68000 the pointers point to the last used location in the stack.

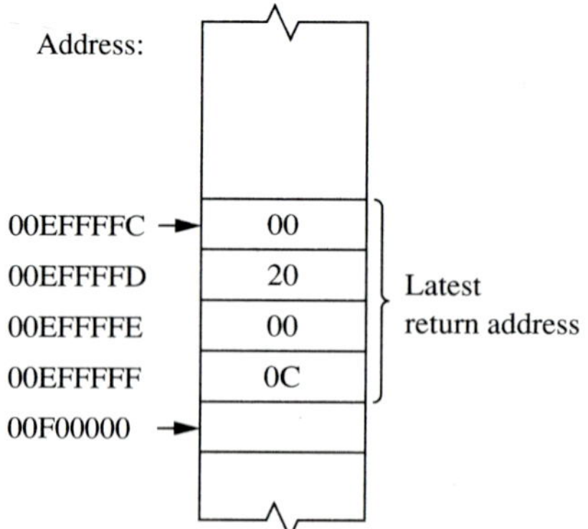

FIGURE 8.16
The MC68000 system stack.

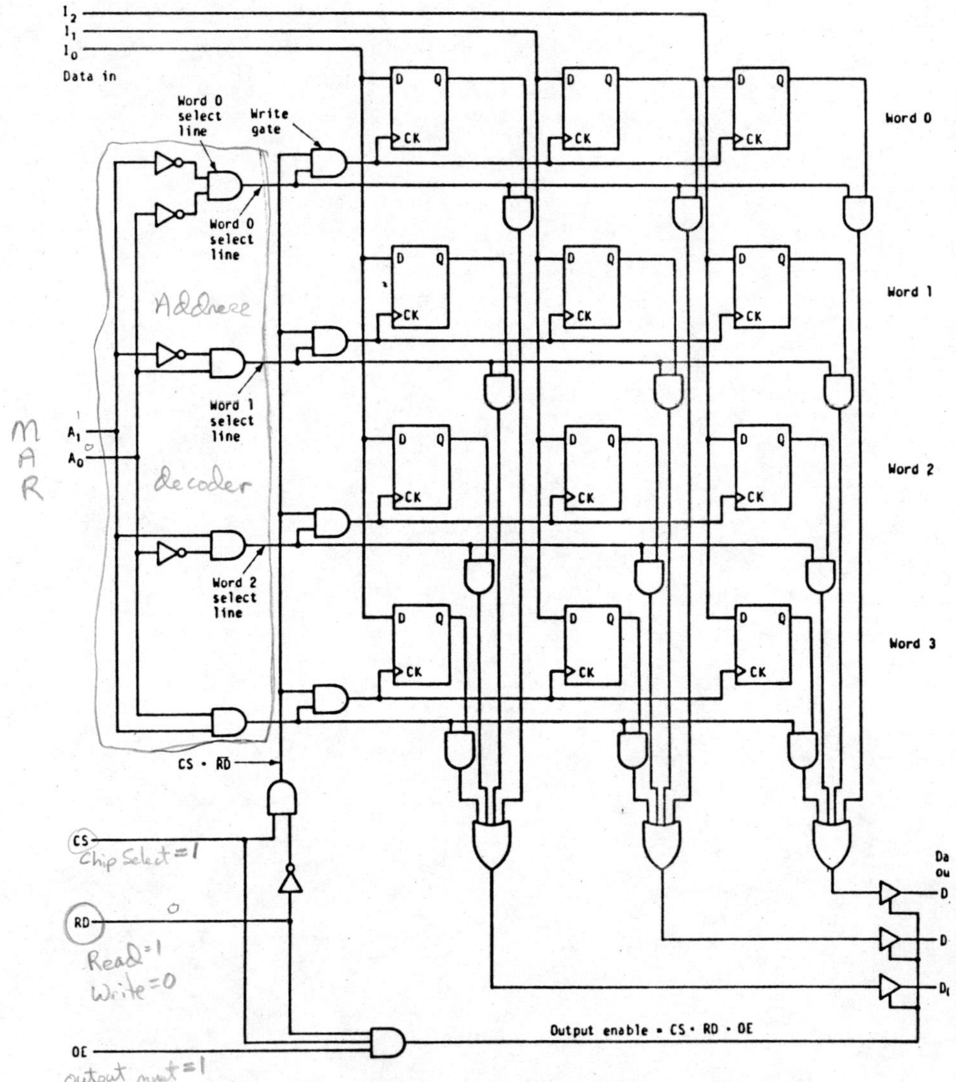

Fig. 3-28. Logic diagram for a 4 × 3 memory. Each row is one of the four 3-bit words. A read or write operation always reads or writes a complete word.

```
MOVE  PARAM1,D0     PASS PARAM1 IN D0 AND PARAM2 IN D1
MOVE  PARAM2,D1
JSR   USEM
```

FIGURE 8.17
Passing parameters in MC68000 registers.

Note also that the system stack pointer must always contain an even number, and that only even numbers of bytes are pushed or pulled with either system stack.

8.7.2 Passing Parameters in the MC68000

One way in which the calling program may pass parameters to a subroutine is to pick up or create the parameters in processor registers and allow them to remain there while calling the subroutine. The program segment in Figure 8.17 illustrates this. Another way to pass parameters is to push them onto the stack prior to calling the subroutine. When this approach is used with the system stack the return address will be pushed on top of the parameters during the call. This requires that the subroutine reach down into the stack to access the parameters, as shown in the sample program listed in Figure 8.18.

Figure 8.19 illustrates the condition of the stack as the routine USEM in the program segment of Figure 8.18 would see it. The last pushed parameter, PARAM8, will be nearest to the top of the stack just below the return address. The others will be below in an order opposite to the stacking order. Another way to pass parameters to a subroutine is to pass a starting address of a list of parameters stored in memory. The starting address may be passed in any address register, or it may be pushed onto the system stack just prior to calling the subroutine. The MC68000 instruction set includes a push instruction designed for this purpose, PEA (push effective address). This instruction causes the processor to calculate the effective address of the single operand (control addressing modes only), and then to push that address onto the system stack. For example, to push the address of the list which starts in a location

In the calling program:

```
    MOVE  PARAM1,-(A7)   STACK PARAM1
    MOVE  PARAM2,-(A7)   STACK PARAM2
    MOVE  PARAM3,-(A7)   STACK PARAM3

          etc.

    MOVE  PARAM8,-(A7)   STACK PARAM8
    JSR   USEM
```

In subroutine USEM:

```
    MOVE  4(A7),D1       PICK UP PARAM8 INTO D1
          :
    MOVE  12A7),D3       PICK UP PARAM4 INTO D1
```

FIGURE 8.18
Passing parameters on the MC68000 stack.

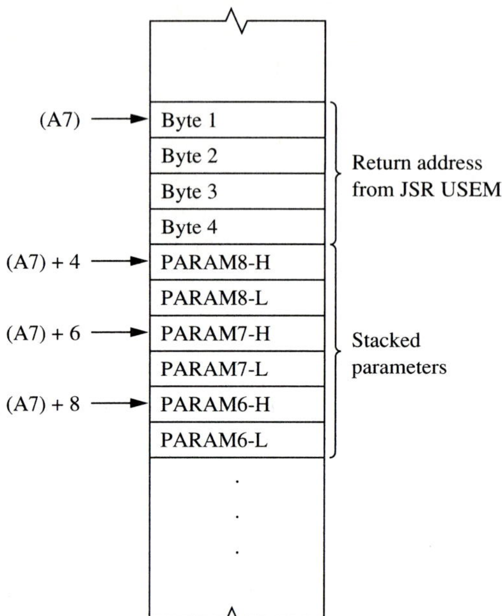

FIGURE 8.19
Passing parameters on the MC68000 system stack.

named PARAM using the PC relative addressing mode, the instruction would be PEA PARAM(PC).

When the calling program uses the PEA instruction to pass the address of a parameter list to the subroutine, the subsequent call to the subroutine will stack the return address on top of the pushed address, as shown in Figure 8.20. The subroutine must reach below this return address in order to retrieve the parameter address. The subroutine may use an instruction such as MOVEA.L 4(SP),A1 to load the pushed parameter address into register A1, which could then be used to access the parameters. The offset of four bytes is required to reach below the return address, as shown in Figure 8.20.

Later on during the subroutine the stack should be cleaned up by moving the return address four locations in memory and incrementing SP by 4. These operations may both be done with the single instruction MOVE.L (SP)+,(SP), since the post-increment takes place after the read but before the write. Alternatively, the calling program could clean up the stack by incrementing SP by 4 with an instruction such as LEA 4(SP),SP immediately after the instruction which calls the subroutine. Cleaning up the stack in either way ensures that it will not fill up with unnecessary information during subsequent calls to the subroutine.

8.7.3 Allocating Memory Space Dynamically in the MC68000

The MC68000 directly supports dynamic memory allocation with two special instructions, LINK and UNLK. The link instruction (LINK) is executed by the subroutine

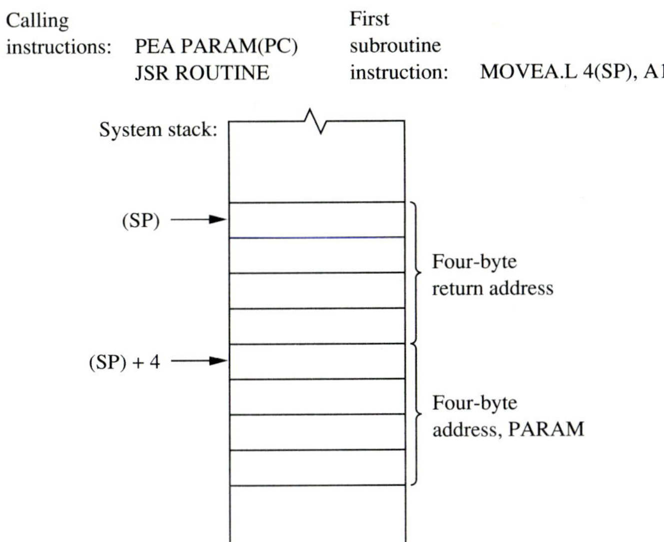

FIGURE 8.20
The MC68000 PEA instruction.

(usually as the first instruction) to set aside a block of locations on the system stack to be used for temporary storage during that specific call. The reserved block is located on top of the return address from the subroutine call. The UNLK instruction is executed just before the return from the subroutine to deallocate the space.

The LINK instruction includes two operands: an address register and a 16-bit signed displacement. During execution, the address register is first pushed onto the system stack above the return address that was saved there when the subroutine was called. This saves the register's contents so that they may be retrieved before the return from the subroutine. The new value of the stack pointer is then loaded into the address register. This register will be used by the subroutine as a pointer to the data area which will be allocated to that instance of the subroutine. The signed displacement operand is then added to the content of the system stack pointer, moving it to a (lower) address, thus freeing up a block of that many locations for the data area. Note that the displacement is *added* to the content of the stack pointer. To reserve a block of n locations, the displacement must be specified as $-n$ to move the pointer to an unused region of the stack space. Note also that the stack pointer must always contain an even address, and so the displacement must be an even number.

Figure 8.21 shows the effect of executing the instruction LINK A0,#−40 to allocate 40 bytes of data area to a subroutine. In order to preserve the address in the register unchanged, the subroutine should access the data area with the address register indirect or the displacement or indexed mode using the specified register. In this case, the subroutine may access the data area by using an address ranging from −1(A0) through −40(A0).

Immediately following the execution of the LINK instruction, the stack pointer is pointing to the top of the reserved area. Therefore, any subsequent subroutine call from within the current one (a nested call) will not affect the reserved area, even if the nested call also employs a link instruction to allocate stack space. This is true even if it uses the same address register.

The unlink instruction (UNLK) is used to undo the link operation. The subroutine should include this instruction just prior to the RTS instruction. The unlink instruction has only one operand, the address register that was designated in the link instruction. When it is executed, it copies the address from the register into the stack pointer and then pulls the top of the stack into that register (while incrementing the stack pointer). An examination of Figure 8.21 will show that the result is a restoration of the situation which prevailed before the execution of the link instruction.

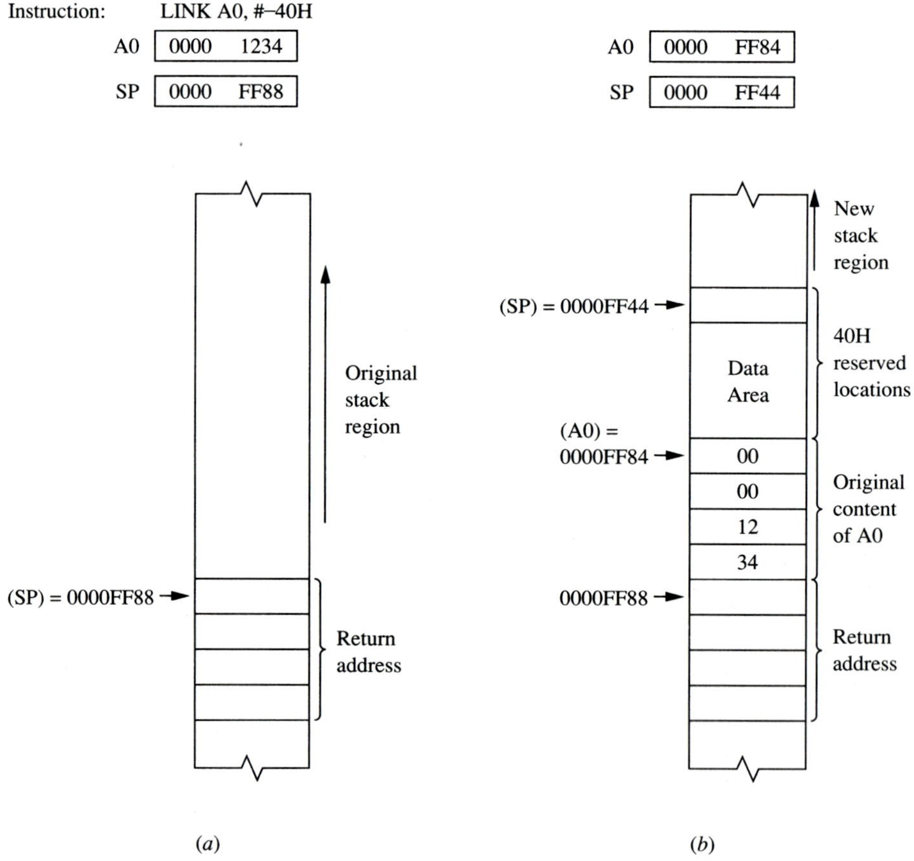

FIGURE 8.21
The MC68000 LINK instruction: (*a*) before execution, (*b*) after execution.

SUMMARY

The LIFO stack was originally devised as a place to save return addresses from subroutine calls which would put no practical restrictions on the depth of nesting. This structure has been found to be very useful for other purposes such as status storage during interrupt servicing, temporary data storage within routines, parameter passing between routines, and dynamic storage allocation within routines.

All microprocessors support the basic stack functions of storing and retrieving subroutine return addresses and saving status during interrupt servicing. Many processors also support the other uses for stacks by means of push/pull or similar types of instructions.

The MC6809 includes push/pull instructions which may be used to stack and retrieve the contents of processor registers. The MC68000 includes a push effective address instruction which can be used to pass the address of a parameter list to a subroutine. In addition, the MC68000 directly supports dynamic memory allocation with link and unlink instructions.

REVIEW PROBLEMS

8.1. Write MC6809 instructions to initialize the top of the user's stack to $77FF and the top of the system stack to $76FF.

8.2. Write MC6809 push and pull instructions to replace the content of register X with the concatenation of registers A and B.

8.3. Write MC6809 push and pull instructions to replace the content of register X with the concatenation of registers DP and CC.

8.4. Write the post byte for the the following MC6809 instruction:

PSHS X,U,B,PC

8.5. Write a series of MC6809 instructions that will call a subroutine named GRTR if the content of register A is greater than the content of a memory location named SPD, subroutine LESS if the content of A is less than that of SPD, and subroutine EQUAL if the content of A equals that of SPD.

8.6. The figure below shows the contents of pertinent MC6809 registers and memory locations before the fetching and execution of the routine DMMY (also shown in Figure P8.6).

(A) = $AA (B) = $BB (X) = $EEEE (Y) = $FFFF
(PC) = $1234 (S) = $5670
($5670) = $00 ($5671) = $11 ($5672) = $22
($5673) = $33 ($5674) = $44

```
DMMY PSHS A
     PSHS B
     PSHS X
     PSHS Y
     PULS A
     PULS B
     PULS X
     PULS Y
```

FIGURE P8.6

a. Before executing the routine what is the content of the top of the stack?
b. After executing the first instruction in the routine what is the content of register A? Of the top of the stack? Of register S?
c. After executing the entire routine what is the content of the program counter? Of the top of the stack? Of register X? Of register Y? Of register B? Of register A?
d. During the execution of the routine what is the minimum content of register *S*? The maximum content?

8.7. Before executing the MC6809 routine shown in Figure P8.7 below, the content of *S* is $1234.

```
        ORG   2000H
        LDD   DPVAL1
        LBSR  GOSUB
        BRA   DOMORE

        ORG   3000H
GOSUB   PSHS  D,CC
        ADDD  DPVAL2
        TFR   D,X
        PULS  D,CC
        RTS
```

FIGURE P8.7

a. Before executing the LBSR instruction what is the content of the program counter?
b. After executing the LBSR instruction what is the content of register *S*? Of the program counter?
c. During the execution of the LBSR instruction what is the value of the address pushed onto the system stack?
d. After executing the RTS instruction what is the address of the next instruction to be executed?

8.8. Determine the hex content of the program counter and the system stack pointer after the fetch and execution of each of the following MC6809 instructions. Use the following initial conditions for each of the parts of this problem. Be sure to return to the same initial conditions before answering each part. Assume that the addresses SUB1 and SUB2 have been defined as $1040 and $1200, respectively.

Processor register contents:

(A) = $AA (B) = $BB (PC) = $1000 (S) = $2000

Memory location contents:

($2001) = $0A ($2002) = $50

Part	*Instruction*
a.	PSHS A,B
b.	BSR SUB1
c.	RTS
d.	JSR SUB1
e.	LBSR SUB2
f.	JSR SUB2
g.	LDS #SUB1

8.9. In an MC6809 system the calling program passes five parameters to the subroutine SUB shown in Figure P8.9 by pushing them onto the stack with the routine PRE as shown.

```
PRE  LDA   PARAM1
     LDB   PARAM2
     TFR   D,X
     LDA   PARAM3
     LDB   PARAM4
     TFR   D,Y
     LDA   PARAM5
     PSHS  A,X,Y
     JSR   SUB
     :
SUB  LDB   LENGTH
     STB   COUNT
     LDX   #ADDR
b.**load A with PARAM1 here
     STA   ,X+
     PSHS  A
c.**load A with PARAM2 here
     STA   5,X
d.**load A with PARAM3 here
     CMPA  #50
     BEQ   FINIS
e.**load A with PARAM4 here
     INCA
     STA   ,X+
f.**load A with PARAM5 here
     :
```

FIGURE P8.9

a. Show the order in which the parameters are stacked in the system stack prior to the execution of the JSR instruction.

b. through *f*: For each case, write one instruction to access the necessary parameter at each of the places indicated in the subroutine.

8.10. Write MC68000 instructions to initialize the top of the user stack to $FF77FF and the top of the supervisor stack to $FF76FF. Assume that the system is in the supervisor mode and privileged instructions may be executed.

8.11. Write MC68000 instructions to push D0 through D5 and A3 and A6 onto the supervisor stack and then to pull them off of the stack. Then repeat the problem with the user stack. Assume that the system is in the supervisor mode.

8.12. Write the post-word in hex for the the following MC68000 instruction:

MOVEM D2-D7/A3-A6,−(A7)

8.13. Write a series of MC68000 instructions which will call a subroutine named GRTR if the content of register D1 is greater than the content of a memory location named SPD, subroutine LESS if the content of D1 is less than that of SPD, and subroutine EQUAL if the content of D1 equals that of SPD.

8.14. Before executing the routine DMMY in the following figure, the contents of pertinent MC68000 registers and location are as shown in Figure P8.14.

(D1) = $0000AAAA (D2) = $0000BBBB (A1) = $0000EEEE
(A2) = $0000FFFF
(PC) = $001234 (A7) = $00005670
($005670) = $00 ($005671) = $11 ($005672) = $22
($005673) = $33 ($005674) = $44 ($005675) = $55

```
DMMY  MOVEM  D1/D2/A1/A2,-(A7)
      MOVEM  (A7)+,A1/A2
      MOVEM  (A7)+,D1/D2
      MOVE.L (A7)+,D3
```

FIGURE P8.14

a. Before executing the routine, what is the content of the top of the system stack?
b. After executing the first instruction in the routine, what is the content of register A7? List the contents of the stack starting at that address and continuing down through location 005670.
c. After executing the entire routine, what is the content of the program counter? Of the top of the stack? Of register D1? Of register D2? Of register D3? Of register A1? Of register A2? Of register A7?
d. During the execution of the routine, what is the minimum column of register A7? The maximum content?

8.15. Before executing the MC68000 routine shown in Figure P8.15, the content of A7 is $00123456.

```
       ORG     002000H
       MOVE.L  D1,DPVAL1
       BSR     GOSUB
       BRA     DOMORE

       ORG     003000H
GOSUB  MOVE.L  D1,-(A7)
       ADD.L   DPVAL2,D1
       EXG.L   D1,D2
LAST   MOVE.L  (A7)+,D1
       RTS
```

FIGURE P8.15

a. Before fetching and executing the BSR instruction, what is the content of the program counter?
b. After executing the BSR instruction, what is the content of register A7? Of the program counter?
c. During the execution of the BSR instruction, what is the value of the address pushed onto the system stack?
d. After executing the first instruction in GOSUB, what is the address of the top of the system stack?
e. After executing the instruction at location LAST, what is the address of the top of the system stack?
f. After executing the RTS instruction, what is the address of the next instruction to be executed?

8.16. Determine the hex content of the program counter and the system stack pointer after the execution of each of the following MC68000 instructions. Use the following initial conditions for each of the parts of this problem. Be sure to return to the same initial conditions before answering each part. Assume that the addresses SUB1 and SUB2 have been defined as $001040 and $003000, respectively.

Processor register contents:

(DO) = $0000AAAA (B) = $0000BBBB (PC) = $001000
(A7) = $00002000

Memory location contents:

($002000 = $00 ($002001) = $50
($002002 = $0B ($002003) = $60

Part	*Instruction*
a.	MOVEM D0/D1,−(A7)
b.	BSR SUB1
c.	RTS
d.	JSR SUB1
e.	BSR SUB2
f.	JSR SUB2
g.	MOVEA.L #SUB1,A7

8.17. In an MC68000 system the calling program passes five parameters to the subroutine SUB shown in Figure P8.17 by pushing them onto the stack with the routine PRE as shown.

```
PRE  MOVE   PARAM1,-(A7)
     MOVE   PARAM2,-(A7)
     MOVE   PARAM3,D0
     MOVE   PARAM4,D1
     MOVE   PARAM5,D2
     MOVEM  D0-D2,-(A7)
     JSR    SUB
       .
       .
SUB  MOVE   LENGTH,D0
     MOVE   D0,COUNT
     MOVEA  #ADDR,A1
b.**load D1 with PARAM1 here
     MOVE   D1,(A1)+
     MOVE   D1,-(A7)
c.**load D1 with PARAM2 here
     MOVE   D1,5(A1)
d.**load D1 with PARAM3 here
     CMPI   #500,D1
     BEQ    FINIS
e.**load D1 with PARAM4 here
     ADDQ   #1,D1
     MOVE   D1,(A1)+
f.**load D1 with PARAM5 here
       .
       .
```

FIGURE P8.17

a. Show the order in which the parameters are stacked in the system stack prior to the execution of the JSR instruction.

b. through *f*: For each case, write one instruction to access the necessary parameter at each of the places indicated in the subroutine.

CHAPTER 9

SOFTWARE DEVELOPMENT

At the heart of every computer application is a problem or series of problems which must be solved. The solutions require a certain hardware configuration and certain programs to make that configuration carry out its necessary tasks. This chapter examines some of the general aspects of preparing programs for use in microprocessor systems. The basic elements of programming languages and various classes of languages are described. The more common programming goals are discussed, and specific requirements for microprocessor software are formulated. To meet these requirements, the modern programming technique of structured modular programming is introduced and illustrated. Finally, several software tools which may be of assistance to the programmer are described.

9.1 THE SOFTWARE DEVELOPMENT PROCESS

The first step in preparing a program is to analyze the problem that the program is intended to solve. This requires a careful consideration of the various inputs and the exact outputs which will be required as well as how they are interrelated. No attempt should be made to write a program until the problem is thoroughly understood.

Following the initial analysis, the programmer must carefully consider the interrelationships between the inputs and the outputs to the system and devise a proper and efficient method to be used in solving the problem. A method or approach followed in solving a problem is called an *algorithm*. Like design skills in so many areas, the ability to devise algorithms to solve programming problems is one which is acquired only by a great deal of practice and experience. By following the steps outlined in later sections in this chapter, some of the necessary skill can begin to be developed. However, an introductory book such as this can only provide a starting point. Additional advanced work in this area is necessary in order to become proficient at the task.

Once the algorithm has been devised, the program must be developed. This entails first writing down the algorithm itself in a clear, easily understood format. In this book, the tool used to describe a program algorithm will be the flowchart.

The process of developing the program from the initial flowchart of the algorithm is usually carried out with several goals or criteria in mind. Among these goals are speed of execution, program size, and memory requirements. These goals and others will be discussed in detail later.

After the program has been designed, it must be written out in a programming language. This step is known as *coding* the program, since the algorithm is coded using a programming language as a cipher.

The coded program is then written into a file with the aid of an editor. This form of the program is known as the *source code*. The source code file is submitted to a program which converts it into machine language. The machine language form is known as the *object code*. The conversion may reveal errors in the coding process, in which case it must be repeated until the source program is successfully converted into machine language.

Following this conversion, the program must be run and tested. This step is seldom performed on the final hardware configuration that will be used in the system. Instead, a larger, more powerful computer is often used to simulate the final system. The running and testing of the program should reveal any logical flaws which may be present. These must then be corrected, the program design changed, the modified source program recoded, and the testing process repeated. This procedure is known as *debugging* the program.

The target hardware is often developed and tested separately as much as possible before being mated with the software. When this hardware design process has been completed, the debugged programs are installed in the hardware memory and tested to see that they work properly in the final configuration.

9.2 PROGRAMMING LANGUAGES

Once the algorithm has been designed and developed in sufficient detail it must be expressed in a language which can be translated into machine code for the target computer. Like any other language, a computer language has its own words and rules (its syntax). Different languages have different words and different rules. Computer programming languages also vary in complexity and in intended applications.

Just as natural languages are divided into related groups, so also are computer languages divided into related groups. The criterion used in grouping computer languages is that of closeness to the processor's internal binary language.

The languages which are exactly the internal language of a processor (usually expressed in hex rather than in binary) are called *machine languages*. Those which use mnemonics and shorthand notations to indicate addressing modes but which are still direct implementations of the machine language of a processor are called *assembly languages*. Those which are independent of the processor and which have been designed to solve specific categories of problems are called *higher-level languages*.

9.2.1 Machine Languages

Earlier chapters in this book have described the machine languages of the MC6809 and the MC68000 processors in detail. Other processors have their own machine languages. Some of them are much simpler than these, others are very much more complex. In fact, two major divisions in machine languages are presently developing.

Until recently, the trend since the earliest days of computers has been toward more and more complex programming models and more and more complex machine languages. Gradually, addressing modes have become more powerful and varied, individual machine instructions have been devised to operate on multiple operands, block mode instructions have been introduced, and major higher-level constructs have been implemented directly in machine language. To distinguish these developments from more recent trends, computers designed with these complex machine languages are now known as *Complex Instruction Set Computers* or *CISC*s.

As these more complex trends have developed, processor designers have become aware of the possibility of improving the overall efficiency of the machine by following an opposite approach. In the so-called *Reduced Instruction Set Computers* (*RISC* machines) each of the simpler instructions can be executed in a very short period of time. The elimination of the need for decoding and implementing complex instructions and complex addressing modes has been found to actually speed up the overall operation of the machine in many applications.

In addition to this subdivision based on instruction set complexity, processors are also classified on the basis of their architectural features. Several different types of processors with a variety of architectures have been designed. One type, the so-called stack processor, includes no address with most instructions but instead operates on the top elements of a last in first out stack. Another type, which includes the MC6809, relies heavily upon the use of an accumulator, and most instructions include a single address. Still others, including the MC68000, have no accumulators but instead use arrays of registers and specify operands by register designation. Instructions in these machines often include two register designations or one register and one memory address. Each of these and other choices in the design of a processor results in an entirely different form of machine language.

9.2.2 Assembly Languages

No programmer will ever write programs in machine language except during the initial programming of a new processor, and then only to prepare the basic support tools such as a program to load machine language programs from a file. Probably the closest that a programmer will get to machine language is when writing programs in assembly language. Assembly language is very closely related to the underlying machine language. Corresponding to each of the wide variety of different machine languages is a counterpart assembly language.

All assembly languages require the programmer to be familiar with all of the details of the target processor, including the programming model, instruction set, addressing modes, and stack structure. In addition, the specific assembler program used to translate the assembly language program into machine language will have its own idiosyncrasies. Each has its own specific field delimiters, limitations on label lengths, allowed character set, and so on. Unfortunately, there is no standardization in this arena, not even for different assemblers for the same processors.

The original assemblers for members of a specific family of processors are somewhat similar. Thus, an MC68000 assembler from Motorola will be more similar to an MC6809 assembler from Motorola than it will be to an assembler for an Intel 8085. However, even that similarity may almost disappear when describing assemblers from sources other than the processor manufacturer.

9.2.3 Higher-Level Languages

Higher-level languages have the common characteristic that they are essentially independent of the particular processor to be used. Once one has learned to program in FORTRAN or Pascal or C, or to prepare SPICE programs, one may code programs in these languages and be (somewhat) confident that they will execute in the same fashion on different target computers.

The translation of a higher-level source program into its related object program is generally done with one of two types of special programs or software tools, a *compiler* or an *interpreter.* A compiler creates an object program in machine language for the entire program. This compiled program can then be loaded into the target processor and executed independently of the original source code. An interpreter translates each instruction of the original source code into machine language and then executes it immediately. The object code for that instruction is then abandoned when the next source code instruction is translated. Thus, the interpreter translates the source code one instruction at a time while the program is executing.

Compilers are longer programs than interpreters since they must keep track of the entire program while they are creating the machine code. Interpreters, although they are much slower, normally require only a fraction of the memory. In fact, interpreters were first introduced in order to provide higher-level language capabilities to microcomputers with very limited memory capacity. There are even microprocessors available which include an interpreter program in ROM on the chip (or at least within the package) and thus are able to execute higher-level code directly from memory.

Because the entire program must be recompiled to accommodate any change or addition to it, using a compiler increases the time to develop programs. However, a compiled program executes much faster than an interpreted one since the entire program has already been converted into machine code prior to its execution.

Procedure-oriented languages are higher-level languages which can be used to solve a wide class of problems. The scope of such languages is often the entire spectrum of several professional disciplines. For example, FORTRAN is oriented toward algebraic procedures and finds wide use in scientific and engineering problems. COBOL is oriented toward commercial procedures and is commonly used in solving accounting and administrative problems. LISP and PROLOG are oriented toward symbol processing and are used in creating computer software tools and in artificial intelligence applications.

Problem-oriented languages are higher-level languages that are applied to the solution of a very narrow category of problems. Various problem-oriented languages are aimed at a specific class of problems, such as SPICE for circuit analysis problems or GPSS for the simulation of systems. Problem-oriented languages are often originally written in a procedure-oriented language and then compiled to run on a computer with a specific processor and certain minimum memory and I/O capabilities.

9.3 PROGRAMMING GOALS

Every assembly language program must meet two basic requirements often overlooked by beginners. First of all, the program *must* be *self-starting*. Every register or memory location that requires initialization must be initialized within the program. Every constant required by the program must be part of the program. The only things that the user should be required to furnish are the items of data required by the program.

The second requirement is that the user should be able to rerun the program immediately by simply reloading the program counter with the starting address. The second running of the program (and any subsequent ones) should be identical to the first. The program should modify neither itself nor any necessary values to which it must have access. If a program does not have these characteristics, it is not even an acceptable program. However, in addition to these basics, certain characteristics of programs have been found to be desirable, and certain criteria or goals are commonly held by programmers when preparing programs.

If an amateur programmer is asked to state some common goals in programming the list will probably look like this:

1. A short execution time.
2. A minimal amount of required memory space.

If a professional is asked the same question the list, although it may include the two above, will probably also include:

3. An easy-to-understand program.
4. An easily modifiable program.

Goals number 1 and 2 are the most obvious and seem almost unquestionably to be desirable. However, this often turns out not to be the case, particularly in microprocessor applications.

In the kinds of applications where microprocessor systems are most often used, execution speed is not a common problem. Consider, for example, the electronic engine controller in an automobile. Based upon the throttle setting, engine speed, vehicle speed, oxygen content in the exhaust gas, and coolant temperature, the processor must compute the fuel mixture required. This computation must be performed ten times per second, or once every 100,000 microseconds. The designers of one such system have stated that the microprocessor is already four times as fast as they could ever anticipate having to run.

Consider applications involving the control of household appliances. The microprocessor must make decisions to turn motors or solenoids on and off based upon temperature or physical position information or human input in the form of switch settings. Again, the processor is working in the sub-microsecond time scale to control processes involving a time scale of seconds or hefty fractions of seconds.

Of course many computer applications involve very lengthy and complex computations which stretch the capabilities of the fastest, most powerful supercomputers. However, these are not typical microprocessor applications. In the typical microprocessor control application, speed of execution will seldom be a meaningful programming goal.

The amount of memory occupied by the program seems to be a worthy goal, but consider this carefully. The programs in a typical control system will be in ROM so that the system will be operative when it is first powered up. As mentioned earlier, solid-state memory including ROM comes in modules of certain sizes. Thus, it makes no sense to hold as a major programming goal the reduction of memory space requirements unless it results in the elimination of a memory chip or the possibility of using a smaller-sized and less expensive memory chip.

Even then, unless many copies of the system are to be built, the savings may be illusory. Consider the cost of attempting to reduce the memory space requirements (perhaps several tens of hours of programming time) versus the cost of the ROM saved (perhaps a dollar or so per system). Thus, goal number 2 is not often a useful goal in programming microprocessor systems.

This leaves programming goals number 3 and 4 as the major ones: to write an easy-to-understand program and to write a program which can be easily modified at some future time by someone, not necessarily the original programmer.

With the plummeting hardware costs that have occurred in the past and which seem evident for the near future, the cost of program preparation has become the major component of total system development costs. In fact, at the present time, typical microprocessor system costs break down into about 20 percent for hardware and 80 percent for software. Thus, any programming goal which results in a reduction of current and future programming time is a worthwhile goal. Goals 3 and 4 do just that.

By concentrating on the goal of understandability, the programmer is discouraged from searching for and implementing "elegant" but difficult-to-understand solutions to problems. Making programs and program segments understandable also reduces the time required by the several members of the typical design team to interface their individual contributions.

The goal of an easy-to-modify program (which, of course, requires also that the program be understandable) ensures that any changes can be implemented with a minimum of time and effort on the part of the programmer. One of the major advantages of the use of a microprocessor in control applications is its versatility. This versatility can best be taken advantage of if the programs can be readily changed to account for different specifications or to accommodate new external requirements. Thus, using the same controller with modified programs to control different models of an appliance or engine makes more economic sense if the programs can be easily modified.

The microprocessor programmer is usually the system designer or a member of the system design team, occasionally a mechanical engineer but more often an electrical or computer engineer. That person must develop a systematic, logical approach to programming. Only through such an approach can the programmer consistently devise straightforward, easy-to-understand, easy-to-modify programs with a reasonable expenditure of time and effort.

9.4 FLOWCHARTS

The preparation of a series of *flowcharts* is often one of the earlier steps in programming. Flowcharts are drawings which consist of specifically shaped symbols or blocks which are labeled and interconnected. They are useful tools for picturing the structure of a program.

Figure 9.1 shows the five most commonly-used flowchart symbols and their uses. These symbols are interconnected by arrows which serve to show the order in

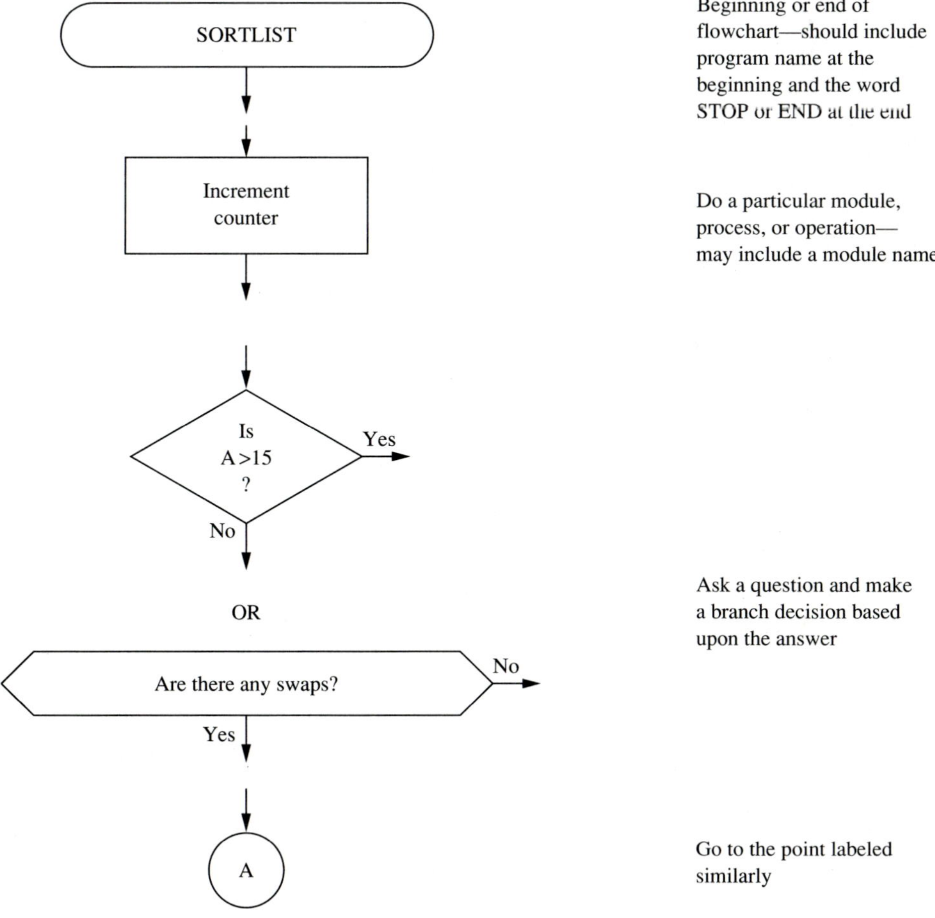

FIGURE 9.1
Flowchart symbols.

which the processes are carried out and the decisions are made. Flowcharts should be restricted to the task of depicting the algorithm or plan of action which the program will follow. They should not include the details of the coding or implementation of the algorithm. These may more readily be understood by referring to the final program listing.

Figure 9.2 is an example of a flowchart showing a program to move a table of numbers. This program was introduced in an earlier chapter as an example of assembly language. The program assumes that the first number in the table is the total number of entries in the table, excluding itself. Thus, in this example program even an empty table is assumed to have one entry, the number 0.

The first block in Figure 9.2, the beginning oval symbol, is labeled with a name for the program, MOVTAB. The same shaped symbol is used to indicate the end of the program, where it is labeled END. The rectangular blocks indicate some procedure or operation. Each of these is labeled with a descriptive name or with sufficient information to identify the process.

It is important not to include details about how the procedures may be implemented. Those details do not belong on a flowchart. For instance, the block labeled "MOVE ONE BYTE" describes a procedure that is self-evident to any proficient assembly language programmer. The actual implementation of this procedure, however, will depend upon the processor used.

If the label does not describe a readily identifiable operation, then it must be expanded in another flowchart on another sheet of paper at a later time. This expansion of procedures into ever more detailed descriptions in successive flowcharts is part of a programming methodology which will be discussed below.

Notice that the flowchart in Figure 9.2 makes no mention of which registers will be used for the pointers and the counter, or even whether registers or memory locations are to be used. These details should be left for when the program is coded.

The primary advantage of a flowchart is that it provides a pictorial representation of the order in which the various steps are carried out. This visual assistance is invaluable to the beginner just learning to program. Although an advanced programmer will often work without the aid of flowcharts, even experts use them to picture unusual algorithms or novel program structures. Until you become an expert or at least very comfortable with programming, you should always start a program by preparing flowcharts in accordance with the recommendations in the following section.

9.5 STRUCTURED MODULAR PROGRAMMING

The key to preparing understandable, easy-to-modify programs lies in a disciplined approach known as *structured modular programming with top-down design and bottom-up implementation*. Although it may sound rather esoteric, the approach is really quite logical and straightforward. Note, however, that it is a *discipline* and that it not only requires that certain kinds of activities and procedures be followed, but that it also restricts the programmer and prohibits certain other activities.

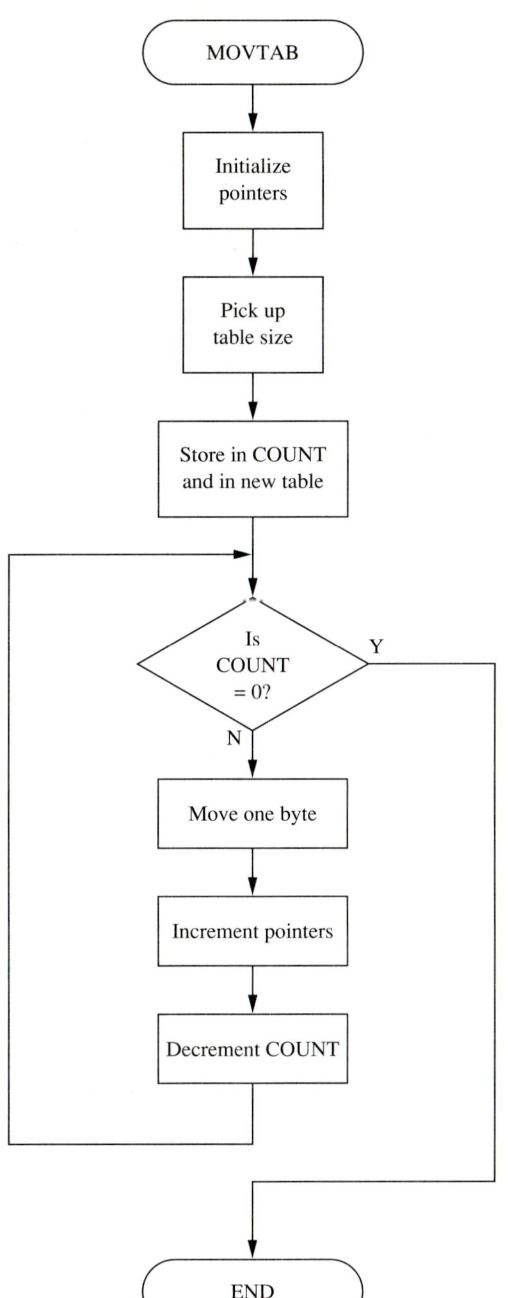

FIGURE 9.2
Flowchart for the program to move a table.

9.5.1 Program Structures

The term *structured programming* means that the flowcharts illustrating an algorithm should contain only basic subunits or structures from a small number of allowed possibilities. The set of allowed structures commonly includes the five shown in Figure 9.3. Although the structures themselves are quite primitive, they can be combined in very complex ways to perform very involved functions in a program.

The LINEAR structure is simply a list of individual operations which are to be done sequentially in a specific order. This is often the form that the initial flowchart for a program will take. That is, the programmer will identify and list by name or function the various steps which must be taken, without concern for the details of how the tasks are to be accomplished. Note that each box showing an individual process has a single line entering it and a single line leaving it. In structured programming, this must be true of every box, every structure, every program segment, and every program.

The second structure, the IF-THEN-ELSE, is a basic decision construction. The rhomboid (or rectangle with pointed ends) represents a test of a condition which may be either true or false. If the condition is true, the "then" operation(s) should take place. If the condition is false, the "else" operation(s) should take place.

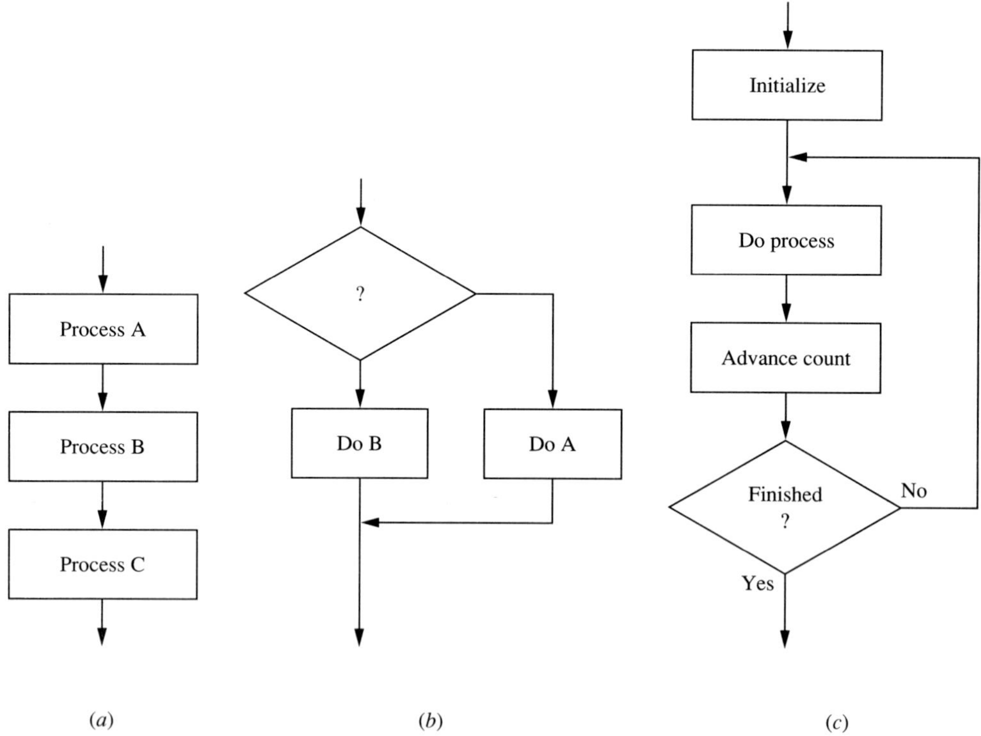

FIGURE 9.3
Basic flowchart structures: (*a*) LINEAR, (*b*) IF-THEN-ELSE, (*c*) DO-UNTIL

The test is often labeled not as a condition, but as a question which has a yes/no answer. A specific example of the IF-THEN-ELSE structure is shown in Figure 9.4 where the condition to be tested is that SPEED is greater than SET. This example implements the structure:

```
IF  SPEED>SET
    THEN  Add 1 to SET
    ELSE  Add 1 to SPEED
```

The condition is shown on the flowchart as the question, "Is SPEED > SET?" with separate branches for the answers "yes" and "no".

Notice that the IF-THEN-ELSE structure has a single entry point and a single exit point. Whatever operations take place along either branch, the two paths must merge into one with no possibility for a branch to some point outside the structure. Having a single entry point and a single exit point is the defining characteristic of each of the structures in structured programming.

The DO-UNTIL and the DO-WHILE are loop structures which allow one or more processes to be repeated a specific number of times. They differ only in the point at which the counting and testing are done. The DO-UNTIL structure performs

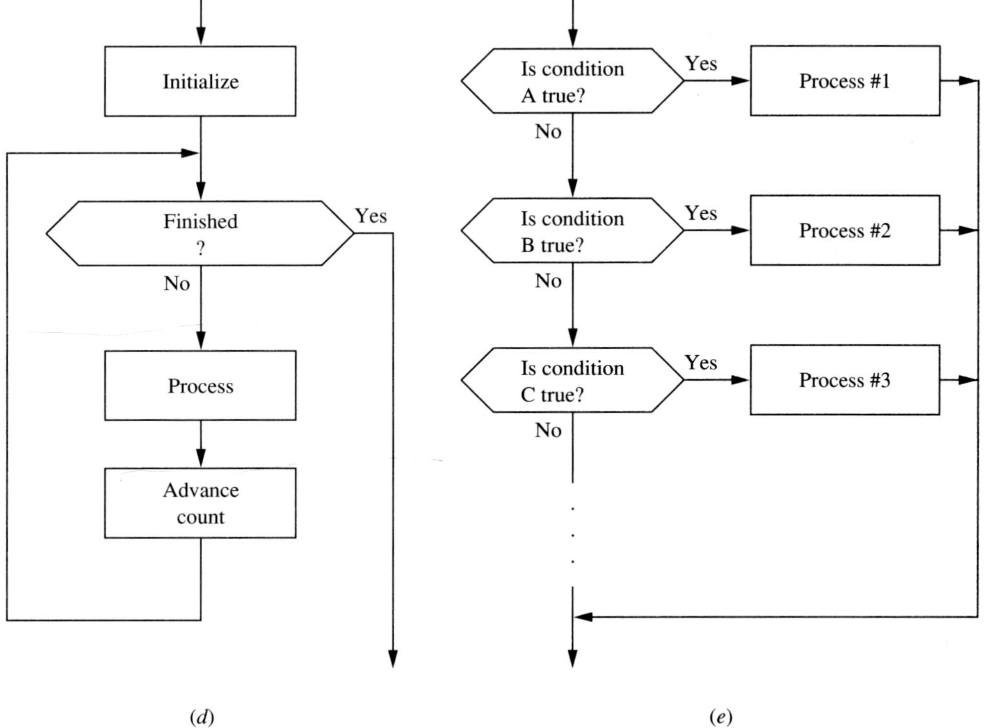

FIGURE 9.3
(*continued*) (*d*) DO-WHILE, (*e*) IN-CASE-OF (PARALLEL PATH).

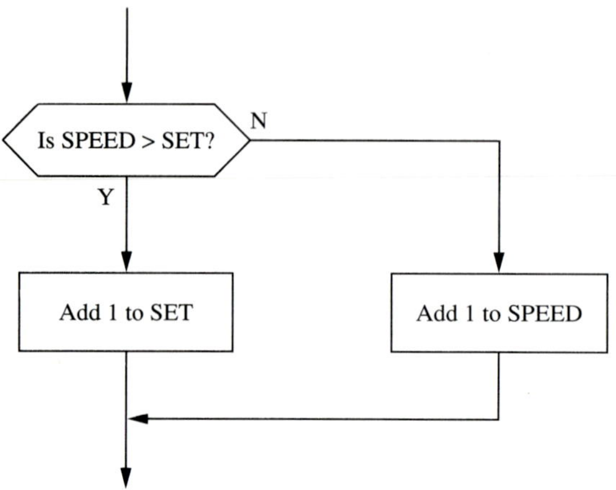

FIGURE 9.4
Example of the IF-THEN-ELSE construct.

the processes and then counts the step and tests the counter. The DO-WHILE structure tests the counter first, and then performs the processes and counts the step prior to returning to repeat the counter test.

The DO-UNTIL approach is commonly used when it is known that the loop will be traversed at least once. It is probably a bit easier to follow in an assembly language program listing, since the counter incrementing and testing take place in adjacent instructions.

The DO-WHILE structure must be used when there is a possibility that under some conditions the loop may not be traversed at all. It is the looping structure which was used in the example flowchart of Figure 9.2. In that example the possibility existed that the table might have been empty and so the loop may not have been traversed at all. Note that the counter was decremented and tested for 0. This is more common in assembly language programming rather than starting at 0 and counting up to a final value. All machine languages have some simple provision for testing for 0. Tests for final values other than 0 are more complex to perform at the machine level.

The DO-UNTIL and DO-WHILE structures may be adapted to test any condition. They are not restricted to testing a counter as shown in these elementary examples. In the DO-UNTIL case the loop will be traversed *until* the condition is true, which implies testing the condition after traversing the loop. In the DO-WHILE case the loop is traversed *while* the condition is true, which implies testing the condition before the loop is traversed. In either structure an operation within the loop itself must change the condition which is being tested. If this is not the case, then when the program is executed the loop will repeat indefinitely and never terminate. A flaw such as this in a program is known as an *infinite loop*.

The final basic structure is known as the IN-CASE-OF or PARALLEL PATH structure. It permits a series of binary tests to be grouped into a screening procedure in order to select one of a set of several possible conditions. Each of the possibilities results in one specific operation (or sequence of operations) being performed. Notice that whichever condition is discovered to be true when it is executed, the structure will always exit to the same point in the program.

Each of the five structures shown earlier in Figure 9.3 has a single entry point and a single exit point. This is the key to structured programming. Since each of the allowed structures has a single entry point and a single exit point, every combination of these structures forming a (sequential) program segment will also have a single entry point and a single exit point. That means that any part of any structured program can be understood as a series of sequential segments. The individual segments may be quite complex and involved, but eventually each will be concluded and the next segment can then take place.

9.5.2 Modular Programming

The term *modular programming* means that the programmer has broken up the overall program into a series of "reasonably-sized" segments or modules, and has then written each module as a separate entity.

The term "reasonably-sized" is an indefinite one. However, in general modules tend to be somewhat small. The resulting coding should seldom require more than about a single page. This usually results in modules which can be readily understood in a single reading. Thus, the primary value of modularity is the segmenting of a complex program into a series of easily understood pieces.

The individual modules are written as subroutines. Each one is written, tested, and debugged independently with no reference to any of the others. The modules are then combined using the main program. The main program is essentially a program segment which accepts outputs from individual modules and provides inputs to others, and calls upon the appropriate modules in the proper order.

It should be emphasized that the modules are written as subroutines regardless of whether they will be called only once or dozens of times. As mentioned earlier, the overhead in program size required for the calling and returning statements does not necessarily translate into higher system costs unless a memory size boundary is crossed. In any case, the overhead is more than compensated for by the ease of modification which accompanies the subroutine structure. Writing the modules as subroutines also has the advantage that they may be used elsewhere in the same or in other system programs if necessary.

9.5.3 Top-Down Design, Bottom-Up Implementation

Top-down design is a process in which the programmer starts with the flowchart equivalent of a block diagram and then expands each block on later diagrams. The first flowchart should merely show the basic steps which must be followed to accomplish the final task. Following this initial outline, each internal "block" in the first flowchart is elaborated upon in successive steps until the individual steps are shown in sufficient detail so as to be readily coded.

This top-down design process is exactly that which is followed in most engineering projects. The first step in any design is to draw a block diagram of the overall structure, which is then progressively developed until the final details are reached. This process is also followed in most projects which have some degree of complexity. Anyone who has ever outlined a report or a speech prior to writing it in detail has used the concept of top-down design.

The initial flowchart is usually a simple linear progression which identifies the basic modules needed to implement the algorithms of the program. A series of successive charts then outlines the details of each of the modules. In this way, the overall structure of the program is shown only roughly while the module details are developed and illustrated in a fashion which is relatively independent of other parts of the program.

Thus, structured modular programming with top-down design requires that the programmer first subdivide the programming task into a nearly linear progression of independent modules. Each of these modules in turn is then shown in more detail on additional flowcharts. If necessary, still other charts are used to develop the finer details of each part of the module. At each step along the way, from the original outline to the finest details, the programmer incorporates only the allowed basic structures into each flowchart. Each of the flowcharts that is generated will show either a large amount of the program in little detail or less of the program in more detail. Therefore, each flowchart should fit on a single page. All of these factors contribute to the understandability of the program.

Bottom-up implementation refers to the process of writing, testing, and debugging the individual modules as subroutines independently of each other. The program is implemented by writing and thoroughly testing the individual modules first (bottom-up). Only after they are working properly are they then tied together with the main calling program.

9.5.4 SORTLIST, A Programming Example

The programming techniques described above will be illustrated by preparing several parts of a program named SORTLIST. This example program is intended to accept a list of unsigned numbers from the user, sort the list into decreasing order, and display the sorted list.

The list, containing up to 255 unsigned 8-bit numbers, will be provided by the user from the console of a computer one 2-digit hex number at a time. The user will terminate the list by entering the letter S. The program is to store the list as it is entered, starting in a memory location named LIST. It is to count the number of entries as the user is providing them and store the length of the list in a memory location named LENGTH.

The list is then to be sorted using a sorting algorithm known as the bubble sort. In this algorithm two adjacent entries in the list are compared; if they are in the incorrect order they are interchanged (swapped) and the interchange is recorded (in a swap recorder). This is repeated for each pair in the list (note that the second entry of a pair is also the first entry of the next pair). After going through the entire list, swapping pairs which are out of order, the swap recorder is tested. If any swaps were recorded, the entire process is repeated. When the entire list can be traversed with no swaps being necessary, the list is sorted.

Figure 9.5 shows an example of the bubble sort algorithm in action. Part (*a*) shows the original list which is to be sorted into ascending order. On the first pass the numbers 25 and 65 are compared and not swapped, and then 65 and 3 are compared and swapped. This swap places 65 down in the list where it is now compared with 92, and no swap is made. The compare/swap process continues (92 with 18, then 92 with 36) until the end of the first pass, when the list is as shown in part (*b*) of Figure 9.5. Notice that at the completion of the first pass, the largest number is at the end of the list, since it was involved in each comparison after it was first encountered.

The second pass results in three swaps and the third, one. After the second and third passes, the list looks like parts (*c*) and (*d*) of Figure 9.5, respectively. The algorithm requires a fourth pass during which no swaps are made since the list is now in order.

The algorithm is named bubble sort because after one pass through the list, at least one correct value will have traversed through the list to the end, somewhat like a bubble rising through a tube of liquid. After two passes, the second value will be in its correct place. After each pass, even if the list is originally in exactly the opposite order, one additional value becomes properly positioned. Of course, several values may be properly positioned as the result of a single pass if the list was originally partially ordered, as in the example of Figure 9.5. This is the reason for testing the swap recorder after each pass through the list.

Figure 9.6 shows the first flowchart of the example program. Notice that it has been subdivided into four primary modules at this stage, INIT, GETLIST, DOSORT, and DISPLAY. The module INIT is used to initialize any I/O devices that require it and to define and set up any special data spaces which may be required by the program. The purpose of GETLIST is to prompt the user to enter the list of values to be sorted and then accept, count, and store the entries. DOSORT sorts the list and DISPLAY displays the sorted list.

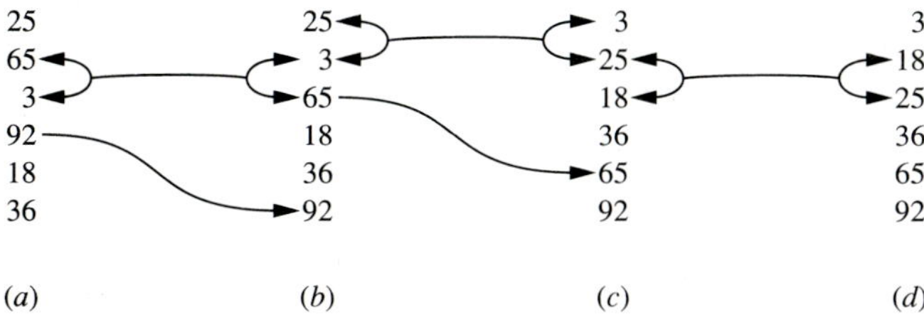

FIGURE 9.5
The Bubble sort algorithm: (*a*) original list, (*b*) first pass, (*c*) second pass, (*d*) third pass.

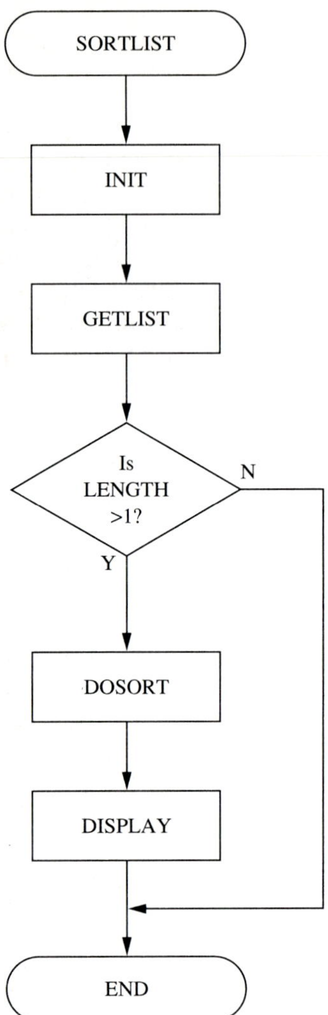

FIGURE 9.6
First flowchart for SORTLIST.

Quite often, the first flowchart of a program is a linear structure. However, in this case, it includes a test of the length of the list. If the list does not include at least two entries, then there is no list to be sorted and the program will terminate.

The next series of charts should develop each of the primary modules in turn. Figure 9.7 illustrates the development of the module DOSORT. Here, a series of initialization steps enters the value of 0 into the swap recorder (SWAPS), the length of the list into a counter (COUNT), and the starting address of the list into a pointer (POINT). Notice that the quantity labeled POINT will probably be an index register or address register in the actual program. In the flowchart its use as a pointer is emphasized by naming it POINT rather than identifying it by its register type or designation.

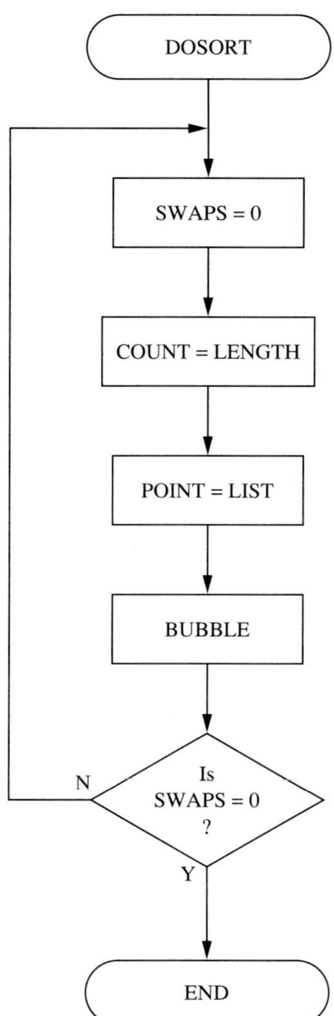

FIGURE 9.7
Flowchart for the module DOSORT.

Following the initialization steps, the module named BUBBLE is called to run through the list comparing pairs and swapping those which are out of order. If the pass through the entire list results in one or more swaps, then the entire DOSORT module will be repeated. If not, DOSORT will terminate and return to the main program, where the primary sequence of modules will continue as shown in Figure 9.6.

At this point, the nature of the BUBBLE module is not obvious, and so it must be clarified in still another more detailed flowchart. This is characteristic of top-down design.

Figure 9.8 shows the details of the module BUBBLE. The module DOSORT initialized COUNT to the number of entries in the list, but the number of pairs to be compared is 1 less than the number of entries. The first step in the module BUBBLE is to decrement the value in COUNT to reflect this observation.

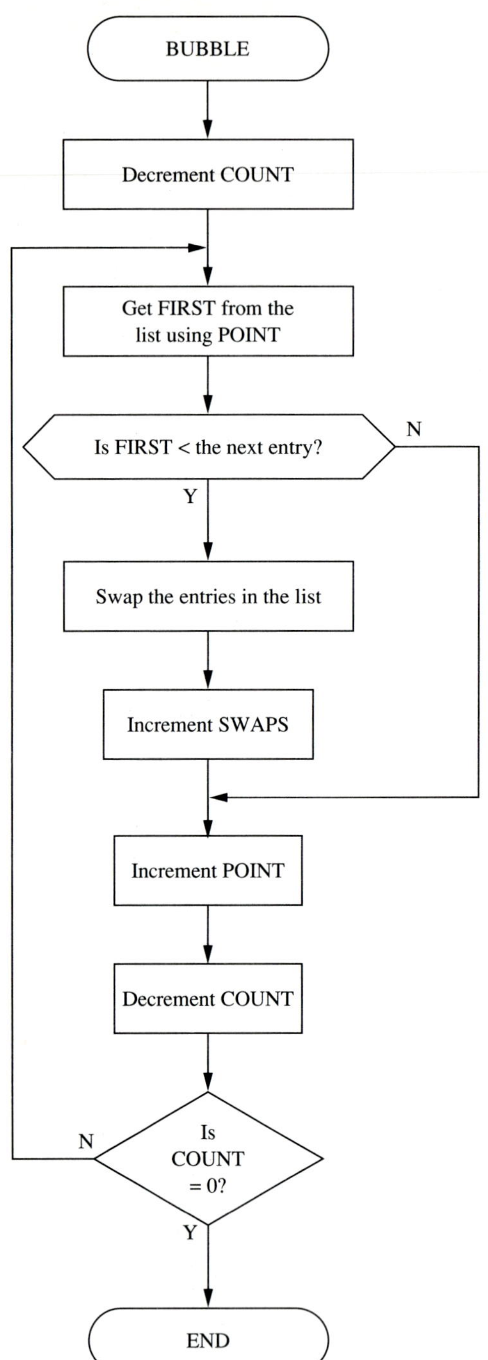

FIGURE 9.8
Flowchart for the Module BUBBLE.

A DO-UNTIL loop then scans through the entries a pair at a time. In this loop, the first of a pair of entries from the list is picked up by the processor (probably in an accumulator or data register). This entry is here labeled FIRST. The value of FIRST is compared to the value of the next entry on the list. Whenever a pair of entries is found to be out of order, they are interchanged in the list.

Notice that the way in which POINT is to be used to pick up the first entry and compare it to the next while leaving the value in POINT unchanged is not explicitly shown here. These kinds of details depend upon the capabilities of the processor which will run the program and upon how the programmer wishes to code the operations.

The interchange decision is carried out in an IF-THEN-ELSE structure imbedded in the middle of the loop, as shown in the flowchart of Figure 9.8. The IF condition is stated in the form of the question "Is FIRST $<$ the next entry?". This question must be considered very carefully. If the question were posed as "Is FIRST $>$ the next entry?" the result would be a possible infinite loop. The problem is that an answer of "No" in the latter case would require swapping the entries, even if they were equal. If equal entries were to be swapped, then whenever the list contained equal entries, a swap would occur at each pass through the list and BUBBLE would never terminate. A valid alternative way to pose the question would be to ask "Is FIRST $>$ or $=$ to the next entry?" Neither that form nor the one shown in the flowchart will result in an infinite loop.

Notice that the IF-THEN-ELSE structure is actually a single process inside the DO-UNTIL loop. It could have been shown by a process block labeled something like "Test a pair and swap and record if necessary". However, that would have then required one more level of top-down expansion. Since the process in question is a single basic structure, it was drawn in detail at its first appearance rather than being shown as a process first and then later developed into its detailed form. This procedure saves time and paper and does not lead to confusion where the expansion is obvious and consists of little more than one of the basic structures.

After comparing a pair of values and, if necessary, swapping the entries in the list and recording the swap, the pointer is incremented to point to the next entry in the list. The standard DO-UNTIL loop then continues with the process of decrementing and testing the counter. If the counter is not yet equal to 0 then another pair is tested. When the entire list has been traversed, the module BUBBLE terminates and the program returns to the module DOSORT.

When preparing flowcharts it is good practice to avoid reference to individual memory locations by number or to registers from the programming model of the processor which will be used to implement the program. The presence of this sort of information in flowcharts serves only to distract the reader from understanding the procedures which are being followed to implement the programmer's solution. Only when coding the program should one need to be concerned with these kinds of details. Thus, in this example, the first entry of each pair is referred to as FIRST rather than as a register content (which it may well be).

The remaining primary modules, INIT, GETLIST, and DISPLAY must now also be developed in detail. The procedure to be followed is similar to that used here with

DOSORT and BUBBLE. The major steps must first be identified and the details filled in to the point where the modules may be readily coded into the language of the processor. The charting and coding of these modules will be left for an exercise.

The parts of the program which have been developed above (modules DOSORT and BUBBLE) are now sufficiently detailed to be coded. They are coded below in assembly language. Figure 9.9 shows the coding for the MC6809 and Figure 9.10 shows the coding for the MC68000. The MC6809 coding is for a list of bytes in memory, while that for the MC68000 assumes a list of words (double-bytes). Most of the comments are the procedure labels from the corresponding operations in the flowcharts in order to make it easier to correlate the listings with the flowcharts.

Each symbolic label in the listings which refers to a memory location must be defined somewhere in the program. These definitions may be included in the main program or in the modules themselves. Here, the assumption is that the locations have all been appropriately defined in the main program.

Notice that the test and branch just before the location DOSWAP in the module BUBBLE is implemented with the single instruction, branch if higher or the same (BHS), in the MC6809 code. This instruction is not available in the MC68000 and so the branch in the MC68000 code is implemented with two instructions, branch if higher (BHI) and branch if equal (BEQ).

```
*
*MODULES DOSORT AND BUBBLE CODED IN MC6809 ASSEMBLY LANGUAGE
*
    DOSORT   CLR  SWAPS     SWAPS = 0
             LDA  LENGTH
             STA  COUNT     COUNT = LENGTH
             LDX  #LIST     X IS USED FOR THE POINTER
             BSR  BUBBLE
             TST  SWAPS     IS SWAPS = 0?
             BNE  DOSORT    NO, GO BACK AND REPEAT DOSORT
    SORTEND  RTS            YES,RETURN
*
*
    BUBBLE   DEC  COUNT     NO OF PAIRS IS LENGTH - 1
    BUBLOOP  LDA  ,X        GET FIRST (A) FROM LIST
             CMPA 1,X       IS FIRST < THE NEXT ENTRY?
             BHS  AROUND    NO, GO AROUND
    DOSWAP   LDB  1,X       YES, SWAP AND RECORD
             STA  1,X       SWAP THE ENTRIES IN THE LIST
             STB  ,X
             INC  SWAPS     INCREMENT SWAPS
    AROUND   LEAX 1,X       INCREMENT POINT
             DEC  COUNT     DECREMENT COUNT; FINISHED?
             BNE  BUBLOOP   NO, GO BACK AGAIN
    BUBEND   RTS            YES, RETURN
```

FIGURE 9.9
MC6809 assembly language coding of example modules.

```
*
*MODULES DOSORT AND BUBBLE CODED IN MC68000 ASSEMBLY LANGUAGE
*
  DOSORT    MOVEQ  #0,D0        USE D0 FOR SWAPS (= 0)
            MOVE   LENGTH,D1    USE D1 FOR COUNT
            MOVEA  #LIST,A0     A0 IS USED FOR THE POINTER
            BSR    BUBBLE
            TST    D0           IS SWAPS = 0?
            BNE    DOSORT       NO, GO BACK AND REPEAT DOSORT
  SORTEND   RTS                 YES, RETURN
*
*
  BUBBLE    SUBQ   #1,D1        NO OF PAIRS IS LENGTH - 1
  BUBLOOP   MOVE   (A0),D2      GET FIRST FROM LIST INTO D2
            CMP    2(A0),D2     IS FIRST < THE NEXT ENTRY?
            BHI    AROUND       NO, GO AROUND
            BEQ    AROUND       NO, GO AROUND
  DOSWAP    MOVE   2(A0),D3     YES, SWAP AND RECORD
            MOVE   D2,2(A0)     SWAP THE ENTRIES IN THE LIST
            MOVE   D3,(A0)
            ADDQ   1,D0         INCREMENT SWAPS
  AROUND    ADDQ   #2,A0        INCREMENT POINT
            SUBQ   #1,D1        DECREMENT COUNT; FINISHED?
            BNE    BUBLOOP      NO, GO BACK AGAIN
  BUBEND    RTS                 YES, RETURN
```

FIGURE 9.10
MC68000 assembly language coding of example modules.

Because of the possibility of interactions between modules, it is more common to complete the detailed flow charting of the entire program before starting to code the modules. The coding of the module DOSORT was done out of order here only because the detailed structure of the remaining modules (INIT, GETLIST, and DISPLAY) has been left as an exercise.

9.6 PROGRAMMING TOOLS

The programmer must be familiar with the basic tools for program preparation. These include editors, assemblers, and compilers. The remaining sections of this chapter describe some of their basic features. A later chapter specifically addressing system design provides a more detailed discussion of these and other important development tools.

9.6.1 Text Editors

Editors are used by the programmer to write the source program into a file which can be read by the computer in preparation for converting it into machine code. The three basic types of editors are line editors, screen editors, and word processors.

Line editors are the simplest of the three. They allow the user to manipulate the symbols on one line of text at a time. Once the user has entered that line into the file, it is not readily available for further manipulation. In order to modify a line, the user must recall that line to the program's working memory space. Line editors are very simple, small, and inexpensive. However, they are seldom used because of their severe limitations.

A screen editor, as opposed to a line editor, provides the user ready access to the entire document. Any part of the file which is displayed on the screen may be easily accessed for manipulation and any part of the document may be readily displayed on the screen. Screen editors use a *cursor* or highlighted block to indicate the location on the screen which is currently available for modification. Special cursor keys move the cursor to a desired location where a new character may be inserted or an old one modified or removed. The screen editor is the most popular type for use in creating source program files. It is much more efficient to use than a line editor and is not as complex as a word processor.

Word processors provide a much greater capability for character manipulation than is needed to prepare program source files. Not only do they support the typical screen editing functions, but they also allow easy font changes, justification capabilities, equation creation, graphics capabilities, footnotes, automatic pagination, hyphenations, and so forth. Most of these functions are not required when preparing source code files, and their presence can be distracting. However, if the programmer is familiar with a specific word processor, it can be a very handy tool to use in preparing source files. When using a word processor the ASCII file output designation must be selected in order that the output may be properly interpreted by the assembler or compiler.

9.6.2 Assemblers and Compilers

In order for a processor to execute any program, it is necessary that the program be represented in binary machine language as a so-called object program. The translation of the original source program into this object program is precisely the sort of process which a computer is particularly well suited to handle. Programs are available to perform this translation for the programmer. If the source program is written in some higher-level language such as FORTRAN or Pascal, then the translation program is called a *compiler*. If the programmer uses assembly language, then the translation program is called an *assembler*.

An assembler or compiler is written for a specific target processor and may not be used with any other processor. However, compilers written for different processors are essentially identical as far as the programmer/user is concerned. It is only necessary that the source program be properly written in the higher-level language with correct syntax and grammar. The compiler itself takes care of all of the details of the target programming model and the final machine language.

Assemblers, on the other hand, require that the programmer be familiar not only with the assembly language of the object program, but also with the specific assembler being used. Unlike compilers, assemblers differ somewhat in their own control statements or assembler directives. They also differ in the types of designations used for constants. In other words, two different assemblers for the same processor may use different directives and/or different constant designations. For example, the directive to include ASCII codes in a list may use the mnemonic FCC (Form Constant Characters) in one assembler, while another assembler may use the mnemonic ASCII, and still another may use the mnemonic FCB (Form Constant Bytes) with a special symbol to indicate that the bytes are to be ASCII codes for a list of characters. Thus, before coding an assembly language program the programmer must become familiar with these kinds of details for the specific assembler which will be used.

The example programs in this chapter as well as those described in the review problems should be prepared with an editor and assembled and run on whatever type of system you have available.

SUMMARY

Regardless of the language used to code a program, certain basic steps may be followed to ensure that the end result will be an easy-to-understand, easy-to-modify program. These steps are summarized in the disciplined approach to programming known as structured modular programming with top-down design and bottom-up implementation. This approach to programming was described in this chapter and exemplified by the design of several modules for a program to sort a list of numbers.

The basic distinctions between the classes of programming languages were discussed and the process of writing programs was described. Finally, some of the basic features of several software development tools were examined.

REVIEW PROBLEMS

For each of the following problems, draw the necessary flowcharts and code the program in assembly language. Try to assemble and run or simulate them on a computer.

9.1. Write a program to build a table of numbers in memory. The table should start at an address named TABST and extend over a total of NUMB locations, and should consist of odd integers in numerical order.

9.2. Expand the module GETLIST as described in Section 9.5.4. Include any "user-friendly" features such as prompts and other messages. Code it into a form corresponding to the I/O capabilities of the system you have available to use. If that system is the ASSYM09 software, use the special SWI monitor features.

9.3. Repeat problem 9.2 for the module DISPLAY.

9.4. The bubble sort routine as it is described in the example of Section 9.4 is inefficient in that the routine always scans the entire list even though it is known to be partially sorted after several scans. Modify the routine to take advantage of the known progress that it is continually making as it runs. For example, after the first pass the last pair needn't be checked, after the second pass the last two pairs needn't be checked, and so on.

9.5. The suggested modification of problem 9.4 may be further improved upon if the algorithm includes a method of keeping track of how many pairs at the end of the list are already in correct order as the program progresses. With this improvement, the terminating of each pass is modified to account for partial sorting which may have been present in the list originally. Modify the algorithm to include this sort of determination.

9.6. Write a program to determine the following single byte quantities for a list of 255 or less signed 2's complement integers:

a. The sum of all of the positive values on the list. Name it PSUM. If PSUM overflows, set a flag byte named POV to FF, otherwise clear POV.
b. The sum of all of the negative values on the list. Name it NSUM. If NSUM overflows, set a flag byte named NOV to FF, otherwise clear NOV.
c. The maximum value on the list. Name it PMAX. If there are no positive values on the list, set this value equal to 00.
d. The minimum value on the list. Name it NMAX. If there are no negative values on the list, set this value equal to 00.

The program should include input and output routines. Enter the list with the list length in the first byte. The input routine should prompt the user and the output routine should label the quantities.

9.7. Repeat problem 9.6 but calculate the values OSUM, ESUM, OOV, EOV, NODD, and NEVN. These are defined as follows: OSUM is the sum of all of the odd numbers with OOV as the overflow flag. ESUM is the sum of all of the even numbers with EOV its overflow flag. NODD and NEVN are the number of odd and even numbers on the list, respectively.

9.8. Write a program which will scan a section of memory starting at a location named START and ending at a location named STOP. The program should count the number of times that the number VALUE appears in that section of memory. The counting should be in a multi-precision form in order to accommodate any possible value for the processor used. The program should include input and output routines and a test for START being less than STOP.

9.9. Write a program which will scan a list of numbers and count the number of entries in the list which have a 1 in bit position number N. First write a program which will work for a specific value of N (0-7 or 0-15) provided by the user and then rewrite the program to count for all values of N during one pass. In the second program store the results in locations named BITN for N = 0 through 7 (or 15). The programs should prompt the user for input and display the output.

9.10. Write a program to accept a series of single-digit decimal numbers from the user and display the running sum in decimal until the value exceeds 99. At this point prompt the user to rerun or terminate the program.

9.11. Repeat problem 9.10 for inputs of two-digit decimal numbers with the display running up to 999.

9.12. Write a program which will accept two unsigned two-digit BCD integers from the user and calculate and display the decimal difference (including the correct sign). To subtract a BCD number in the MC6809 you must add its *10's complement*. The 10's complement of a two-digit decimal number is found by subtracting it from 99 and then adding 1. The subtraction may be carried out in hex since no borrow is ever necessary. However, the addition of the 1 must be followed by a decimal adjust instruction. After calculating the 10's complement of the subtrahend, it must be added to the minuend (also using the decimal adjust). If you implement this program on the MC68000, you may use the BCD subtract instruction.

9.13. Write a program to accept a two-digit unsigned BCD dividend and a 1-bit unsigned BCD divisor from the user, and calculate and display the decimal quotient and remainder. The program should then prompt the user to rerun or terminate the program.

9.14. Write a program to convert a list of unsigned two-digit hex integers into their BCD equivalents. The program should prompt the user for the list and test each entry to see that it is less than $64 (decimal 100). Values equaling or exceeding this should be rejected. The input module should count the number of entries in the list.

9.15. Write a program consisting of three modules LIST, NSUM, and DSPL together with a main program BUSY. The modules should modify no registers. The module LIST should store the BCD integers 1 through 30 in memory starting at a location named BCD. The module NSUM is to receive a value of N from BUSY in the system stack, add every Nth number stored in the list and return a double-precision decimal sum in the system stack. BUSY is to initialize the system (including the stack), call LIST once, and then call NSUM 15 times to calculate the sums for each value of N from 1 through 15. BUSY should then call DSPL to display the results in a meaningful (labeled) format.

CHAPTER 10

INPUT/OUTPUT STRUCTURES

The input/output (I/O) section of a computer handles the transfer of information between the computer and the devices which communicate with the outside world. The input and output directions are from the point of view of the computer. Output flows from the computer to the devices; input flows from the devices to the computer. The devices, called *peripheral devices* or *peripherals*, include such things as keyboards, switches, display lamps, character displays, cathode ray tube displays, pen plotters, teleprinters, analog-to-digital (A/D) converters, digital-to-analog (D/A) converters, solenoids, motor starters, and the like.

Peripheral devices are connected to the processor through special electronic circuits known as *interfaces*, as shown in Figure 10.1. These circuits access a selected peripheral and take care of any special timing requirements or signal level adjustments which may be necessary.

Both data and control information must be transferred between the computer and a peripheral. Data comprises the bits which encode the pattern to be displayed, the key which was pressed, the character to be printed, the lights to be lit, and so forth. Control signals keep the computer informed as to the status or availability of the peripheral and the timing of events concerning the peripheral. They also initiate certain specific controlled activities in the peripheral such as turning on a drive motor or lifting a pen. Control also refers to the function of ensuring that the data has been properly transferred. Thus, control information includes acknowledgement signals which may travel in either direction.

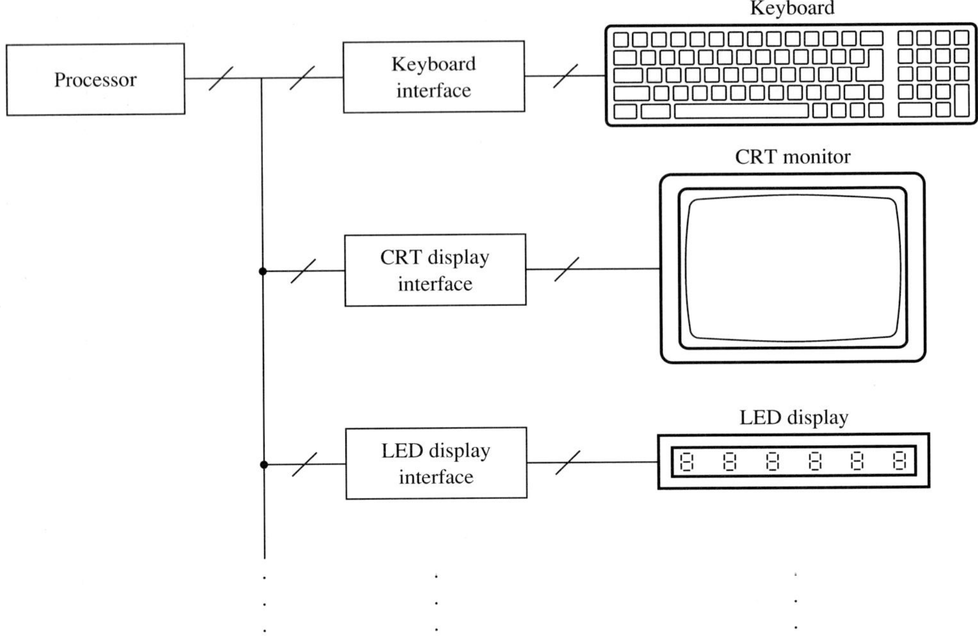

FIGURE 10.1
Interfacing with peripherals

10.1 ACCESSING I/O

The processor may access the interface circuits associated with a particular peripheral using either of two basic methods. The first method, which must be designed into the processor, is known as *special I/O* (sometimes referred as *I/O-mapped I/O*). The other method, which requires no special considerations in the processor, is called *memory-mapped I/O*.

10.1.1 Special I/O

Special I/O refers to a configuration in which the I/O circuitry has its own address space separate from that of memory. The interface circuits are accessed by special I/O instructions. These instructions are intended specifically for I/O operations and they refer to the special I/O address space. Special I/O must be designed into the processor, since it requires, among other things, that the special instructions must be a part of the instruction set for the processor.

The number of I/O locations in any computer system is very much smaller than the number of memory locations, so the I/O address space is always smaller than the memory address space. It is quite common for the I/O address bus to be a subset of the memory address bus. In 8-bit microprocessors which implement special I/O, bits

0 through 7 of the address bus serve both memory and I/O, while the remaining bits are used in memory accesses only.

The byte (or in some cases integral multiples of it) is the common block of information transferred in an I/O instruction. An 8-bit microprocessor can readily accommodate this with its data bus. A 16-bit processor may transfer 16 bits at a time or, alternatively, may transfer a single byte at a time on the lower-ordered eight bits of its data bus.

As a consequence of the limited space on microprocessor chips, only very simple instructions are available to support special I/O. These commonly include only such operations as "input a byte from device number *N* to an accumulator" or "output a byte from an accumulator to device number *N*". In these examples *N* would be the I/O space address of the interface circuit.

A microprocessor which implements special I/O must devote one of its pins to a signal which identifies whether the current bus cycle is for the I/O space or for the memory space. Thus, a logic level of 1 on the pin may mean that the address and data on the bus are to be used for a transfer to/from memory, while a logic level of 0 would mean that the data bus and the lower bits of the address bus are to be used for an I/O transfer.

A typical special I/O system is shown in Figure 10.2. In order to simplify the diagram, the control line MEM/$\overline{\text{I/O}}$ is decoded into two separate control lines, MEM and I/O, which serve to separate the two address spaces. Note that memory and interface circuits each require the control line labeled R/$\overline{\text{W}}$ in order to establish the direction of information transfer.

The MC6809 and the MC68000 do not use special I/O. They have neither I/O instructions nor a separate I/O address space, nor do they generate I/O-memory

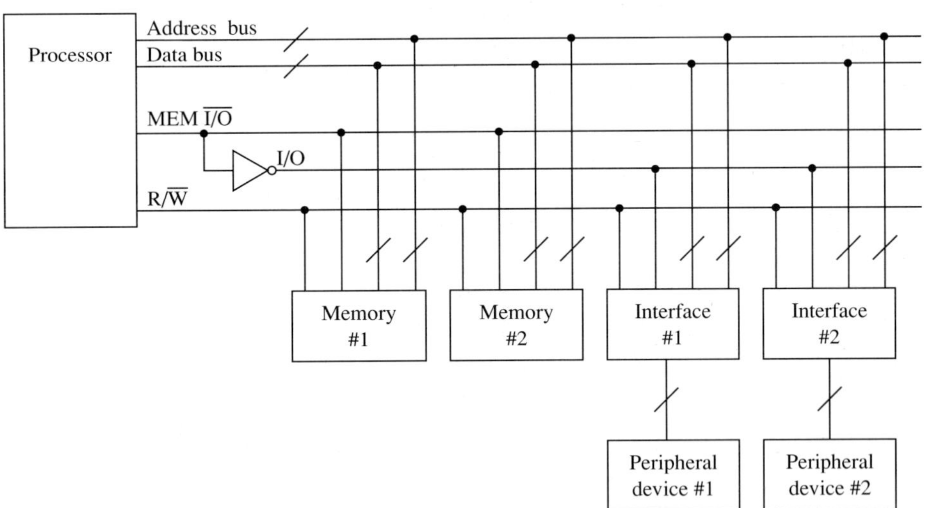

FIGURE 10.2
Special I/O.

control signals. Instead, systems based on either of these processors must use *memory-mapped I/O*.

10.1.2 Memory-Mapped I/O

Whether a processor includes provisions for special I/O or not, an alternative way for it to access the I/O interface circuits is by including them in the system in exactly the same way that memory is included. In that case, the I/O circuits share the single address space of the processor with the memory devices. This approach, known as memory-mapped I/O, is illustrated in Figure 10.3.

Since the interface circuits look exactly like memory locations to the processor, any of the regular instructions which operate upon the contents of memory locations can be brought to bear upon the I/O devices. All of the rich and varied memory reference operations and addressing modes are available for use in I/O instructions. This is a major advantage of memory-mapped I/O over that of special I/O with its limited instruction set.

A disadvantage of memory-mapped I/O is that the interface circuits occupy a portion of the common address space which would ordinarily be available for memory. Even though there may be only a few I/O devices in a system, memory comes in fairly sizable modules, on the order of 1024 or more bytes per chip. As a consequence, even one or two I/O interface locations in a memory-mapped system will displace at least 1024 memory locations. However, control applications which use 8- or 16-bit processors usually have more than enough memory space available to provide for memory-mapped I/O.

Note that any processor may implement memory-mapped I/O. Addresses associated with I/O devices need only be decoded in the hardware to access the associated

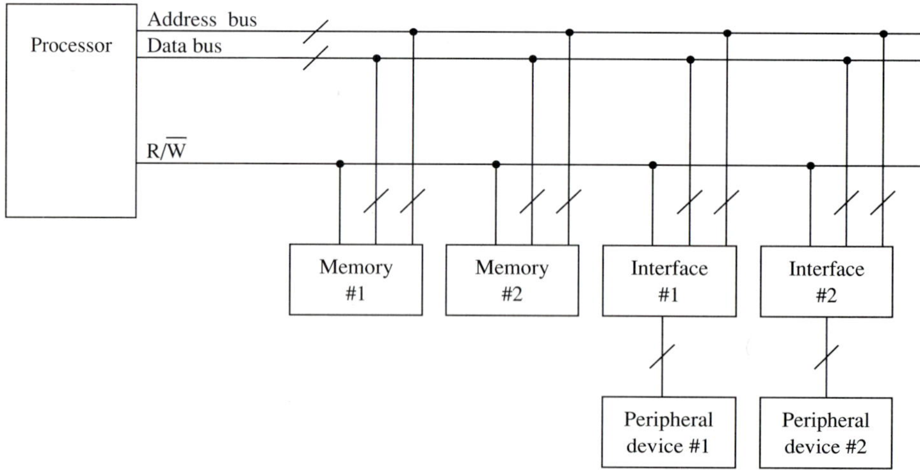

FIGURE 10.3
Memory-mapped I/O.

interface circuitry rather than memory devices. It is not uncommon to use memory-mapped I/O even with processors which have special I/O available. When there is a choice to be made, the usual deciding factor is the need for memory space. If it leaves sufficient memory space for the system program needs, the memory-mapped approach will often be selected in order to allow the use of the entire instruction set for I/O. On the other hand, when the system memory requirements preclude using memory-mapped I/O, special I/O provides a good fallback approach if it is available.

Programming examples in this chapter assume memory-mapped I/O. Instructions such as LDA $1234, CLR $5678 or MOVE D0,$123456 may be ordinary memory reference instructions or they may be I/O instructions. To distinguish the latter, we will use symbolic addresses such as KBD1 or CRT2 to identify the device and register number in the interface. The above examples might be written as LDA KBD1, CLR CRT2, or MOVE D0,CRT3. Comments and meaningful labels such as these are the only means of identifying I/O instructions in a system with memory-mapped I/O.

10.2 INITIATION AND CONTROL OF I/O

Both the processor and the peripheral device (through its interface circuitry) are involved in the transfer of I/O data and control information. Several alternatives have been devised for initiating and controlling the transfer. The alternatives differ in the relative involvement of the processor and the interface, and in which part of the system initiates the transfer and which part controls the transfer.

10.2.1 Programmed I/O

In *programmed I/O* the processor, by executing program instructions, both initiates and controls the transfer of information. The program tells the peripheral interface exactly what to do and when to do it. Lighting up a pattern on an LED display may be accomplished by a pair of instructions such as LDA #PTRN and STA DSPL (or the single instruction MOVE #PTRN,DSPL), where PTRN is the binary pattern to be sent to the display interface and DSPL is the address of the interface. These instructions could be included in the program wherever the programmer decides that it is appropriate to do so.

In some cases, it may be necessary to test the peripheral to determine whether it is ready to communicate. If so, the program will perform the test with a simple procedure called a *polling loop*. The processor fetches a byte from the interface and tests a bit in it. If the result of this test indicates that the peripheral is not ready for data transfer, then the program loops back to repeat the fetch and test (polling) sequence. The polling continues until the peripheral is ready to transfer data. At that time the program proceeds with the data transfer operation.

The polling process is necessary when programmed I/O is used with a peripheral such as a keyboard which must wait for an external operation to take place or for a device such as a printing mechanism, which may require some time to complete a previous I/O operation.

Examples of polling loops for a keyboard are shown in Figure 10.4. KBST is the symbolic address for a status register associated with the keyboard. The interface has been designed so that bit 7 (the sign bit) in this register will become a 1 whenever a new key is pushed. At the same time, the code associated with the key will be put into the interface register whose symbolic address is KCOD. Lines 2 and 3 repeatedly fetch the status byte from KBST and test bit 7. As long as bit 7 is a 0 the program will loop back to line 2. When a key is pushed and bit 7 becomes a 1, the program continues to line 4, where the value from the key code register is loaded into the processor for further processing.

Of the three methods described here for initiating and controlling the transfer of information between the computer and its peripherals, programmed I/O is the slowest. However, it is the best approach to use if it is fast enough to meet the system requirements, since it requires the least amount of interface logic to implement. With this method, the programmer has complete control over the entire process. As a consequence, it is also the easiest method to test and debug. Whenever it can keep up with the application at hand, programmed I/O should be the first method of choice.

10.2.2 Interrupt I/O

Notice in the example programs in Figure 10.4 that the processor may spend a large part of its time waiting for a key to be pushed. This is a consequence of programmed I/O when dealing with peripherals which may not always be ready for data transfer. If the peripheral is not ready for data transfer when the program is, then the processor must wait in a loop of this sort. In systems with several peripherals of this type, the time spent waiting in these loops is often not tolerable. There may be other, more important things which the processor should be doing rather than waiting for peripherals. In such cases, an alternative is to use *interrupt I/O*.

With interrupt I/O the peripheral initiates the transfer of data. It does this by signaling its readiness on a special input to the processor called an interrupt request line. This action normally occurs while the processor is executing a program. Thus,

```
1.*MC6809 POLLING LOOP EXAMPLE
2.  TEST  LDA   KBST     KBST IS THE KBD STATUS REGISTER
3.        BPL   TEST     BIT 7 = 1 WHEN KEY IS PUSHED
4.  PSHD  LDA   KCOD     KCOD CONTAINS THE KEYCODE
5.         .             DO SOMETHING WITH KEYCODE
           .
           .

1.*MC68000 POLLING LOOP EXAMPLE
2.  TEST  BTST
3.        BEQ   TEST     BIT 7 = 1 WHEN KEY IS PUSHED
4.  PSHD  MOVE  KCOD,D0  KCOD CONTAINS THE KEYCODE
5.         .             DO SOMETHING WITH THE KEYCODE
           .
           .
```

FIGURE 10.4
Keyboard polling loops.

the processor needn't wait until the peripheral is ready for data transfer. Instead, it can be doing some productive work until the peripheral signals that it is ready for service.

The interrupt process is illustrated in Figure 10.5. The interrupt is indicated by the IRQ (Interrupt ReQuest) signal coming in from outside of the processor while it is executing the main program sequence at point A.

The processor responds to the interrupt request by completing the execution of the current instruction and saving information concerning the status of the current program on the stack. Included in this information must be at least the content of the program counter so that the processor will know where to return after completion of the I/O operation.

The processor then turns off the interrupt system so that it can execute instructions with no additional interrupt occurring. Then it branches to the beginning of a special program segment called an interrupt service routine. This is shown in Figure 10.5 as point X. The interrupt service routine transfers the data or otherwise services the peripheral in accordance with its needs. Upon the completion of the service routine at point Y, the processor restores the status which was saved, turns the interrupt system back on, and resumes its execution of the main program.

As shown in Figure 10.5, the interrupt could occur at any point in the program, perhaps at point B instead of point A. The process is the same. The interrupt service routine would be executed in exactly the same fashion. The only difference is that the return address which is saved in the stack when the processor responds to the interrupt would be for the location at point B rather than for that at point A.

Note the similarity of the interrupt process to a subroutine as shown earlier in Figure 8.1. In each case, the execution of the main program is temporarily suspended while an auxiliary routine is executed, the return address is saved on the stack during the execution of the auxiliary routine, and execution along the main program sequence is resumed once the auxiliary routine is completed. The primary difference is that the interrupt may occur at any unpredictable time whereas the subroutine call is under the complete control of the programmer.

Because of the elimination of the polling loops, interrupt I/O is faster than programmed I/O. However, the complexity of the system and the difficulty of debugging programs which may be interrupted at any point should encourage a system designer to

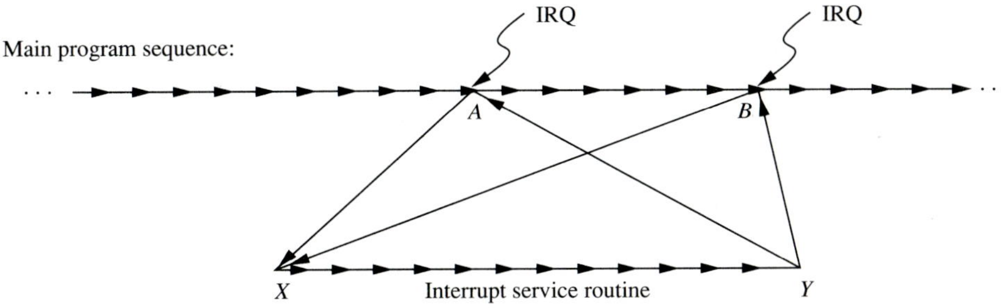

FIGURE 10.5
Interrupt I/O.

avoid using this approach unless the time savings warrant it. A wide variety of interrupt support structures, both hardware and software, exist in microprocessors. Many of these will be discussed in a later chapter of this book.

With programmed I/O the transfer of information is both initiated and controlled by the program. With interrupt I/O, the peripheral initiates the transfer and the program (through the interrupt service routine) controls the transfer. Program control of the transfer of information means that the processor must fetch and execute instructions in order to carry out the transfer. The next approach to be described relieves the processor of this duty and achieves the maximum data transfer rate possible.

10.2.3 Direct Memory Access

The absolute maximum I/O transfer rate for a given system occurs when the memory is accessed at every cycle and a word is transferred at each access. This corresponds to a transfer rate of one word per memory cycle time. This rate cannot be achieved when the transfer is under program control because the instructions to transfer the data must also be fetched during memory cycles. In the MC6809, for example, the shortest time to transfer a single byte of data under program control is the time it takes to fetch and execute two instructions, a load instruction and a store instruction. This takes at least four memory cycles using the shortest possible forms of these instructions. In this case the maximum transfer rate with programmed control is only one-fourth of the theoretical maximum. The data transfer rate in the MC68000 using the MOVE instruction is one byte in 4 to 12 memory cycles, depending on the operand size and the addressing mode used.

The maximum data transfer rate can be achieved only by removing the processor from the system and transferring data directly between the peripheral (through its interface) and memory. This technique is known as *direct memory access* or *DMA*. It requires a complex interface and a certain amount of initialization time. As a consequence, it is used only when large blocks of data must be transferred in the shortest possible time. Examples of peripherals which may use DMA are video displays and disks.

With DMA the peripheral device initiates the transfer by signaling the processor that it wishes to take over control of the address and data buses. This signaling takes place over a special line called a bus request or a DMA request line. When the processor reaches a place in its sequence where it can do so, it will cease fetching and executing instructions. It will then release control of the bus lines and signal the peripheral that it may now use them. The peripheral (through its interface) takes over the buses, placing the required address and data on them and controlling the transfer directly with memory with no intervention from the processor.

Most processors support several alternatives for the timing of a DMA data transfer. In *block transfer*, the peripheral takes over the bus for the duration of the transfer of an entire block of data. This may result in large gaps of time during which the processor is not executing instructions. If that is a problem, an alternative is *cycle stealing*. With cycle stealing, the processor gives up the bus for one memory cycle of DMA, or at most a few such cycles. Following that, the processor resumes control for one instruction cycle. The process repeats, alternating instruction cycles with DMA memory cycles until the entire block is transferred. Another alternative is *cycle stretching*. When using this approach the processor adds one memory cycle to each part of the instruction cycle. During that added memory cycle, the peripheral executes DMA. The result is several DMA cycles interwoven into each instruction.

In contrast to programmed I/O, where the program initiates and controls the transfer of data, and to interrupt I/O, where the peripheral initiates but the program controls the transfer of data, with DMA the peripheral both initiates and controls the transfer of data.

10.3 FORMATS FOR DATA TRANSFER

When data is transferred between the computer and a peripheral, it may be transmitted in one of two different ways: the bits may be transmitted simultaneously or one at a time. In the latter case, several choices are available for maintaining synchronism between the computer and the peripheral. This section will compare these various alternatives.

10.3.1 Parallel Data Transfer

When a high data transfer rate is desired the data bits in a single word or byte are transferred simultaneously over a group of data lines called the peripheral data bus. This data bus is a part of the I/O bus which interconnects the computer interface circuits with the peripherals. In the *parallel format*, many bits are moved in a single cycle. For 8-bit microprocessors such as the MC6809, the size of the transferred word is one byte. Even in processors having a larger word size, often only one byte at a time is transferred. This is because the byte is the standard size for alphanumeric data.

In addition to transferring the data, the I/O bus must serve to access the desired peripheral, to control both the timing and the direction of the transfer, and to provide support for the interrupt system. It must therefore include control lines and address lines as well as the peripheral data lines. The parallel format requires that the bus be extended between the computer and each of the peripherals, using the format illustrated in Figure 10.6.

The high data transfer rate in the parallel format comes at the cost of the multiple-line bus running around the system. When the peripherals are relatively close to the processor, say within a few meters of it, this cost is so small as not to be a concern.

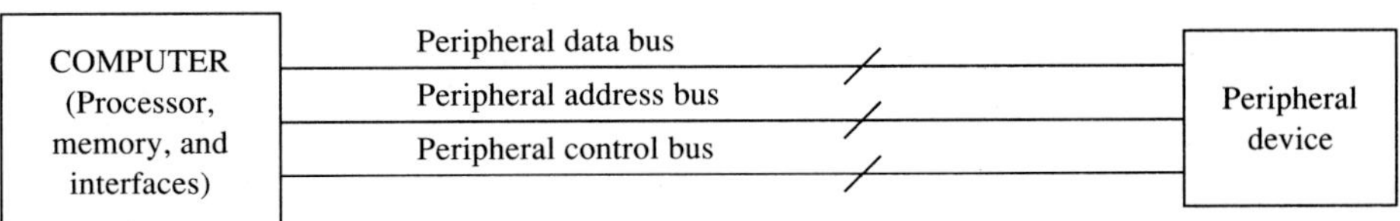

FIGURE 10.6
Parallel data transfer.

However, when the peripherals are at a greater distance from the processor this cost may become prohibitive and an alternate approach must be used.

10.3.2 Serial Data Transfer

When the high data transfer rate associated with the parallel format is not necessary, or when a peripheral is at too great a distance from the computer, then a *serial format* may be used. In cases when the computer must communicate with another device over a telephone line, the serial format is mandatory. With this format, the data is transferred one bit at a time over a single data line. Thus, the interconnecting cables between the peripherals and the computer can have far fewer lines than the corresponding cables required with the parallel format. However, the data transfer rate is also considerably slower.

Since the receiving device and the transmitting device are remote from one another, it is seldom feasible to include synchronizing signals within the interconnecting cable. However, a practical serial transmission scheme nevertheless requires that the receiver be in synchronism with the transmitter in order to sort out the message bits.

Two timing problems must be resolved with serial data transmission. The first is that of bit synchronization, the identification and separation of each individual bit in the data stream. The other is that of word boundary identification, or the separation of the individual bit-groups in the data stream. These problems may be handled in either one of two ways, the *synchronous* approach and the so-called *asynchronous* approach.

10.3.3 Synchronous Serial Data Transfer

With synchronous serial data transfer, bit synchronization is accomplished by extracting the bit frequency from the data stream itself. This is made possible by the use of a special coding scheme which results in one signal transition per bit. The bit stream can be processed at the receiver in a special electronic circuit known as a *phase-locked loop*. This circuit enables a clock at the receiver to lock in on the bit clock back at the transmitter and remain in phase synchronism with it. Once the clocks are locked in phase with each other, it is a straightforward matter to identify the individual bits in the data stream.

Word boundary identification is accomplished by reserving a unique 8-bit pattern for the identification of the beginning of the message. This special pattern (called a *flag* in one particular synchronous scheme) can be picked out of the message at the receiver by attempting to match a group of incoming bits with the expected pattern. The group is shifted one bit at a time through the message until a match is found. When the match is successful, the first word in the message has been located and the separation of the bit stream into words can proceed.

The principles of the synchronous serial data transmission system are illustrated in Figure 10.7. In this system the transmitter transmits the bit stream using the coding mentioned above. The phase-locked loop extracts the necessary information from

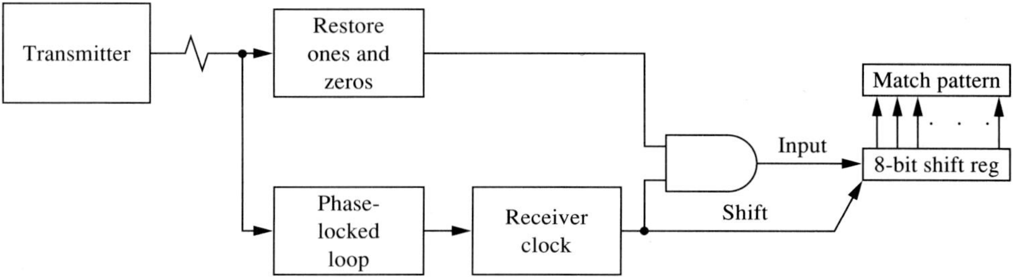

FIGURE 10.7
Synchronous serial data transfer.

the bit stream to lock the receiver bit clock into synchronism with the transmitted bits. The Restore circuit decodes the bit stream back into the standard 1/0 pattern it had before it was encoded at the transmitter. The individual bits can then be readily separated by the AND gate and the shift register. The pattern in the shift register is shifted until it matches the expected special pattern. From that point on, every successive group of eight bits constitutes a separate byte of the message.

10.3.4 Asynchronous Serial Data Transfer

The asynchronous approach to serial data transfer sacrifices data transmission rate for system simplicity by introducing extra bits into the data stream. These extra bits (two or three per word) reduce the data rate but enable the receiver to use an asynchronous bit clock which is effectively resynchronized once per word with the transmitter clock.

The principle of the asynchronous approach is illustrated by the transmitted bit stream shown in Figure 10.8. The idle state of the data line between messages is logic level 1. At point *A*, the transmitter signals to the receiver that it is about to transmit a word (eight bits in this example) by placing a 0 on the line. This initial 0 is called the *start bit* and lasts for one bit duration until point *B* where the message bits begin. The leading edge of the start bit acts as a signal to the receiver that it should start timing bits from this point.

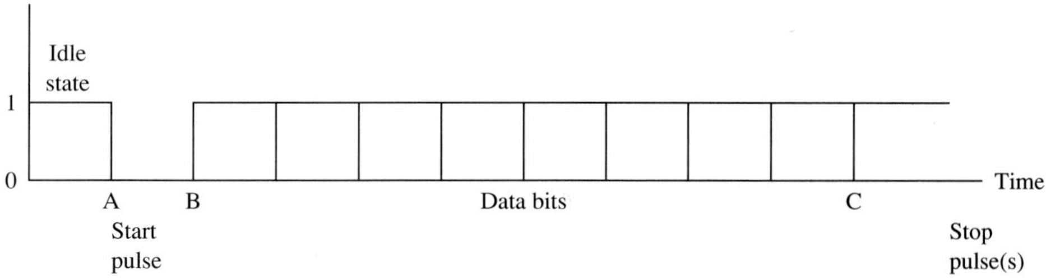

FIGURE 10.8
Asynchronous serial data format.

Starting at point A, the receiver times and extracts the start bit and the eight signal bits using its own (asynchronous) clock and the bit rate which it expects to see in the message. At point C, the end of the last data bit, the transmitter sends two bits at logic level 0. These bits, called the *stop bits*, are used by the receiver to verify that it is still properly separating the signal into individual bits.

If the receiver's clock is close enough in frequency to the transmitter's clock, then the receiver will be able to extract the eight signal bits and identify the stop bits even though its clock is not in exact synchronism with that of the transmitter. Notice that after the stop bits, the transmitter may send a new start bit to signal the start of a new word to the receiver. In essence, this system is word-synchronous (the receiver starts each word in synchronism with the transmitter) but bit-asynchronous.

10.3.5 Data Rate versus Bit Rate

The asynchronous system is much simpler than the synchronous system. However, the extra start and stop bits in the example shown mean that 11 bits must be transmitted in order to convey the 8 data bits. This means that the data rate will not equal the bit rate.

Signal transmission in a serial transmission scheme is measured in actual signal bits per second regardless of whether they are data bits or not. To distinguish this from the data rate, the number of bits per second is called the *Baud rate* when applied to all of the signal bits but the *data rate* when applied only to the data bits. Thus, in the asynchronous system shown in Figure 10.8, if 10 eight-bit words per second are transmitted, the *data rate* would be 80 bits per second, while the *bit rate* would be 110 Baud (10 words per second times 11 actual bits transmitted per word). In the case of a synchronous scheme, the Baud rate is essentially equal to the data rate in bits per second. The slight overhead of the special pattern which must occasionally be transmitted is divided over many words of the message and so has a negligible effect on the overall rate.

10.4 INTERFACES

The special circuitry which fits into the gap between the processor and the peripheral is called an *interface*. As was shown in Figure 10.2 and Figure 10.3, the interface is connected to the processor's data bus, address bus, and control bus. It monitors the signals on these buses and passes on information between the processor and the peripheral.

Every interface must perform certain common functions such as address decoding, data transfer synchronization, speed matching, and signal conditioning. In addition, each interface must meet the individual requirements of its associated peripheral.

Although at one time interface circuits were designed for each specific peripheral as needed, that is no longer the practice. Instead, special purpose integrated circuits are used. These integrated circuits are called *interface chips*. This section examines some of the basic requirements for interfaces and describes in a general way some of the interface chips which support the more common peripherals.

10.4.1 Functions Required of Interfaces

Each interface must perform an *address decoding* or *I/O device selection* function. This means that the interface must respond in a desired fashion when it is addressed by the processor and not respond at any other time. Address decoding is accomplished by the use of logic gates connected to the address bus and/or the special I/O control line in the control bus. These gates generate a signal which is used to access an interface whenever its identifying address appears on the bus. The interface itself must include an enable input to which this signal is connected. On interface chips, this input is called a *chip select* input.

The interface must respond in the proper fashion when it is accessed by the microprocessor. This means that it must distinguish between the two directions of data transfer and react accordingly. In addition, it must sense the timing signals and place data on the data bus or read data from the data bus at the appropriate points in time. These functions, too, are accomplished with the use of control lines on the interface chip which cause it to respond to the read/write signals and the timing signals in the microprocessor's control bus.

A second function which the interface must perform is that of matching the speed of the microprocessor with that of the peripheral. The microprocessor operates on a sub-microsecond time scale while most peripherals operate in a much slower time frame. Typical peripherals in microprocessor control systems are simply not capable of responding to the fleeting signals which the microprocessor generates. Thus, the interface must capture these signals and hold them for the peripheral. This is accomplished with flip-flops and registers contained within the interface chip.

Another function of the interface is to match the microprocessor signal characteristics to the requirements of the peripheral. The peripheral may need a different voltage than the processor provides or it may present too large a load to be driven directly by the processor. The processor in turn requires a very specific range of input signals from the peripheral if it is to operate properly. The interface must satisfy these needs by converting between the two categories of signals.

In addition to these general requirements certain peripherals may require support for special functions such as generating an interrupt signal, prioritizing interrupt signals, responding to polling inquiries from the processor, converting between the microprocessor's parallel signals and an external serial signal, detecting certain types of anomalous conditions (parity errors, stop-bit overruns in serial transmission), or a large number of other peripheral-specific functions. These additional requirements are beyond the scope of this book and would be the proper subject of a textbook on microprocessor interfacing.

10.4.2 Interface Chips

Special integrated circuits are available to support almost any peripheral device which one may need to incorporate into a system. These integrated circuits are called programmable interface chips. As their name implies, they are programmable in order to make them more universally useful.

By making the interface chips programmable, the chip manufacturer ensures a wider market for them. That is, more applications for the specific type of peripheral are likely to be supported by the chip. The wider market means more sales, which in turn means lower prices. As a consequence, programmable interface chips are relatively inexpensive, considering their capabilities.

While their programmability results in lower costs for the chips, it also makes them more difficult to use than might otherwise be the case. Before an interface can be used to support the input or output of information, it must first be programmed or told how it must operate in that specific application. Thus, the first part of a system program must include initialization routines to program the various interfaces used in the system.

The system designer must include any necessary interface chips in the overall plan for the system. An example of an I/O interface chip incorporated into a memory-mapped system is shown in Figure 10.9. Interface chips support address decoding by means of one or more chip select pins. The higher-ordered bits of the address bus are decoded by external address decoding logic so as to select the interface whenever its address appears on the bus.

Figure 10.10 shows an example of an address decoding circuit which selects an interface whenever an address (16 bits) within the range of A000 through A007 appears on the bus. Notice that the bit pattern which is common to this range of addresses (1010 0000 0000 0---) must be present to select the interface. Other address decoding circuits are described in a later chapter on memory chips.

The individual registers within the interface chip are selected by on-chip address pins connected to the lower-ordered bits of the address bus. The number of locations on a typical interface chip is much smaller than on a memory chip, on the order of 2 to 16, and these locations are referred to as I/O registers. Thus, the on-chip address pins are commonly referred to as register select pins (RS pins). In the example of Figure 10.10, where the interface chip occupies eight locations in the address space, it would have three register select pins.

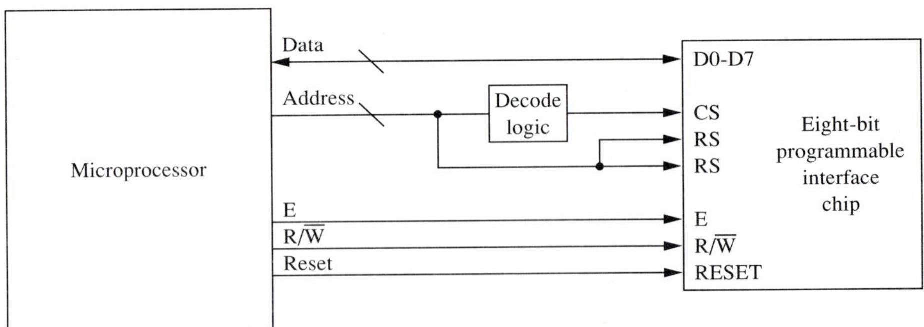

FIGURE 10.9
Wiring to a programmable interface chip.

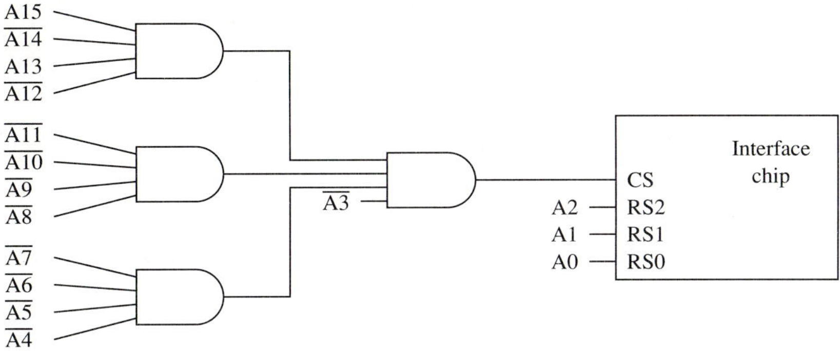

FIGURE 10.10
Address decoding.

As was shown in Figure 10.9, the data bus, the read/write directional control line, the timing signal line (E), and the system reset lines round out the complement of signals which are required for the processor to communicate with an interface chip. The system reset line is used by the interface to ensure a safe initial condition prior to initialization. In cases where the interface supports interrupts, one or more of the processor interrupt lines would also be connected to a corresponding pin on the interface chip.

The following sections briefly describe the features of some of the more commonly-used Motorola interface chips. The reader should consult the manufacturer's specification sheets or a text on microprocessor interfacing for more specific details and programming information.

10.4.3 The MC6821 Peripheral Interface Adapter

One of the most commonly-used interface chips in control applications is the *parallel I/O chip*. The Motorola version is the MC6821 *Peripheral Interface Adapter (PIA)* shown in Figure 10.11. The pins shown on the left are used for communication with the processor and those on the right connect to the peripheral device(s) with which the chip interfaces.

Access from the processor is via the standard bi-directional data bus, read/write pin, timing pin (E), chip select, and register-select pins. The chip select pins (CS0, CS1, and CS2) are ANDed internally to provide part of the address decoding circuitry (see Figure 10.10). As the presence of the two register select pins indicates, the PIA occupies four locations in the address space.

The PIA connects to peripherals with 16 peripheral data lines (PA0-PA7 and PB0-PB7), each of which can be individually programmed to be an input or an output. It also includes four programmable control lines (peripheral control lines: CA1, CA2, CB1, and CB2). These lines can be used by peripherals to trigger interrupts to the

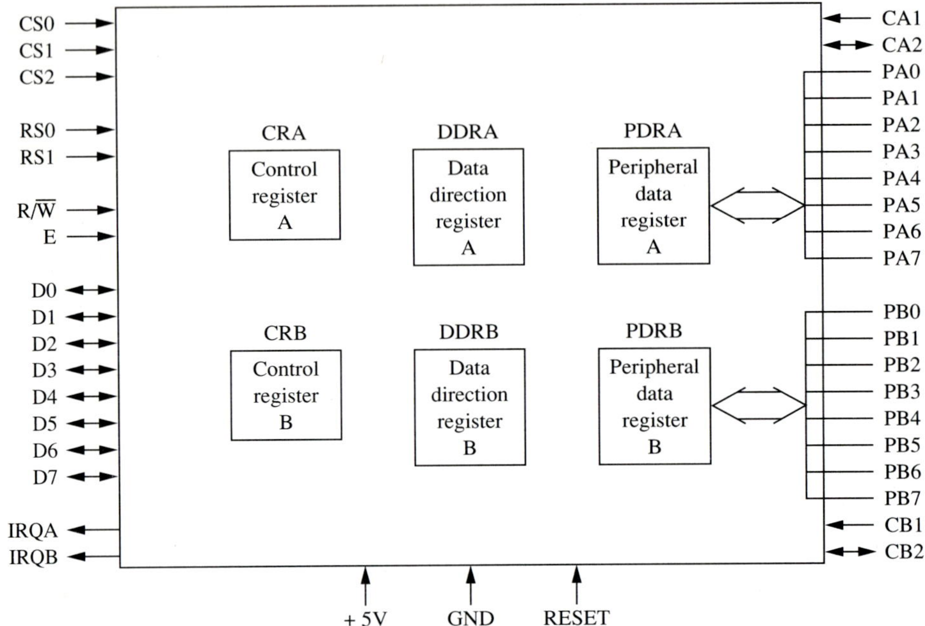

FIGURE 10.11
The MC6821 peripheral interface adapter.

processor (if so programmed) on either the rising edge or the falling edge of a pulse. Alternatively, CA2 and CB2 may be used as additional data outputs. Thus, the PIA can serve a variety of applications including providing signals to scan keyboards or character displays, turning equipment off and on, and sensing the state of operator-actuated or machine-actuated switches.

The PIA is divided into two almost identical halves, side A and side B. Each half includes three registers, the control register (CRA/CRB), the data direction register (DDRA/DDRB), and the peripheral data register (PDRA/PDRB). The control registers retain the programming, which the processor must install to tell each side how its control lines are to operate, whether interrupts are to be triggered, and so forth. The peripheral data registers contain the input or output data which appears on the peripheral data lines. The direction registers retain a bit pattern which programs the direction for each data line.

Included in the control registers are status bits which the processor may read in order to determine the status of input control lines or of any interrupts which may be pending from this chip. Thus, these bits support the polling operations described earlier in this chapter as well as in a later chapter on interrupts.

As will be seen in a later chapter, microprocessors typically include several interrupt inputs, each of which has different characteristics. The interrupt signals from the PIA appear on separate pins to allow flexibility in the choice of these. Thus, side A may be connected to one interrupt input through IRQA, while side B is connected to another through IRQB.

10.4.4 The MC6840 Programmable Timer Module

Another commonly used Motorola interface chip is the MC6840 *Programmable Timer Module (PTM)*. This chip incorporates three 16-bit counters which can be programmed to generate a variety of output waveforms, to measure pulse durations, or to compare the frequencies of two inputs. It also supports interrupts for various programmable conditions. The PTM can be used to time events over periods ranging from a fraction of a microsecond to thousands of days.

A block diagram for the PTM is shown in Figure 10.12. The chip includes two chip select pins and three register select pins and occupies eight locations in the address space. The three counter latches can be pre-loaded by the processor with starting values with which the counters will be loaded. Each counter counts down from its starting value to 0 with a wide variety of options. The count rate may be established by the processor's clock (input on pin E) or by an external clock (C1, C2, C3). The count may be stopped or started by an external input (G1, G2, G3). The counter may generate outputs to peripherals or to other counters on the same chip through an output pin (01, 02, 03). The counter may trigger an interrupt to the processor (on IRQ) when reaching 0. These and other options must be selected for each counter and programmed into its control register by the processor. The control registers also contain flags or status bits which the processor may consult during polling operations.

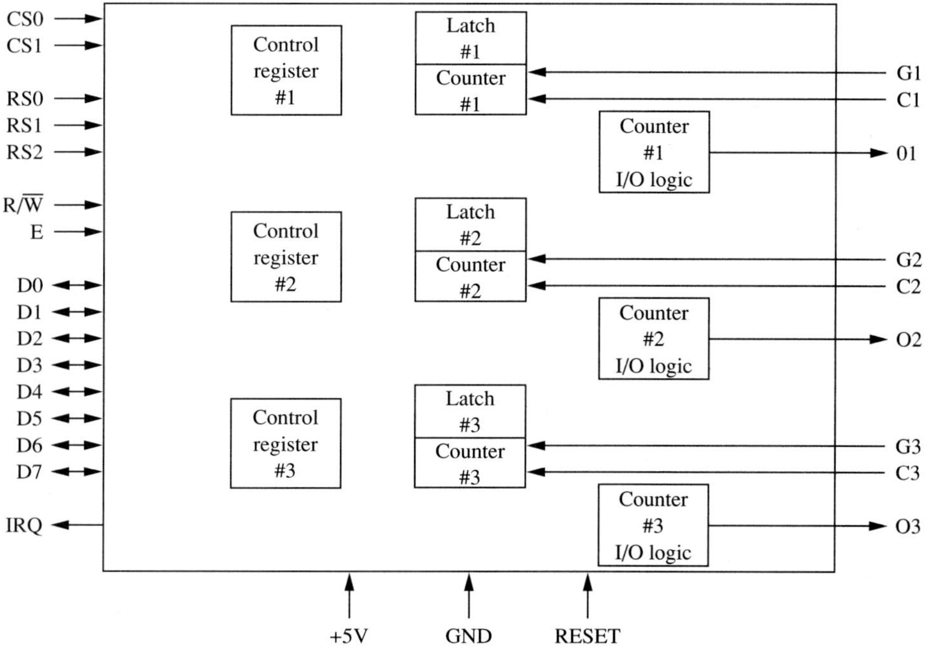

FIGURE 10.12
The MC6840 programmable timer module.

10.4.5 The MC6850 Asynchronous Communications Interface Adapter

A third important Motorola interface chip is the MC6850 *Asynchronous Communications Interface Adapter (ACIA)*. The ACIA supports the serial data format described earlier in Section 10.3.2 and shown in Figure 10.8. It converts the parallel data from the processor into one of several choices of serial form for transmission. Among the selections available are the number of data bits (seven or eight), the choice of parity (odd, even, or none), and one or two stop bits. The chip also performs the counterpart operation of converting the serial input stream into a parallel form for transfer into the processor. It also supports several interrupt conditions. Figure 10.13 shows a block diagram for the ACIA. The chip includes three chip select lines and occupies two locations in the memory space.

The parallel data from the processor is first loaded into the transmit data register. When the transmit shift register is empty and available for use, it is automatically loaded with the data from the transmit data register. Thus, the transmitter is *double buffered*, that is, two bytes of outgoing data may be in the chip simultaneously, one being transmitted and the other waiting its turn. When the data register is empty, the chip immediately signals this fact to the processor, which can then load another byte into it. This ensures no delay between the transmission of consecutive bytes. The bit rate is established by the input signal on the transmit clock pin and a divide ratio established during the programming of the control register by the processor.

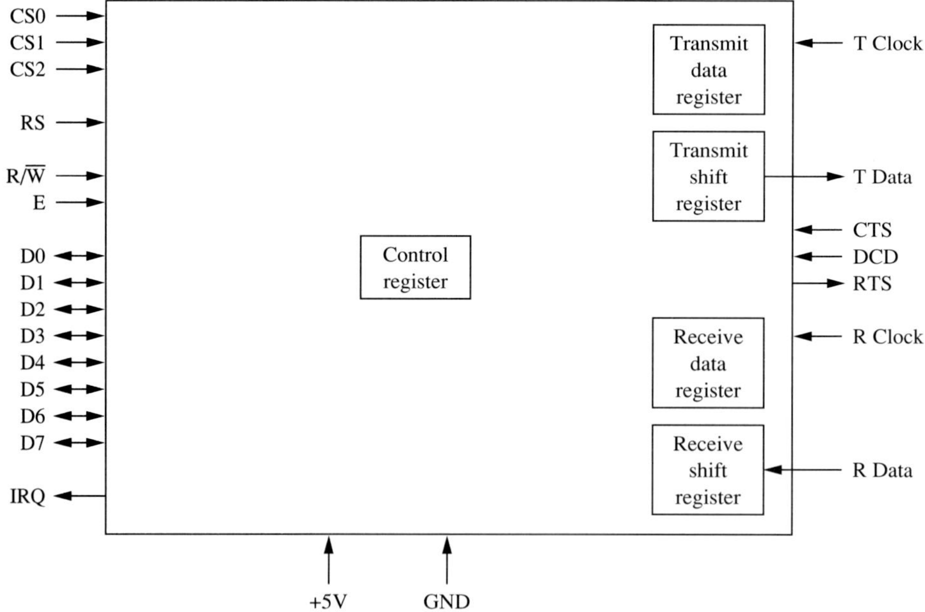

FIGURE 10.13
The MC6850 asynchronous communication interface adapter.

Received data is handled in an analogous fashion. Data coming in on the receive data pin is shifted into the receive shift register at a rate determined by the receive clock signal. When the shift register is full, the byte is automatically loaded into the receive data register and the chip signals the processor.

The three control lines, CTS (clear to send), DCD (data carrier decode), and RTS (request to send), are used to interface with a modulator/demodulator device or *modem*. A modem is used to convert between the logic signals in the serial data stream and a sequence of audio tones. These tones can be transmitted over the telephone network, unlike the normal 0/1 logic signals, which cannot. The modem uses the control lines to communicate with the microprocessor through the ACIA and to convey information concerning the status of the telephone link itself.

As in most interface chips, the control register includes status bits to inform the processor as to the condition of the chip itself: whether it needs more transmitter data or whether it contains valid receiver data, the status of any interrupt request, error conditions in the receiver such as overrun or a parity error, and so forth. These conditions may be detected by polling routines similar to those described earlier.

10.4.6 Other Programmable Interface Chips

The integrated circuits mentioned above are only a few of the more commonly-used Motorola interface chips. Others include real-time clocks, synchronous serial communications support devices, color TV modulators, and controllers for cathode ray tube displays, keyboards, and video display terminals. These and other interface chips are described in textbooks on the interfacing of microprocessors.

10.5 STANDARD BUSES

When all of the components of a microprocessor control system can be placed onto one printed circuit board, the designer need not be concerned about any bus structure beyond that of the microprocessor being used and the I/O bus for the peripherals concerned. However, when the system overflows to more than a single board, then an *inter-board bus* must be considered. Many inter-board buses have been designed that have been subjected to industrial standards.

When selecting such a standard bus, the user can be somewhat assured that the several boards comprising a system will be interconnected properly and will interact properly in a system. Another advantage in selecting a standard bus is that many boards have been designed to work with the standard buses. Thus, the designer can specify building blocks which have already been designed, built, and tested. Often, the entire system hardware can be assembled from standard boards. Such a system would include the basic housing, which contains the bus wires and the sockets into which the cards are inserted. The bus and sockets are mounted on a printed circuit board called a *back plane* or a *motherboard*.

Among the hundreds of standard buses which have been used from time to time, only about a dozen are currently specified to any great extent in control systems. Table 10.1 lists some of the more popular control system standard buses, together with a few of their basic characteristics. As with the interface chips, standard buses are more

TABLE 10.1
Characteristics of some standard buses.

Name/ IEEE standard	Data bits	Address bits	Board size	Number of pins
S100/696	8	16	5.3×10 In.	100
STD/P961	8	16	4.5×6.5 In.	56
VMEbus/1014	16/32	23/31	100×160/233×220 mm	96/192
Multibus/796	16	24	6.75×12 In.	86/146
Futurebus/P896	32	32	337×280 mm	96
ISA/None	16	24	4.8×13.2 In.	98
EISA*/None	8/16/32	32	4.8×13.2 In.	188

*ISA cards may be used an in EISA system with some restrictions. The extra 90 pins in EISA are contacted at a deeper insertion depth.

properly the subject of an interfacing text, and will not be discussed in any detail in this book.

SUMMARY

Special I/O must be designed into the processor itself. When it is available, it provides an alternative approach for a system in which the memory requirements preclude using memory-mapped I/O. Either approach provides the means for the processor to access its peripheral devices through their associated interface circuits.

Programmed I/O, both the simplest method of transferring data and the slowest, requires the program to initiate and control the transfer of data. With interrupt I/O the peripheral initiates the transfer, but the program still controls it. The result is a faster and more complex system but not the ultimate in speed. With direct memory access, the peripheral both initiates and controls the transfer of data through its interface circuitry. This provides the highest speed of data transfer, but at the price of added system complexity.

An alternative to the parallel transfer of data bits when large distances are involved is to use a serial data format. Either a more complex synchronous serial data transmission scheme or the slower but simpler asynchronous scheme may be selected.

The design of microprocessor control systems is supported by the availability of special-purpose programmable interface chips which can be used to interface with a wide variety of peripheral devices. Standard bus cards provide similar support and may be used to design entire systems using interconnected pre-designed and tested printed circuit boards.

REVIEW PROBLEMS

10.1. Name the two choices of I/O mapping and list one advantage and one disadvantage of each.

10.2. Contrast the three commonly-used data transfer techniques (programmed I/O, interrupt I/O, and DMA) as to which part of the system initiates the data transfer and which part controls the data transfer.

10.3. List the three data transfer techniques in the order of increasing speed of operation.

10.4. Write an MC6809 or an MC68000 assembly language routine which will poll both a keyboard and a printer as follows:

a. The keyboard status register has been defined as KEYSR. When a key is pushed, bit 7 in KEYSR will be set and the code for the key will be loaded into a defined location. When the code is read by the processor, the bit will be cleared.

b. The printer status register has been defined as PRNSR. When the printer is idle and ready to print a character, bit 7 in PRNSR will be set. While it is in the process of printing a character, the bit will be cleared.

c. The routine must scan both peripherals. When a key has been pushed, the routine should call the defined subroutine KYBRD. When the printer is idle, the routine should call the defined subroutine PRINT.

d. Upon returning from either subroutine, the polling routine should continue to scan both peripherals.

10.5. Describe the differences between synchronous and asynchronous serial data transmission.

10.6. An asynchronous serial data transmitter uses the format of one start bit, eight data bits, and two stop bits. Each bit transmitted has a duration of one millisecond.

a. What is the bit rate in Baud?

b. What is the data rate in bits per second?

10.7. An asynchronous serial transmitter transmits one start bit, eight data bits, and two stop bits, at a rate of 9600 Baud. Calculate the minimum frequency and the maximum frequency which the receiver bit clock may have if the system is to work properly. Assume that the receiver must detect both of the stop bits properly in order for the system to work.

10.8. Design an address decoder circuit for the following system which includes two memory-mapped I/O chips. Use any method which will implement the required scheme for either an MC6809 or an MC68000 system. Assume that each chip has a single active high chip select line. If you use a decoder, assume that it has an active high enable input and that its outputs are also active high.

Chip	*Address Range*
I/O #1	2000–2003
I/O #2	2010–2017
RAM #1	5000–5FFF
RAM #2	6000–6FFF
RAM #3	7000–7FFF
ROM #1	A000–BFFF
ROM #2	C000–DFFF

10.9. List the three functions which must be performed by an I/O interface circuit.

10.10. List as many applications as you can for each of the three programmable interface chips described in this chapter (the PIA, the PTM, and the ACIA).

CHAPTER 11

INTERRUPTS AND EXCEPTION PROCESSING

When using the interrupt method of input/output control, the peripheral initiates the transfer of information through its interface by means of one or more interrupt lines to the processor. Subsequently, the processor controls the transfer of information by means of a program module called an interrupt service routine. The procedure followed by the processor as it transfers control of the system from the interrupted program to the interrupt service routine is known as exception processing.

Various structures and schemes have been devised to implement and support exception processing and to extend and improve upon it. This chapter introduces some of the interrupt structures commonly found in microprocessors. In addition, it discusses some of the basic requirements that the interrupt service routine must satisfy. Finally, it describes the primary features of both the MC6809 and the MC68000 interrupt systems.

11.1 THE INTERRUPT PROCESS

An interrupt is a forced branch in the sequence of a program in response to a hardware-initiated signal which may occur at any time that the system is in operation. To give the designer some control over this process, a software method is commonly provided for turning the interrupt system on and off. Most processors provide this control by means of an interrupt system mask bit in the condition code register. When the bit is set, the interrupt system is off; when it is cleared, the system is on. A processor having multiple interrupt inputs may have a mask that contains several bits. The bit pattern in the mask determines which of the interrupts are enabled and which are not.

If an interrupt occurs during a time when it has not been enabled by the program, the processor ignores it and continues fetching and executing instructions as usual. If at a later time the program enables the interrupt, it will then be detected and the processor will respond appropriately.

In order to allow more than one interrupting device to use a single interrupt input to the processor, interrupt inputs are commonly designed to be active-low. With this type of input, several interrupting sources can use *open collector gates* to pull the line low without interfering with each other. The output of an open collector gate is either low (0) or it is not connected to any source inside of the gate. In the latter case, it is said to be in the *high impedance* state, and its signal level is free to be determined by some other external source connected to the same line. Outputs from several open collector gates may be safely tied together with no interference. Any one of the gates can drive the control line low but none can drive it high.

Figure 11.1 shows how several open collector gates may be connected to a common interrupt line. The resistor holds the line high in the absence of an interrupt signal while allowing any of the gates to pull it low.

When a peripheral device signals an interrupt, the processor suspends its normal fetch/execute cycle and begins so-called *exception processing* if the interrupt has been enabled by the program (see Figure 11.2). In this figure the processor is executing instructions in the main program at the time that the interrupt occurs.

Prior to recognizing the interrupt and initiating exception processing, the processor completes the execution of the current instruction. Whatever the current data

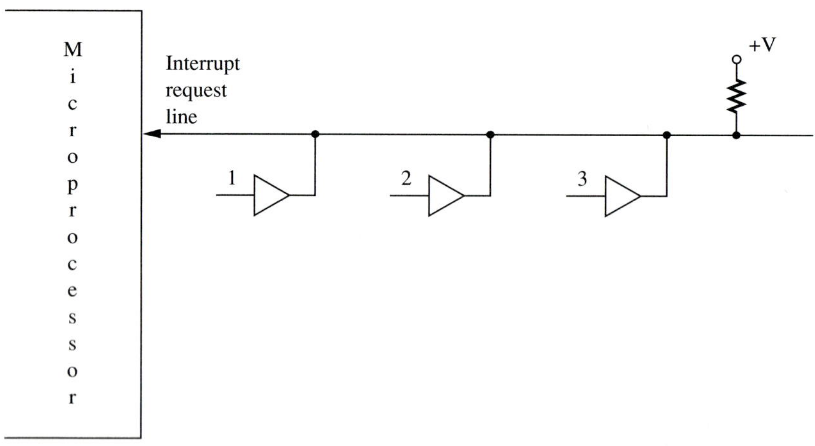

FIGURE 11.1
Open-collector gates driving a common interrupt input.

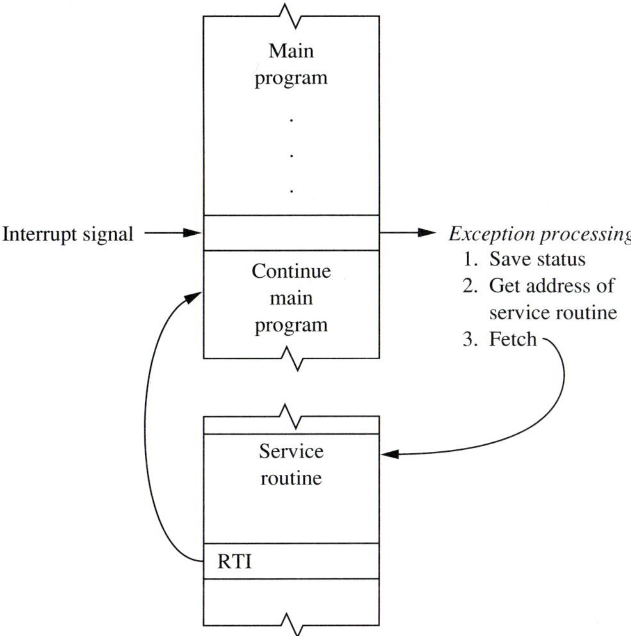

FIGURE 11.2
The interrupt sequence.

manipulation or branch decision, it is first concluded and the contents of the pertinent registers and locations are updated. This is necessary so that the interrupt does not interfere in any way with that part of the program being executed at the time that the interrupt occurs.

The processor then saves some or all of its current status in a stack. The contents of each register which may be changed while the peripheral is being serviced must be saved before it is changed, so that, upon returning from the service routine, the interrupted program will be able to resume where it left off with no loss of information.

Some processors automatically save the contents of all processor registers in the stack prior to the transfer of control to the interrupt service routine. This approach ensures that every register will be saved and properly restored before returning to the original program. An alternative approach followed by other processors is to save only the program counter and the condition code register—the two registers changed by almost every instruction. These processors leave the responsibility for the remaining registers to the programmer.

Stacking all of the registers takes time and delays the transition from the main program to the interrupt service routine. However, it may actually save time in many cases, because all of the registers are stacked automatically by the hardware. The alternative approach requires the interrupt service routine to fetch and execute extra instructions if any registers must be stacked.

After stacking whichever registers it does, the processor must then disable the interrupt system before it can start to execute the instructions in the interrupt service routine. If the interrupt system were not turned off, as soon as the processor began to service the interrupting device the interrupt signal that this device sends would immediately interrupt the processor again. The result would be an infinite interrupting loop that would lock up the processor.

After turning off the interrupt system the processor determines the starting address of the interrupt service routine and loads that address into the program counter. Exception processing has now concluded and the processor continues the standard fetch/execute cycle as though nothing unusual had happened. That is, the processor does not keep track of the fact that it is servicing an interrupt. It simply fetches and executes instructions in the normal fashion.

The interrupt service routine ends with a special instruction that turns the interrupt system back on and causes the processor to return to the main program. In Figure 11.2 the instruction is shown as the return from interrupt (RTI). When executing the return the processor restores all of the status that it had originally saved, including the original mask, which has the effect of turning the interrupt system back on. Also included as a part of the restored status is the address that was in the program counter at the completion of the interrupted instruction. That address will be pulled off the stack and loaded into the program counter. In this way the processor is able to continue the execution of the main program.

11.2 VECTORED INTERRUPT

The location to which a particular processor branches when responding to a specific interrupt signal may be a fixed location in memory. This type of processor has a non-vectored interrupt system. The interrupt service routine must always be written to start in that particular location. The processor will automatically start fetching and executing the interrupt service routine from that location whenever an interrupt occurs.

A more flexible approach is for the processor to obtain an address for the service routine by reading a specified location in memory whenever an interrupt is detected. The location is called an interrupt vector location and such a processor is said to have a vectored interrupt system. When using vectored interrupt, the designer must be certain that the correct starting address is fetched when the vector is read. One way to ensure this is to store the address in that location permanently as part of the system software. An alternative is to have the interface hardware intervene and supply the starting address during the cycle when the processor reads the vector location. With this approach each of several interrupting devices could supply a starting address specific to its own interrupt service routine.

Vectored interrupt is illustrated in Figure 11.3. The main program is interrupted at point A. The processor completes the current instruction and saves the status on the stack (including the return address to the next instruction following point A). The processor then fetches the starting address for the interrupt service routine from the vector location and loads it into the program counter. This causes the transition to the service routine at point B. The return instruction at point C returns execution to the main program just after point A.

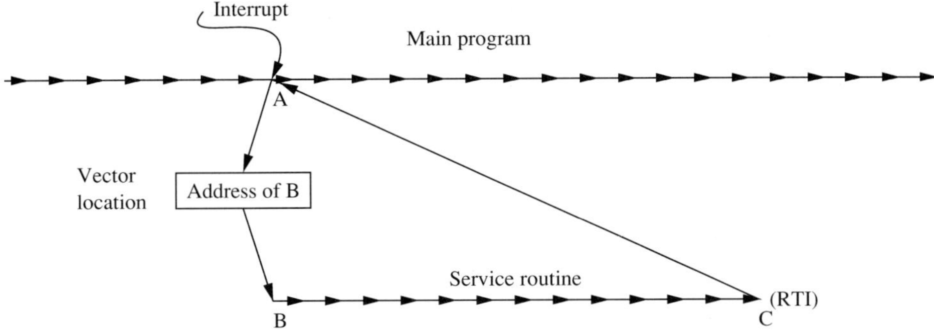

FIGURE 11.3
Vectored interrupt.

11.3 PRIORITIZATION AND POLLING

When a system has two or more interrupting peripherals, they must be *prioritized* in order of importance or in order of need. When two peripherals interrupt simultaneously, the higher-priority device should be tended to first. Ideally, the higher-priority device should be allowed to interrupt the other's service routine while it is in progress, but not vice-versa. Thus, prioritization involves both the consideration of tie-breaking and of disabling competing interrupts in some sort of ranked order.

Many processors provide multiple interrupt input lines numbered in order of priority. Such processors include a multi-bit mask that can be loaded under program control with a priority number. The system will respond to any interrupt with a higher priority than the number in the mask. Clearing the mask has the effect of turning on all of the interrupts.

With processors that support only a single priority but that have vectored interrupt, external hardware can be used to sort out the priorities in case of a tie and to vector to the appropriate service routine by providing the address during the processor's vector fetch cycle. The hardware can also be used to stop lower-priority interrupt signals from reaching the processor until the completion of the higher-priority service routine. Special programmable interface chips called *priority interrupt encoders* are available to implement these features.

In cases where prioritization is not provided and two or more peripherals must use the same interrupt request line, the service routine itself must determine which peripheral has triggered the current interrupt. A routine to do this is called a *polling routine*.[1] The routine "polls" the various peripheral interfaces, asking each one in turn whether it triggered the interrupt. With this approach, the prioritization is determined by the order in which the polling routine interrogates the peripherals. The next section discusses polling in more detail and also includes examples of polling routines.

---

[1]This should not be confused with the polling loop used with programmed I/O as described in Section 10.2.1.

11.4 THE INTERRUPT SERVICE ROUTINE

The program that the processor executes in responding to the interrupt is called the interrupt service routine. This routine must satisfy certain specific requirements of both the interrupting peripheral and the interrupt system of the microprocessor.

If the processor does not automatically save the contents of all of the registers when responding to the interrupt, then the first task of the interrupt service routine must be to save all necessary registers. That is, it must save on the stack the contents of each register to be used during the service routine before it is used. This is readily done with data movement instruction such as PUSH or MOVEM.

If more than one device is connected to the same interrupt line, each must be polled to determine the source of the current interrupt. The service routine must include a polling routine immediately following the stacking of the registers. It consists of a series of tests similar to the one described in the polling loop routine of section 10.2.1. Examples of such a routine are shown in Figure 11.4.

In the program segment of Figure 11.4, STATn is a status register (or a control register) in the interface for peripheral device number n. Each status register is designed so that if its associated peripheral is interrupting the processor, bit number 7 of the register will be set; that is, the value in the register will look like a negative number. The use of bit 7 in this way is very common in programmable interfaces.

In lines 2, 4, and 6 of Figure 11.4, each status register in turn is fetched into the processor and bit number 7 tested. The order in which the status registers are tested establishes the priority of the devices. In line 3 the actual test/branch is carried out for the first peripheral device. If that device triggered the interrupt, the branch will be taken to the location whose symbolic address is DEV1. Starting in location DEV1 should be the service routine for the first peripheral device. If that device did not trigger the interrupt, the polling routine will continue and test the second device, and so on.

```
1.  *MC6809 INTERRUPT POLLING ROUTINE
    *
2.  POLL  LDA  STAT1      STAT1 IS A STATUS REGISTER
3.        BMI  DEV1       SERVICE DEVICE †1
4.        LDA  STAT2      POLL DEVICE †2
5.        BMI  DEV2       SERVICE DEVICE †2
6.        LDA  STAT3      POLL DEVICE †3
7.        etc.
    *
    *

1.  MC68000 INTERRUPT POLLING ROUTINE
    *
2.  POLL  BTST †7,S TAT1  STAT1 IS A STATUS REGISTER
3.        BNE  DEV1       SERVICE DEVICE †1
4.        BTST †7, STAT2  POLL DEVICE †2
5.        BNE  DEV2       SERVICE DEVICE †2
6.        BTST †7, STAT3  POLL DEVICE †3
7.        etc.
```

FIGURE 11.4
Interrupt polling routines.

Each of the DEVn service routines ends with a return from interrupt instruction, so the polling routine will not be reentered until the next interrupt. However, it is good practice to terminate the polling routine with a return from interrupt instruction as a precaution against spurious interrupt signals appearing on the interrupt line.

The device service routine, reached either through polling or vectoring, must service its peripheral. That is, it must perform the necessary functions called for by the interrupt. The routine together with the interface must ensure that the action taken in servicing the peripheral clears the interrupt request. If the request is not cleared during the service routine, when the processor turns the interrupt system back on before resuming execution of the main program the same interrupt will be immediately detected again. This would result in an infinite loop of repeated execution of the service routine.

After servicing the peripheral, the interrupt service routine must proceed with the orderly return to the program that was interrupted. If the routine itself saved processor registers on the stack, it must now reload these registers with their original contents by executing the appropriate PULL or MOVEM instruction. If the processor saved the contents of the registers automatically when responding to the interrupt, it will also reload them automatically when it returns to the interrupted program.

Finally, the service routine must end with the instruction that tells the processor to return from the interrupt service routine to the interrupted program. This is a return from interrupt instruction, which is similar to the return from subroutine instruction in that it has no address specification; the processor gets the return address from the top of the stack.

11.5 OTHER EXCEPTIONS

In addition to the interrupts used by peripheral devices to initiate I/O transfers, many processors provide interrupt-like support for other functions. These include such things as reset, software interrupts, traps, tracing support, and hardware error interrupts. Together with the regular interrupts, these functions are referred to as exceptions, since they require the processor to do exception processing. Each exception with which a particular processor is equipped has its own associated vector location. Some processors include several hundred exception vectors.

Each exception to be used in a particular application requires its own service routine to take the appropriate action called for by the exception. Each of these routines must satisfy the requirements described earlier for the interrupt service routine, including the final return from interrupt instruction, which returns the processor to its location at the time the exception was initiated.

11.5.1 Reset

Every processor includes a reset function as its highest-priority exception. The reset input is used to start the processor in a predictable fashion when it is first turned on. It may also be used as a "panic button" input to terminate an infinite loop or other such catastrophic problem arising during program debugging.

When a processor detects an active-low signal on its reset input line, it immediately ceases operation and waits for the line to go high. When the line goes high, the processor fetches a starting address from the reset vector (or it generates a fixed starting address) and loads that value into the program counter. It then begins fetching and executing instructions in the normal fashion. With this exception the processor saves neither status nor return address. Its intended use precludes any need to return to an interrupted sequence of operations.

When it responds to the reset the processor adjusts the interrupt mask to ensure that interrupts will be ignored until the point in time when the program specifically unmasks them. This prevents any spurious signals from unprogrammed interfaces or un-initialized peripherals from interfering with proper system start-up.

A circuit such as that shown in Figure 11.5 is often connected to the reset input. The capacitor in the circuit ensures that when the power supply is first turned on, the microprocessor circuits are energized but the reset line remains low. This allows the processor to recognize the presence of the reset signal, thus holding itself inactive. After a few milliseconds, the capacitor charges up to logic level one and the processor initiates the start-up procedure. To terminate operation and restart the system at any time, the user closes the abort switch. This shorts the reset line to ground and triggers the regular reset exception sequence.

11.5.2 Traps

A trap is an exception that is initiated internally by the processor itself. It occurs when the processor recognizes a specific condition during the execution of certain instructions. The condition may be an abnormal one, such as an attempt to divide by zero or an attempt to execute a restricted instruction or an undefined instruction. On the other hand, the condition may be a normal one for which the instruction is testing. An example of the latter is an instruction that traps when a specific CCR bit is set or one that tests a number in a register against limits and traps if the value is outside of the limits.

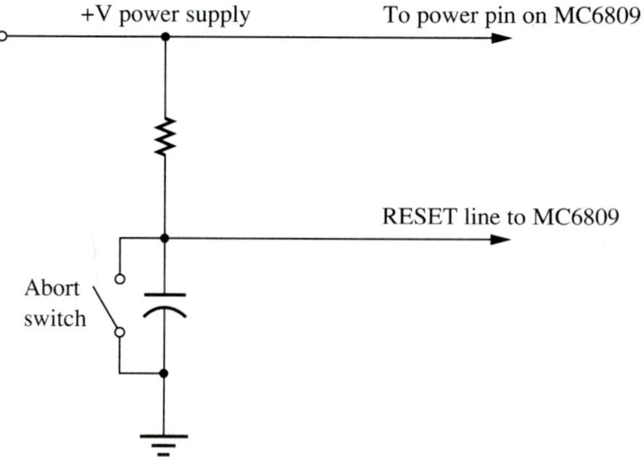

FIGURE 11.5
Reset circuit.

11.5.3 Software Interrupts

A processor may include instructions that trap unconditionally; they cause the processor to do exception processing whenever they are executed. These are referred to as trap instructions (TRAPn) or software interrupt instructions (SWIn), since they initiate an interrupt-like procedure whenever they are executed.

Trap instructions or software interrupt instructions are used by a programmer to call upon the resources of an operating system or monitor program. They provide a means whereby a user's program may make use of the I/O capabilities of these system programs. They are also used to assist in debugging user's programs.

11.5.4 The Trace Exception

A processor may support program debugging by providing the user with the option of interrupting the system automatically after the execution of each instruction. When this option is selected (by setting a CCR bit or by signaling on an input pin) the processor executes one instruction and then enters exception processing. The service routine for this exception normally includes calls to an operating system or a monitor, which could provide the user with some sort of debugging support such as a display of register contents or of recent memory accesses. The return instruction at the end of the exception routine allows the processor to fetch and execute the next user's instruction, which is again followed by the trace exception.

11.5.5 System Failure Exceptions

Many processors support the detection of certain types of failures in the hardware of the computer itself. These may include such things as power failure or improper response of memory circuits to a data transfer. When such hardware problems are detected, the processor enters exception processing. The service routines may then take protective action to minimize the harmful effects to the procedures in progress at the time of the failure.

11.6 THE MC6809 INTERRUPT STRUCTURE

In comparison with other eight-bit microprocessors, the MC6809 has a fairly complex interrupt system. It includes both hardware and software interrupts in a vectored and partially prioritized scheme.

11.6.1 General Structure of the MC6809 Interrupt System

The exception system of the MC6809 includes four separate hardware interrupts. Each has its own individual interrupt input pin on the processor and its own specific vector location in the high end of the memory space. In addition to these interrupts, which are caused by conditions external to the processor, exception processing will be initiated whenever any one of three software interrupt instructions is executed.

The four hardware interrupts are named reset, nonmaskable interrupt, normal maskable interrupt, and fast maskable interrupt. The corresponding input pins to the processor are RESET, NMI, IRQ, and FIRQ, respectively. Each of these interrupt inputs is active-low. The software interrupt instructions are SWI, SWI2, and SWI3.

Because it is used to start the processor properly, the reset signal has priority over the other exceptions. The others have the following priority from highest to lowest: nonmaskable, SWI, fast maskable, normal maskable, SWI2, and SWI3. The vector addresses are all in the high end of memory, as listed in Table 11.1.

Bits I, E, and F in the condition code register are used by the interrupt system. I and F are the mask bits for the normal and fast maskable interrupts, respectively. If the I-bit is set, the processor will ignore an interrupt signal on the IRQ pin, and if the F-bit is set, it will ignore an interrupt signal on the FIRQ pin.

The E-bit is used by the processor to keep track of how many registers were stacked during the most recent interrupt request. If the E-bit is a one, the entire status was stacked; all of the registers except the system stack pointer itself were saved on the system stack. If the E-bit is a zero, only the program counter and the condition code register were saved. When executing the RTI (return from interrupt) instruction, the processor first restores the condition code register and then tests the E-bit to determine the number of additional registers to be restored. The processor's use of the E-bit will be described in detail in the following sections.

11.6.2 The MC6809 Reset

The MC6809 immediately ceases operation when it detects a zero on its reset line. When the line is returned to one, the processor fetches a starting address from the reset vector ($FFFE and $FFFF) and loads it into the program counter. It then begins fetching and executing instructions in the normal fashion, saving no status whatsoever.

While responding to the reset signal, the processor clears both interrupt mask bits (I and F) to ensure that neither interrupt will be allowed to interfere with the start-

TABLE 11.1
Interrupt vector locations in the MC6809

Interrupt	Vector address
RESET	FFFE and FFFF
NMI	FFFC and FFFD
SWI	FFFA and FFFB
IRQ	FFF8 and FFF9
FIRQ	FFF6 and FFF7
SWI2	FFF4 and FFF5
SWI3	FFF2 and FFF3
Unused but reserved	FFF0 and FFF1

up procedure. The processor also clears the direct page register in order to provide compatibility with the MC6800, an earlier Motorola microprocessor that has no direct page register and instead uses 00 for the upper half of all direct addresses.

11.6.3 The MC6809 Nonmaskable Interrupt

The nonmaskable interrupt is edge-triggered. This prevents the continuing presence of a zero on the NMI input from triggering repeated interrupts before the service routine has a chance to clear the interrupt request. The processor will always respond to a one-to-zero transition on the NMI pin—there is no way to force the processor to ignore it. In response to such a transition, the processor sets the E-bit in the condition code register to indicate that the entire status was saved. It then saves the contents of all of the processor registers (except the system stack pointer) on the system stack. Note that this includes the E-bit, which was just set. The processor then fetches the starting address for the NMI service routine from the NMI vector locations ($FFFC and $FFFD), loads it into the program counter, and starts a standard fetch cycle.

The NMI interrupt is used in special situations where its non-maskable feature is required. For example, it may be connected to a power-failure detector on the line side of the system power supply. After a power failure there is often an appreciable delay before the output of the power supply drops below the value necessary for the computer system to operate properly. This delay may be several tens of milliseconds—sufficient time to interrupt the current program and to terminate operations in such a way as to minimize the harm that might otherwise occur. Critical information may be saved, or necessary termination sequences may be instituted.

Another example of an application for a non-maskable interrupt is a real-time clock. If the interrupt associated with a clock signal happens to be masked off when the interrupt occurs, the clock time being maintained in the system could miss the signal and thus be incorrect. Using a non-maskable interrupt ensures that this does not occur.

11.6.4 The MC6809 Maskable Interrupts

The normal maskable interrupt is the standard I/O interrupt for the MC6809. It can be masked off by setting the I-bit in the condition code register. When the I-bit is clear and the IRQ line is low, the processor recognizes the interrupt. It sets the E-bit and saves the entire status on the system stack. After having saved the original contents, the processor sets the I-bit in the condition code register in order to turn off the IRQ, so that the service routine will have a chance to service the interrupt without the processor's immediately responding to the same interrupt request (or another one) again. The processor then fetches the service routine starting address from the IRQ vector. Note that this procedure will automatically result in a cleared I-bit (its original value) when the original condition code register is restored during the execution of the return from interrupt instruction at the end of the interrupt service routine.

The fast maskable interrupt is an alternative to the normal interrupt. In response to a fast interrupt request, the processor saves only the condition code register and the program counter on the system stack. The processor responds more quickly to this interrupt because of the time saved in not stacking the other processor registers.

When the F-bit is clear and the FIRQ pin is pulled low, the processor recognizes the fast interrupt request, clears the E-bit, and saves only the condition code register and the program counter on the system stack. It then sets both I and F to mask any further interrupts and to allow the system to respond to the current interrupt. When the return from interrupt instruction is executed at the end of the service routine, the original content of the condition code register is retrieved from the stack. At that time the original values of the I and F bits are automatically restored.

The ASSYM09 assembler/simulator available for use with this text simulates the maskable hardware interrupts with the use of two keys on the PC keyboard. Pressing the I key simulates the presence of a normal interrupt signal. Pressing the F key simulates the presence of a fast interrupt. When using simulated interrupts, all of the usual requirements concerning the interrupt service routine and the mask bits must be satisfied. Any error in their use may result in the premature termination of the simulated program. The simulator uses the standard ASSIST09 monitor vector swap routine described in the following paragraphs.

When using interrupts with an MC6809 system (or a simulated system) that includes the ASSIST09 monitor program, the user must inform the monitor of the starting address for the service routine. Thereafter, the monitor retains this address and refers to it whenever an interrupt occurs.

To inform ASSIST09 (or the simulator), the user's program must include instructions that load the X register with the desired address and accumulator A with either the code 0AH (for the FIRQ vector) or the code 0CH (for the IRQ vector). The program must then execute the following two-byte sequence:

```
SWI
FCB 9
```

This sequence is known in ASSIST09 as the SWI vector swap service and is used to install the interrupt vectors. This and other SWI services are described in more detail in the following section.

11.6.5 The MC6809 Software Interrupts

Each of the three MC6809 software interrupt instructions causes the processor first to set the E-bit and then to save the entire status on the system stack. The SWI instruction then sets the I-bit and F-bit in the (new) condition code register, thus masking these two lower-priority hardware interrupts while the service routine for the SWI is being executed. The other two software interrupt instructions, SWI2 and SWI3, have a lower priority and so they do not mask the two hardware interrupts.

The ASSIST09 monitor program uses the SWI instruction to support calls to the monitor from a user's program. The monitor makes use of the stacked program counter (stacked during execution of the SWI) to locate a single byte following SWI in the user's program. The value of this byte determines which of several available services the monitor will perform for the user. After performing the service, the monitor skips over this code byte and returns to the next location in the user's program. The MC6809 Microprocessor Programming Manual available from Motorola Inc. describes these services in detail.

The ASSYM09 assembler/simulator software supports many of the ASSIST09 services and a few additional ones. The services available in ASSYM09 are listed in Table 11.2. They are described in the file named 6809USER.DOC included with the software. The code referred to in the table is the content of the location in the user's program immediately following the SWI instruction. This code may be included in the user's source program with the FCB assembler directive. For example, to have a user's program pause and wait for a key to be pushed and its code to be loaded into accumulator A, the program need only include the following two lines:

```
SWI
FCB 0
```

11.6.6 Special Interrupt Instructions in the MC6809

In certain applications the main program may run to completion before the occurrence of an anticipated hardware interrupt. No additional program activity is possible until an interrupt occurs. In order to speed up the response to an interrupt when it does occur under these circumstances, the MC6809 includes the special instruction CWAI, clear CC bits and wait for interrupt. The instruction includes one byte of immediate data.

When the CWAI instruction is executed, the processor ANDs the immediate data byte with the content of the condition code register. This provides a means for clearing the interrupt mask bits. The processor then sets the E-bit before saving the entire status on the system stack, including the modified condition code register with the E-bit set. It remains inactive while waiting for an interrupt to occur.

TABLE 11.2
ASSYM09 SWI user services

Code	Service
0	Input a character from the keyboard
1	Display a character on the simulated screen
2	Display a string on the simulated screen
3	Output CR and LF then display a string on the simulated screen
4	Display a byte in hex on the simulated screen
5	Display a double-byte in hex on the simulated screen
6	Output CR and LF
8	End of user's program
9	Change IRQ or FIRQ vector
10	Clear simulated screen and reset cursor
11	Move cursor on simulated screen
12	Get cursor position on simulated screen
13	Produce an audible tone (beep)

```
1. WRDISK LDX   DATA  ADDRESS OF BLOCK
2.        LDB   SIZE  SIZE OF BLOCK
3. NEXT   LDA   ,X+   GET NEXT BYTE
4. WAIT   SYNC        WAIT FOR INTERRUPT
5.        Interrupt Occurs
6. WRITE  STA   DISK  WRITE BYTE
7.        DECB        COUNT IT. FINISHED?
8.        BNE   NEXT  IF NOT, GO BACK FOR MORE
```

FIGURE 11.6
Use of the MC6809 SYNC instruction.

When a subsequent interrupt does occur, the delay associated with saving the status is eliminated. Note that whichever type of interrupt occurs following this instruction, including the fast maskable interrupt, the entire status will have already been saved on the stack. The processor fetches the starting address for the interrupt service routine and services the interrupt. At the completion of the service routine, the RTI instruction will cause the entire status to be restored and program execution will continue from the instruction following the CWAI instruction.

The only way that the processor can continue any activity following the execution of the CWAI instruction is to respond to a hardware interrupt; this includes the nonmaskable interrupt, the two maskable interrupts, and the reset.

Another special MC6809 interrupt instruction is SYNC, synchronize to an external event. When this single-byte instruction is executed, the processor stops processing instructions and waits for an interrupt. When any interrupt occurs, the processor resumes processing instructions. If the interrupt that occurs is enabled, the processor will perform the standard exception processing. If the interrupt is masked, the processor will simply continue fetching and executing the instructions following the SYNC instruction. SYNC is often used with a masked interrupt and no interrupt service routine. It synchronizes program execution with hardware events taking place outside the processor.

The program segment shown in Figure 11.6 illustrates how the SYNC instruction is used to wait for an external device to be ready to transfer data. In this example, the SYNC instruction serves as an alternative to a polling loop.

The segment of code in Figure 11.6 transfers a block of data from memory to a disk. The starting address of the block is stored in a location named DATA, and the block length is stored in a location named SIZE. The address of the interface to the disk input buffer is named DISK. The system will receive a masked interrupt from the disk when the disk buffer is ready to receive a byte of data.

After initializing the pointer and the counter and picking up the first byte in lines 1 through 3, the SYNC instruction in line 4 causes the program to wait for the disk to become ready for data transfer. When it is, the interrupt restarts the processing at line 6, where the byte is written and counted (line 7). Line 8 is the usual test for repeating the loop.

11.7 THE MC68000 EXCEPTION STRUCTURE

The MC68000 includes externally generated interrupts, software interrupt (trap) instructions, hardware- and software-initiated conditional traps, and a single-instruction tracing option. These exceptions are organized into a complex prioritized system that supports 256 vectors and three priority groups with a total of 14 priority levels.

11.7.1 General Structure of the MC68000 Exception System

The external exception system of the MC68000 includes a three-pin interrupt input bus, which is used to trigger an interrupt and to identify the interrupting device. This interrupt bus allows the encoding of up to seven separate external sources by priority level. In addition, a *bus error* (BERR) pin may be used with external logic to inform the processor of an unusual condition, such as an illegal memory access or a failure of a device to respond. These, together with the reset input, provide a total of nine external exceptions.

The interrupt mask consists of the three least significant bits in the system byte of the status register. These bits indicate the current priority status of the system, and they may be changed under program control while the processor is in the supervisor state. Interrupts at a priority level less than or equal to the current priority status are masked off and will be ignored by the processor, except for the fact that a level seven interrupt request is nonmaskable and will always be recognized each time the request level changes from some lower value to seven.

Certain internal conditions can also initiate exception processing. These include an attempt to execute an illegal instruction or one having certain special op-words, an attempt to do a word or long-word memory access with an odd address, an attempt to execute a privileged instruction while in the user state, the execution of a trap instruction, and the occurrence of specific trap conditions. These are the trap conditions: attempting to divide by zero, having a one in the V-bit during the execution of the trap on overflow instruction (TRAPV), and the register content being out of bounds during the execution of the check register against bounds instruction (CHK). Exception processing will also be initiated after the execution of any instruction whenever the trace bit in the supervisor's status register is set. Table 11.3 lists the various MC68000 exceptions, which are grouped by priority and by the way in which they are handled by the processor. Group 0, the highest-priority group, includes the reset, bus

TABLE 11.3
MC68000 exception types

Exception type	Source
Interrupts	Interrupt bus
Reset	RESET input
Bus error	BERR input
Illegal instruction	Invalid op-word pattern
Special op-word	Op-word of 1010 or 1111
Address error	Odd address access with word or long word size
Privilege violation	Execute privileged instruction while in user state
Instructions	TRAP, TRAPV, CHK, DIVS, DIVU
Trace	T-bit set in CCR

TABLE 11.4
MC68000 exception groups and priorities

Group	Exception type	Exception processing
0	Reset Bus error Address error	Aborts current instruction
1	Trace Interrupt Illegal and special op-words Privilege violation	Completes current instruction
2	Instructions	Called for by the current instruction

error, and address error exceptions. With these exceptions, the processor aborts the current instruction and responds immediately. With Group 1 exceptions, the processor completes the execution of the current instruction before initiating exception processing. This group includes trace, interrupts, illegal instructions, special op-words, and privilege violations. Group 2 exceptions occur as a result of the routine execution of instructions, and they have the lowest priority. Table 11.4 lists the exceptions by group and in decreasing order of priority within each group.

The MC68000 exception vectors are in the low end of the supervisor memory space at addresses determined by an eight-bit *vector number*. Internal logic determines the vector number associated with each of the non-interrupt exceptions. For interrupt vectors, the external circuitry must supply a *user interrupt vector number* on the lowest eight bits of the data bus during a special read cycle (the interrupt acknowledge cycle), which the processor executes when it responds to an interrupt. Alternatively, the external circuitry may signal to the processor that it is to use an internal vector number (an *autovector* number) for a particular interrupt.

The vector address is obtained by multiplying the vector number by four (shifting left by two bits) and appending 14 zeros, as shown in Figure 11.7. The long word (24 bits of it) found at that address is the service routine starting address, which is loaded into the program counter to service the exception.

The exception vector number assignments and their associated vector addresses are listed in Table 11.5. Note that the reset exception has two vectors—one vector for

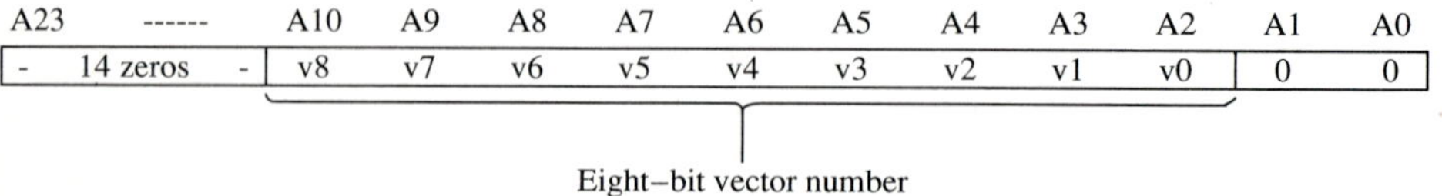

FIGURE 11.7
Translation of an MC68000 vector number to a vector address.

TABLE 11.5
MC68000 exception vector number assignments

Number	Address (Dec/Hex)	Assignment
0	0/000	Reset—initial SSP
1	4/004	Reset—initial PC
2	8/008	Bus error
3	12/00C	Address error
4	16/010	Illegal instruction
5	20/014	Divide by zero
6	24/018	CHK instruction
7	28/01C	TRAPV instruction
8	32/020	Privilege violation
9	36/024	Trace
10	40/028	Op-code 1010
11	44/02C	Op-code 1111
12–14[1]	48/030–59/03B	Unassigned, reserved
15	60/03C	Uninitialized interrupt
16–23[1]	64/040–95/05F	Unassigned, reserved
24	96/060	Spurious interrupt[2]
25–31	100/064–127/07F	Autovectors 1 through 7
32–47	128/080–191/0BF	TRAPn for $n = 0$ to $n = 15$
48–63[1]	192/0C0–255/0FF	Unassigned, reserved
64–255	256/100–1023/3FF	User interrupt vectors

[1]Vector numbers 12–14, 16–23, and 48–63 are reserved for future enhancements by the manufacturer and should not be used.

[2]A spurious interrupt is indicated by a bus error during the interrupt acknowledge cycle.

the initial value of the supervisor stack pointer and one for the starting address of the reset routine.

Exception processing in the MC68000 proceeds through the steps shown in Figure 11.8. The processor first makes a temporary copy of the current status register. It then sets the status register for exception processing by clearing the T-bit and setting the S-bit. This will have the effect of turning off the trace mode and putting the processor into the supervisor privilege state during the execution of the service routine. If the exception is an interrupt, the interrupt mask will also be set to the priority level of the interrupt being acknowledged. Next, the exception vector number is determined and is used to generate the vector address. The processor then saves the status by pushing (onto the supervisor's stack) the original program counter and the copy of the original status register. Finally, the starting address for the exception service routine is fetched from the exception vector and loaded into the program counter. The processor then resumes its normal operation and executes the exception service routine. The service routine must end with the *return from exception* instruction (RTE). When executing this instruction, the processor restores the original status register and program counter from the supervisor's stack and returns to the interrupted program sequence.

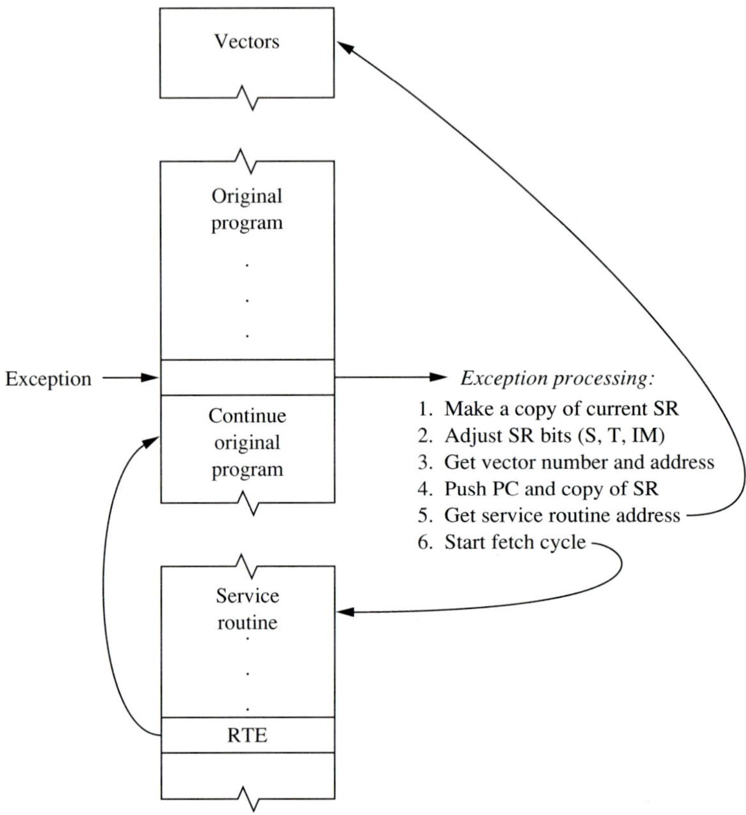

FIGURE 11.8
MC68000 exception processing.

11.7.2 The MC68000 Reset

The MC68000 immediately stops fetching and executing whenever it detects a zero on its reset line. When the line is returned to one, the processor fetches two addresses from the reset vectors; one is loaded into the supervisor's stack pointer and the other into the program counter. The trace bit is cleared to turn the trace mode off, and the supervisor bit is set to the supervisor privilege state. The interrupt mask is set to level seven to ensure that none of the maskable interrupts will be allowed to interrupt the start-up procedure before the point where the program unmasks them. The processor then begins fetching and executing instructions in the normal fashion, having saved no status whatsoever.

The RESET instruction (a privileged instruction) does not reset the processor but merely asserts the reset pin in order to reset external devices.

11.7.3 The MC68000 Interrupts

The three-bit interrupt bus and the interrupt mask provide seven levels of interrupt priorities numbered from one to seven, with level seven having the highest priority.

An external device signals an interrupt request to the processor by placing its encoded interrupt level on the interrupt bus. A code of zero means that no request is pending.

When the level specified in the interrupt mask is greater than or equal to the level of the request, the processor ignores the request. However, a level-seven request will always be honored whenever it is first initiated, regardless of the mask level. If a request is pending at some later time when the mask is changed to a value lower than the requesting level, exception processing will be initiated.

If the request level is greater than the mask level (or if it has just changed to level seven), the processor initiates exception processing. It first saves a temporary copy of the current status register and then sets the status to supervisor with tracing suppressed and priority level equal to that of the interrupt being acknowledged. Then it reads a vector number from the interrupting device on the low half of the data bus. This should be some value between 64 and 255, since user interrupt vector numbers fall within that range (see Table 11.5). Alternatively, the interface circuitry may request autovectoring instead of providing a vector number. It does so by returning a signal on the VPA line during the vector number read cycle. In that case, a fixed number corresponding to the request level is used (numbers 25 through 31—see Table 11.5).

If the interface circuitry determines that no device requires an interrupt service, it must return a bus error signal on the BERR line during the vector number read cycle. The processor assumes that the interrupt signal was spurious and it uses vector number 24 (the spurious interrupt vector).

Following the generation of the vector address from the vector number, the processor continues the standard exception processing steps. It saves the program counter and original status register contents on the supervisor stack and fetches and loads the starting address of the service routine from the appropriate vector address.

The nonmaskable interrupt level (level seven) is edge-triggered. That is, whenever the request level *changes* to level seven, it is acknowledged. This prevents the continuing presence of a level seven request from triggering repeated interrupts before the service routine has had a chance to service the interrupt. Section 11.6.3, which discusses the nonmaskable interrupt in the MC6809, describes several instances where the nonmaskable characteristic of the level seven interrupt would be desirable.

The ASSYM000 assembler/simulator available for use with this book simulates autovector interrupts in an MC68000 system with keys Alt-1 through Alt-7 for levels one through seven, respectively. When using the simulated interrupts, all of the usual requirements concerning the interrupt service routine and the mask bits must be satisfied. Any error in their use may result in the premature termination of the simulated program. Before implementing a simulated interrupt, the user must inform the simulator of the service routine starting address. In order to do this, the Options/Add selection must be used. The simulator menu for this selection is self-explanatory.

11.7.4 The MC68000 Instruction Exceptions

A Group 2 exception in the MC68000 is one caused by an instruction. The exception may occur either because the processor recognizes a specific abnormal condition or because the instruction itself requests the exception as a part of its normal operation.

The sixteen TRAP #n instructions (TRAPn with some assemblers) unconditionally force exception processing with vector number $32+n$. Similarly, instructions having op-words starting with bit patterns 1010 or 1111 (known as *unimplemented instructions*) force exception processing with special vectors assigned to them (numbers 10 and 11, respectively). The former are often used for operating system calls, while the latter are used for emulating in software instructions that are not available in the processor's instruction set. When one of these instructions is executed, the status register is temporarily saved, the supervisor state is selected, and tracing is turned off. The vector number is generated internally, and the original status register and program counter are saved on the supervisor's stack. The program counter address saved is that of the subsequent instruction. The exception service routine starting address is fetched from the vector and loaded into the program counter, and the processor enters the fetch cycle.

The special instruction ILLEGAL ($48FC) and all other instructions that do not include a legal op-word unconditionally force exception processing in a similar fashion with vector number 4. However, these instruction exceptions cause the processor to save the address of the first word of the instruction itself rather than that of the subsequent instruction.

The remaining Group 2 exceptions are conditional; exception processing is initiated only when particular conditions prevail during the execution of specific instructions. These conditions include attempting to divide by zero during the execution of the DIVS or the DIVU instruction, the overflow bit (V) being equal to one during the execution of the TRAPV instruction, and a data register content being out-of-bounds during the execution of the CHK instruction. The address saved for each of these is that of the instruction following the one that initiates the exception.

Another conditional exception, privilege violation, is initiated whenever one of the privileged instructions listed in Table 11.6 is executed while in the user state. The privilege violation exception causes the processor to save the address of the first word of the instruction itself.

The ASSYM000 assembler/simulator simulates the zero divide, CHK, TRAPV, and TRAPn instruction exceptions. The user must inform the simulator of the starting address for each service routine using the Options/Add selection. The simulator does not support the other instruction exceptions.

TABLE 11.6
MC68000 privileged instructions

AND to SR
EOR to SR
OR to SR
MOVE to SR
MOVE USP
RESET
RTE
STOP

11.7.5 The MC68000 Trace Exception

The MC68000 includes a trace mode of operation during which exception processing is forced after each instruction is executed. This supports the implementation of a single-step debugging procedure as part of a monitor system to assist in program development.

The trace mode is selected whenever the T-bit in the status register is set and disabled whenever the T-bit is cleared. When the T-bit is set, a trace exception (vector number 9) will be initiated after the execution of each instruction. The standard exception processing occurs with the address of the next instruction in sequence being saved. Of course, during this transition the T-bit is cleared so that the service routine may execute without attempting to trace itself. The return at the end of the trace service routine resets the T-bit to its original value and returns the processor to the original (traced) program.

11.7.6 The MC68000 Hardware Exceptions

The MC68000 hardware exceptions, bus error (vector number 2) and address error (vector number 3), abort the memory cycle during which they occur and immediately force exception processing. Bus error is signaled by external circuitry through a special input pin (BERR). Address error is detected internally when the processor is about to attempt to access an instruction or a word or long-word operand at an odd address.

When either of these exceptions occurs, the processor follows the usual practice of copying the status register, turning on the supervisor state, turning off the trace state, and generating the vector address. However, in addition to saving the program counter and status register on the supervisor's stack, the processor saves the address of the memory location that was being accessed during the aborted memory cycle, the first word of the instruction being executed during the aborted instruction cycle, and information about the processing state at the time of the exception (read or write, instruction or data, exception or vector fetch, and so forth).

If either a bus error or an address error occurs while the processor is doing exception processing for any Group 0 exception (reset, bus error, or address error), the processor halts and remains inactive. It can be restarted only with a new reset signal on the RESET pin. This behavior minimizes the damage that might be done if the processor were to continue to attempt to operate in the face of some apparently catastrophic failure.

SUMMARY

Exception processing is an exception to the standard fetch/execute cycling of the processor. It provides a convenient means for a computer system to handle the out-of-the-ordinary procedures for which the programmer cannot precisely plan. It can support the transfer of information between the system and peripheral devices, provide a means of detecting and responding to run-time errors occurring in calculations or to hardware problems arising during system operation, provide for the orderly start-up of programs, and provide an easy-to-use software switch to allow context changes between widely differing programs.

This chapter has examined several exception structures and many of their pertinent hardware and software features. It has also described the major features of the MC6809 and the MC68000 systems: the interrupts and other exceptions, their special characteristics, some applications for them, and the special interrupt-related instructions.

REVIEW PROBLEMS

11.1. a. Write an MC6809 assembly language instruction that can be used to enable each of the following interrupts: IRQ, FIRQ, NMI, RESET, and all of the SWIs

b. Write an MC6809 assembly language instruction that can be used to disable each of these interrupts. IRQ, FIRQ, NMI, RESET, all of the SWIs

11.2. List the seven MC6809 interrupts by name (not by mnemonic) and state whether each saves the entire status of the machine.

11.3. List the MC6809 registers that will be stacked in the order in which they will be stacked during exception processing in each of the following circumstances. Whenever the CCR is stacked, state the values of the E-, I-, and F-bits. Whenever the PC is stacked, state the address value.

a. An FIRQ is recognized during the execution of an SWI instruction at location $1234.

b. An IRQ is recognized during the execution of an SWI instruction at location $1234.

c. An NMI is recognized during the execution of an SWI instruction at location $1234.

d. An FIRQ is recognized during the execution of an SWI3 instruction at location $1234.

e. An IRQ is recognized during the execution of an SWI2 instruction at location $1234.

f. An NMI is recognized during the execution of an SWI3 instruction at location $1234.

11.4. Write an interrupt service routine in MC6809 assembly language for the NMI interrupt wired to detect power failures. The routine should save the contents of all of the processor registers and of the locations named TEMP*n* for $n = 1$ to 8 in a nonvolatile block of memory that starts in location $A100. Include statements that specify the NMI vector value (in ASSIST09) for the routine.

11.5. Write an interrupt service routine in MC6809 assembly language for the FIRQ interrupt that is wired to an external timer signal. The routine should add one to the content of a location named COUNT, and if the unsigned value overflows, the routine should execute an SWI2 instruction before returning from the service routine. In order to clear the timer interrupt request, the routine must write something (any value) to location TMRSTAT. Include statements specifying the FIRQ vector value for the routine (in ASSIST09).

11.6. Write an interrupt service routine in MC6809 assembly language that adds one to a counter that is to count the number of seconds in a day (86,400). When the count reaches 86,400, the routine is to add one to a location named DAYS and reset the counter. An external clock circuit will drive the nonmaskable interrupt line with a one cycle per second square-wave. Because this interrupt is edge-triggered, it need not be cleared by the service routine. Include all necessary defining directives and instructions.

11.7. List all of the exceptions in the MC68000 processor with as many details of each as you can ascertain.

11.8. The reset, bus error, and address error exceptions in the MC68000 cannot be masked. For each one, explain why the designers of the processor chose not to allow it to be masked.

11.9. Write an interrupt service routine in MC68000 assembly language for the level 7 autovectored interrupt wired to detect power failures. The routine should save the contents of all of the processor registers and of the locations named TEMP*n* for $n = 1$ to 8 in a nonvolatile block of memory starting in location $AB1000.

11.10. Write an exception service routine in MC68000 assembly language for the divide by zero exception. The routine should replace the divisor (DVR) by the smallest possible nonzero single precision binary value having the same sign as the dividend (DVD) and return to execute the divide instruction that initiated the exception.

11.11. Write an interrupt service routine in MC68000 assembly language for the level 7 interrupt that uses vector number 83 and is wired to an external timer signal. The routine should add one to the content of a location named COUNT, and if the unsigned value overflows, the routine should execute a TRAP5 instruction before returning from the service routine. In order to clear the timer interrupt request, the routine must write something (any value) to location TMRSTAT. Include statements specifying the content of vector number 83.

11.12. Write an MC68000 interrupt service routine in assembly language that adds one to a counter that is to count the number of seconds in a day (86,400). When the count reaches 86,400, the routine is to add one to a location named DAYS and reset the counter. An external clock circuit will place a low level on all three interrupt lines simultaneously, generating a level-seven interrupt once per second. Because a level-seven interrupt is edge-triggered, it need not be cleared by the service routine. Use autovectoring and include all necessary defining directives and instructions.

CHAPTER 12

MEMORY STRUCTURES

The two primary types of memory, ROM and RAM, are distinguished on the basis of whether the contents can be changed by the processor during program execution. Additional classifications of each are based mainly on details of their internal structure. Although the detailed internal structure of a memory integrated circuit (memory chip) varies widely from type to type, they are functionally very similar. That is, each memory chip includes the same few basic structures that are used for the same few basic tasks.

This chapter will examine the basic structure of memory circuits and the differences between various classifications of memory: ROM, RAM, and several types of programmable ROMs and nonvolatile RAMs. The chapter will also discuss the task of decoding the address provided by the processor in order to select a desired location out of several memory chips within a computer system. It will conclude by examining several alternative circuit approaches to address decoding.

12.1 INTEGRATED CIRCUIT MEMORY

The circuits that make up the main memory of a computer system are available in the form of integrated circuits, or chips. These chips are similar to those encountered earlier in this book—for example, those containing gates, decoders, flip-flops, microprocessors, and so forth—in that they require a source of power and additional support chips in order to operate properly.

The memory on a given integrated circuit usually comprises one specific type. Among the different types available are those that contain information in a permanent form and can only be read by the processor, those that can be altered and reprogrammed off-line but still only read by the processor, and those into which the processor can write information as well. Regardless of this read/write behavior, all types of memory chips have certain common characteristics which will be examined in the following section.

12.1.1 The Functional Structure of a Memory Chip

The size of a memory chip is specified by the number of locations it contains and the number of bits per location. The total number of bits per chip may be less than one thousand to as many as several million and is always an integer power of two. The number of locations varies from 128 to 4 MB (1 MB equals 2^{20}), while the number of bits per location may be 1, 2, 4, or 8. For example, one popular 32 K-bit memory chip is specified as 4K×8 (4096 eight-bit locations) in size.

The bits in a specific location on a memory chip are accessed by means of pins which are grouped into an address bus, a data bus, and a control bus. The bit pattern corresponding to the address of the location is placed on the address bus and the necessary control signals are placed on the control bus. The memory will then respond by placing the content of that location on the data bus (a read operation) or by writing the data bus content into that location (a write operation).

The address bus on a memory chip contains exactly the number of lines necessary to access the number of locations present, that is, $\log_2$ of the number of locations. Thus, a 1K×8 memory chip has 10 address lines ($2^{10} = 1024 = 1K$), while a 64K×8 chip has 16 address lines ($2^{16} = 64K$). The data bus contains one line for each bit in a location, so each of these chips has an eight-bit data bus.

All memory chips are functionally similar, even though the actual circuit implementation of the structure and the electronic details of the memory bit-cells may differ between memory types. Figure 12.1 shows the structure of a typical 1024×8 ROM. Every solid-state memory chip includes the functional structures shown therein.

The following sections will describe the functions performed by the various blocks in Figure 12.1.

12.1.2 The Address Decoder

The *address decoder* in Figure 12.1 implements the decode function that was first introduced in Chapter 2. The signals on the n-bit address bus entering the memory chip are interpreted as a binary number. The one out of the 2^n outputs of the decoder corresponding to that number will have logic level 1 on it. The other outputs will remain at level 0. Thus, the decoder selects a desired location on the memory chip and focuses on it to the exclusion of all others.

The large size of the memory chip address decoder makes it impractical to implement it in the standard AND gate structure discussed in Chapter 2 and shown in

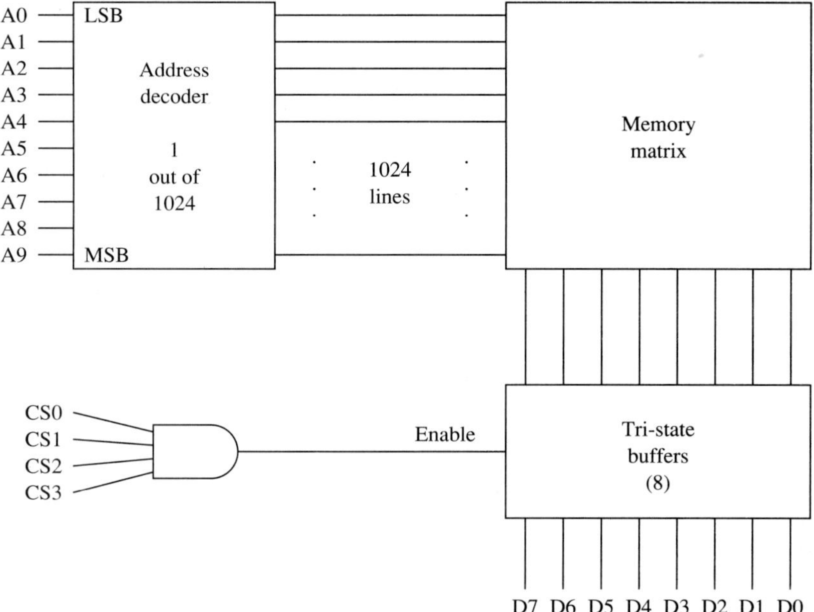

FIGURE 12.1
Functional block diagram of a memory chip.

Figure 2.15. For example, a one-out-of-1048 decoder would require 1048 gates with 10 inputs each! Instead, a matrix approach similar to that shown in Figure 12.2 is commonly used.

In the matrix decoder, the five bits of the upper half-address are decoded by a one-out-of-32 decoder into a *row address* and the five bits of the lower half-address are decoded by a similar decoder into a *column address*. These two sets of decoder outputs become row and column lines into the AND gate matrix as shown. At each of the 1024 intersections, a two-input AND gate implements the final one-out-of-1024 decoding selection.

The matrix decoder approach is used with all sizes of memories, and in some cases the address may not be subdivided into equal parts. For example, in a chip with 8 K locations the 13 address pins may be subdivided into groups of seven upper pins that define a row address and six lower pins that define a column address. In that case, the matrix would be 128 (2^7) rows by 64 (2^6) columns in size. The upper partial-address is referred to as the row address and the lower partial-address as the column address.

12.1.3 The Memory Matrix

As shown in Figure 12.1, the 1024 outputs from the decoder go to the *memory matrix*, an array of special electronic circuits or devices that implement the actual bit-by-bit

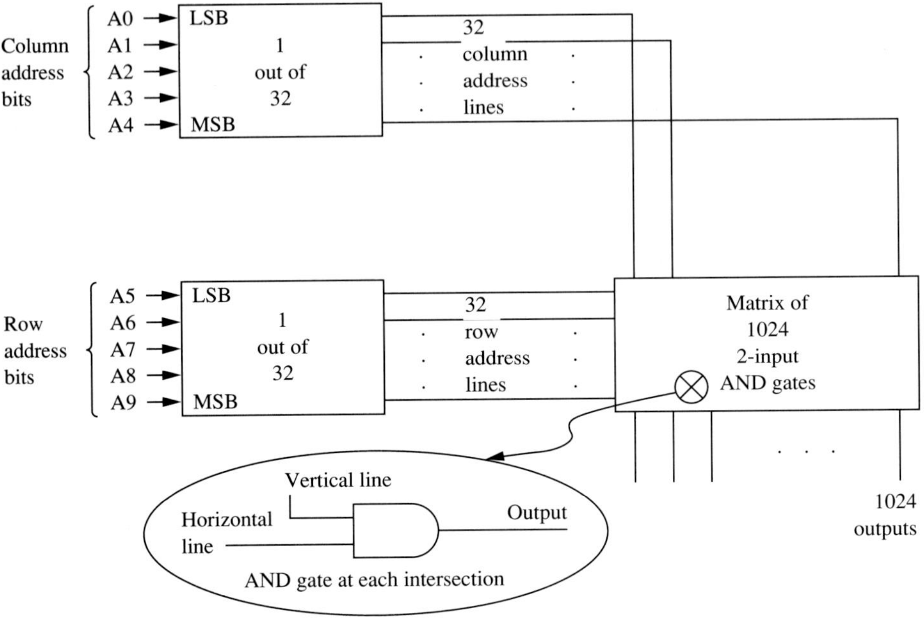

FIGURE 12.2
Matrix decoder circuit.

memory function. The size of the matrix is 2^n rows by m columns, where n is the number of lines in the chip's address bus and m is the number of lines in the chip's data bus. The 1K×8 example ROM used here has ten address pins, eight data pins, and a 1024×8 memory matrix.

Part of the memory matrix of the ROM chip is shown functionally in Figure 12.3. In that figure, R_0 through R_7 are resistors that hold the data output leads at logic level 0 (0 volts, or ground) in the absence of any other signal. The other components in the figure are electronic devices called *diodes*. A diode will pass a positive signal (logic level 1) through in the direction of its arrow but will not pass such a signal in the opposite direction.

The address decoder in the memory chip allows the input address to access a specific horizontal row in the memory matrix by applying logic level 1 to it. The diodes in only that row of the matrix will pass the 1 through from that horizontal line to certain vertical lines. Each row intersection in the matrix containing a diode will pass the 1 to that particular vertical line. Each intersection that does not contain a diode will not pass a 1, so that vertical line will remain at 0, held there by its resistor.

In Figure 12.3 the location corresponding to Address #0 contains one in bit 7, one in bit 6, zero in bit 5, one in bit 4, zero in bit 3, zero in bit 2, one in bit 1, and one in bit 0. That is, location #0 contains the pattern 11010011 (D3 in hex). The figure also shows that location #1 contains 00110110 (36 in hex) and location #1023 contains 11110000 (F0). The ROM shown in Figure 12.1 can thus be programmed by including diodes in its memory matrix where ones are necessary and omitting

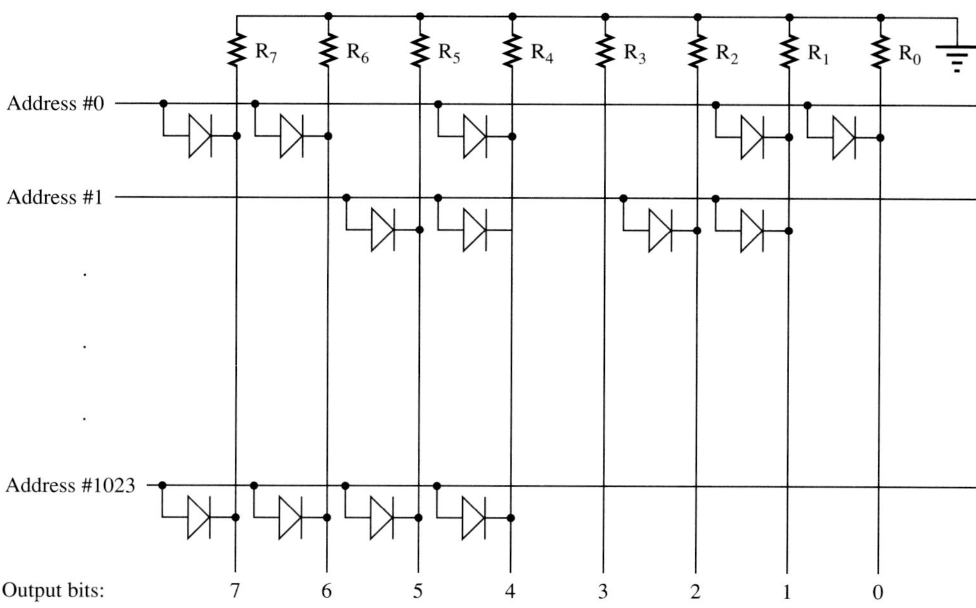

FIGURE 12.3
Memory matrix circuit for a ROM.

diodes where zeros are necessary. It is the physical presence or absence of a diode that implements the memory function on a bit-by-bit basis in this type of ROM.

12.1.4 Tri-State Buffers and Chip-Select Inputs

The bit pattern in the selected row appears on the vertical data output lines from the memory matrix. This pattern does not go directly to the chip's data bus because of the conflict that may occur there when several memory chips are included in a system.

If two or more chips were to place signals on a common microprocessor data bus, one chip might place a zero on a line when another places a one on the same line. This results in a conflict known as *bus contention*. When this occurs, the result is unpredictable. Any circuit required to place signals on the data bus must be equipped with special output gates known as *tri-state buffers* to prevent bus contention.

A tri-state buffer is a logic circuit having two inputs—*data* and *enable*—and a single output. Figure 12.4 shows its logic symbol and truth table. Whenever the enable input is high, the output follows the data input—1 when the data input is 1, 0 when the data input is 0. In this condition the tri-state buffer is said to be enabled. When the enable input is low, the output is placed at neither logic level 0 nor logic level 1. Instead, it is said to be disabled, or in a third state—a high-impedance state. In this state the output is not connected to any source inside the chip but is free to be determined by some other external source connected to the output line.

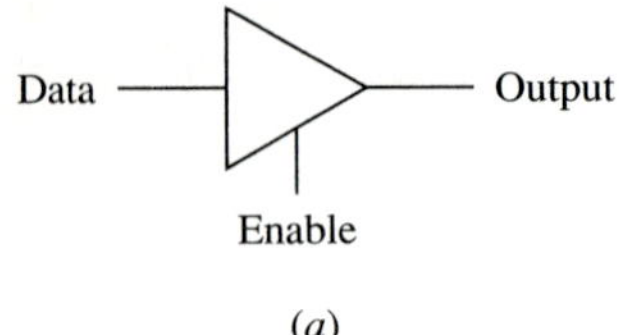

(*a*)

Enable	data	Output
0	0	Hi-Z*
0	1	Hi-Z*
1	0	0
1	1	1

*In the Hi-Z (high-impedance) state, the output is disconnected.

(*b*)

FIGURE 12.4
The tri-state buffer: (*a*) symbol, (*b*) truth table.

The data signals from the memory matrix in a memory chip are connected to the data bus through a bank of tri-state buffers having a common enable line. This enable line is brought out on a pin from the chip and is called the *chip-select pin*. In order for the memory chip to place signals on its data bus in response to an address on its address bus, the chip select pin must be held high (enabled).

In some memory chips the enable line into the tri-state buffers is the output from an AND gate on the memory chip itself. The inputs to this gate are then brought out from the memory chip as a series of several chip-select pins. This is the case in the example of Figure 12.1, where the chip-select lines are shown as CS0, CS1, CS2, and CS3.

Every memory chip must have at least one chip-select pin. All of the spare pins available on the integrated circuit package housing the memory chip are commonly used to provide the user with as many chip-select lines as possible. Often, one or more of these chip select lines will be active low. That line must be low AND the other lines must be at their appropriate levels in order to select that particular memory chip and have its output data appear on the data bus.

The 1024×8 ROM in our example would require a 24-pin package: ten address pins, eight data pins, two power pins, and four chip-select pins. Because it is a ROM, it needs no read/write control line. If it were a RAM, the matrix would differ, and it would require an input to select the direction of the data (probably in the form of a READ/WRITE control line). One of the chip-selects would be eliminated to make room for this input so that the resulting RAM would still fit into a 24-pin package.

12.2 READ ONLY MEMORY TYPES

The ROM used as an example in the previous section contains its information in the form of a physical structure, the diode memory matrix. As long as the ROM remains intact and functional, the content of the memory will not change, regardless of the presence or absence of power to the chip. A memory chip exhibiting such behavior is said to be *nonvolatile*. A nonvolatile memory retains its information regardless of whether the system is powered up or not. This type of memory is necessary if a system is to start up properly when the power is first turned on. Every computer system must have a minimum amount of nonvolatile memory.

12.2.1 Custom-Masked ROMs

The diodes in the memory matrix of a ROM may be installed in the required patterns when the integrated circuit is manufactured. Usually such a memory circuit is first made with every diode in place and wired into the matrix. The connections that are not necessary are then etched away during a final step in the manufacturing process. To carry out this step the manufacturer must construct a special jig that is custom designed to incorporate the customer's information into the memory. This jig is called a *mask*, and the resulting memory is called a *mask-programmed* or *custom-masked* ROM.

Of all of the types of nonvolatile memory available, the custom-masked ROM has the lowest cost per bit. However, the special mask is very expensive, on the order of several thousand dollars. In addition to this high initial cost, the turnaround time is quite long. It may take several weeks for the manufacturer to construct the mask and deliver the first ROM. These factors have led to the development of other types of ROMs that can be programmed by the user in the field, called *field programmable ROMs* or simply *programmable ROMs* (PROMs).

12.2.2 Fused-Link PROMs

The original programmable ROM is the *fused-link PROM*. This PROM has all of its diodes wired into the matrix, but the connections to them are made of a fusible material that can be readily melted or burned out. The integrated circuit package has an extra pin that must be brought to a high voltage in order to transfer the data applied to the data lines into the location addressed by the address lines.

The task of programming the thousands of bits in a PROM is only feasible with the aid of a computerized tool known as a *PROM programmer*, which can program a variety of different PROMs directly from hex files. Because a physical change takes place when it is programmed (the melting of the links), the fused-link PROM can be programmed only once. Its inability to be reprogrammed makes this type of PROM less popular than others. Although not used as often as it once was, it has contributed an enduring expression to computer jargon. The phrase "burning a PROM" is a common way of describing the activity of programming any PROM, even though in many cases it no longer involves burning out fused links.

12.2.3 Ultraviolet Erasable PROMs

A second type of PROM is one that can be erased by ultraviolet light and reprogrammed many times. The complete name for this device is the *UltraViolet Erasable*

Programmable Read Only Memory (UVEPROM). When the unqualified term EPROM is used, it usually refers to this device. The term PROM is reserved for one-time-programmable memories such as the fused-link devices.

The components in the memory matrix of the UVEPROM are complex electronic devices known as *floating gate avalanche injection metal oxide field effect transistors*. These devices act like diodes that can be turned on or off (effectively inserted or removed from the circuit) by the presence or absence of minute amounts of electrical charge. These small bits of charge are deposited on the devices by a programming scheme that uses one of the pins on the integrated circuit to control the process. Because of the nearly perfect isolation of the charge, it remains in place indefinitely, thus retaining the program in the EPROM for many years.

Unlike fused link devices, EPROMs are not physically changed when they are programmed. The change is a reversible electrical one, which can be undone by exposing the memory matrix to ultraviolet light. To make this possible, the integrated circuit package containing the EPROM includes a clear quartz window transparent to ultraviolet light. The presence of such a window is an indication of an ultraviolet erasable device.

Before it can be programmed, the entire EPROM must first be erased by exposing it to the proper wavelength of ultraviolet light. This process takes anywhere from approximately 20 minutes to an hour, depending upon the intensity of the light source and the specifications of the memory chip. Following erasure, the memory can be programmed with the aid of a PROM programmer capable of working with that specific EPROM. The programming process itself takes on the order of tens of milliseconds per location.

After the chip is programmed, the quartz window is covered with tape to prevent the inadvertent loss of content by exposure to stray sources of ultraviolet radiation. Such loss can occur in as short a time as one week in direct sunlight. If the contents of the memory must be changed, the entire process may simply be repeated. EPROMs have reportedly been reprogrammed hundreds of times with no loss of performance.

A special version of the UVEPROM is available that competes directly with the fused-link PROM. It is useful in applications in which reprogramming the memory after the initial time will not be necessary, but in which the mask cost or turnaround time precludes the use of a mask-programmed ROM. This is a so-called *One Time Programmable EPROM* (OTP EPROM). The OTP EPROM is a standard UVEPROM mounted in a non-hermetically sealed package without a quartz window. The device is furnished completely erased and can be programmed one time only, since no erasing window is provided. The savings in packaging results in a cost that compares favorably to the ROM, while the technology of the EPROM construction still provides field programmability.

12.2.4 Electrically Erasable PROMs

A relatively recent nonvolatile memory development is the *Electrically Erasable PROM* (EEPROM or E-squared PROM). It uses components that are somewhat similar to those in the UVEPROM in that they act like diodes that can be inserted into or removed from the matrix by the presence of small amounts of electrical charge. However, the components in the EEPROM can be disconnected (thus erasing the memory) electrically rather than by exposure to ultraviolet light. This memory device can be erased and written into by the computer system itself and need not be removed from the circuit in order to be reprogrammed. Individual locations can also be modified in isolation without erasing the entire chip at once.

Unlike most other solid-state devices, EEPROMs wear out with use. They may be relied upon for only a few thousand erase/write cycles. A typical specification is a 3 percent failure rate per 10,000 cycles. In addition, their erase and write times are on the order of several milliseconds per location. Thus, the devices are not true read/write memories (RAMs), which can respond in the submicrosecond cycle time of a processor. However, their reprogramming times are much faster than the time it would take to erase and reprogram an EPROM, and they can be reprogrammed on a location-by-location basis by the host computer system.

A memory type that differs only superficially from the EEPROM is the *Electrically Alterable ROM (EAROM)*. This, too, is a ROM whose contents can be erased and rewritten electrically by the host computer system, and erase and write times are comparable to those for the EEPROM. The feature that distinguishes the EAROM from the EEPROM is the number of locations that can be erased and written into at one time. Locations in EAROMs must be erased in blocks having a common address segment.

The relatively high costs of EEPROMs and EAROMs have limited their use except in applications where it is necessary to be able to alter the program while the system remains at some remote location. They are often used in conjunction with a telephone link, which permits modifying their contents from a distance.

12.3 READ/WRITE MEMORY TYPES

Read/write memory (RAM) must be able to respond to requests to accept or deliver information in the submicrosecond scale of a processor's cycle time and must be capable of millions of read/write cycles with no degradation in performance. All of the currently popular solid-state read/write memory chips have one particularly annoying characteristic — they are *volatile*, which means that they lose their information content whenever the power to the system is turned off. Later we will examine some attempts to overcome this drawback.

RAM is necessary in a computer system in order to provide a place for the processor to store information temporarily while the program is being executed. Some larger systems, such as personal computers, also run programs from RAM. In such cases, the volatility of RAM requires that the programs must first be loaded into the RAM space by the processor from some secondary storage device, such as a disk.

12.3.1 Dynamic RAMs

The memory matrix circuit of Figure 12.3 may be modified to describe the functioning of a RAM by removing the diodes and resistors and including the circuit of Figure

12.5 at each intersection. The component labeled C is a capacitor, a device that can retain an electrical charge for a period of time. The presence of a positive charge on the capacitor (a positive voltage) can be interpreted as a one, and its absence (zero voltage) as a zero. The component labeled S is an electronic switch that connects the capacitor to the data line when the address input is at logic level one and disconnects it when at level zero.

Referring to Figures 12.3 and 12.5, whenever a particular address on a RAM chip is decoded, a set of eight switches connects a bank of eight capacitors to the data leads. If it is a read cycle, the charges on the capacitors are delivered through the tri-state buffers to the chip's data leads. If it is a write cycle, the data leads must become inputs to the same capacitors and must charge or discharge them to the proper voltages.

The read/write capability of a RAM requires that the buffers be bi-directional with the direction controlled by a READ/WRITE control line and access enabled by one or more chip select lines. A circuit such as the one shown in Figure 12.6 must replace each tri-state buffer to provide this capability.

Thus, the structure of Figures 12.1 and 12.3 can be used to describe the operation of a RAM as well as a ROM. It is only necessary to replace the single diode of the

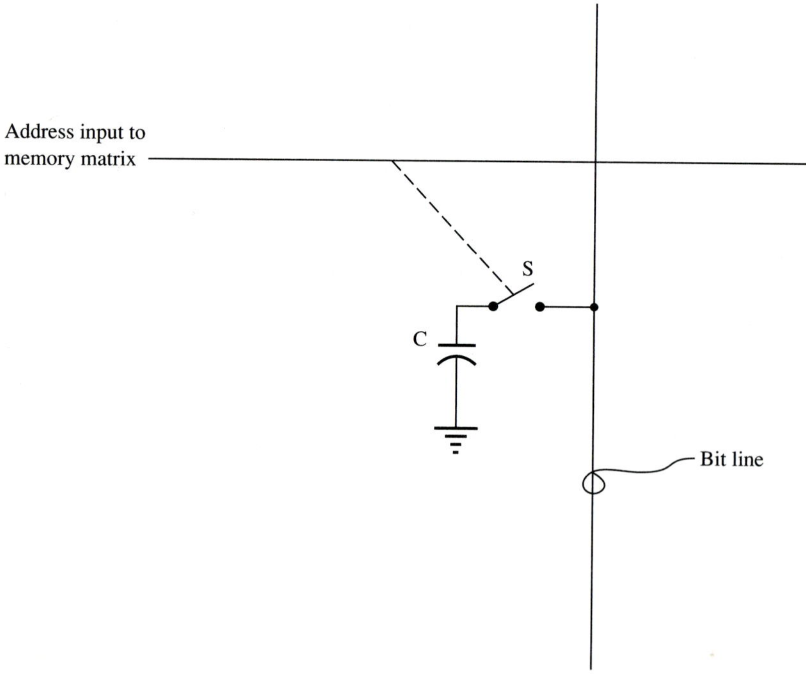

FIGURE 12.5
Functional diagram of a bit cell in DRAM.

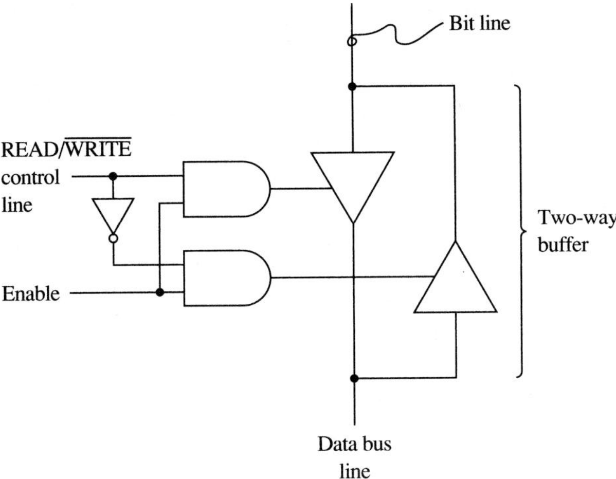

FIGURE 12.6
Read-write control in a RAM.

typical ROM memory matrix cell with the two components of Figure 12.5 and to replace the uni-directional tri-state buffers with the bi-directional ones of Figure 12.6. However, it is important to remember that this is a functional description and that circuit details will differ.

A RAM that uses a capacitor at each point in the matrix suffers from a major drawback. A capacitor can retain its charge for only a limited duration of time, and with the sizes used in actual RAM chips, this time is on the order of five milliseconds! A RAM having such a limited storage time is known as a *Dynamic RAM* (DRAM). The DRAM has a very short-term memory that must be refreshed periodically, on the order of once every two to five milliseconds. The actual circuits in DRAMs are designed in such a way that the recharging will take place any time a location is read. Furthermore, each location in a group having a common upper half-address will be refreshed simultaneously whenever any location in the group is read. Thus, only $2^{n/2}$ refresh cycles must be included during the specified time, where 2^n is the number of locations in the DRAM.

A common DRAM is 64K×1 in size (a byte-organized memory requires eight of these chips to construct a 64K×8 memory). This sized memory chip has 16 address leads. The refresh process consists of doing dummy reads of 256 locations, hex locations 0000, 0100, 0200, . . . , FD00, FE00, and FF00. If the refresh time is four milliseconds, these dummy reads must be performed at the rate of approximately one per 16 microseconds, and they must be interleaved in such a way as not to interfere with the normal behavior of the system.

The cost per bit for DRAM is lower than for any other type of read/write memory. However, the overhead costs (in both time and circuitry) involved in the refreshing process limits its use to systems requiring large amounts of RAM. The typical personal computer memory, for example, consists of hundreds of thousands or millions of bytes of DRAM.

The most popular sizes of DRAMs are 64K×1, 256K×1, and 1M×1, with current sizes up to 4M×1 (2^{22}×1). They are most commonly organized on a one bit per location size in order to minimize the number of pins on each package. This further restricts their use to large systems. For example, eight of the 256K×1 chips must be combined to implement a 256K×8 RAM, with each chip providing only a single data bit. This is the smallest byte-wide block of memory that can be implemented with chips of this size.

One solution to the need for refresh circuitry is to include it on the DRAM chip itself. Several manufacturers provide DRAMs that include the refresh circuitry as well as circuitry to detect conflicts between the refresh process and the requirements of the computer system. The refresh process takes place automatically during the time between memory accesses to the chip. These *pseudo-static RAMs* are typically byte-organized and provide an intermediate cost level between DRAM and the static RAM described below.

12.3.2 Static RAMs

If the capacitors in the DRAM matrix are replaced by flip-flops, the result is a true *static RAM* (SRAM), in which the contents of the memory remain unchanged for an indefinite period of time as long as the power is on. Because each flip-flop requires on the order of four or more components, the result is a memory chip that contains significantly fewer bits than a typical DRAM, with a correspondingly higher cost per bit.

Popular SRAM sizes and organizations are 16K bits (2K × 8), 64K bits (8K × 8) and 256K bits (32K × 8). Because of their relatively high cost per bit, they are used primarily in smaller systems, a fact reflected in their byte-wide organization. RAM chips used in typical microprocessor control applications are often static RAM.

12.4 OTHER TYPES OF MAIN MEMORY

Many attempts have been made to overcome the volatility inherent in the RAM chips described. These attempts have been met with little enthusiasm on the part of system designers. The ideal nonvolatile RAM should be as fast as ROM with a similar cost and packing density but with the read/write capability and the simplicity of use of SRAM. Although none of the following devices approaches this ideal, each is used in situations where a nonvolatile read/write memory is required.

12.4.1 Core Memory

The memory used in earlier electronic computers (pre-1970*s*) was *magnetic core memory*. It is still occasionally used, particularly in certain military systems where its (nuclear) radiation resistance is a major advantage. It consists of tiny doughnuts of ferromagnetic material, each of which is magnetized circumferentially (in the direction around the doughnut). The direction of the magnetic flux determines the binary value of the bit. These cores are pierced by several conductors, which are used to sense and change the direction of the flux. Core memory is extremely expensive, since it is not made in integrated circuit form but must be assembled bit by bit with most of the operations involving hand labor. Of course, this also results in a large size and low speed. It is much slower than solid-state memory devices, with response times on the order of about one-half of a microsecond.

12.4.2 Battery-Backed CMOS RAM

The power consumption of RAM implemented in *Complementary Metal Oxide Semiconductor* (CMOS) technology is low enough that the use of battery backup to provide nonvolatility becomes feasible. CMOS RAM chips are often provided with a separate stand-by power supply connection that maintains the content of the RAM but does not provide the capability of accessing it. This reduces the consumption to a few microamperes from a five-volt supply.

Of course, the use of batteries has major drawbacks. In a microprocessor system using battery backup, the battery will be the least reliable and shortest-lived component. If a storage battery is to be used, charger circuitry must be included; if a primary cell is used, its life is even shorter. Special circuits must sense when the primary power is turned off (or lost) and must switch over to the backup power. These limitations have restricted the use of the approach primarily to applications where the primary power source itself may be a battery—in vehicles and other mobile equipment, for instance.

12.4.3 Shadow RAM

RAM chips are available that incorporate EEPROM backup along with a standard SRAM memory matrix in the same integrated circuit package. During normal use this so-called *shadow RAM* has all of the characteristics of SRAM with its high speed of data transfer in both the read and write directions. A control pin is used to tell the chip when the power is about to be removed. In response to this signal, the chip automatically dumps the current content of the RAM matrix into the EEPROM, requiring a time on the order of about ten milliseconds. When the chip power is restored, the internal circuitry automatically restores the RAM to the content of the EEPROM without changing the content of the EEPROM. Some chips provide the additional capability of allowing the system to restore the entire content of the RAM to the current content of the EEPROM at any time through the use of another control pin.

A system using such memory must include a sense circuit to warn the shadow RAM when power failure is imminent, and it must ensure that the power to the chip remains within standard specifications during the time it takes to dump the RAM into the EEPROM. These extra requirements and the relatively limited sizes available have restricted the use of shadow RAM. It is found primarily in situations where no battery is available in the system for other needs and only a limited amount of nonvolatile RAM is necessary.

12.5 CHIP-SELECT DECODING

The address pins on each memory chip are connected to the lowest-ordered pins of the microprocessor's address bus. This is necessary so that, as the microprocessor progresses through a program or a list of data, the locations accessed will be in consecutive locations on the same chip.

The higher-ordered pins of the microprocessor's address bus are used to select the desired chip from among the several memory chips in the system. This selection process is made possible by the chip-select pins on each memory chip.

When designing the memory system for a computer, the system designer must first specify the desired address ranges for each of the memory chips in the system. These ranges are not purely arbitrary but must meet certain requirements that differ from processor to processor. Some processors require that the information in certain locations be available at all times to the system (exception vectors, for instance). These locations (usually at the very beginning or the very end of the memory space) must fall within a ROM address range in order to satisfy this requirement. In addition, certain chips must have consecutive address ranges.

Ranges for the ROM chips containing programs must be consecutive so that a program may progress smoothly across chip boundaries. Consider a system that uses three 1K×8 ROMs to implement program memory. Each chip has 10 address lines, so each chip has an address range in hex of 000 through 3FF within the chip itself. A reasonable selection of 16-bit address ranges for the three might be F400 through F7FF, F800 through FBFF, and FC00 through FFFF, respectively, as shown in Figure 12.7. The initial (binary) address in each of these ranges ends in 10 zeros. The final

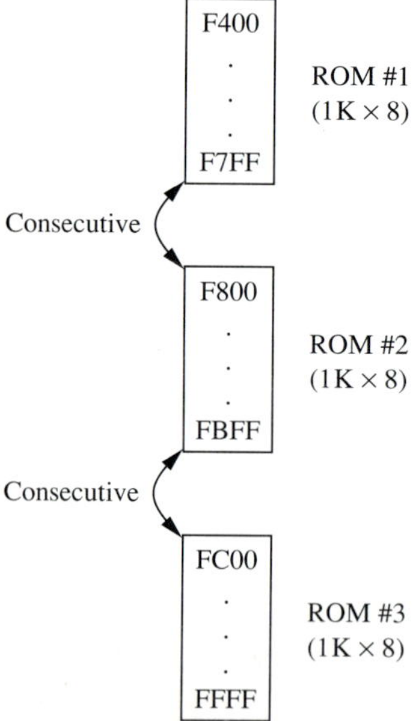

FIGURE 12.7
Consecutive address ranges for multiple ROM chips.

address in each range ends in 10 ones. These 10 bits correspond to the 10 address lines on each individual memory chip.

If a nonconsecutive selection such as that shown in Figure 12.8 were made, with ranges of E000 through E3FF, F000 through F3FF, and FC00 through FFFF, the program would have to skip from E3FF to F000 and from F3FF to FC00 in order to find the next consecutive ROM locations; this is nonsensical. The programmer would have to be aware of this and prepare the program accordingly. The only reasonable choice is to make the ROM addresses sequential.

RAM addresses should also be sequential for cases in which the program must access sequential locations in RAM—with data arrays or stacks, for example. However, it is not necessary that the ROM space and the RAM space be adjacent to each other or to any memory-mapped I/O circuits that may appear as memory locations.

Once the address range for each chip has been selected, a logic circuit must be designed to select the single appropriate chip when an address within its range appears on the microprocessor's address bus. This circuit will use AND gates or decoder chips to drive the chip-select pin or pins on each memory chip.

Figure 12.9 shows one possible circuit that could be used to access the three ROMs with the consecutive address ranges listed in Figure 12.7. Notice that none of the chips will respond unless the four most significant bits in the address bus are all 1. This means that each chip's address space starts with the hex digit F. The first chip responds to any address having bits A11 and A10 equal to zero and one, respectively. Its address range is then established as F400 through F7FF. The remaining chips are similarly decoded, as shown in Table 12.1.

Notice that a portion of the logic that implements the chip-select function in Figure 12.9 is accomplished by the AND gates on the memory chips. In each case, the CS inputs are ANDed on the memory chip itself.

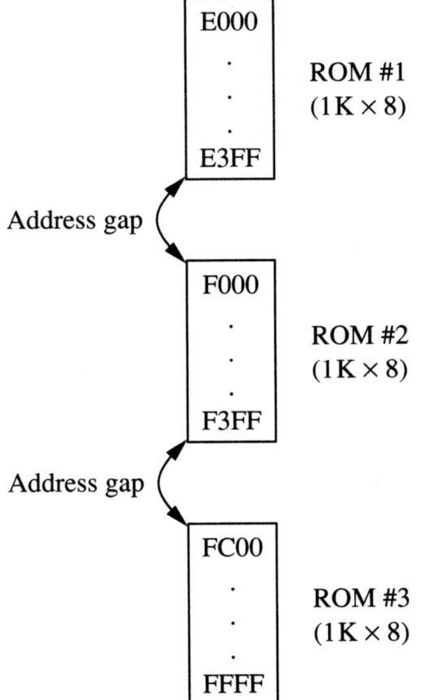

FIGURE 12.8
Nonconsecutive address ranges for multiple ROM chips.

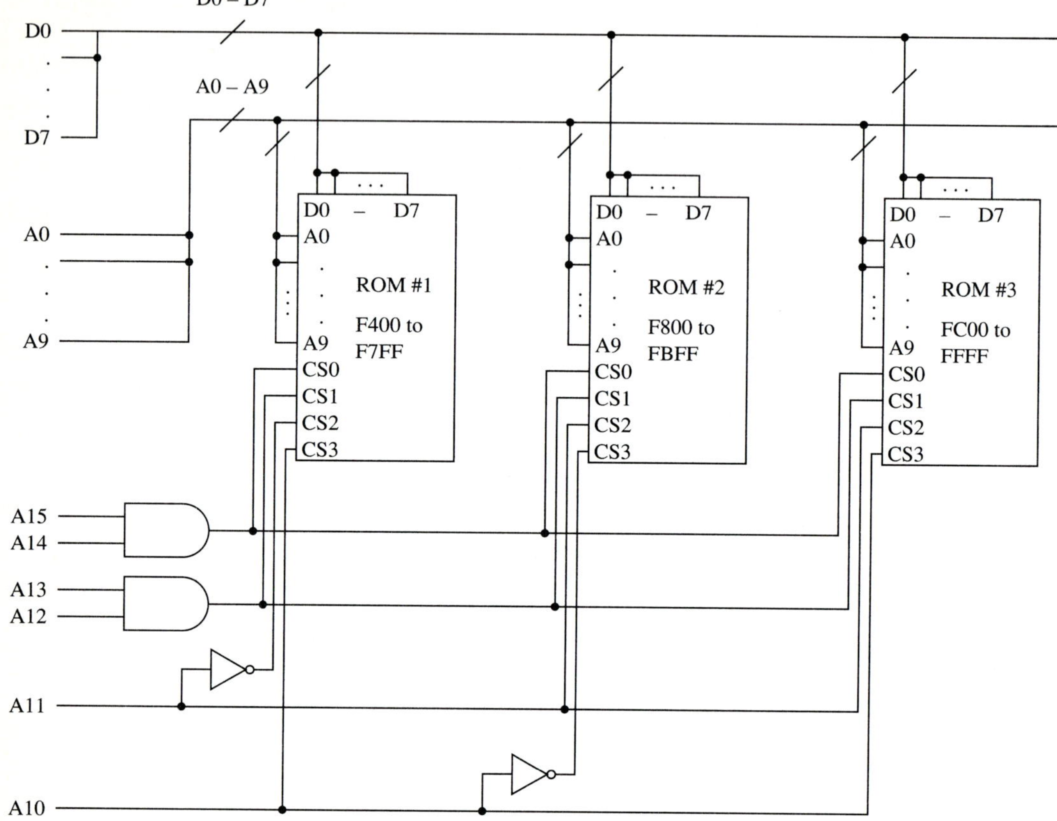

FIGURE 12.9
Memory addressing circuit.

An alternative to using AND gates for address decoding is to use a decoder circuit as shown in Figure 12.10. The decoder selects one of the four outputs Y0 through Y3 based on a decoding of the inputs A and B (connected to A11 and A10 in this example), but only if the enable input (A12) is high. Each of three of the outputs goes to select one of the ROMs by asserting one of its chip-select pins. The other chip

TABLE 12.1
Address ranges for the chips in Figure 12.9

Chip selected	A15	- - - - - -	A10	- - - others	Hex Address Range
ROM chip #1	1	1 1 1 0	1	X X . . .	F400–F7FF
ROM chip #2	1	1 1 1 1	0	X X . . .	F800–FBFF
ROM chip #3	1	1 1 1 1	1	X X . . .	FC00–FFFF

X = don't care (not used in the chip select circuits)

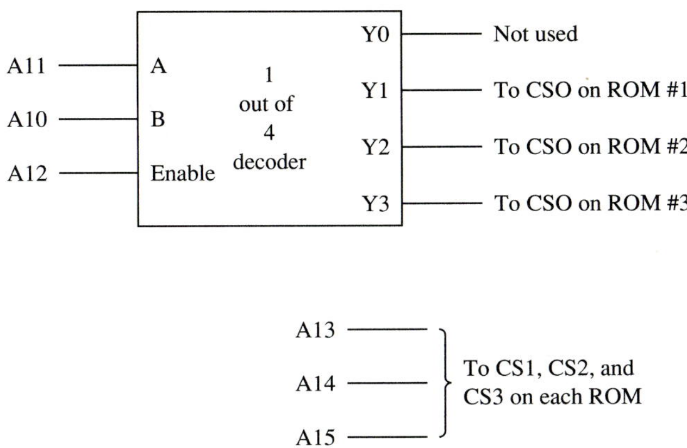

FIGURE 12.10
A decoder used for memory addressing.

selects on the ROM are asserted only if the bits A15, A14, and A13 are also high. The circuit in Figure 12.10 thus decodes the ROMs to the same address ranges as that in Figure 12.9. Notice that the use of the decoder simplifies the task of adding another similar ROM chip (accessed with Y0) if necessary.

Many different schemes have been devised for address decoding to select memory chips. The details and relative advantages and disadvantages of these approaches are appropriate subjects for a text on system design or interfacing and are beyond the scope of this book.

SUMMARY

The operation of all memory chips can be understood on the basis of a similar structural form in which the on-chip address is first decoded in a matrix decoder and is then used to select the appropriate memory devices in a memory matrix. The components in the memory matrix determine the type of memory implemented.

The memory chips used to implement ROM or RAM must be located sequentially within the memory space of the processor. The address decoding circuits that access these chips determine the actual addresses to be used by the software. These circuits must be capable of selecting the proper chip from among several in the system.

REVIEW PROBLEMS

12.1. "All ROMs are nonvolatile." If this is a true statement, justify it. If the statement is false, refute it.

12.2. How many address and data leads are necessary on a 32 K × 8 memory chip?

12.3. How many address pins are necessary on a 4 M-bit memory chip that is organized with a single bit per location?

12.4. a. In which of the following memory types may the content of a location be changed once it has been originally established?

b. In which may the change be under ordinary program control?

c. Which are random access?

d. Which are volatile?

Mask-programmed ROM	Fusible-link PROM
UVEPROM	Dynamic RAM
Static RAM	Shadow RAM
EEPROM	EAROM

12.5. Show the internal functional structure of a 1 K × 8 ROM that uses a matrix decoder.

12.6. Each of four 4096 × 8 memory chips used in a system has its 12 address pins connected to bits A0 through A11 of the address bus. The chip select pins (all are active-high) are wired as shown in Figure P12.6. List in hex the address range to which each memory chip will respond. (Assume that the processor has a total of 16 address lines.)

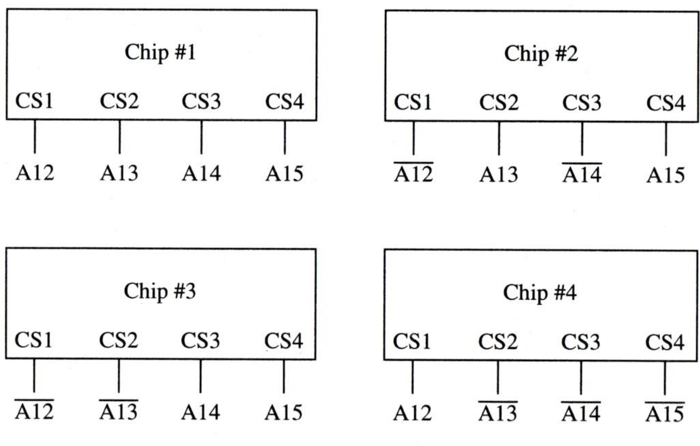

FIGURE P12.6

12.7. Repeat Problem 12.6 for the case in which all of the chip select pins on the memory chips are active-low.

12.8. Each of four 4096 × 8 memory chips used in a system has its 12 address pins connected to pins A0 through A11 of the address bus. The active-high chip-select pins are wired as shown in Figure P12.8, where +5 is logic level 1. List in hex *each 4 K address range* to which each chip will respond. Assume that the processor has a total of 16 address lines. Note that some of the chips may respond to more than one 4096-location address range.

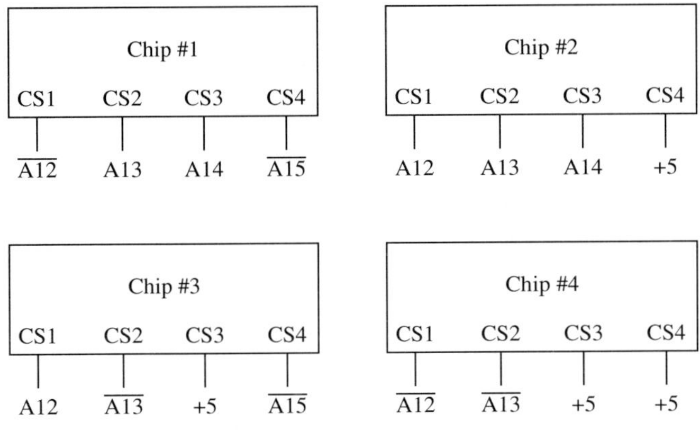

FIGURE P12.8

12.9. In a microprocessor system the address and data buses are connected to a particular memory chip, as shown in Figure P12.9. The address leads not shown are not used.

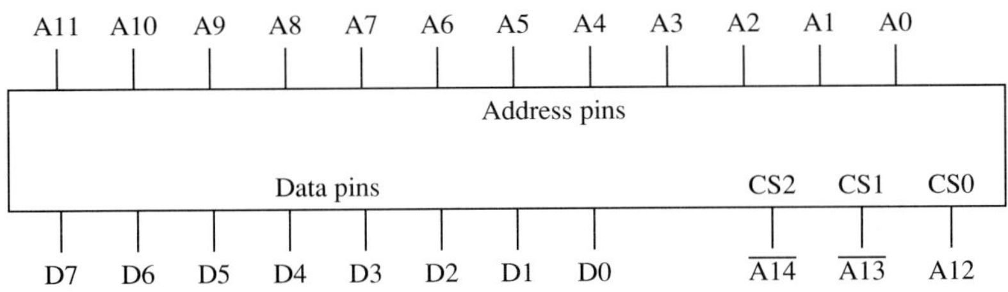

FIGURE P12.9

a. What is the standard designation of the size of the memory chip?

b. What is the total number of bits of memory in this chip?

c. List all of the blocks of addresses to which this chip will respond. Assume that the processor has a total of 16 address lines. Note that there is more than a single block of addresses.

12.10. A ROM is connected to the (16-bit) address bus of a microprocessor system, as shown in Figure P12.10. MSB and LSB are the most significant and least significant bits, respectively, of the decoded inputs to the one-out-of-eight decoder. The Enable input to the decoder is active-high, as are the chip-select inputs to the ROM.

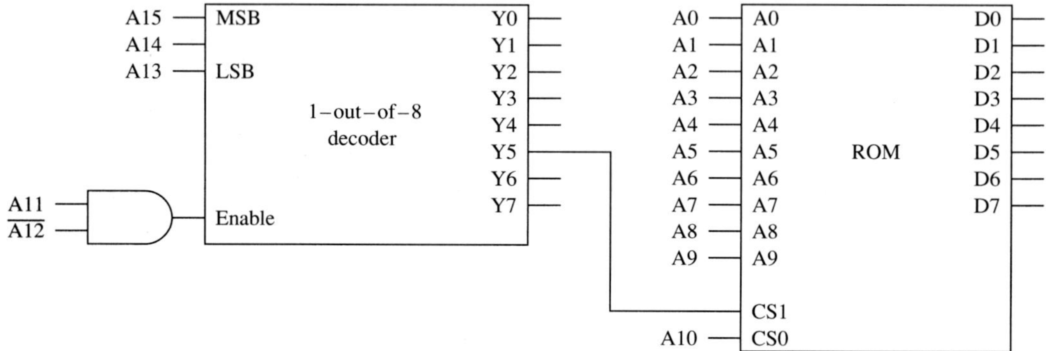

FIGURE P12.10

a. What is the pattern of address bits A15–A10 that will select the ROM?

b. What is the standard designation of the size of the ROM?

c. What is the range of hex addresses to which the ROM will respond?

12.11. Design an address decoder circuit for the memory map shown in Figure P12.11. Use any scheme that will implement the requirements shown. Assume that each memory chip has a single active-high chip-select input. If you use a decoder, assume that it has an active-high enable input. Assume that the processor has a total of 16 address lines.

Memory chip	Address range
RAM #1	4000-5FFF
RAM #2	6000-7FFF
RAM #3	8000-9FFF
ROM #1	E000-EFFF
ROM #2	F000-FFFF

FIGURE P12.11

12.12. Design a 2 K × 8 memory (PROM) using 1 K × 4 chips, each of which has four chip select pins. The memory should be completely decoded to an address range of F800 to FFFF in a system having a 16-bit address bus. Show the data bus as well as the address bus.

12.13. The ROM memory of a microprocessor system consists of four 2048 × 8 chips that are to be connected to the 16-bit address using a one-out-of-four decoder, as partially

Decoder truth table:

B	A	Y3	Y2	Y1	Y0
0	0	0	0	0	1
0	1	0	0	1	0
1	0	0	1	0	0
1	1	1	0	0	0

ROM address table

Chip #	Address range
1	0000 - 07FF
2	0800 - 0FFF
3	1000 - 17FF
4	1800 - 1FFF

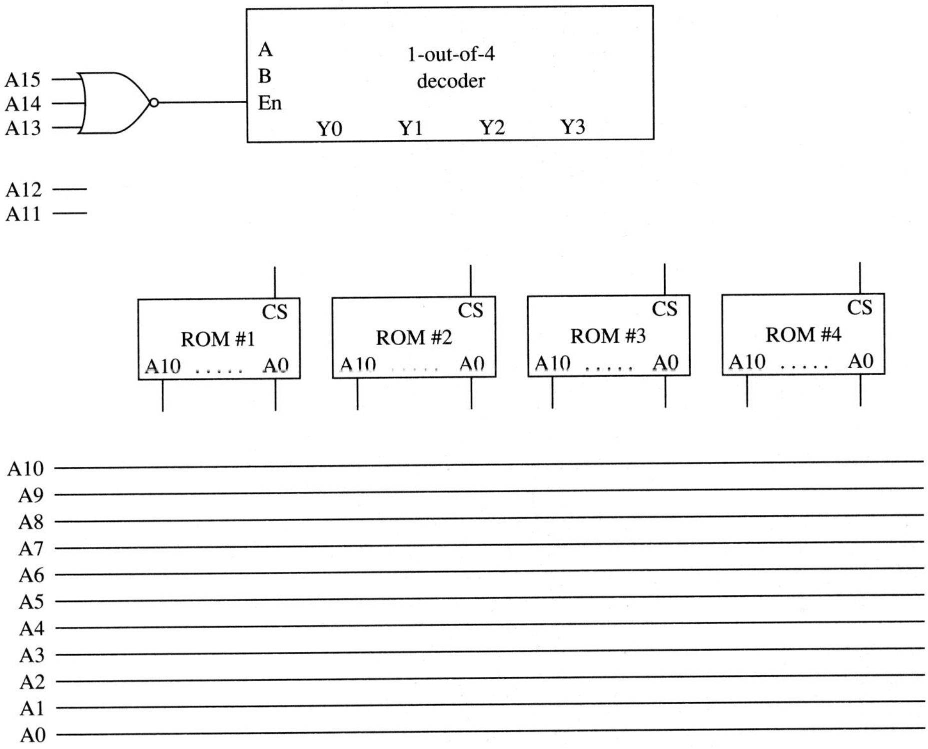

FIGURE P12.13

shown in Figure P12.13. Complete the diagram using the decoder description shown, so that the blocks of addresses shown in the ROM address table are assigned to each chip. Assume that all chip selects and enable inputs are active-high.

CHAPTER 13

MICROPROCESSOR CHIP HARDWARE

This chapter will introduce some of the basic characteristics and hardware behavior of microprocessor chips, including the timing of data transfers, pin designations, and speed limitations. For the detailed specifications of any integrated circuit, including a microprocessor, one must consult the manufacturer's data sheets. These will provide such pertinent information as the definitions of the zero and one input signal levels, the driving capabilities of the output pins, power supply tolerance and current drain, minimum and maximum pulse durations, minimum and maximum rise and fall times, setup times required prior to anticipated changes, and so forth.

13.1 INSTRUCTION TIMING

The general philosophy followed by the chip designers in controlling the transfer of data into and out of Motorola microprocessor chips is to relegate direction information and timing information to separate pins. This is not necessarily the approach used in all microprocessors. In the Intel microprocessors, for example, timing and directional information are combined on the same pins. For reasons such as this, although memory and I/O chips intended for use with one particular microprocessor may often be made to work with others, a simpler system will result if the support chips selected are specifically designed to be used with the system's processor.

Both the MC6809 and the MC68000 processors convey directional information on a read/write pin, $R/\overline{W}$. During the times when the information on this pin is valid, the presence of a one indicates that the present bus cycle is a read cycle (input to the processor), and the presence of a zero indicates that it is a write cycle (output from the processor). The specific times when this read/write information is valid as well as the times when address and data on the processor's buses are valid are indicated by transitions that take place on several other timing pins. Thus, whichever processor is used, the R/$\overline{W}$ pin may be used to inform memory and I/O chips as to whether a read or a write cycle is taking place.

All microprocessors obtain the timing for their various activities from the clock signal, which alternates back and forth between zero and one at a fixed rate. The rate of this clock signal is accurately determined (to only a few parts in a million) by a component called a *piezoelectric crystal*. Some microprocessors include the clock circuitry on the chip and require only that the crystal be attached to a pair of terminals. Others require a complete clock circuit, including the crystal, to be added outside of the processor. Whichever the case, the specifications for the microprocessor chip include a maximum clock frequency and often a minimum as well. Clock frequencies for typical microprocessor systems range from a million cycles per second (one megahertz or MHz) to several tens of millions of cycles per second.

The activities of a processor are such that they typically require four complete cycles of the clock signal to complete one read or write bus cycle. Thus, the standard bus frequency both for the MC6809 microprocessor and for the MC68000 microprocessor is one-fourth of the crystal frequency. The following sections describe the clock and timing signals for each of the processors.

13.1.1 Timing in the MC6809

The MC6809 includes an on-chip clock circuit and provides two pins, EXTAL and XTAL, to connect to the external crystal. The maximum crystal frequency allowed is 4 MHz, although special versions of the chip (designated MC68A09 and MC68B09) allow the use of frequencies as high as 8 MHz. All versions of the 6809 require a minimum crystal frequency of 400 kHz. To facilitate the use of the processor in synchronized multiprocessor systems, one of the external crystal pins (XTAL) may be grounded, and an external clock signal may be applied to the other pin (EXTAL).

The timing of data transfers on the MC6809 bus is accomplished with two output signals, Q and E, sometimes referred as the Q-clock and the E-clock. Other names are the quadrature and enable signals. The phase relationship between these two signals is shown in Figure 13.1. Note that Q is one-fourth of a cycle ahead of E—hence the name *quadrature signal*. Note also that each of these signals is at a frequency equal to one-fourth of the crystal frequency. Thus, in the standard MC6809, the E- and Q-clocks are at a frequency between 100 kHz and 1 MHz, depending on the crystal frequency. These establish the standard bus cycle (read/write) frequency of the processor.

The Q and E signals define four points in each bus cycle, labeled 1 through 4 in Figure 13.1. The time interval between any two successive points is equal to one period of the crystal frequency. The support circuitry in the microprocessor system

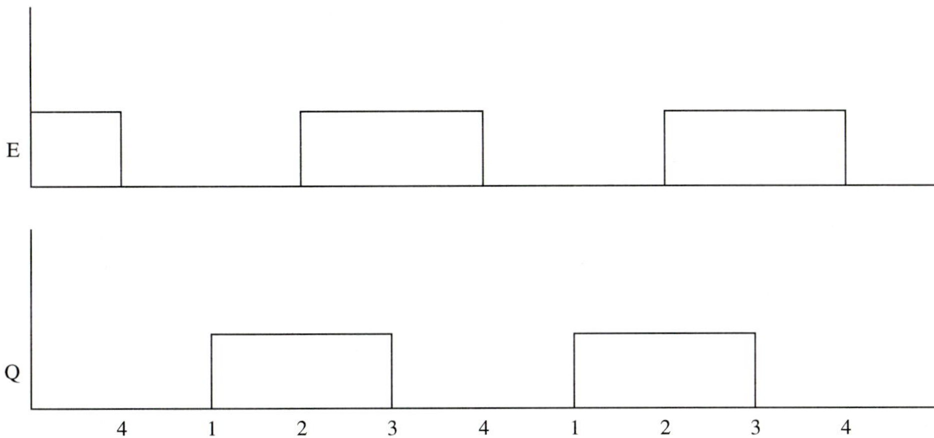

FIGURE 13.1
The MC6809 enable and quadrature signals.

must be designed to identify these points and to use them to time all accesses to the various memory and I/O chips in the system. The significance of each of these points is listed in Table 13.1.

The time between adjacent points 4 and 1 in Figure 13.1 is the time during which the processor is changing the values on the R/$\overline{W}$ line and the address and data buses. Thus, these signals are not valid during that interval. Immediately prior to point 1, these signals become valid. The transition in Q at point 1 is the signal that these signals may be accepted by the external circuitry and address decoding may proceed.

Point 2 indicates that any data on the processor's data bus during a write cycle may be accepted as valid. Thus, it marks the point at which an external device may begin to write this data. The data is valid until the termination of the bus cycle at point 4.

TABLE 13.1
MC6809 timing signals

Point (from Figure 13.1)	Internal significance		External significance	
	Read	**Write**	**Read**	**Write**
1	Address and R/$\overline{W}$ valid	None	Decode address and direction	
2	None	Data valid	None	Start to write
3	None	None	None	None
4	End of cycle	End of cycle	End of cycle	Latch data

Points defined as follows:

1—E stable low, Q going high
2—Q stable high, E going high
3—E stable high, Q going low
4—Q stable low, E going low

Point 3 indicates nothing of significance to the support circuitry. However, sometime between points 3 and 4 the processor will begin to set up the latches that will accept the data from a memory location or an I/O register during a read cycle. At point 4, this input data is latched into the processor and the bus cycle terminates.

From Figure 13.1 and Table 13.1 it can be seen that the address bus contains a valid address during the interval between points 1 and 4. During that interval either Q is a one or E is a one. Thus, the system will have the maximum time for decoding the address if it uses the OR of Q and E to enable address decoding, perhaps by connecting this signal to the enable input of a decoder chip used in address decoding. The circuit shown in Figure 13.2, for example, might be used to implement this.

In order to permit the use of slow memory or I/O circuits with the MC6809 processor, the chip includes a special input pin designated MRDY which stands for "memory ready". When MRDY is high, the Q and E signals operate as described above, with one period of the crystal clock between the adjacent points labeled in Figure 13.1. In that case, the valid address interval (between points 1 and 4 in Figure 13.1) is three clock periods. When MRDY is held low, the processor stretches out the interval between points 3 and 4 in integral multiples of the clock period, as shown in Figure 13.3.

For slow memory or I/O circuits to have sufficient time to respond to the MC6809, the address decoding circuitry must provide a temporary zero on MRDY whenever a valid address for a location in the slow device first appears on the bus. The zero signal on MRDY must last long enough for the device to respond, and then it must return to one. This will stretch the bus cycle to the duration required by the slow memory or I/O circuit.

13.1.2 MC6809 Instruction Execution Time

Simple systems such as those using the MC6809 often take advantage of the accuracy of the processor's clock frequency to time certain activities. Thus, it may be necessary to determine the execution time for a program segment or to tailor a segment to have a specific execution time. This is done by first referring to the programmer's aid (Appendix A) to obtain the number of bus cycles required for fetching and executing each instruction (with its specified addressing mode) in the segment. These numbers are listed in the columns labeled with the single-cycle sine wave.

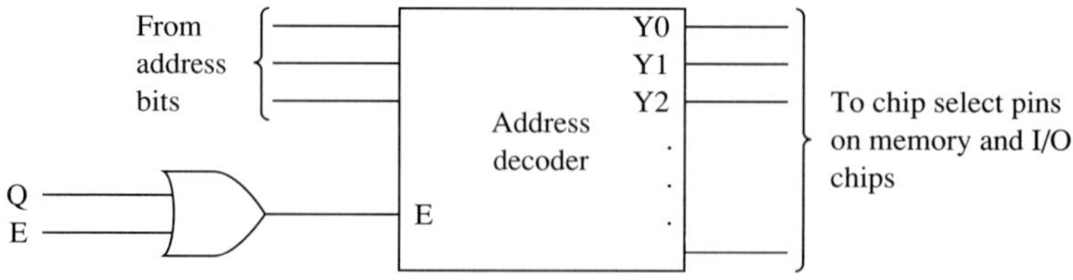

FIGURE 13.2
The MC6809 timing signals used in address decoding.

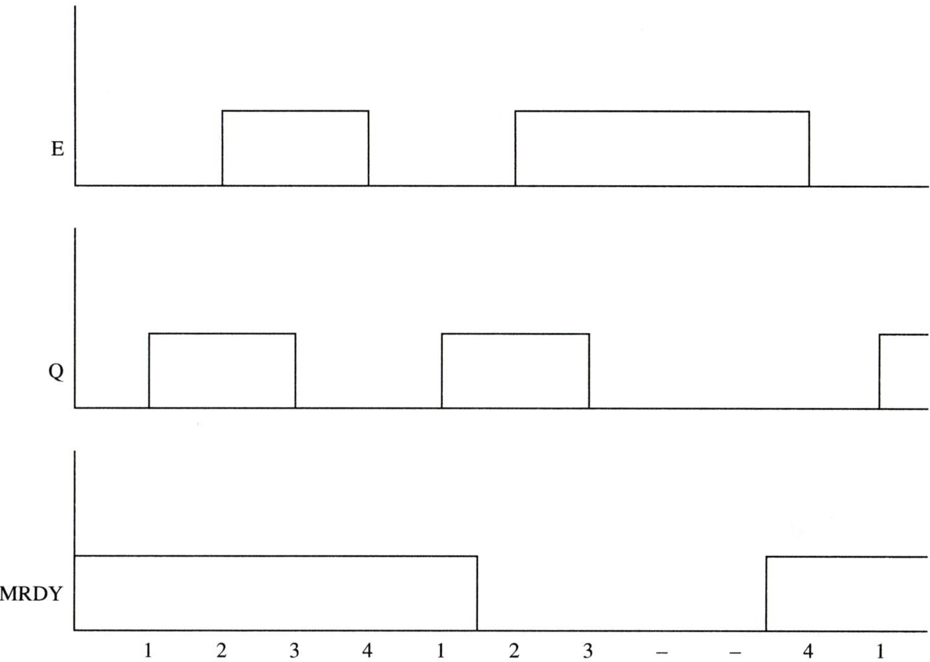

FIGURE 13.3
Stretching the MC6809 bus cycle with MRDY.

For example, consider the segment in Figure 13.4 that contains a DO UNTIL loop. The number of bus cycles for each instruction as listed in the programming aid is included in the comment column. Notice that the loop consists of the three instructions in lines 2 through 4. These three instructions require a total of seven bus cycles to be fetched and executed. The loop is repeated until the content of A is decremented to zero, a total of 50 repetitions. Thus, the loop portion of the segment requires 50×7, or 350, bus cycles, and the entire segment (including line 1) requires a total of 352 cycles.

Because the clock frequency is four times the bus frequency, one unstretched bus cycle lasts four clock periods and this segment will be executed in a total of 4×352 clock periods. Assuming a crystal frequency of 1 MHz and a corresponding clock period of 1 microsecond (μs), the segment would be executed in a time period of 352×4, or 1408 μs.

```
1.  START  LDA   #50    2 cycles
2.  LOOP   NOP          2 cycles
3.         DECA         2 cycles
4.         BNE   LOOP   3 cycles
5.         CONTINUE
```

FIGURE 13.4
Illustrations of MC6809 instruction cycle times.

13.1.3 Timing in the MC68000

The MC68000 does not include an on-chip clock circuit. The support system must generate the clock signal externally and provide a proper fixed-frequency digital signal to the microprocessor on a clock input pin (CLK). Integrated circuits that can generate such a signal are available; they use a crystal to maintain a fixed frequency. The same clock signal may be used with several processors in synchronized multiprocessor systems.

Four versions of the MC68000 microprocessor are currently available, allowing different maximum clock frequencies: 8, 10, 12.5, and 16.67 MHz. The three slowest versions require a minimum clock frequency of 4 MHz, while the 16.67-MHz version requires a minimum frequency of 8 MHz.

The normal timing of data transfers on the MC68000 bus is accomplished with three output signals: address strobe ($\overline{AS}$), upper data strobe ($\overline{UDS}$), and lower data strobe ($\overline{LDS}$). These signals are all active-low, as indicated by the bar over each of their designations. In addition, the MC68000 uses an input signal, *data transfer acknowledge* ($\overline{DTACK}$), to vary its bus cycle time to accommodate memory and I/O circuits with widely varying access times. In essence, the 68000 can slow down its bus cycles for memory or I/O circuits having longer access times.

The MC68000 is capable of addressing individual (16-bit) words at even-numbered locations in its memory space with a 23-bit address bus containing bits 1 through 23 of the address of the location. However, the processor can also access individual bytes in its address space by means of the data strobe signals. When the access is for only the upper byte of the word (an even address), the processor grounds $\overline{UDS}$, and the data is transferred on the upper half of the data bus. When the access is for only the lower byte of the word (an odd address), the processor grounds $\overline{LDS}$, and the data is transferred on the lower half of the data bus. When the access is to the entire word, both data strobes are grounded and the entire word is transferred on the 16-bit data bus.

Figure 13.5 shows how the processor uses its signals to time the transfer of data between itself and the memory or I/O circuits. The processor sets $\overline{AS}$ low to signal that the R/$\overline{W}$ line and the address on the address bus are valid. If the $\overline{DTACK}$ signal is returned (low) by the addressed device during the one and a half clock cycles immediately following the address strobe (before the end of state S4 in the figure), the bus cycle lasts exactly four clock cycles. This cycle, shown here as a read cycle, is the shortest bus cycle possible. If the $\overline{DTACK}$ signal is not returned low within the expected time, the processor stretches out the cycle in integer multiples of the clock period by inserting wait states between states S4 and S5, as shown in the stretched write cycle.

It is possible to include in an MC68000 system I/O peripheral interface circuits that were originally designed for use with the slower eight-bit Motorola processors. For this purpose, the 68000 includes special timing signals: two output signals—enable (E) and valid memory address ($\overline{VMA}$)—and one input signal—valid peripheral address ($\overline{VPA}$). When the address-decoding circuitry detects that the valid address on the MC68000 address bus is for one of these slow interface circuits, it must return a low signal on the $\overline{VPA}$ line. Upon detecting this signal, the processor asserts the

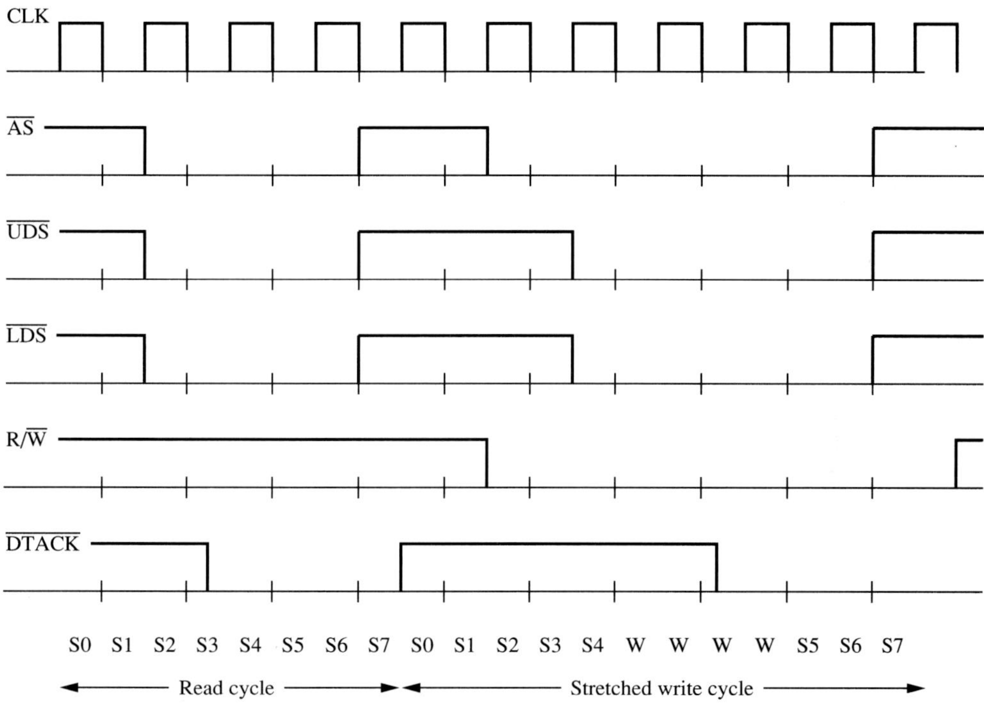

FIGURE 13.5
Short and stretched MC68000 bus cycles.

$\overline{\text{VMA}}$ line, which is then used by the slow interface together with the enable signal (E) to time the transfer. The enable signal (E) is synchronized with the MC68000 clock but runs at one-tenth the frequency, thus more closely matching the interface circuit's capabilities.

13.2 PIN DESIGNATIONS AND USES

Many microprocessors, including both the MC6809 and the MC68000, are mounted in a rectangular package with the pins protruding downward from the long edges, the so-called *dual in-line package*, or DIP. Since there are no standards for pin connections to microprocessors, each one must be described by an appropriately labeled diagram. Pin designations, or *pin-outs*, for integrated circuits are normally shown on a diagram representing the top view of the circuit package. Such a diagram is called the *footprint* for the circuit.

Most current microprocessor chips must be powered by a five-volt DC supply with the positive end connected to a pin labeled V_{CC} and the negative end connected

Signal	Pin	Pin	Signal
V_{SS}	1	40	$\overline{HALT}$
$\overline{NMI}$	2	39	XTAL
$\overline{IRQ}$	3	38	EXTAL
$\overline{FIRQ}$	4	37	$\overline{RESET}$
BS	5	36	MRDY
BA	6	35	Q
V_{CC}	7	34	E
A0	8	33	$\overline{DMA/BREQ}$
A1	9	32	$R/\overline{W}$
A2	10	31	D0
A3	11	30	D1
A4	12	29	D2
A5	13	28	D3
A6	14	27	D4
A7	15	26	D5
A8	16	25	D6
A9	17	24	D7
A10	18	23	A15
A11	19	22	A14
A12	20	21	A13

FIGURE 13.6
MC6809 pin connections.

to a pin labeled either ground (GND) or V_{SS}. The subscripts refer to the names for internal electronic structures, CC for collector and SS for substrate.

In addition to the address and data bus pins, the footprints show the locations of the various clock and timing pins, the read/write pin, and the interrupt request pins, as well as other pins that are specific to that processor; these include special outputs that provide information about the internal status of the processor, and input pins that request special responses of the processor, such as DMA operation.

13.2.1 The MC6809 Chip

The MC6809 microprocessor is mounted in a 40-pin DIP having the footprint shown in Figure 13.6. In addition to the bus pins described earlier, the MC6809 includes two output signals: bus available and bus status (BA and BS), which provide information about the current status of the processor. Bus available indicates when the processor has relinquished its buses by placing them in a high-impedance state (when it has *tri-stated* them), thereby making them available for use by external devices. Table 13.2 lists the current status corresponding to each combination of the BS and BA signals.

TABLE 13.2
MC6809 status signals

BA	BS	Internal status of 6809
0	0	Normal (fetching and executing)
0	1	Hardware interrupt vector fetch
1	0	Waiting during SYNC instruction
1	1	Halted (buses granted to others)

Two special inputs to the MC6809 are the *halt* and the *DMA/break request* pins ($\overline{\text{HALT}}$ and $\overline{\text{DMA/BREQ}}$). The $\overline{\text{DMA/BREQ}}$ input is used by a peripheral device to signal its intent to use the processor's buses to do direct memory access I/O. A low level on this pin causes the processor to cease normal operation at the end of the current instruction and then to tri-state its buses. The processor signals that it has done so by setting both BA and BS high. When responding to this request, the processor reclaims its buses every 15 cycles for internal self-refresh, an operation that takes three bus cycles.

Alternatively, an external request for the buses may be made by placing a low level on the halt pin. In that case, the processor will give up its buses and may remain halted indefinitely. This input may be used to turn off the processor permanently or to turn it off and on periodically, allowing it to start only long enough to execute one instruction at a time, for example.

13.2.2 The MC68000 Chip

The MC68000 microprocessor is mounted in a 64-pin DIP having the footprint shown in Figure 13.7. In addition to the address, data, timing, interrupt, and power pins

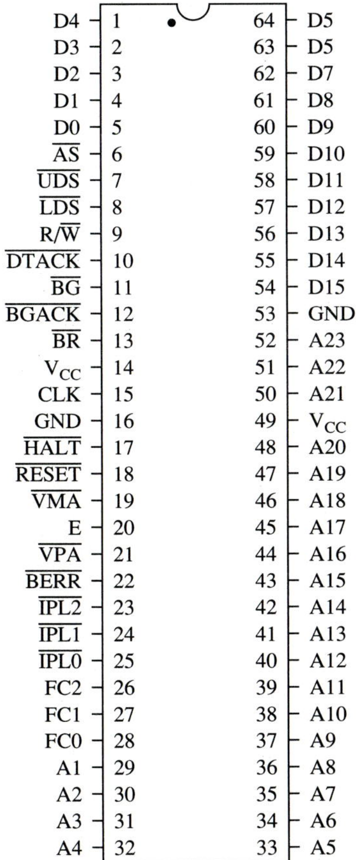

FIGURE 13.7
MC68000 pin connections.

described earlier, the MC68000 processor includes input and output signals that may be used to inform the outside world about internal activities and to mediate external requests for special responses from the processor.

The *function code* output signals (FC0, FC1, and FC2) are used to inform the external world whether the current bus cycle is intended for program or data space and whether the processor is in the user or supervisor state. They thus define four separate spaces known as *user's program, user's data, supervisor's program,* and *supervisor's data* memory spaces.

The function code signals provide valid information whenever the AS signal is asserted, with any necessary changes occurring at the beginning of state S0 (see Figure 13.5). Table 13.3 lists the various interpretations of these three signals. From the table it is evident that FC2 encodes the privilege state (0 = user, 1 = supervisor), while FC0 and FC1 encode the type of access.

Whenever the source of the current memory address is the program counter, the function code pins indicate a program type of access. For any other address source, they indicate a data type of access. Note from Table 13.3 that one function code combination is reserved for the indication that the interrupt vector is being fetched. This combination may be used to provide for the external vectoring of interrupts.

Several *bus arbitration* pins are used to control DMA I/O operations and to assist in transferring the control of the processor's buses from the MC68000 to external devices. The bus request ($\overline{\text{BR}}$) is the signal used by an external device to requisition the processor's buses. A low level on this input pin causes the processor to cease normal operation at the end of the current instruction and then to tri-state its buses. The processor signals that it has done so by asserting the bus grant output pin ($\overline{\text{BG}}$), that is, by making it low. The requesting device then signals that it has accepted the processor's buses by placing a low level on the input bus grant acknowledge pin ($\overline{\text{BGACK}}$). Following this exchange of signals (known as *hand-shaking*), the external device may take control of the buses for as long as necessary. The device signals when it is through by negating the bus request pin, placing a one on it.

Alternatively, an external request for the buses may be made by placing a low level on the *halt* pin ($\overline{\text{HALT}}$). In that case, the processor will give up its buses and

TABLE 13.3
MC68000 function code signals

			Current bus cycle	
FC2	**FC1**	**FC0**	**Type**	**Privilege state**
0	0	0	(Reserved)	User
0	0	1	Data	User
0	1	0	Program	User
0	1	1	(Reserved)	User
1	0	0	(Reserved)	Supervisor
1	0	1	Data	Supervisor
1	1	0	Program	Supervisor
1	1	1	Interrupt acknowledge	Supervisor

may remain halted indefinitely. This input may be used to turn off the processor permanently or to turn it off and on periodically, allowing it to start only long enough to execute one instruction at a time, for example. The halt pin is bi-directional and is also used as an output by the processor to signal to the system that it has stopped processing because it has detected a catastrophic failure.

SUMMARY

The details of the electrical and timing specifications for a microprocessor and its support and memory chips are available from the manufacturer in the form of specification sheets. These sheets include not only the pertinent details of the physical operation and limitations of the integrated circuits, but also a complete description of the software features for the programmable components.

REVIEW PROBLEMS

13.1. Sketch a timing diagram showing the MC6809 bus signals during a write cycle in which the MRDY signal is asserted by the memory circuits during the third cycle of the clock following the one to zero transition of Q. Show the following signals for at least one complete bus cycle: EXTAL, E, Q, R/$\overline{W}$, and MRDY.

13.2. a. Calculate the number of bus cycles required for the execution of the following MC6809 program segment.

b. Calculate the total time required to execute the segment if the system operates with no wait states and the crystal frequency is 2 MHz.

```
        PSHS  A
        LDA   #$28
LOOP    DECA
        NOP
        NOP
        BNE   LOOP
        PULS  A
```

13.3. The three MC6809 instructions listed below are to be executed exactly 50 times.

```
EXT   LDA   ,X
      ADDA  #13
      STA   ,X+
```

a. How many bus cycles will the processor take to execute the three instructions 50 times?

b. How many microseconds is that in a system that has a crystal frequency of 3 MHz and operates with no memory delays?

c. Write the necessary assembly language instructions to precede and follow the sequence in order to cause it to be executed 50 times and then return to the ASSIST09 monitor. Include an initialization of index register X to a value of 1000H.

13.4. Write an MC6809 assembly language subroutine named DELAY that will perform no meaningful task except provide a fixed execution time of 5 ms ($\pm 50 \mu s$). The system runs with a crystal frequency of 2.5 MHz with no wait states caused by slow memory. DELAY is not to change the content of any processor registers with the possible exception of the condition code register.

13.5. Repeat Problem 4 with a required delay time of 1 second ($\pm 100 \mu s$).

13.6. Write an MC6809 program to determine the duration of a pulse input as a one in bit 7 in location 1234H. The start of the pulse is signaled by a fast maskable interrupt and has a maximum duration of one minute. Your result should be the duration in milliseconds. Assume that the MC6809 system uses a 4-MHz crystal.

13.7. Design a combinational logic circuit that can be used to decode the MC68000 function code signals and provide the necessary chip-select signals to extend the address space of the processor to four 16 MB segments—one each for user's data, user's programs, supervisor's data, and supervisor's programs.

13.8. Sketch a timing diagram showing the MC68000 bus signals during a (short) read cycle in which only the lower byte of a user's data memory location is read. Show the following signals for states S0 through S7: CLK, $\overline{AS}$, $\overline{UDS}$, $\overline{LDS}$, R/$\overline{W}$, $\overline{DTACK}$, FC0, FC1, and FC2.

13.9. Repeat Problem 7 for a write cycle in which the $\overline{DTACK}$ signal is asserted by the memory circuits during the fifth wait state after state S4.

13.10. Explain why the MC68000 does not include address pin A0 in its address bus.

CHAPTER 14

TOOLS FOR SYSTEM DESIGN

Whether the application is an automobile engine controller or a desktop personal computer, every microprocessor-based system has two parts—the hardware and the software. The design of such a system requires the separate development of these two discrete parts and their integration into a coherent working system. In order to make the design process as efficient as possible, several tools are available to assist in this endeavor.

Software tools include *compilers, assemblers, debuggers,* and *simulators*. Hardware development tools include *evaluation kits, hardware emulators,* and *logic analyzers*. One tool that defies classification, the *PROM programmer*, is included here under the hardware category. Several of these tools may be combined with generic software support (editors, an operating system, and so forth) into a single computer-based piece of equipment known as a *microprocessor development system*. This chapter describes these various tools and their uses in the design of a microprocessor-based system, referred to here as a *prototype system*.

14.1 SOFTWARE DESIGN TOOLS

All of the tools used in the development of the software component of a prototype system are programs that must be run on a host computer system. These programs are used to develop software aimed at a specific target microprocessor. For example, a compiler that will compile a Pascal program to run on the MC6809 processor cannot be used to help in the design of an Intel 8085-based system. Each software support tool, then, is specific to two processors—that of the *host computer*, which will run the program used to develop the software, and the *target microprocessor*, which will run the software being developed.

These software development tools may be used in a general-purpose computer system such as a personal computer or a work station. Alternatively, they may be incorporated into a computer system specifically intended to support the development of microprocessor-based application systems. Such so-called *microprocessor development systems* will be the subject of a later section in this chapter.

14.1.1 Compilers and Assemblers

The primary software development tools are the compilers and assemblers that are used to convert the source program into the machine code that will be executed by the target processor. As discussed in Chapter 6, higher-level language programs are translated by compilers, and assembly language programs are translated by assemblers.

The host computer on which a compiler will run is often itself based on a microprocessor, so the possibility exists that the host processor will be the same type as the target processor. When this is the case, the development tool is described as a *resident compiler*. Most personal computers have resident compilers available only for the preparation of their own machine code. That is, computers using the MC68000 processor often have compilers available to translate various higher-level languages into MC68000 machine code, but not into, say, 8086 machine code. Because the target processor is identical to the host processor, the object code output of the resident compiler can be executed, tested, and debugged on the host machine.

The smaller control-type microprocessors such as the MC6809 are not found as host processors in computer systems that support compilers. Thus, compilers targeting these microprocessors must use a host machine that has a different processor. These compilers are called *cross-compilers*, since they compile into a machine language different from that of the host processor.

Similarly, both *host-assemblers* and *cross-assemblers* are available. They, too, have the characteristic of targeting either the host processor itself or another, respectively.

Host-compilers or assemblers often include a program module called a *loader*. The function of the loader is to load the object code into the host system's memory so that the programmer may run and debug it using the host processor. Once this initial debugging is completed, the machine code may be dumped into a file that can then be used to program the ROM for the prototype system.

14.1.2 Debuggers

A software development tool that is inherently a resident tool is a *debugger program*. A debugger is used to execute, test, and debug the prototype machine code on the host system. Thus, the host processor must be of the same type as the target processor. Resident assemblers often incorporate debugging support as part of an integrated software package. The package may even include an editor to incorporate changes into the prototype source program as the need for such changes is discovered.

Debugger programs assist the user in loading the prototype program into the host system's memory and executing it. They often have a users' command structure that is similar to a monitor program's command structure. They typically include such features as examining and changing memory and register contents and executing programs with break points or in single-step form. At the same time, they allow the prototype program to incorporate some of the host's I/O capabilities.

Ideally, the user should be able to control the debugger by using whatever source language was used in writing the prototype program. He or she should be able to specify starting and stopping addresses or memory contents to be displayed by their symbolic names in the case of assembly language. With higher-level languages, the user should be able to specify these things by line number or variable name. Unfortunately, the ideal is also the exception. Most debuggers are not so sophisticated. Instead, they more often require the user to specify machine level information—addresses in hex, for example. Many debugger programs do go so far as to display the current instruction (pointed to by the program counter) in machine code or in source code form or both. They may also allow the user to specify a source code listing as one of the formats used to display blocks of memory.

The debugging process is a tedious one, requiring the user to run the prototype program with various variable values starting at various points with various initial register contents. The program or a segment thereof is run and the results are examined. Errors or unanticipated results must be analyzed, and program modifications must be devised to correct these situations. These modifications must be incorporated into the program, either in machine code form or by returning to the source code file, modifying, and then recompiling or reassembling it. The entire process must be repeated until the user is satisfied that the prototype program is error-free.

When a cross-compiler or a cross-assembler is used with a general-purpose host computer, the prototype software must be tested in some way other than by using a debugger and executing it directly with the host processor. One choice would be to execute it indirectly on the host system with a simulator program. An alternative would be to transfer the software directly to the prototype system for testing. The latter approach may require the use of an output port from the host to a hardware tool such as an evaluation kit or a simple development system. As a third alternative, the host system may include a PROM programmer that can be used to write the machine code into a memory chip, which can then be inserted into the prototype system. These alternatives and their associated development tools will be discussed in the following sections.

14.1.3 Simulators

Once the prototype machine code has been obtained from a cross-compiler or a cross-assembler, the problem of debugging it arises. Since the host processor differs from the target processor, a debugger program cannot be used to test the code on the host processor. If the prototype hardware does not include the necessary peripheral devices, it may be extremely difficult to debug the program using the prototype system itself. One solution is to use another type of software tool known as a *simulator*.

A simulator is a program that runs on a host computer and makes it imitate the prototype. It uses software to force the host system (host processor and host memory) to behave as though it were the prototype system (prototype processor and prototype memory). The user can load the object program into the simulated prototype memory and execute and debug it.

Simulators not only simulate the prototype system, but they also provide various debugging capabilities. They allow the user to specify the prototype memory by location and type. They support the use of break points to interrupt the program when it reaches a certain place. They allow the user to execute one instruction at a time, stopping in between to allow the examination of various register and memory contents. They often provide the simulated system with additional I/O capabilities, calling upon the host system's peripherals to do so. A simulator is often found as a part of an integrated software development package that includes a cross-assembler and, in some cases, an editor to incorporate changes into the source program as the need for such changes is discovered.

Many simulators imitate the machine-level behavior of the target processor by fetching, decoding, and executing the actual machine code that an assembler or compiler has generated. The prototype program which is to be simulated must be provided as input to the simulator program in the form of an object code file. Such *object code simulators* have the advantage of carrying no link with the original source code program, so they may be used with a variety of compilers or assemblers. In addition, machine code patches and corrections may be inserted by the programmer during the debugging process without the need for recompiling or reassembling the program. Of course, an object code simulator can provide the user only with binary or hex information during the debugging process. It provides so little user support that its use is not recommended except with the simplest prototype programs.

An alternative is a *source code simulator*, in which the simulator program actually fetches and interprets the instructions from the original source code file itself. This type of simulator must be written to accompany the specific compiler or assembler being used. The advantage here is that the simulator may easily keep track of various parts of the original program and prevent the programmer from making certain elementary errors, such as attempting to execute data or attempting to write over parts of a program. It can also display the original source code (labels and all) while the program is running, a feature that is invaluable during the debugging process.

The simulator parts of the ASSYM09 and ASSYM000 software available for use with this book are source code simulators. They can only simulate the execution of programs that have been previously assembled with the corresponding assembler part of the software. That is, they simulate the target system directly from the source code and not from the machine code that the associated assembler generates.

Between the source code simulators and the object code simulators falls another category of simulators. Some object code simulators fetch and execute the target instructions at the machine code level (hex op-codes, hex addresses, and so forth) but do so with access to the complete source code file. They are able to provide the aforementioned desirable features, since they have access to such things as symbolic names, labels, variable names, line numbers, and so on. Of course, the user must supply both the source code file and the assembled machine code file to such a simulator.

14.2 HARDWARE DESIGN TOOLS

The major tools available for use in developing the hardware component of a prototype system are evaluation kits, hardware emulators, logic analyzers, and PROM programmers. The first two are always target-processor specific; the others are more general in nature and may be used with a variety of target processors.

Whereas software development programs are often available for use on an ordinary personal computer or work station system, the hardware support tools are seldom so used. More often they are noncomputerized stand-alone instruments, or they are found as parts of a completely integrated computer system, called a *development system*. Development systems will be discussed in Section 14.3. This section will describe the pertinent features of the hardware support tools divorced from any consideration of their incorporation into a development system.

14.2.1 Evaluation Kits

An evaluation kit is a small stand-alone microprocessor system consisting of one or two printed circuit boards. It contains all of the necessary components to make up a complete system, including the clock circuits, crystal, address decoder circuitry, I/O chips, memory chips, and some rudimentary peripheral devices such as hex keypad and character displays.

Evaluation kits are intended primarily to be used as educational tools to introduce the designer to the pertinent characteristics of a specific target microprocessor. As such, they are available at reasonable cost, usually from sources associated with the manufacturer of the microprocessor. They are the systems most commonly used in teaching introductory courses in microprocessors. Educational intent aside, the evaluation kit provides a reasonable platform around which many small microprocessor systems have been designed. The kit itself, perhaps with some minor modifications, has become the prototype system, or at least has been used to test some of the basic design features of the system.

Evaluation kits fall into two categories of complexity. The simpler, smaller ones provide very limited on-board memory and I/O capabilities and have little provision for expansion. These may be useful in testing simple system configurations with very small programs. Others can be quite powerful, including provisions for connection to a video display terminal or even to a larger computer system for software development support.

Each evaluation kit comes equipped with a ROM containing a monitor program that supports simple program debugging tasks. The ROM in a more complex kit may include an assembler with somewhat limited features with respect to the use of labels and forward references. It may also include a disassembler to convert machine code into at least the rudiments of assembly language so as to ease the task of interpreting the software as it is displayed on the user's screen.

A prototype system built around an evaluation kit often includes the monitor ROM intact, even if it is not used during normal prototype operation. The ROM occupies only a small part of the memory space, and it may be of use during repair or maintenance procedures.

Most kits include one or more extra I/O ports that are not used by the monitor and that may readily be incorporated into the prototype system. They can often support both parallel and serial I/O data transfer as well as I/O and RESET interrupts. Many kits include space on the circuit board where additional I/O support chips may be mounted.

The major limitation of even a more complex evaluation kit is its memory capability. Typical on-board RAM rarely exceeds a few KB, although some limited amount of expansion RAM may be added. Most boards include extra address decoding capabilities that can be tapped for this purpose, as well as space into which to mount the memory chips themselves. Another common feature is the inclusion of (address-decoded) sockets into which EPROMs containing users' programs may be inserted.

14.2.2 Logic Analyzers

A logic analyzer is a piece of laboratory test equipment that is used to troubleshoot defective digital equipment. It includes a series of input leads that can be connected into the circuit being tested to capture the very short-duration signals that are flitting back and forth while the system is operating.

The analyzer includes a programmable capability to store and display the captured information in various formats on a video display screen. The capture may be specified as the last *n* patterns immediately before the appearance of a specific pattern, or as the next *n* patterns immediately following the appearance of a specific pattern. Thus, it may be used to monitor the buses in a microprocessor system and capture signals before or after an access to a particular location or before or after a specific value is present on the data bus. It is a powerful and indispensable tool for repairing computer systems.

The logic analyzer has also been found to be a valuable tool in the development and initial testing of the hardware configuration for a prototype system. It serves the role there that the oscilloscope serves in the development of complex analog systems. That is, it is primarily used to verify the order in which certain specific events occur and to capture and display signals of very short durations.

An analyzer used with a microprocessor system may be able to display information in many alternative formats, including binary, hex, and octal. The display includes many channels that can be used to portray timing diagrams depicting the time relationships between many binary signals, typically as many as twenty or more.

Although the logic analyzer was originally a stand-alone item, it is now often found as an optional part of the integrated development system that will be described in more detail later. When it is included in such a system, its internal programming is controlled by the system host and may be changed as the testing of the prototype system progresses.

14.2.3 PROM Programmers

The PROM programmer is a device used to insert a user's program, data, or both into a programmable memory chip. It may be capable of programming various types of chips or only one particular type. The more popular models can each program a wide variety of chips of one generic family (UVEPROMs, fused-link PROMs, EEPROMs, or EAROMs). The programmer is adapted to each specific chip in the family by inserting the specific plug-in *personality module*.

The PROM programmer may be a stand-alone device or part of a microprocessor development system or some other computer system. The stand-alone programmer must have a means of accepting the binary code from the user. A simple stand-alone programmer may require the user to key in the code through a hex keypad. Such a crude approach is obviously impractical except for very short blocks of code. More commonly, the device includes a serial input port through which the code may be downloaded from an independent computer containing the machine language file.

When the PROM programmer is a part of a development system or some other computer system, the binary code is resident within the system in hex form and may be programmed into the chip without external intervention. The user need only provide the commands necessary to initiate the programming activity.

14.2.4 Emulators

An emulator is an integrated development tool (hardware and software) that allows a powerful host system to reach into a prototype system and monitor and control its behavior while it is actively processing instructions.

When an emulator is used, the target microprocessor is removed from the prototype system and replaced by a plug connected to a *processor pod*, which in turn is connected to the host computer through an *umbilical cord*. The processor pod contains a replacement target processor and monitoring circuits that continuously feed signals back and forth between the pod and the host. In this way, the host becomes linked through hardware with the prototype. It monitors and interprets the actual binary signals on the target processor's buses and can take various types of action based upon these signals.

Through the emulator, the host computer is able to capture and store information from the buses for display at a later time. Depending upon the complexity of the emulator, it may be able to substitute host memory for certain blocks of the target address space, stop whenever a specific bus condition exists, time the duration of specific segments of the program, disassemble the object code into assembly language for display, or interrupt the system whenever a specific sequence of events has occurred.

The emulator ties the host computer (often a development system) into whatever parts of the prototype hardware happen to exist at the time. It can replace any or all of the parts of the prototype system with other factory-provided emulator parts that are known to be operable. Initially, no prototype hardware is necessary; the entire system may be represented by the emulator hardware. As the design of the prototype system progresses, the designer may replace more and more of the hardware with the actual prototype system resources.

The emulator merges the software and the hardware components of the prototype system. It allows the user to designate certain address blocks to be referred to the internal emulator memory, and others to the prototype system's memory. While it is in operation, the emulator continuously monitors the address bus and shunts each bus transaction to the designated memory. Thus, the target programs may be run from emulator RAM as they are being developed and tested. When they are fully tested, they can be programmed into a PROM and inserted into the prototype hardware. From then on, these programs can be executed directly from the prototype.

The user may select to use the emulator clock or the prototype system clock during an emulation run. The emulator clock frequency is often software-selectable, or at least it may easily be modified by replacing the crystal. The user may also be able to use some of the emulator-host I/O capabilities before the corresponding prototype I/O circuitry is developed.

In addition, the emulator provides the usual monitor-type support functions, such as downloading and executing prototype programs, examining and changing memory and register contents, and so forth. Thus, it provides complete software debugging support while aiding in the testing and development of the hardware.

So that the emulator may work with any prototype system using its processor, it will always include as part of its hardware the highest-speed version of the target processor that is available. The host system must be even faster so that it can monitor and modify the target processor's behavior when necessary.

Because it works within the hardware of the prototype system, the emulator is often referred to as a *hardware emulator*. This title helps to distinguish it from a simulator that provides only a software imitation of the target system. It may also be referred to as an *in-circuit emulator* (ICE), since it operates within the circuit of the prototype system.

14.3 DEVELOPMENT SYSTEMS

The premier design tool used in the development of microprocessor systems is, obviously enough, the microprocessor development system. It consists of a host computer equipped with many, if not all, of the software and hardware tools described earlier. Development systems range from simple single-user systems comprising little more than a single circuit board and a terminal to sophisticated networks in which multiple

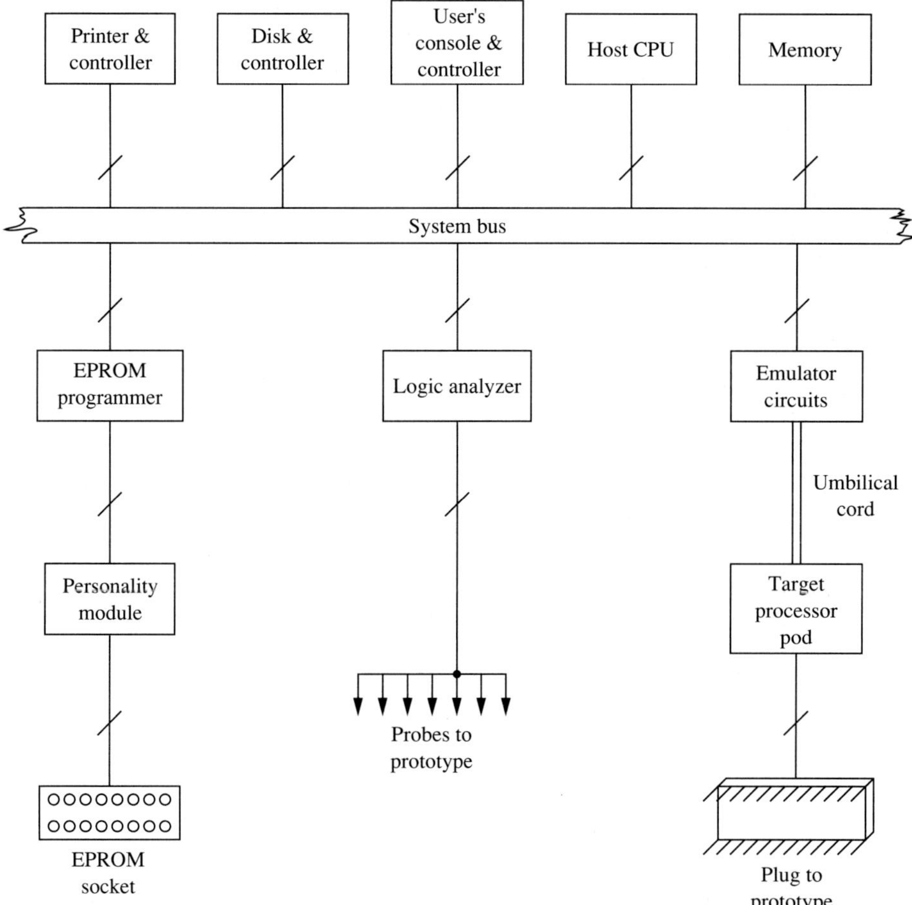

FIGURE 14.1
A typical single-station microprocessor development system.

work stations allow a team of engineers to collaborate on a single project. The configuration of a typical single-station system is shown in Figure 14.1, and a multi-station system is shown in Figure 14.2.

Development systems are subdivided into two categories: the single microprocessor family versions and the universal systems. These two classes of development systems are available from two different sources — microprocessor chip manufacturers and laboratory instrument manufacturers, respectively.

Systems made by the chip manufacturer cannot be expected to support another manufacturer's processors. Such systems support a single microprocessor or family of processors and can usually be easily extended to include most of that manufacturer's microprocessors. On the other hand, universal systems support a wide variety

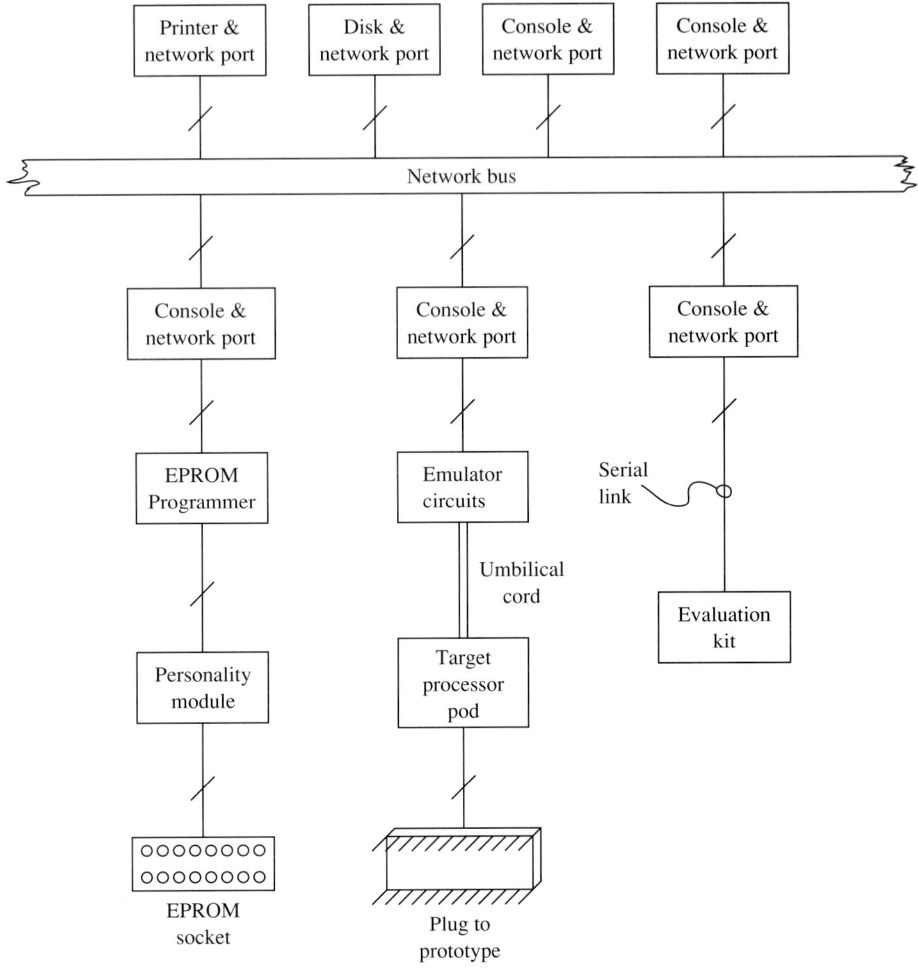

FIGURE 14.2
A multiple-station development system.

of microprocessors. They can be extended to encompass many different processors (within certain size and speed ranges) by means of optional plug-in cards and software packages.

A minimal development system includes such software as operating system support for file manipulation and I/O control, a text editor for preparing programs, assemblers and compilers, a linker/loader (used to merge separate program modules into a single entity, which is then loaded into memory), and a debugger. It commonly includes hardware tools such as a PROM programmer for a variety of EPROMs and an emulator system for each supported processor. A very simple system may be connected to an evaluation kit through a serial port as an alternative to an emulator.

Many development systems include a logic analyzer with a wide variety of optional capabilities.

A multiple-station system, such as the one shown in Figure 14.2, typically shares system I/O resources such as a printer and hard disk over a local network while supporting specific development tasks locally at individual consoles. Each console itself is a complete computer with self-contained CPU and memory. Each one can be equipped with various hardware development tools of its own and can call up various software development tools from the network.

Such a multistation configuration allows several designers to cooperate by working simultaneously on different parts of the same prototype system. They are able to access software development tools as well as other team members' results. Alternatively, such a development system can allow several designers to work separately on different prototype systems that do not necessarily involve the same microprocessor or even the same family of microprocessors.

SUMMARY

Almost any task that makes use of a computer requires common computer tools such as an operating system, a text editor, file-manipulating software, and so forth. When the task is to develop software for a prototype microprocessor system, specific software development tools such as compilers, assemblers, debuggers, and simulators are also necessary. Similarly, in addition to the standard types of electronic laboratory equipment such as meters, power supplies, and oscilloscopes, the design of the prototype hardware requires such things as evaluation kits, hardware emulators, logic analyzers, and PROM programmers.

Development systems include both types of tools in one integrated package supervised and controlled by a host computer. Such systems are invaluable in the design and integration of both of the major components of a prototype microprocessor system.

REVIEW PROBLEMS

14.1. a. What is the difference between an emulator and a simulator?

b. Discuss the disadvantages of attempting to use only a simulator (without an emulator) in designing a prototype system.

14.2. List the typical software and hardware tools included in a development system and describe each one briefly.

14.3. a. List a minimum set of the tools described in this chapter that you would find necessary to design a prototype system.

b. State your reasons for including each item on your list.

c. State your reasons for not including those tools that you omitted from your list.

APPENDIX

SELECTED TABLES FROM THE PROGRAMMING REFERENCE CARD FOR THE MC6809 MICROPROCESSOR

Instruction	Forms	Addressing Modes															Description	5	3	2	1	0
		Immediate			Direct			Indexed[1]			Extended			Inherent				H	N	Z	V	C
		Op	~	#	Op	~	#	Op	~	#	Op	~	#	Op	~	#						
ABX														3A	3	1	B + X → X (Unsigned)	•	•	•	•	•
ADC	ADCA	89	2	2	99	4	2	A9	4 +	2 +	B9	5	3				A + M + C → A	↕	↕	↕	↕	↕
	ADCB	C9	2	2	D9	4	2	E9	4 +	2 +	F9	5	3				B + M + C → B	↕	↕	↕	↕	↕
ADD	ADDA	8B	2	2	9B	4	2	AB	4 +	2 +	BB	5	3				A + M → A	↕	↕	↕	↕	↕
	ADDB	CB	2	2	DB	4	2	EB	4 +	2 +	FB	5	3				B + M → B	↕	↕	↕	↕	↕
	ADDD	C3	4	3	D3	6	2	E3	6 +	2 +	F3	7	3				D + M:M + 1 → D	•	↕	↕	↕	↕
AND	ANDA	84	2	2	94	4	2	A4	4 +	2 +	B4	5	3				A Λ M → A	•	↕	↕	0	•
	ANDB	C4	2	2	D4	4	2	E4	4 +	2 +	F4	5	3				B Λ M → B	•	↕	↕	0	•
	ANDCC	1C	3	2													CC Λ IMM → CC					6
ASL	ASLA													48	2	1	A } c ← b7 … b0 ← 0	7	↕	↕	↕	↕
	ASLB													58	2	1	B	7	↕	↕	↕	↕
	ASL				08	6	2	68	6 +	2 +	78	7	3				M	7	↕	↕	↕	↕
ASR	ASRA													47	2	1	A } b7 … b0 → c	7	↕	↕	•	↕
	ASRB													57	2	1	B	7	↕	↕	•	↕
	ASR				07	6	2	67	6 +	2 +	77	7	3				M	7	↕	↕	•	↕
BIT	BITA	85	2	2	95	4	2	A5	4 +	2 +	B5	5	3				Bit Test A (M Λ A)	•	↕	↕	0	•
	BITB	C5	2	2	D5	4	2	E5	4 +	2 +	F5	5	3				Bit Test B (M Λ B)	•	↕	↕	0	•
CLR	CLRA													4F	2	1	0 → A	•	0	1	0	0
	CLRB													5F	2	1	0 → B	•	0	1	0	0
	CLR				0F	6	2	6F	6 +	2 +	7F	7	3				0 → M	•	0	1	0	0
CMP	CMPA	81	2	2	91	4	2	A1	4 +	2 +	B1	5	3				Compare M from A	7	↕	↕	↕	↕
	CMPB	C1	2	2	D1	4	2	E1	4 +	2 +	F1	5	3				Compare M from B	7	↕	↕	↕	↕
	CMPD	10 83	5	4	10 93	7	3	10 A3	7 +	3 +	10 B3	8	4				Compare M:M + 1 from D	•	↕	↕	↕	↕
	CMPS	11 8C	5	4	11 9C	7	3	11 AC	7 +	3 +	11 BC	8	4				Compare M:M + 1 from S	•	↕	↕	↕	↕
	CMPU	11 83	5	4	11 93	7	3	11 A3	7 +	3 +	11 B3	8	4				Compare M:M + 1 from U	•	↕	↕	↕	↕
	CMPX	8C	4	3	9C	6	2	AC	6 +	2 +	BC	7	3				Compare M:M + 1 from X	•	↕	↕	↕	↕
	CMPY	10 8C	5	4	10 9C	7	3	10 AC	7 +	3 +	10 BC	8	4				Compare M:M + 1 from Y	•	↕	↕	↕	↕

Instruction	Forms	Addressing Modes															Description	5	3	2	1	0
		Immediate			Direct			Indexed[1]			Extended			Inherent				H	N	Z	V	C
		Op	~	#	Op	~	#	Op	~	#	Op	~	#	Op	~	#						
COM	COMA													43	2	1	$\overline{A}$ → A	•	↕	↕	0	1
	COMB													53	2	1	$\overline{B}$ → B	•	↕	↕	0	1
	COM				03	6	2	63	6 +	2 +	73	7	3				$\overline{M}$ → M	•	↕	↕	0	1
CWAI		3C	≥20	2													CC Λ IMM → CC Wait for Interrupt					7
DAA														19	2	1	Decimal Adjust A	•	↕	↕	0	↕
DEC	DECA													4A	2	1	A − 1 → A	•	↕	↕	↕	•
	DECB													5A	2	1	B − 1 → B	•	↕	↕	↕	•
	DEC				0A	6	2	6A	6 +	2 +	7A	7	3				M − 1 → M	•	↕	↕	↕	•
EOR	EORA	88	2	2	98	4	2	A8	4 +	2 +	B8	5	3				A ⊻ M → A	•	↕	↕	0	•
	EORB	C8	2	2	D8	4	2	E8	4 +	2 +	F8	5	3				B ⊻ M → B	•	↕	↕	0	•
EXG	R1, R2	1E	8	2													R1 → R2[2]	•	•	•	•	•
INC	INCA													4C	2	1	A + 1 → A	•	↕	↕	↕	•
	INCB													5C	2	1	B + 1 → B	•	↕	↕	↕	•
	INC				0C	6	2	6C	6 +	2 +	7C	7	3				M + 1 → M	•	↕	↕	↕	•
JMP					0E	3	2	6E	3 +	2 +	7E	4	3				EA[3] → PC	•	•	•	•	•
JSR					9D	7	2	AD	7 +	2 +	BD	8	3				Jump to Subroutine	•	•	•	•	•
LD	LDA	86	2	2	96	4	2	A6	4 +	2 +	B6	5	3				M → A	•	↕	↕	0	•
	LDB	C6	2	2	D6	4	2	E6	4 +	2 +	F6	5	3				M → B	•	↕	↕	0	•
	LDD	CC	3	3	DC	5	2	EC	5 +	2 +	FC	6	3				M:M + 1 → D	•	↕	↕	0	•
	LDS	10 CE	4	4	10 DE	6	3	10 EE	6 +	3 +	10 FE	7	4				M:M + 1 → S	•	↕	↕	0	•
	LDU	CE	3	3	DE	5	2	EE	5 +	2 +	FE	6	3				M:M + 1 → U	•	↕	↕	0	•
	LDX	8E	3	3	9E	5	2	AE	5 +	2 +	BE	6	3				M:M + 1 → X	•	↕	↕	0	•
	LDY	10 8E	4	4	10 9E	6	3	10 AE	6 +	3 +	10 BE	7	4				M:M + 1 → Y	•	↕	↕	0	•
LEA	LEAS							32	4 +	2 +							EA[3] → S	•	•	•	•	•
	LEAU							33	4 +	2 +							EA[3] → U	•	•	•	•	•
	LEAX							30	4 +	2 +							EA[3] → X	•	•	↕	•	•
	LEAY							31	4 +	2 +							EA[3] → Y	•	•	↕	•	•

Instruction	Forms	Immediate			Direct			Indexed[1]			Extended			Inherent			Description	5 H	3 N	2 Z	1 V	0 C
		Op	~	#	Op	~	#	Op	~	#	Op	~	#	Op	~	#						
LSL	LSLA													48	2	1	A B M: C ← b7 … b0 ← 0	•	↕	↕	↕	↕
	LSLB													58	2	1		•	↕	↕	↕	↕
	LSL				08	6	2	68	6+	2+	78	7	3					•	↕	↕	↕	↕
LSR	LSRA													44	2	1	A B M: 0 → b7 … b0 → C	•	0	↕	•	↕
	LSRB													54	2	1		•	0	↕	•	↕
	LSR				04	6	2	64	6+	2+	74		3					•	0	↕	•	↕
MUL														3D	11	1	A × B → D (Unsigned)	•	•	↕	•	8
NEG	NEGA													40	2	1	$\overline{A}$ + 1 → A	7	↕	↕	↕	↕
	NEGB													50	2	1	$\overline{B}$ + 1 → B	7	↕	↕	↕	↕
	NEG				00	6	2	60	6+	2+	70	7	3				$\overline{M}$ + 1 → M	7	↕	↕	↕	↕
NOP														12	2	1	No Operation	•	•	•	•	•
OR	ORA	8A	2	2	9A	4	2	AA	4+	2+	BA	5	3				A V M → A	•	↕	↕	0	•
	ORB	CA	2	2	DA	4	2	EA	4-	2-	FA	5	3				B V M → B	•	↕	↕	0	•
	ORCC	1A	3	2													CC V IMM → CC				6	
PSH	PSHS	34	5+[4]	2													Push Registers on S Stack	•	•	•	•	•
	PSHU	36	5+[4]	2													Push Registers on U Stack	•	•	•	•	•
PUL	PULS	35	5+[4]	2													Pull Registers from S Stack	•	•	•	•	•
	PULU	37	5+[4]	2													Pull Registers from U Stack	•	•	•	•	•
ROL	ROLA													49	2	1	A B M: C ← b7 … b0 ← C	•	↕	↕	↕	↕
	ROLB													59	2	1		•	↕	↕	↕	↕
	ROL				09	6	2	69	6+	2+	79	7	3					•	↕	↕	↕	↕
ROR	RORA													46	2	1	A B M: C → b7 … b0 → C	•	↕	↕	•	↕
	RORB													56	2	1		•	↕	↕	•	↕
	ROR				06	6	2	66	6+	2+	76	7	3					•	↕	↕	•	↕
RTI														3B	6/15	1	Return From Interrupt					6
RTS														39	5	1	Return from Subroutine	•	•	•	•	•
SBC	SBCA	82	2	2	92	4	2	A2	4+	2+	B2	5	3				A − M − C → A	8	↕	↕	↕	↕
	SBCB	C2	2	2	D2	4	2	E2	4+	2+	F2	5	3				B − M − C → B	8	↕	↕	↕	↕
SEX														1D	2	1	Sign Extend B into A	•	↕	↕	0	•

Instruction	Forms	Immediate			Direct			Indexed[1]			Extended			Inherent			Description	5 H	3 N	2 Z	1 V	0 C
		Op	~	#	Op	~	#	Op	~	#	Op	~	#	Op	~	#						
ST	STA				97	4	2	A7	4+	2+	B7	5	3				A → M	•	↕	↕	0	•
	STB				D7	4	2	E7	4+	2+	F7	5	3				B → M	•	↕	↕	0	•
	STD				DD	5	2	ED	5+	2+	FD	6	3				D → M:M + 1	•	↕	↕	0	•
	STS				10 DF	6	3	10 EF	6+	3+	10 FF	7	4				S → M:M + 1	•	↕	↕	0	•
	STU				DF	5	2	EF	5+	2+	FF	6	3				U → M:M + 1	•	↕	↕	0	•
	STX				9F	5	2	AF	5+	2+	BF	6	3				X → M:M + 1	•	↕	↕	0	•
	STY				10 9F	6	3	10 AF	6+	3+	10 BF	7	4				Y → M:M + 1	•	↕	↕	0	•
SUB	SUBA	80	2	2	90	4	2	A0	4+	2+	B0	5	3				A − M → A	7	↕	↕	↕	↕
	SUBB	C0	2	2	D0	4	2	E0	4+	2+	F0	5	3				B − M → B	7	↕	↕	↕	↕
	SUBD	83	4	3	93	6	2	A3	6+	2+	B3	7	3				D − M:M + 1 → D	•	↕	↕	↕	↕
SWI	SWI[5]													3F	19	1	Software Interrupt 1	•	•	•	•	•
	SWI2[5]													10 3F	20	2	Software Interrupt 2	•	•	•	•	•
	SWI3[5]													11 3F	20	1	Software Interrupt 3	•	•	•	•	•
SYNC														13	≥4	1	Synchronize to Interrupt	•	•	•	•	•
TFR	R1, R2	1F	6	2													R1 → R2[2]	•	•	•	•	•
TST	TSTA													4D	2	1	Test A	•	↕	↕	0	•
	TSTB													5D	2	1	Test B	•	↕	↕	0	•
	TST				0D	6	2	6D	6+	2+	7D	7	3				Test M	•	↕	↕	0	•

Legend:

- OP Operation Code (Hexadecimal)
- ~ Number of MPU Cycles
- \# Number of Program Bytes
- \+ Arithmetic Plus
- − Arithmetic Minus
- • Multiply
- $\overline{M}$ Complement of M
- → Transfer Into
- H Half-carry (from bit 3)
- N Negative (sign bit)
- Z Zero Result
- V Overflow, 2s complement
- C Carry from ALU
- ↕ Test and set if true, cleared otherwise
- • Not Affected
- CC Condition Code Register
- : Concatenation
- V Logical or
- Λ Logical and
- ⊻ Logical Exclusive or

Notes:

1. This column gives a base cycle and byte count. To obtain total count, add the values obtained from the INDEXED ADDRESSING MODES table.
2. R1 and R2 may be any pair of 8 bit or any pair of 16 bit registers.
   The 8 bit registers are: A, B, CC, DP
   The 16 bit registers are: X, Y, U, S, D, PC
3. EA is the effective address.
4. The PSH and PUL instructions require 5 cycles plus 1 cycle for each **byte** pushed or pulled.
5. SWI sets I and F bits. SWI2 and SWI3 do not affect I and F.
6. Conditions Codes set as a direct result of the instruction.
7. Value of half-carry flag is undefined.
8. Special Case — Carry set if b7 is SET.

PUSH/PULL POST BYTE

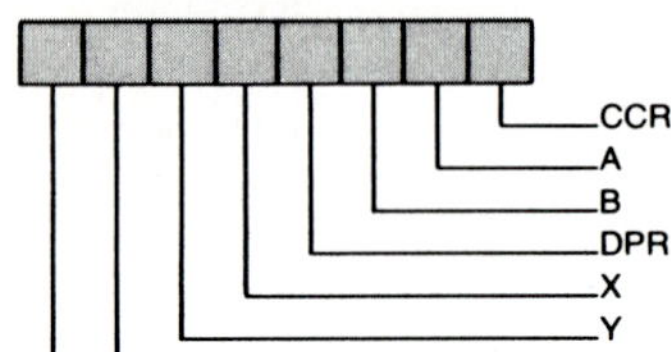

TRANSFER/EXCHANGE POST BYTE

SOURCE	DESTINATION

REGISTER FIELD (Source or Destination)

0000 = D (A:B)	0101 = PC
0001 = X	1000 = A
0010 = Y	1001 = B
0011 = U	1010 = CCR
0100 = S	1011 = DPR

INDEXED ADDRESSING MODES

Type	Forms	Non Indirect				Indirect			
		Assembler Form	Postbyte OP Code	+ ~	+ #	Assembler Form	Postbyte OP Code	+ ~	+ #
Constant Offset From R (twos complement offset)	No Offset	,R	1RR00100	0	0	[,R]	1RR10100	3	0
	5 Bit Offset	n, R	0RRnnnnn	1	0	defaults to 8-bit			
	8 Bit Offset	n, R	1RR01000	1	1	[n, R]	1RR11000	4	1
	16 Bit Offset	n, R	1RR01001	4	2	[n, R]	1RR11001	7	2
Accumulator Offset From R (twos complement offset)	A — Register Offset	A, R	1RR00110	1	0	[A, R]	1RR10110	4	0
	B — Register Offset	B, R	1RR00101	1	0	[B, R]	1RR10101	4	0
	D — Register Offset	D, R	1RR01011	4	0	[D, R]	1RR11011	7	0
Auto Increment/Decrement R	Increment By 1	,R+	1RR00000	2	0	not allowed			
	Increment By 2	,R++	1RR00001	3	0	[,R++]	1RR10001	6	0
	Decrement By 1	,-R	1RR00010	2	0	not allowed			
	Decrement By 2	,--R	1RR00011	3	0	[,--R]	1RR10011	6	0
Constant Offset From PC (twos complement offset)	8 Bit Offset	n, PCR	1XX01100	1	1	[n, PCR]	1XX11100	4	1
	16 Bit Offset	n, PCR	1XX01101	5	2	[n, PCR]	1XX11101	8	2
Extended Indirect	16 Bit Address	—	—	—	--	[n]	10011111	5	2

R = X, Y, U or S X = 00 Y = 01
X = Don't Care U = 10 S = 11

+~ and +# Indicate the number of additional cycles and bytes for the particular variation.

Reprinted with permission of Motorola.

BRANCH INSTRUCTIONS

Instruction	Forms	Addressing Mode Relative OP	~	#	Description	5 H	3 N	2 Z	1 V	0 C
BCC	BCC	24	3	2	Branch C=0	•	•	•	•	•
	LBCC	10 24	5(6)	4	Long Branch C=0	•	•	•	•	•
BCS	BCS	25	3	2	Branch C=1	•	•	•	•	•
	LBCS	10 25	5(6)	4	Long Branch C=1	•	•	•	•	•
BEQ	BEQ	27	3	2	Branch Z=1	•	•	•	•	•
	LBEQ	10 27	5(6)	4	Long Branch Z=1	•	•	•	•	•
BGE	BGE	2C	3	2	Branch≥Zero	•	•	•	•	•
	LBGE	10 2C	5(6)	4	Long Branch≥Zero	•	•	•	•	•
BGT	BGT	2E	3	2	Branch>Zero	•	•	•	•	•
	LBGT	10 2E	5(6)	4	Long Branch>Zero	•	•	•	•	•
BHI	BHI	22	3	2	Branch Higher	•	•	•	•	•
	LBHI	10 22	5(6)	4	Long Branch Higher	•	•	•	•	•
BHS	BHS	24	3	2	Branch Higher or Same	•	•	•	•	•
	LBHS	10 24	5(6)	4	Long Branch Higher or Same	•	•	•	•	•
BLE	BLE	2F	3	2	Branch≤Zero	•	•	•	•	•
	LBLE	10 2F	5(6)	4	Long Branch≤Zero	•	•	•	•	•
BLO	BLO	25	3	2	Branch lower	•	•	•	•	•
	LBLO	10 25	5(6)	4	Long Branch Lower	•	•	•	•	•

Instruction	Forms	Addressing Mode Relative OP	~	#	Description	5 H	3 N	2 Z	1 V	0 C
BLS	BLS	23	3	2	Branch Lower or Same	•	•	•	•	•
	LBLS	10 23	5(6)	4	Long Branch Lower or Same	•	•	•	•	•
BLT	BLT	2D	3	2	Branch<Zero	•	•	•	•	•
	LBLT	10 2D	5(6)	4	Long Branch<Zero	•	•	•	•	•
BMI	BMI	2B	3	2	Branch Minus	•	•	•	•	•
	LBMI	10 2B	5(6)	4	Long Branch Minus	•	•	•	•	•
BNE	BNE	26	3	2	Branch Z=0	•	•	•	•	•
	LBNE	10 26	5(6)	4	Long Branch Z=0	•	•	•	•	•
BPL	BPL	2A	2	2	Branch Plus	•	•	•	•	•
	LBPL	10 2A	5(6)	4	Long Branch Plus	•	•	•	•	•
BRA	BRA	20	3	2	Branch Always	•	•	•	•	•
	LBRA	16	5	3	Long Branch Always	•	•	•	•	•
BRN	BRN	21	3	2	Branch Never	•	•	•	•	•
	LBRN	10 21	5	4	Long Branch Never	•	•	•	•	•
BSR	BSR	8D	7	2	Branch to Subroutine	•	•	•	•	•
	LBSR	17	9	3	Long Branch to Subroutine	•	•	•	•	•
BVC	BVC	28	3	2	Branch V=0	•	•	•	•	•
	LBVC	10 28	5(6)	4	Long Branch V=0	•	•	•	•	•
BVS	BVS	29	3	2	Branch V=1	•	•	•	•	•
	LBVS	10 29	5(6)	4	Long Branch V=1	•	•	•	•	•

SIMPLE BRANCHES

	OP	~	#
BRA	20	3	2
LBRA	16	5	3
BRN	21	3	2
LBRN	1021	5	4
BSR	8D	7	2
LBSR	17	9	3

SIMPLE CONDITIONAL BRANCHES (NOTES 1-4)

Test	True	OP	False	OP
N=1	BMI	2B	BPL	2A
Z=1	BEQ	27	BNE	26
V=1	BVS	29	BVC	28
C=1	BCS	25	BCC	24

SIGNED CONDITIONAL BRANCHES (NOTES 1-4)

Test	True	OP	False	OP
r>m	BGT	2E	BLE	2F
r≥m	BGE	2C	BLT	2D
r=m	BEQ	27	BNE	26
r≤m	BLE	2F	BGT	2E
r<m	BLT	2D	BGE	2C

UNSIGNED CONDITIONAL BRANCHES (NOTES 1-4)

Test	True	OP	False	OP
r>m	BHI	22	BLS	23
r≥m	BHS	24	BLO	25
r=m	BEQ	27	BNE	26
r≤m	BLS	23	BHI	22
r<m	BLO	25	BHS	24

Notes:

1. All conditional branches have both short and long variations.
2. All short branches are 2 bytes and require 3 cycles.
3. All conditional long branches are formed by prefixing the short branch opcode with $10 and using a 16-bit destination offset.
4. All conditional long branches require 4 bytes and 6 cycles if the branch is taken or 5 cycles if the branch is not taken.

APPENDIX B

MC6809 INSTRUCTION SET

This appendix describes the MC6809 instructions in alphabetical order by mnemonic. Unless otherwise stated, nonbranch memory reference instructions that do not write to memory allow any of the standard modes (immediate, direct, indexed, and extended). Instructions that do write a value to memory allow only the writable modes (direct, indexed, and extended).

ABX Add the content of register B to the content of register X. Inherent mode only.

ADC Add with carry—add the content of the memory location identified in one of the standard modes to the content of the accumulator designated in the mnemonic and add to that sum the content of the carry flag in the condition codes register.

ADD Add the content of the memory location identified in one of the standard modes to the content of the accumulator (or double accumulator, D) designated in the mnemonic.

AND AND the content of the memory location identified in one of the standard modes to the content of the accumulator designated in the mnemonic.

ANDCC AND the immediate operand to the content of the CC register.

ASL Arithmetic shift left—shift left by one bit the pattern in the designated accumulator or in the memory location identified in one of the writable modes. Shift a zero in from the right and shift the leftmost bit into the carry.

ASR Arithmetic shift right—shift right by one bit the pattern in the designated accumulator or in the memory location identified in one of the writable modes. Shift a copy of bit seven (the sign bit) into the leftmost position and shift the rightmost bit into the carry.

BCC (LBCC) Branch if carry is clear.

BCS (LBCS) Branch if carry is set.

BEQ (LBEQ) Branch if equal—branch if the Z-bit is set.

BGE (LBGE) Branch if greater than or equal—after SUB or CMP branch if the signed number in the accumulator was greater than or equal to the signed number in the memory location.

BGT (LBGT) Branch if greater than—after SUB or CMP branch if the signed number in the accumulator was greater than the signed number in the memory location.

BHI (LBHI) Branch if higher—after SUB or CMP branch if the unsigned number in the accumulator was greater than the unsigned number in the memory location.

BIT Bit test—AND the content of the location identified in one of the standard modes with the content of the designated accumulator but discard the result after using it to update the condition code bits.

BHS (LBHS) Branch if higher than or the same—after SUB or CMP branch if the unsigned number in the accumulator was greater than or equal to the unsigned number in the memory location.

BLE (LBLE) Branch if less than or equal—after SUB or CMP branch if the signed number in the accumulator was less than or equal to the signed number in the memory location.

BLO (LBLO) Branch if lower—after SUB or CMP branch if the unsigned number in the accumulator was less than the unsigned number in the memory location.

BLS (LBLS) Branch if lower than or the same—after SUB or CMP branch if the unsigned number in the accumulator was less than or equal to the unsigned number in the memory location.

BLT (LBLT) Branch if less than—after SUB or CMP branch if the signed number in the accumulator was less than the signed number in the memory location.

BMI (LBMI) Branch if minus—branch if the N-bit is set.

BNE (LBNE) Branch if not equal—branch if the Z-bit is cleared.

BPL (LBPL) Branch if plus—branch if the N-bit is cleared.

BRA (LBRA) Branch always—unconditionally branch.

BRN (LBRN) Branch never—never branch.

BSR (LBSR) Branch to subroutine and save the content of the PC on the system stack.

BVC (LBVC) Branch if V-bit is cleared.

BVS (LBVS) Branch if V-bit is set.

CLR Clear each bit in the designated accumulator or in the location identified in one of the writable modes.

CMP Compare—subtract the value in the memory location identified in one of the standard modes from the register designated in the mnemonic (A, B, D, S, U, X, or Y) and discard the result after using it to update the condition code bits.

COM Complement each bit in the designated accumulator or in the memory location identified in one of the writable modes.

CWAI Change condition codes and wait for interrupt—AND the immediate data with the CC register to modify its content and then cease fetching and executing instructions and wait for an interrupt.

DAA Decimal adjust accumulator A—adjust the value in A to the correct BCD code. (This instruction works properly only immediately after the execution of an ADDA or an ADCA instruction in which both operands are BCD values.)

DEC Decrement—subtract one from the content of the designated accumulator or the memory location identified in one of the writable modes.

EOR EXCLUSIVE OR the content of the memory location identified in one of the standard modes to the content of the designated accumulator.

EXG Exchange the contents of two registers (immediate * mode only). The operand consists of a register pair designated by letters from the following set: A, B, D, CC, DP, X, Y, U, S, or PC. The two registers designated must be of the same size.

INC Increment—add one to the content of the designated accumulator or the memory location identified in one of the writable modes.

JMP Jump to the location whose address is identified in one of the writable modes.

JSR Jump to the subroutine whose starting address is identified in one of the writable modes. Save the content of the PC on the system stack.

LBcc Long branch on condition cc. See **Bcc** branches.

LD Load the register designated in the mnemonic (A, B, D, S, U, X, or Y) with the content of the location in memory identified in one of the standard modes.

LEA Load effective address—load the double register designated in the mnemonic (S, U, X, or Y) with the address obtained from the indexed address calculation as specified in this instruction's addressing option. Requires the indexed addressing mode.

---

*Motorola's designation. The two registers are identified in a single byte *immediately* following the op-code. The source code does not include the # symbol.

LSL Logic shift left—shift left by one bit the pattern in the designated accumulator or in the memory location identified in one of the writable modes while bringing a zero in from the right. The leftmost bit shifts into the carry. This instruction is identical to the arithmetic shift left (ASL) in machine code.

LSR Logic shift right—shift right by one bit the pattern in the designated accumulator or in the memory location identified in one of the writable modes while bringing a zero in from the left. The rightmost bit shifts into the carry.

MUL Multiply the content of accumulator A by the content of accumulator B (unsigned) and load the 16-bit product into the double register D (A concatenated with B).

NEG Negate—change the sign (twos complement) of the value in the designated accumulator or in the memory location identified in one of the writable modes.

NOP No operation—do nothing.

OR OR the content of the memory location identified in one of the standard modes to the content of the designated accumulator.

ORCC OR the immediate operand to the content of the CC register.

PSH Push—immediate* mode only. The operand consists of any number of registers from the following set: A, B, D, CC, DP, X, Y, U/S (not the pointer to the target stack), or PC. Write the contents of the registers designated in the operand into the top of the target stack designated in the mnemonic.

PUL Pull—immediate* mode only. The operand consists of any number of registers from the following set: A, B, D, CC, DP, X, Y, U/S (not the pointer to the target stack), or PC. Write the contents of the top of the target stack designated in the mnemonic into the registers designated in the operand.

ROL Rotate left—shift left by one bit the pattern in the designated accumulator or in the memory location identified in one of the writable modes while bringing the carry bit into the rightmost position and moving the leftmost bit into the carry.

ROR Rotate right—shift right by one bit the pattern in the designated accumulator or in the memory location identified in one of the writable modes while bringing the carry bit into the leftmost position and moving the rightmost bit into the carry.

RTI Return from interrupt—retrieve the contents of the registers that were saved on the system stack during the latest interrupt.

RTS Return from subroutine—retrieve the content of the top of the system stack into the PC.

SBC Subtract with carry—subtract the content of the memory location identified in one of the standard modes from the content of the accumulator designated in the mnemonic and subtract from that difference the content of the carry flag in the condition codes register.

SEX Sign-extend the value of accumulator B into accumulator A by copying the sign bit from B into every bit position in A.

---

*Motorola's designation. The two registers are identified in a single byte *immediately* following the op-code. The source code does not include the # symbol.

ST Store the content of the register designated in the mnemonic (A, B, D, S, U, X, or Y) into the location whose address is identified in one of the writable modes.

SUB Subtract the content of the memory location identified in one of the standard modes from the content of the designated accumulator (or double accumulator, D).

SWI Software interrupt—branch to one of three locations as determined by the interrupt vector specified by the mnemonic while saving the contents of the processor registers on the system stack.

SYNC Synchronize to external event—cease fetching and executing instructions and wait for an interrupt.

TFR Transfer the content of the first designated register into the second designated register (immediate* mode only). The operand consists of a register pair designated by letters from the following set: A, B, D, CC, DP, X, Y, U, S, or PC. The two registers designated must be of the same size.

TST Test—subtract zero from the value in the accumulator designated in the mnemonic or from the value in the memory location identified in one of the writable modes. Use the result to update the N- and Z-flags in the condition code register.

---

*Motorola's designation. The two registers are identified in a single byte *immediately* following the op-code. The source code does not include the # symbol.

APPENDIX C

SELECTED TABLES FROM THE PROGRAMMING REFERENCE CARD FOR THE MC68000 MICROPROCESSOR

Addressing Modes

Mnemonic	Size	Address Mode	Dn #	Dn ~	An #	An ~	(An) #	(An) ~	(An)+ #	(An)+ ~	−(An) #	−(An) ~	d_{16}(An) #	d_{16}(An) ~	d_8(An,Xn) #	d_8(An,Xn) ~	Abs.W #	Abs.W ~	Abs.L #	Abs.L ~	d_{16}(PC) #	d_{16}(PC) ~	d_8(PC,Xn) #	d_8(PC,Xn) ~	s = Immed d = SR/CC #	s = Immed d = SR/CC ~	Opcode Bit Pattern 1111 11 / 5432 1098 7654 3210	Boolean	Condition Codes X N Z V C
ABCD	B	s = Dn d =	2	6																							1100 RRR1 0000 0rrr	d10 + s10 + X → d	* U * U *
		s = −(An) d =									2	18															1100 RRR1 0000 1rrr		
ADD	B/W	s = Dn d =	2	4		ADDA	2	12	2	12	2	14	4	16	4	18	4	16	6	20							1101 DDD1 SSEE EEEE	d + Dn → d	* * * * *
		d = Dn s =	2	4	2*	4	2	8	2	8	2	10	4	12	4	14	4	12	6	16	4	12	4	14	4	8	1101 DDD0 SSee eeee	Dn + s → Dn	
	L	s = Dn d =	2	8		ADDA	2	20	2	20	2	22	4	24	4	26	4	24	6	28							1101 DDD1 10EE EEEE	d + Dn → d	
		d = Dn s =	2	8	2	8	2	14	2	14	2	16	4	18	4	20	4	18	6	22	4	18	4	20	6	16	1101 DDD0 10ee eeee	Dn + s → Dn	
ADDA	W	d = An s =	2	8	2	8	2	12	2	12	2	14	4	16	4	18	4	16	6	20	4	16	4	18	4	12	1101 AAA0 11ee eeee	An + s → An	- - - - -
	L	d = An s =	2	8	2	8	2	14	2	14	2	16	4	18	4	20	4	18	6	22	4	18	4	20	6	16	1101 AAA1 11ee eeee		
ADDI	B/W	s = Imm d =	4	8		ADDA	4	16	4	16	4	18	6	20	6	22	6	20	8	24							0000 0110 SSEE EEEE	d + # → d	* * * * *
	L	s = Imm d =	6	16		ADDA	6	28	6	28	6	30	8	32	8	34	8	32	10	36									
ADDQ	B/W	s = Imm3 d =	2	4	2*	8	2	12	2	12	2	14	4	16	4	18	4	16	6	20							0101 QQQ0 SSEE EEEE	d + # → d	* * * * *
	L	s = Imm3 d =	2	8	2	8	2	20	2	20	2	22	4	24	4	26	4	24	6	28									
ADDX	B/W	s = Dn d =	2	4																							1101 RRR1 SS00 0rrr	d + s + X → d	* * * * *
		s = −(An) d =									2	18															1101 RRR1 SS00 1rrr		
	L	s = Dn d =	2	8																							1101 RRR1 1000 0rrr		
		s = −(An) d =									2	30															1101 RRR1 1000 1rrr		
AND	B/W	s = Dn d =	2	4			2	12	2	12	2	14	4	16	4	18	4	16	6	20							1100 DDD1 SSEE EEEE	d<and>Dn → d	- * * 0 0
		d = Dn s =	2	4			2	8	2	8	2	10	4	12	4	14	4	12	6	16	4	12	4	14	4	8	1100 DDD0 SSee eeee	Dn<and>s → Dn	
	L	s = Dn d =	2	8			2	20	2	20	2	22	4	24	4	26	4	24	6	28							1100 DDD1 10EE EEEE	d<and>Dn → d	
		d = Dn s =	2	8			2	14	2	14	2	16	4	18	4	20	4	18	6	22	4	18	4	20	6	16	1100 DDD0 10ee eeee	Dn<and>s → Dn	
ANDI	B/W	s = Imm d =	4	8			4	16	4	16	4	18	6	20	6	22	6	20	8	24							0000 0010 SSEE EEEE	d<and># → d	- * * 0 0
	L	s = Imm d =	6	16			6	28	6	28	6	30	8	32	8	34	8	32	10	36									
ANDI CCR	B	s = Imm d =																							4	20	0000 0010 0011 1100	s<and>CCR → CCR	* * * * *
ANDI SR	W	s = Imm d =																							4	20	0000 0010 0111 1100	s<and>SR → SR	* * * * *
ASL, ASR	B/W	count = Dn d =	2	6 + 2n																							1110 rrrf SS10 0DDD	C, X ← Left ← 0	* * * * *
		count = #1–8 d =	2	6 + 2n																							1110 QQQf SS00 0DDD		
	L	count = Dn d =	2	8 + 2n																							1110 rrrf 1010 0DDD	Right → C, X	
		count = #1–8 d =	2	8 + 2n																							1110 QQQf 1000 0DDD		
Memory	W	count = 1 d =					2*	12	2*	12	2*	14	4*	16	4*	18	4*	16	6*	20							1110 000f 11EE EEEE		

Bcc	B	d8 =																					branch taken 2	10	0110 CCCC PPPP PPPP	If cc true, then PC + disp → PC	- - - - -
																							branch not taken 2	8			
	W	d16 =																					branch taken 4	10			
																							branch not taken 4	12			
BCHG	B	bit# = Dn d =					2	12	2	12	2	14	4	16	4	18	4	16	6	20					0000 rrr1 01EE EEEE	'(bit#) of d → Z,	- - * - -
		bit# = Imm d =					4	16	4	16	4	18	6	20	6	22	6	20	8	24					0000 1000 01EE EEEE	'(bit#) of d → (bit#) of d	
	L	bit# = Dn d =	2	<8																					0000 rrr1 01EE EEEE		
		bit# = Imm d =	4	<12																					0000 1000 01EE EEEE		
BCLR	B	bit# = Dn d =					2	12	2	12	2	14	4	16	4	18	4	16	6	20					0000 rrr1 10EE EEEE	'(bit#) of d → Z,	- - * - -
		bit# = Imm d =					4	16	4	16	4	18	6	20	6	22	6	20	8	24					0000 1000 10EE EEEE	0 → (bit#) of d	
	L	bit# = Dn d =	2	<10																					0000 rrr1 10EE EEEE		
		bit# = Imm d =	4	<14																					0000 1000 10EE EEEE		
BRA	B	d8 =																					2	10	0110 0000 PPPP PPPP	PC + disp → PC	- - - - -
	W	d16 =																					4	10			
BSET	B	bit# = Dn d =					2	12	2	12	2	14	4	16	4	18	4	16	6	20					0000 rrr1 11EE EEEE	'(bit#) of d → Z,	- - * - -
		bit# = Imm d =					4	16	4	16	4	18	6	20	6	22	6	20	8	24					0000 1000 11EE EEEE	1 → (bit#) of d	
	L	bit# = Dn d =	2	<8																					0000 rrr1 11EE EEEE		
		bit# = Imm d =	4	<12																					0000 1000 11EE EEEE		
BSR	B	d8 =																					2	18	0110 0001 PPPP PPPP	PC → − (SP), PC + disp → PC	- - - - -
	W	d16 =																					4	18			
BTST	B	bit# = Dn d =					2	8	2	8	2	10	4	12	4	14	4	12	6	16	4	12	4	14			0000 rrr1 00EE EEEE	'(bit#) of d → Z	- - * - -
		bit# = Imm d =					4	12	4	12	4	14	6	16	6	18	6	16	8	20	6	16	6	18			0000 1000 00EE EEEE		
	L	bit# = Dn d =	2	<6																					0000 rrr1 00EE EEEE		
		bit# = Imm d =	4	<10																					0000 1000 00EE EEEE		
CHK	W	d = Dn s(bound) =	2	<44 trap			2	<48	2	<48	2	<50	4	<52	4	<54	4	<52	6	<56	4	<52	4	<54	4	<48	0100 DDD1 10ee eeee	If Dn<0 or Dn>(bound),	- * U U U
			2	10 no trap			2	14	2	14	2	16	4	18	4	20	4	18	6	22	4	18	4	20	4	14		then trap	
CLR	B/W	d =	2	4			2	12	2	12	2	14	4	16	4	18	4	16	6	20							0100 0010 SSEE EEEE	0 → d	- 0 1 0 0
	L	d =	2	6			2	20	2	20	2	22	4	24	4	26	4	24	6	28									
CMP	B/W	d = Dn s =	2	4	2*	4	2	8	2	8	2	10	4	12	4	14	4	12	6	16	4	12	4	14	4	8	1011 DDD0 SSee eeee	Dn − s	- * * * *
	L	d = Dn s =	2	6	2	6	2	14	2	14	2	16	4	18	4	20	4	18	6	22	4	18	4	20	6	14			
CMPA	W	d = An s =	2	6	2	6	2	10	2	10	2	12	4	14	4	16	4	12	6	18	4	14	4	16	4	10	1011 AAA0 11ee eeee	An − s	- * * * *
	L	d = An s =	2	6	2	6	2	14	2	14	2	16	4	18	4	20	4	18	6	22	4	18	4	20	6	14	1011 AAA1 11ee eeee		
CMPI	B/W	s = Imm d =	4	8		CMPA	4	12	4	12	4	14	6	16	6	18	6	16	8	20							0000 1100 SSEE EEEE	d − #	- * * * *
	L	s = Imm d =	6	14		CMPA	6	20	6	20	6	22	8	24	8	26	8	24	10	28									
CMPM	B/W	s = (An)+ d =							2	12																	1011 RRR1 SS00 1rrr	d − s	- * * * *
	L	s = (An)+ d =							2	20																			

Reprinted with permission of Motorola.

Mnemonic	Size	Address Mode	Dn #	Dn ~	An #	An ~	(An) #	(An) ~	(An)+ #	(An)+ ~	−(An) #	−(An) ~	d16(An) #	d16(An) ~	d8(An,Xn) #	d8(An,Xn) ~	Abs.W #	Abs.W ~	Abs.L #	Abs.L ~	d16(PC) #	d16(PC) N	d8(PC,Xn) #	d8(PC,Xn) N	s = Immed d = SR/CC #	s = Immed d = SR/CC N	Opcode Bit Pattern 1111 11 5432 1098 7654 3210	Boolean	Condition Codes X N Z V C
DBcc	W	d16 = Imm			cc	Counter	Branch																				0101 CCCC 1100 1DDD	If cc true, then NOP else Dn − 1 → Dn, If Dn ≠ −1, then PC + disp → PC	- - - - -
		counter =	4	10	false	≠ −1	yes																						
				12	true	N/A	no																						
				14	false	expired	no																						
DIVS	W	d = Dn s =	2	<158			2	<162	2	<162	2	<164	4	<166	4	<168	4	<166	6	<170	4	<166	4	<168	4	<162	1000 DDD1 11ee eeee	Dn32/s16 → Dn(r : q)	- * * * 0
DIVU	W	d = Dn s =	2	<140			2	<144	2	<144	2	<146	4	<148	4	<150	4	<148	6	<152	4	<148	4	<150	4	<144	1000 DDD0 11ee eeee	Dn32/s16 → Dn(r : q)	- * * * 0
EOR	B/W	s = Dn d =	2	4			2	12	2	12	2	14	4	16	4	18	4	16	6	20							1011 rrr1 SSEE EEEE	d ⊕ Dn → d	- * * 0 0
	L	s = Dn d =	2	8			2	16	2	16	2	18	4	20	4	22	4	20	6	24									
EORI	B	s = Imm d =	4	8			4	16	4	16	4	18	6	20	6	22	6	20	8	24							0000 1010 SSEE EEEE	d ⊕ # → d	- * * 0 0
	L	s = Imm d =	6	16			6	28	6	28	6	30	8	32	8	34	8	32	10	36									
EORI CCR	B	s = Imm d =																							4	20	0000 1010 0011 1100	s ⊕ CCR → CCR	* * * * *
EORI SR	W	s = Imm d =																							4	20	0000 1010 0111 1100	s ⊕ SR → SR	* * * * *
EXG	L	s = Dn d =	2	6	2	6																					1100 DDD1 0100 0DDD	s ↔ d	- - - - -
		s = An d =	2	6	2	6																					1100 AAA1 0100 1AAA		
																											1100 DDD1 1000 1AAA		
EXT	W	d =	2	4																							0100 1000 1000 0DDD	bit 7 → bits 15 : 8	- * * 0 0
	L	d =	2	4																							0100 1000 1100 0DDD	bit 15 → bits 31 : 16	
ILLEGAL			2	34																							0100 1010 1111 1100	PC → −(SSP), SR → −(SSP), (illegal vector) → PC	- - - - -
JMP		d =					2	8					4	10	4	14	4	10	6	12	4	10	4	14			0100 1110 11EE EEEE	d → PC	- - - - -
JSR		d =					2	16					4	18	4	22	4	18	6	20	4	18	4	22			0100 1110 10EE EEEE	PC → −(SP),d → PC	- - - - -
LEA	L	d = An s =					2	4					4	8	4	12	4	8	6	12	4	8	4	12			0100 AAA1 11ee eeee	s → An	- - - - -
LINK		d16 = Imm s =			4	16																					0100 1110 0101 0AAA	An → −(SP), SP → An, SP + disp → SP	- - - - -
LSL, LSR	B/W	count = Dn d =	2	6 + 2n																							1110 rrrf SS10 1DDD	C ← [ ] ← 0; X ← Left	* * * 0 *
		count = #1–8 d =	2	6 + 2n																							1110 QQQf SS00 1DDD	0 → [ ] → C, → X; Right	
	L	count = Dn d =	2	8 + 2n																							1110 rrrf 1010 1DDD		
		count = #1–8 d =	2	8 + 2n																							1110 QQQf 1000 1DDD		
Memory	W	count = 1 d =					2*	12	2*	12	2*	14	4*	16	4*	18	4*	16	6*	20							1110 001f 11EE EEEE		

MOVE	B/W	d=Dn	s=	2	4	2	4	2	8	2	8	2	10	4	12	4	14	4	12	6	16	4	12	4	14	4	8	00XX RRRM MMee eeee	s→d	-**00
		d=An	s=	MOVEA		MOVEA		MOVEA		MOVEA		MOVEA		MOVEA		MOVEA		MOVEA		MOVEA		MOVEA		MOVEA		MOVEA				
		d=(An)	s=	2	8	2	8	2	12	2	12	2	14	4	16	4	18	4	16	6	20	4	16	4	18	4	12			
		d=(An)+	s=	2	8	2	8	2	12	2	12	2	14	4	16	4	18	4	16	4	20	4	16	4	18	4	12			
		d=−(An)	s=	2	8	2	8	2	12	2	12	2	14	4	16	4	18	4	16	6	20	4	16	4	18	4	12			
		d=d16(An)	s=	4	12	4	12	4	16	4	16	4	18	6	20	6	22	6	20	8	24	6	20	6	22	6	16			
		d=d8(An,Xn)	s=	4	14	4	14	4	18	4	18	4	20	6	22	6	24	6	22	8	26	6	22	6	24	6	18			
		d=Abs.W	s=	4	12	4	12	4	16	4	16	4	18	6	20	6	22	6	20	8	24	6	20	6	22	6	16			
		d=Abs.L	s=	6	16	6	16	6	20	6	20	6	22	8	24	8	26	8	24	10	28	8	24	8	26	8	20			
MOVE	L	d=Dn	s=	2	4	2	4	2	12	2	12	2	14	4	16	4	18	4	16	6	20	4	16	4	18	6	12	0010 RRRM MMee eeee	s→d	-**00
		d=An	s=	MOVEA		MOVEA		MOVEA		MOVEA		MOVEA		MOVEA		MOVEA		MOVEA		MOVEA		MOVEA		MOVEA		MOVEA				
		d=(An)	s=	2	12	2	12	2	20	2	20	2	22	4	24	4	26	4	24	6	28	4	24	4	26	6	20			
		d=(An)+	s=	2	12	2	12	2	20	2	20	2	22	4	24	4	26	4	24	4	28	4	24	4	26	6	20			
		d=−(An)	s=	2	12	2	12	2	20	2	20	2	22	4	24	4	26	4	24	6	28	4	24	4	26	6	20			
		d=d16(An)	s=	4	16	4	16	4	24	4	24	4	26	6	28	6	30	6	28	8	32	6	28	6	30	8	24			
		d=d8(An,Xn)	s=	4	18	4	18	4	26	4	26	4	28	6	30	6	32	6	30	8	34	6	30	6	32	8	26			
		d=Abs.W	s=	4	16	4	16	4	24	4	24	4	26	6	28	6	30	6	28	8	32	6	28	6	30	8	24			
		d=Abs.L	s=	6	20	6	20	6	28	6	28	6	30	8	32	8	34	8	32	10	36	8	32	8	34	10	28			
MOVE CCR	W	d=CCR	s=	2	12			2	16	2	16	2	18	4	20	4	22	4	20	6	24	4	20	4	22	4	16	0100 0100 11ee eeee	s→CCR	*****
MOVE SR	W	d=SR	s=	2	12			2	16	2	16	2	18	4	20	4	22	4	20	6	24	4	20	4	22	4	16	0100 0110 11ee eeee	s→SR	*****
		s=SR	d=	2	6			2	12	2	12	2	14	4	16	4	18	4	16	6	20							0100 0000 11EE EEEE	SR→d	-----
MOVE USP	L	s=USP	d=			2	4																					0100 1110 0110 1AAA	USP→An	-----
		d=USP	s=			2	4																					0100 1110 0110 0AAA	An→USP	
MOVEA	W	d=An	s=	2	4	2	4	2	8	2	8	2	10	4	12	4	14	4	12	6	16	4	12	4	14	4	8	0011 AAA0 01ee eeee	s→An	-----
	L	d=An	s=	2	4	2	4	2	12	2	12	2	14	4	16	4	18	4	16	6	20	4	16	4	18	6	12	0010 AAA0 01ee eeee		
MOVEM	W	s=Xn	d=					4	8+4n			4	8+4n	6	12+4n	6	14+4n	6	12+4n	8	16+4n							0100 1000 10EE EEEE a7 a0 d7 d0	Xn→d	-----
		d=Xn	s=					4	12+4n	4	12+4n			6	16+4n	6	18+4n	6	16+4n	8	20+4n	6	16+4n	6	18+4n			0100 1100 10ee eeee a7 a0 d7 d0	s→Xn	
	L	s=Xn	d=					4	8+8n			4	8+8n	6	12+8n	6	14+8n	6	12+8n	8	16+8n							0100 1000 11EE EEEE a7 a0 d7 d0	Xn→d	
		d=Xn	s=					4	12+8n	4	12+8n			6	16+8n	6	18+8n	6	16+8n	8	20+8n	6	16+8n	6	18+8n			0100 1100 11ee eeee a7 a0 d7 d0	s→Xn	
MOVEP	W	s=Dn	d=											4	16													0000 DDD1 1000 1AAA	Dn→d by bytes	-----
		s=d16(An)	d=	4	16																							0000 DDD1 0000 1AAA	s→Dn by bytes	
	L	s=Dn	d=											4	24													0000 DDD1 1100 1AAA	Dn→d by bytes	
		s=d16(An)	d=	4	24																							0000 DDD1 0100 1AAA	s→Dn by bytes	

Reprinted with permission of Motorola.

Mnemonic	Size	Address Mode	Dn		An		(An)		(An)+		−(An)		d_{16}(An)		d_8(An,Xn)		Abs.W		Abs.L		d_{16}(PC)		d_8(PC,Xn)		s = Immed d = SR/CC		Opcode Bit Pattern 1111 11 5432 1098 7654 3210	Boolean	Condition Codes X N Z V C
			#	~	#	~	#	~	#	~	#	~	#	~	#	~	#	~	#	~	#	N	#	N	#	N			
MOVEQ	L	s = Imm8 d =	2	4																							0111 DDD0 QQQQ QQQQ	# → Dn	- * * 0 0
MULS	W	d = Dn s =	2	<70			2	<74	2	<74	2	<76	4	<78	4	<80	4	<78	6	<82	4	<78	4	<80	4	<74	1100 DDD1 11ee eeee	Dn × s → Dn	- * * 0 0
MULU	W	d = Dn s =	2	<70			2	<74	2	<74	2	<76	4	<78	4	<80	4	<78	6	<82	4	<78	4	<80	4	<74	1100 DDD0 11ee eeee	Dn × s → Dn	- * * 0 0
NBCD	B	d =	2	6			2	12	2	12	2	14	4	16	4	18	4	16	6	20							0100 1000 00EE EEEE	0 − d10 − X → d	* U * U *
NEG	B/W	d =	2	4			2	12	2	12	2	14	4	16	4	18	4	16	6	20							0100 0100 SSEE EEEE	0 − d → d	* * * * *
	L	d =	2	6			2	20	2	20	2	22	4	24	4	26	4	24	6	28									
NEGX	B/W	d =	2	4			2	12	2	12	2	14	4	16	4	18	4	16	6	20							0100 0000 SSEE EEEE	0 − d − X → d	* * * * *
	L	d =	2	6			2	20	2	20	2	22	4	24	4	26	4	24	6	28									
NOP			2	4																							0100 1110 0111 0001	none	- - - - -
NOT	B/W	d =	2	4			2	12	2	12	2	14	4	16	4	18	4	16	6	20							0100 0110 SSEE EEEE	'd → d	- * * 0 0
	L	d =	2	6			2	20	2	20	2	22	4	24	4	26	4	24	6	28									
OR	B/W	s = Dn d =					2	12	2	12	2	14	4	16	4	18	4	16	6	20							1000 DDD1 SSEE EEEE	d<or>Dn → d	- * * 0 0
		d = Dn s =	2	4			2	8	2	8	2	10	4	12	4	14	4	12	6	16	4	12	4	14	4	8	1000 DDD0 SSee eeee	Dn<or>s → Dn	
	L	s = Dn d =					2	20	2	20	2	22	4	24	4	26	4	24	6	28							1000 DDD1 10EE EEEE	d<or>Dn → d	
		d = Dn s =	2	8			2	14	2	14	2	16	4	18	4	20	4	18	6	22	4	18	4	20	6	16	1000 DDD0 10ee eeee	Dn<or>s → Dn	
ORI	B/W	s = Imm d =	4	8			4	16	4	16	4	18	6	20	6	22	6	20	8	24							0000 0000 SSEE EEEE	d<or># → D	- * * 0 0
	L	s = Imm d =	6	16			6	28	6	28	6	30	8	32	8	34	8	32	10	36									
ORI CCR	B	s = Imm d =																							4	20	0000 0000 0011 1100	s<or>CCR → CCR	* * * * *
ORI SR	W	s = Imm d =																							4	20	0000 0000 0111 1100	s<or>SR → SR	* * * * *
PEA	L	s =					2	12					4	16	4	20	4	16	6	20	4	16	4	20			0100 1000 01ee eeee	s → −(SP)	- - - - -
RESET			2	132																							0100 1110 0111 0000	assert RESET pin	- - - - -
ROL, ROR	B/W	count = Dn d =	2	6+2n																							1110 rrrf SS11 1DDD	Right n → C	- * * 0 0
		count = #1–8 d =	2	6+2n																							1110 QQQf SS01 1DDD		
	L	count = Dn d =	2	8+2n																							1110 rrrf 1011 1DDD		
		count = #1–8 d =	2	8+2n																							1110 QQQf 1001 1DDD	C ← Left n	
Memory	W	count = 1 d =					2*	12	2*	12	2*	14	4*	16	4*	18	4*	16	6*	20							1100 011f 11EE EEEE		
ROXL, ROXR	B/W	count = Dn d =	2	6+2n																							1110 rrrf SS11 0DDD	Right n → C, X	* * * 0 *
		count = #1–8 d =	2	6+2n																							1110 QQQf SS01 0DDD		
	L	count = Dn d =	2	8+2n																							1110 rrrf 1011 0DDD		
		count = #1–8 d =	2	8+2n																							1110 QQQf 1001 0DDD	C, X ← Left n	
Memory	W	count = 1					2*	12	2*	12	2*	14	4*	16	4*	18	4*	16	6*	20							1110 010f 11EE EEEE		
RTE			2	20																							0100 1110 0111 0011	(SP)+ → SR, (SP)+ → PC	* * * * *
RTR			2	20																							0100 1110 0111 0111	(SP)+ → CC, (SP)+ → PC	* * * * *
RTS			2	16																							0100 1110 0111 0101	(SP)+ → PC	- - - - -

SBCD	B	s = Dn	d =	2	6																							1000 RRR1 0000 0rrr	d10 − s10 − X → d	* U * U *
		s = −(An)	d =									2	18															1000 RRR1 0000 1rrr		
Scc	B	cc = True	d =	2	6			2	12	2	12	2	14	4	16	4	18	4	16	6	20							0101 CCCC 11EE EEEE	If cc true, then 1s → d	- - - - -
		cc = False	d =	2	4			2	12	2	12	2	14	4	16	4	18	4	16	6	20								else 0s → d	
STOP																										4	4	0100 1110 0111 0010	# → SR, wait for interrupt	* * * * *
SUB	B/W	s = Dn	d =	2	4	SUBA		2	12	2	12	2	14	4	16	4	18	4	16	6	20							1001 DDD1 SSEE EEEE	d − Dn → d	* * * * *
		d = Dn	s =	2	4	2*	4	2	8	2	8	2	10	4	12	4	14	4	12	6	16	4	12	4	14	4	8	1001 DDD0 SSee eeee	Dn − s → Dn	
	L	s = Dn	d =	2	8	SUBA		2	20	2	20	2	22	4	24	4	26	4	24	6	28							1001 DDD1 10EE EEEE	d − Dn → d	
		d = Dn	s =	2	8	2	8	2	14	2	14	2	16	4	18	4	20	4	18	6	22	4	18	4	20	6	16	1001 DDD0 10ee eeee	Dn − s → Dn	
SUBA	W	d = An	s =	2	8	2	8	2	12	2	12	2	14	4	16	4	18	4	16	6	20	4	16	4	18	4	12	1001 AAA0 11ee eeee	An − s → An	- - - - -
	L	d = An	s =	2	8	2	8	2	14	2	14	2	16	4	18	4	20	4	18	6	22	4	18	4	20	6	16	1001 AAA1 11ee eeee		
SUBI	B/W	s = Imm	d =	4	8	SUBA		4	16	4	16	4	18	6	20	6	22	6	20	8	24							0000 0100 SSEE EEEE	d − # → d	* * * * *
	L	s = Imm	d =	6	16	SUBA		6	28	6	28	6	30	8	32	8	34	8	32	10	36									
SUBQ	B/W	s = Imm3	d =	2	4	2*	8	2	12	2	12	2	14	4	16	4	18	4	16	6	20							0101 QQQ1 SSEE EEEE	d − # → d	* * * * *
	L	s = Imm3	d =	2	8	2	8	2	20	2	20	2	22	4	24	4	26	4	24	6	28									
SUBX	B/W	s = Dn	d =	2	4																							1001 RRR1 SS00 0rrr	d − s − X → d	* * * * *
		s = −(An)	d =									2	18															1001 RRR1 SS00 1rrr		
	L	s = Dn	d =	2	8																							1001 RRR1 1000 0rrr		
		s = −(An)	d =									2	30															1001 RRR1 1000 1rrr		
SWAP	W		d =	2	4																							0100 1000 0100 0DDD	Dn(31:16) ←→ Dn(15:0)	- * * 0 0
TAS	B		d =	2	4			2	14	2	14	2	16	4	18	4	20	4	18	6	22							0100 1010 11EE EEEE	test d → cc, 1 → bit 7 of d	- * * 0 0
TRAP				2	38																							0100 1110 0100 VVVV	PC → −(SSP), SR → −(SSP), (1 of 16 trap vectors) → PC	- - - - -
TRAPV				2	34	trap taken																						0100 1110 0111 0110	If V = 1, then PC → −(SSP), SR → −(SSP), (TRAPV vector) → PC, else NOP	- - - - -
				2	4	trap not taken																								
TST	B/W		d =	2	4			2	8	2	8	2	10	4	12	4	14	4	12	6	16							0100 1010 SSEE EEEE	test d → cc	- * * 0 0
	L		d =	2	4			2	12	2	12	2	14	4	16	4	18	4	16	6	20									
UNLK						2	12																					0100 1110 0101 1AAA	An → SP, (SP)+ → An	- - - - -

General Notes:

- * Word Only
- \# Number of Bytes in Instruction
- ~ Execution Time in Clock Periods
- s Source (s10 = base 10 operand)
- d Destination (d10 = base 10 operand)
- < Value is Maximum Number

Complement (invert)
- d_8 8-Bit Displacement
- d_{16} 16-Bit Displacement
- Imm Immediate Data
- Imm3 Immediate Data, 3 Bits
- Imm8 Immediate Data, 8 Bits

Opcode Bit Pattern Codes:

- A Address Register Number
- C Test Condition
- D Data Register Number
- E Destination Effective Address
- e Source Effective Address
- f Direction: 0 = Right 1 = Left
- M Destination EA Mode
- P Displacement
- Q Quick Immediate Data
- R Destination Register
- r Source Register
- S Size: 00 = Byte 01 = Word 10 = Long
- V Vector Number
- XX Move size: 01 = Byte 11 = Word

Condition Code Notation:

- * Set according to result of operation.
- — Not affected by operation.
- 0 Cleared
- 1 Set
- U Undefined after operation.
- ? Other — See Special Definition

Condition Code Computations

Operations	X	N	Z	V	C	Special Definition
ABCD	*	U	?	U	?	C = Decimal Carry $Z = Z \cdot \overline{Rm} \cdot \ldots \cdot \overline{R0}$
ADD, ADDI, ADDQ	*	*	*	?	?	$V = Sm \cdot Dm \cdot \overline{Rm} + \overline{Sm} \cdot \overline{Dm} \cdot Rm$ $C = Sm \cdot Dm + \overline{Rm} \cdot Dm + Sm \cdot \overline{Rm}$
ADDX	*	*	?	?	?	$V = Sm \cdot Dm \cdot \overline{Rm} + \overline{Sm} \cdot \overline{Dm} \cdot Rm$ $C = Sm \cdot Dm + Rm \cdot Dm + Sm \cdot \overline{Rm}$ $Z = Z \cdot \overline{Rm} \cdot \ldots \cdot \overline{R0}$
AND, ANDI, EOR, EORI, MOVEQ, MOVE, OR, ORI, CLR, EXT, NOT, TAS, TST	—	*	*	0	0	
CHK	—	*	U	U	U	
SUB, SUBI, SUBQ	*	*	*	?	?	$V = \overline{Sm} \cdot Dm \cdot \overline{Rm} + Sm \cdot \overline{Dm} \cdot Rm$ $C = Sm \cdot \overline{Dm} + Rm \cdot \overline{Dm} + Sm \cdot Rm$
SUBX	*	*	?	?	?	$V = \overline{Sm} \cdot Dm \cdot \overline{Rm} + Sm \cdot \overline{Dm} \cdot Rm$ $C = Sm \cdot \overline{Dm} + Rm \cdot \overline{Dm} + Sm \cdot Rm$ $Z = Z \cdot \overline{Rm} \cdot \ldots \cdot R0$
CMP, CMPI, CMPM	—	*	*	?	?	$V = \overline{Sm} \cdot Dm \cdot \overline{Rm} + Sm \cdot \overline{Dm} \cdot Rm$ $C = Sm \cdot \overline{Dm} + Rm \cdot \overline{Dm} + Sm \cdot Rm$
DIVS, DIVU	—	*	*	?	0	V = Division Overflow
MULS, MULU	—	*	*	0	0	
SBCD, NBCD	*	U	?	U	?	C = Decimal Borrow $Z = Z \cdot \overline{Rm} \cdot \ldots \cdot \overline{R0}$

Operations	X	N	Z	V	C	Special Definition
NEG	*	*	*	?	?	$V = Dm \cdot Rm$, $C = Dm + Rm$
NEGX	*	*	?	?	?	$V = Dm \cdot Rm$, $C = Dm + Rm$ $Z = Z \cdot \overline{Rm} \cdot \ldots \cdot \overline{R0}$
BTST, BCHG, BSET, BCLR	—	—	?	—	—	$Z = \overline{Dn}$
ASL	*	*	*	?	?	$V = Dm \cdot (\overline{D_{m-1}} + \ldots + \overline{D_{m-r}})$ $+ \overline{Dm} \cdot (D_{m-1} + \ldots + D_{m-r})$ $C = D_{m-r+1}$
ASL (r=0)	—	*	*	0	0	
LSL, ROXL	*	*	*	0	?	$C = D_{m-r+1}$
LSR (r=0)	—	*	*	0	0	
ROXL (r=0)	—	*	*	0	?	C=X
ROL	—	*	*	0	?	$C = D_{m-r+1}$
ROL (r=0)	—	*	*	0	0	
ASR, LSR, ROXR	*	*	*	0	?	$C = D_{r-1}$
ASR, LSR (r=0)	—	*	*	0	0	
ROXR (r=0)	—	*	*	0	?	C=X
ROR	—	*	*	0	?	$C = D_{r-1}$
ROR (r=0)	—	*	*	0	0	

NOTES:

Sm Source Operated — most significant bit

Dm Destination operand — most significant bit

? See Special Definition

Rm Result operand — most significant bit

n bit number

r shift count

Effective Addressing Mode Categories

Type	Mode	Register	Generation	Assembler Syntax
Data Register Direct	000	reg. no.	EA=Dn	Dn
Address Register Direct	001	reg. no.	EA=An	An
Register Indirect	010	reg. no.	EA=(An)	(An)
Postincrement Register Indirect	011	reg. no.	EA=(An), An←An+N	(An)+
Predecrement Register Indirect	100	reg. no.	An←An−N, EA=(An)	−(An)
Register Indirect With Offset	101	reg. no.	EA=(An)+d_{16}	d_{16}(An)
Indexed Register Indirect With Offset	110	reg. no.	EA=(An)+(Xn)+d_8	d_8(An, Xn)
Absolute Short	111	000	EA=(Next Word)	xxx
Absolute Long	111	001	EA=(Next Two Words)	xxxxxx
PC Relative With Offset	111	010	EA=(PC)+d_{16}	d_{16}(PC)
PC Relative With Index and Offset	111	011	EA=(PC)+(Xn)+d_8	d_8(PC+Xn)
Immediate	111	100	Data=Next Word(s)	#xxx
Quick Immediate	—	—	Inherent Data	#xxx (1–8)
Implied Register	—	—	EA=SR, USP, SP, PC	—

NOTES:
EA = Effective Address
An = Address Register
Dn = Data Register
Xn = Address or Data Register used as Index Register
SR = Status Register
PC = Program Counter
d_8 = Eight bit Offset (displacement)
d_{16} = Sixteen bit Offset (displacement)
N = 1 for Byte, 2 for Words and 4 for Long Words
( ) = Contents of
← = Replaces

APPENDIX D

MC68000 INSTRUCTION SET

The listing in this appendix describes the entire instruction set for the MC68000 in alphabetical order by mnemonic. Only certain groups of addressing modes are permitted with each operand of each instruction. See the tables in Appendix C for the details concerning these restrictions.

Certain instructions include special versions as indicated by an extra letter at the end of the mnemonic. Examples include ADDA, ADDI, ADDQ, and ADDX. The suffix A calls for an address register as the destination and as such is limited to a size of word or long. The suffix I (immediate) calls for an immediate source operand (byte, word, or long), and the suffix Q (quick) for an immediate source value ranging from 1 through 8 with the three size options for the destination. A special version will only be described separately when it involves a major difference in the effect of the instruction.

ABCD Add BCD—add the source operand and the extend bit to the destination operand using BCD arithmetic (byte only). Both operands must be in either the data register direct or the address register indirect with predecrement mode.

ADD Add the source operand to the destination operand.

ADDX Add the source operand and the content of the extend bit to the destination operand.

AND AND the source operand to the destination operand.

ANDI (to CCR) AND the immediate operand to the content of the lower byte of the status register (byte only).

ANDI (to SR) AND the immediate operand to the content of the entire status register (word only, privileged).

ASL Arithmetic shift left—shift left the pattern in the destination location. Shift a zero in from the right, and shift the leftmost bit into the carry and the extend bit. If the destination is a data register, the shift count may be specified by an immediate source value (1 through 8) or by the content of a source data register. If the destination is specified as a data value in memory, the shift count is one and no source operand is allowed.

ASR Arithmetic shift right—shift right the pattern in the destination location while bringing a copy of the most significant bit (the sign bit of the size selected) into the leftmost position. Shift the rightmost bit into the carry and the extend bit. If the destination is a data register, the shift count may be specified by an immediate source value (1 through 8) or by the content of a source data register. If the destination is specified as a data value in memory, the shift count is one and no source operand is allowed.

Bcc Branch on condition (cc)—branch if the condition is true.

BCHG Test a bit and change—test a bit in the destination operand and update the Z-bit to a copy of it; then complement the bit in the destination. The bit number may be specified by an immediate source value or by the content of a source data register (byte or long only).

BCLR Test a bit and clear—test a bit in the destination operand and update the Z-bit to a copy of it; then clear the bit in the destination. The bit number may be specified by an immediate source value or by the content of a source data register (byte or long only).

BRA Branch always—unconditionally branch.

BSET Test a bit and set—test a bit in the destination operand and update the Z-bit to a copy of it; then set the bit in the destination. The bit number may be specified by an immediate source value or by the content of a source data register (byte or long only).

BSR Branch to subroutine and save the content of the PC on the system stack.

BTST Test a bit—Test a bit in the destination operand and update the Z-bit to a copy of it. The bit number may be specified by an immediate source value or by the content of a source data register (byte or long only).

CHK Check register against bounds—check the (signed) value in the low half of the destination data register. If it is negative or greater than the source operand, initiate exception processing using the CHK trap vector (word only).

CLR Clear each bit in the destination operand.

CMP Compare—subtract the source operand from the destination operand and discard the result after using it to update the condition code bits.

CMPM Compare memory—subtract the source operand from the destination operand and discard the result after using it to update the condition code bits. Both operands must use the address register indirect with post increment mode.

DBcc Decrement and branch on condition (cc)—if the condition is true, do nothing. If it is false, decrement the source data register. If the result is not −1, branch to the destination (label in source code, 16-bit PC offset in machine code).

DIVS Signed division—divide the destination data register operand (32 bits) by the word-sized source operand and store the remainder/quotient in the destination data register (word only).

DIVU Unsigned division—see DIVS.

EOR EXCLUSIVE OR the source operand to the destination operand.

EORI (to CCR) EXCLUSIVE OR the immediate operand to the content of the lower byte of the status register (byte only).

EORI (to SR) EXCLUSIVE OR the immediate operand to the content of the status register (word only, privileged).

EXG Exchange the contents of the two operand registers (data registers, address registers, or one of each—long only).

EXT Sign extend the byte (word) in the destination data register into a word (long)—word or long only.

ILLEGAL Initiate exception processing using the Illegal Instruction trap vector.

JMP Jump—unconditionally branch.

JSR Jump to subroutine and save the content of the PC on the system stack.

LEA Load effective address—calculate the effective source address and load it into the destination address register (long only).

LINK Save the content of the source address register on the system stack; then load that register with the content of the system stack pointer. Add the immediate constant specified as the destination operand to the system stack pointer (unsized).

LSL Logic shift left—shift left the pattern in the destination location. Shift a zero in from the right and shift the leftmost bit into the carry and the extend bit. If the destination is a data register, the shift count may be specified by an immediate source value (1 through 8) or by the content of a source data register. If the destination is specified as a data value in memory, the shift count is one and no source operand is allowed.

LSR Logic shift right—shift right the pattern in the destination location. Shift a zero in from the left, and shift the rightmost bit into the carry and the extend bit. If the destination is a data register, the shift count may be specified by an immediate source value (1 through 8) or by the content of a source data register. If the destination is specified as a data value in memory, the shift count is one and no source operand is allowed.

MOVE Copy the source operand into the destination location.

MOVE (to CCR) Copy the low-order byte of the word-sized source operand into the lower byte of the status register (word only).

MOVE (to SR) Copy the source operand into the status register (word only, privileged).

MOVE (from SR) Copy the content of the status register into the destination location (word only).

MOVEUSP Copy the content of the user stack pointer into the destination address register (long only, privileged).

MOVEM Move multiple registers—copy the register list in the source operand to consecutive locations in memory starting at the destination location, or copy the contents of the consecutive memory locations starting at the source location into the registers listed in the destination operand. Both options allow any control mode. In addition, the former allows predecrement, and the latter allows postincrement (word or long only).

MOVEP Move peripheral data—copy the data from the source data register into alternate memory locations starting at the destination location, or copy the data from alternate memory locations starting at the source location into the destination data register (word or long only).

MULS Signed multiplication—multiply the word-sized source operand by the lower word in the destination data register and store the long word product in the destination data register (word only).

MULU Unsigned multiplication—see MULS.

NBCD Negate decimal—subtract the destination operand and the content of the extend bit from zero using BCD arithmetic. Store the difference in the destination (byte only). If X = 0 the result is the tens complement of the destination operand; if X = 1 the result is the nines complement.

NEG Negate—subtract the destination operand from zero using binary arithmetic. Store the difference in the destination.

NEGX Negate with extend—subtract the destination operand and the content of the extend bit from zero using binary arithmetic. Store the result in the destination. If X = 0 the result is the twos complement of the destination operand; if X = 1 the result is the ones complement.

NOP No operation—do nothing.

NOT Complement each bit in the destination operand.

OR OR the source operand to the destination operand.

ORI (to CCR) OR the immediate operand to the content of the lower byte of the status register (byte only).

ORI (to SR) OR the immediate operand to the content of the entire status register (word only, privileged).

PEA Push effective address—calculate the effective destination address and store it on the system stack (long only).

RESET Reset external devices—assert the reset line on the processor to reset I/O interface chips, but not the processor itself (privileged).

ROL Rotate left—rotate left the pattern in the destination location. Shift the leftmost bit into the rightmost bit position and into the carry bit. If the destination is a data register, the shift count may be specified by an immediate source value (1 through 8) or by the content of a source data register. If the destination is specified as a data value in memory, the shift count is one and no source operand is allowed.

ROR Rotate right—rotate right the pattern in the destination location. Shift the rightmost bit into the leftmost bit position and into the carry bit. If the destination is a data register, the shift count may be specified by an immediate source value (1 through 8) or by the content of a source data register. If the destination is specified as a data value in memory, the shift count is one and no source operand is allowed.

ROXL Rotate left through extend—rotate left the pattern in the destination location and extend bit. Shift the leftmost destination bit into the carry bit and the extend bit and shift the extend bit into the rightmost destination bit position. If the destination is a data register, the shift count may be specified by an immediate source value (1 through 8) or by the content of a source data register. If the destination is specified as a data value in memory, the shift count is one and no source operand is allowed.

ROXR Rotate right through extend—rotate right the pattern in the destination location and extend bit. Shift the rightmost destination bit into the carry bit and the extend bit and shift the extend bit into the leftmost destination bit position. If the destination is a data register, the shift count may be specified by an immediate source value (1 through 8) or by the content of a source data register. If the destination is specified as a data value in memory, the shift count is one and no source operand is allowed.

RTE Return from exception—load the status register and program counter from the system stack (privileged).

RTR Return and restore—load the condition codes and program counter from the system stack.

RTS Return from subroutine—load the program counter from the system stack.

SBCD Subtract BCD—subtract the source operand and the extend bit from the destination operand using BCD arithmetic. Byte only. Both operands must be in either the data register direct or the address register indirect with predecrement mode.

Scc Set on condition (cc)—if the condition is true, write all ones into the destination; if not, write all zeros.

STOP Load the immediate operand into the status register and then cease fetching and executing instructions and wait for an interrupt or a reset (word only, privileged).

SUB Subtract the source operand from the destination operand.

SUBX Subtract the source operand and the content of the extend bit from the destination operand.

SWAP Interchange the contents of each half of the destination data register (word only).

TAS Test and set—update the N- and Z-bits to reflect the value of the destination operand; then set the highest ordered bit of the destination operand (byte only).

TRAP*n* Initiate exception processing using the exception vector specified by the (four-bit) immediate operand, *n*.

TRAPV If the V-bit is set, initiate exception processing using the TRAPV exception vector.

TST Test—subtract the destination operand from zero and discard the result after using it to update the condition code bits.

UNLK Unlink—load the stack pointer with the content of the source address register; then load that register with the long word from the top of the stack (unsized).

BIBLIOGRAPHY

Cassell, Douglas A. *Microcomputers & Modern Control Engineering*. Reston Publishing Company, Reston, VA, 1983.

Clements, Alan. *Microcomputer Design and Construction*. Prentice-Hall International, London, 1982.

Comer, David J. *Microprocessor-Based System Design*. Holt, Rinehart and Winston, New York, 1986.

Fohl, Mark E. *A Microprocessor Course*. Petrocelli Books, New York, 1979.

Gault, James W. and Russell L. Pimmel. *Microcomputer-Based Digital Systems*. McGraw-Hill, New York, 1982.

Givone, Donald D. and Robert P. Roesser. *Microprocessors/Microcomputers: An Introduction*. McGraw-Hill, New York, 1980.

Hamacher, V. Carl, Zvonko G. Vranesic, and Safwat G. Zaky. *Computer Organization*. 2d ed. McGraw-Hill, New York, 1984.

Hennessy, John L. and David A. Patterson. *Computer Architecture: A Quantitative Approach*. Morgan Kaufmann Publishers, Inc., San Mateo, CA, 1990.

Hillburn, John L. and Paul M. Julich. *Microcomputers/Microprocessors: Hardware, Software, and Applications*. Prentice Hall, Inc., Englewood Cliffs, NJ, 1976.

Kimberley, Paul. *Microprocessors An Introduction*. McGraw-Hill, New York, 1982.

Krieger, Morris, Charles Popper, Robert Radcliffe, and David Ripps. *Structured Microprocessor Programming*. Yourdon Inc., New York, 1979.

Leventhal, Lance A. *6809 Assembly Language Programming*. Osborne/McGraw-Hill, Berkeley, CA, 1981.

Lipovski, G. Jack. *Microcomputer Interfacing*. Lexington Books, Lexington, MA, 1980.

———. *Single- and Multiple-Chip Microcomputer Interfacing*. Prentice Hall, Inc., Englewood Cliffs, NJ, 1988.

Mano, M. Morris. *Computer System Architecture*. 2d ed. Prentice Hall, Inc., Englewood Cliffs, NJ, 1982.

Motorola Semiconductor Products, Inc. *MC6809-MC6809E Microprocessor Programming Manual*. Motorola Inc., Austin, TX, 1983.

———. *Microprocessor, Microcontroller and Peripheral Data*. Motorola Inc., Phoenix, AZ, 1988.

———. *M68000 16/32-Bit Microprocessor Programmer's Reference Manual*. 4th ed. Prentice Hall, Inc., Englewood Cliffs, NJ, 1988.

Pooch, Udo W. and Rahul Chattergy. *Minicomputers: Hardware, Software, and Selection*. West Publishing Company, St. Paul, MN, 1980.

Scanlon, Leo J. *The 68000: Principles and Programming*. Howard W. Sams & Co., Inc., Indianapolis, IN, 1981.

Shiva, Sajjan G. *Introduction to Logic Design*. Scott, Foresman and Company, Glenview, IL, 1988.

Short, Kenneth L. *Microprocessors and Programmed Logic*. Prentice Hall, Inc., Englewood Cliffs, NJ, 1981.

Slater, Michael. *Microprocessor-Based Design*. Mayfield Publishing Company, Mountain View, CA, 1987.

Wakerly, John F. *Microcomputer Architecture and Programming*. John Wiley & Sons, Inc., New York, 1981.

Wiatrowski, Claude A. and Charles H. House. *Logic Circuits and Microcomputer Systems*. McGraw-Hill, New York, 1980.

Zaks, Rodnay and William Labiak. *Programming the 6809*. Sybex, Berkeley, CA, 1982.

Zaks, Rodnay and Austin Lesea. *Microprocessor Interfacing Techniques*. 3rd ed. Sybex, Berkeley, CA, 1979.

INDEX